# Communication in the Jewish Diaspora

*Two Thousand Years of Saying Goodbye without Leaving*

Edited by

## Menahem Blondheim
Hebrew University of Jerusalem

## Hananel Rosenberg
Ariel University

# Communication in the Jewish Diaspora
## *Two Thousand Years of Saying Goodbye without Leaving*

Menahem Blondheim and Hananel Rosenberg, Editors

**Published by ISRAEL ACADEMIC PRESS, New York**

(A subsidiary of MultiEducator, Inc.)

553 North Avenue • New Rochelle, NY 10801

Email: info@Israelacademicpress.com

ISBN # 978-1-885881-57-1

Cover illustration  by Amy Erani. The featured world map is from
Hillel Kahana, *Glilot haAretz* (Bucharest: Dfus haYoetz, 1880).

*In memory of Tamar Liebes*

# Table of Contents

# Acknowledgements

It's a very pleasant duty to thank the many people who took part in this project and the institutions that made the publication of this volume possible. The project was launched as the theme of a research group that was hosted in the inspiring environment of the Institute for Advanced Studies at the Hebrew University of Jerusalem, headed at the time by Benjamin Z. Kedar. Yaron Eliav, Shmuel Feiner, William Labov, Derek Penslar, John Peters, Annabelle Sreberny and Dror Wahrman, together with most of the authors of chapters in this volume, were part of the team.

Two other institutions took over the responsibility for bringing this project to completion: The Da'at Hamakom Excellence Center in Israel and the Enhancing Life Project headed by Bill Shweiker at the University of Chicago and Günter Thomas at Ruhr-University Bochum. The Hebrew University of Jerusalem's Authority for Research and Development was generous in providing funds that enabled the publishing of this volume. The publication process itself, however protracted, was a pleasant and harmonious affair. Credit is due to the volume's expert copy-editors, Kalia Vogelman-Natan and Greg John, and to the personnel of Israel Academic Press and its heads, Yitzhak Reiter and Marc Schulman. It was a pleasure to work with IAP's graphic designer Amy Erani.

From its beginnings and throughout its subsequent stages, three scholars joined me in leading this project: Elihu Katz, one of the founding fathers of communication studies; Doron Mendels, the steadfast bridge between historical studies and communications; and our brilliant and profound dynamo and friend, the late Tamar Liebes. This volume is dedicated to her memory.

— Menahem Blondheim

INTRODUCTION
# 'One People, Scattered'
## Jewish Diasporic Communications 200-2000 CE
### MENAHEM BLONDHEIM AND HANANEL ROSENBERG

## *Communications and the Dynamics of Diaspora*

Transformations in the media environment at the turn of the 20th century have directed considerable attention to the problem of extending community through geographical space. Much of this attention has focused on processes of globalization. They enable the dramatic extension of dominant economic, political, and cultural regimes, with far reaching implications for social and political organization and for cultural identity. But thinking about new communications and emerging world order gradually shifted its focus to the other side of globalization: to the possibilities that new media afford for linking social enclaves over the globe. Hence the burst of talk about diaspora.

New media enhances contact and cohesion among individuals, groups, and social entities dispersed in space, countering or even reversing local forces. They can point instead to a dynamic of diversity and the shaping of multiplicity of identities. This project of virtual community building, maintenance, and enhancement, by means of effective new tools and networks of communication, has particular relevance to the nature and meaning of diasporas.

Diasporas are a fact of geography, of history, and of identity. Processes of communication are the dynamic mechanism that negotiates the interplay of these factors of space, time, and culture, as they define the diasporic experience.

The construction of diasporas can vary considerably: in geography they may be thinly scattered or densely spread over several or many locations, regions, or countries. They can represent different demographic balances between emigrants and their homeland, between immigrants and their host societies, certainly between various immigrant groups in a specific society. In their temporality diasporas may reflect short-term military, economic, or political dislocations, or represent the permanent transplantation of populations, or anything in-between. Culturally, a diasporic condition can launch a process of assimilation into the host culture, or conversely, a process of cultural colonialism. Alternatively, and more commonly, diasporas may engage in a continuous quest for cultural survival within one or more alien cultural environments in an attempt to defer assimilation or prepare for return.

In all such varied constructions of diaspora and its dynamics, communications serve as a key factor in their build-up and development. As John Peters has pointed out, "diaspora suggests real or imagined relationships among scattered fellows whose sense of community is sustained by forms of communication and contact."[1] Communication channels thus underpin the variety of links between diasporic peripheries and their center, between diasporas and their host societies, and most importantly perhaps, within each community of exiles and between them.

## Jewish Diasporic Communications

On all the dimensions just suggested for profiling diasporas in their dependence on communication, the Jewish diaspora stands out. Some would tag it "the mother of all diasporas." Jewish exceptionalism as a diasporic experience pertains to the fundamental dimensions of space, time and culture, as outlined above. To put it most simply and most glaringly, Jewish communities in diaspora managed to maintain cultural distinction across an ecumenical scattering, and managed to do so over nearly two millennia.

But beyond its considerable spread and staying power, the Jewish diasporic experience is historically unique with regard to a crucial factor: the relationship between center and periphery. For unlike most other diasporas, Jews, through most of their exilic experience, did not have a geographical center to which they could orient themselves. Until the latter 20th century, they had only an imagined homeland, carefully crafted by historical memory[2] and an elaborate vision of destiny, sustained by a pervasive system of beliefs and appropriate praxis, shared to a remarkable extent across geography. Nevertheless, without a concrete homeland, one could say that the center of the Jewish diaspora was the communicative network that linked its scattered communities.[3] That network sustained a common flow of shared content between Jews and Jewish communities, let alone the imagination of connection. To invoke John Dewey (though not Benedict Anderson), diaspora Jews as Jews, as well as their nation, existed "in communication."[4]

Understanding the Jewish diaspora as an extreme specimen of diasporic existence may help shed light on diasporas generally. Since diasporas exist through communications, focusing on communicative aspects of the Jewish diasporic past may well provide a key to such a general understanding. Conversely, and at least as significantly, since Jews and Judaism existed in diaspora over nearly two millennia, and much of that time without a concrete geographical center, understanding diasporic communications is crucial for understanding Jewish history and cohesion. The present volume is geared to this double-pronged quest of understanding diasporas and understanding Jewish national persistence, by focusing on communicative mechanisms and patterns that anchored Jewish diasporic history.

Such a framework must take into account the structure, operation, and meaning of both lateral and hierarchical networks of social organization and communication. It must also consider processes of transfer of content, experience and meaning over time, space, and social environment. The articles in this volume do so by investigating specific historical periods, communication processes, institutions, media and texts, and they span antiquity to modernity. Their common thrust is to explore the lateral and temporal dimensions of Jewish interconnectedness. They study the role of travel and trade, transportation and transmission, but also the unity and diversity of language among Jews, the duality of oral and written modes of the cultural heritage (affording a mix of fixity and flexibility); the interplay of nation, community, public and family as the loci of ritual; the multifaceted approach to time—sacred, historical, communal and individual—and, of course, specific communicative institutions that evolved to sustain inter-diasporic communications.

## *Methodological Premises*

The project of viewing and discussing the Jewish diaspora from a communications perspective implies an encounter between two distinct disciplinary clusters: History and communications. Both are notoriously ambitious: History, after all, aspires to trace all aspects of the human lifeworld and to understand it in all its complexity. Communications is one such significant, albeit neglected, aspect of human history; however, it understands itself as the potential key to grasping and untangling human complexity—past, present and future. By its nature, communication is the story of links, of interconnections and relations, and it therefore sees itself as the nerve-center of human activity.

Inevitably, the relationship between the study of history and the study of communications potentially points to a two-way affair. History, as the great warehouse of human experience, is the ultimate data-base, and thus a giant multi-function laboratory for testing and fine-tuning ideas and theories about communication. Moreover, it is potentially an indispensable site for generating such ideas. It can and should serve as a powerful resource for generating theories as well as the ultimate site for their verification. At the same time, communication theory can serve as a useful tool for improving the understanding of a key aspect of history. After all, although one of the most fundamental human activities, communications was not conceptualized as a category of the human lifeworld until late modernity. Nor was communication institutionalized as an academic discipline until the middle of the 20th century. Thus, the historical discipline has an urgent project of updating itself through factoring communications—one of its former blindspots—into its developmental account of the human experience.

Translating this interdisciplinary rationale to the study of the Jewish diaspora, the present volume points to an inevitable corrective in understanding the diasporic past of the Jews, and its meaning as a communicative process. At the same time it points to the Jewish experience as a leading example for the role of communications in shaping personal, communal and national identities.

Focusing on diaspora, a pervasive social phenomenon, this volume isolates one national experience for the study of its communicative and historical meaning, over the *longue duree*. As noted, the Jewish diasporic experience is outstanding in its time frame: In the longevity of the people, of their religious culture and their memory. It is outstanding also in the spatial distribution and organization of Jews in the diasporic phase of their history. Both of these outstanding characteristics of the Jewish experience, can be construed as aspects of communications. It could even be argued that Jewish history cannot be properly traced and understood without resort to the theme of communications. At the same time Jewish history can provide communication scholars with unique lessons on the ideology and mechanisms of transmitting information, texts, and ideas—as well as feelings and identities—from place to place and from generation to generation, through a variety of channels and a comprehensive gallery of media, to a powerful effect.

Within historical study, there have been conflicting tendencies in approaching the Jewish experience. One dominant approach has been "internal," viewing Jewish history as a story unto itself, zooming in on themes unique to it and its particularities, disconnected from general history and historical research themes. A contrasting approach has been to consider Jewish history as an aspect of the social, political and cultural history of nations and regions. The theme of this volume, touching among other foci on the interface between Jewish and gentile societies, merges these two approaches—the internal and the general. Aside from linking the two contrasting traditions of Jewish historiography, it also adds a third: the analysis of a specific theme of history—communication in our case—which has considerable contemporary implications.

## Structure of the Volume

The construction of Jewish diasporic communications as proposed above, and the agenda for its study is broad indeed. Its historiographic orientation spans intellectual, social, religious, and institutional history; and it envisions the application of many strands of communication theory as well. The programmatic approach proposed here may be seen as recasting Jewish exilic history as a study of diasporic segments in communication. Given the enormous scope of such a project, and the limits of this publication, we have telescoped the investigation by focusing on a number of key chapters in Jewish history. We are well aware that this is only a first step in incorporating communications into the description and analysis of the texture, techniques, institutions, processes, and connections that have sustained the Jewish world in distinct eras.

It is doubtful whether generalizations can be made across the case studies presented here. However, they may suggest directions for studying continuities in Jewish ways and means of communication over its diasporic experience. After all, the articles in this volume span biblical to modern times, and consider a plethora of media, from primary orality to the novel.

The first chapter in the volume connects the fundamental text of the Jews, the Bible, to their dominant experience of Diaspora. The Five Scrolls, individually and as a corpus, are analyzed in Katz and Blondheim's chapter as a guide to ways Jews could construct Diaspora and relate to it through the ages and throughout the world. These approaches to coping with diaspora, or "diaspora dreams," include *return, revenge, remain* and *take over*, or *rule*.

The Bible itself as a written corpus, with the five scrolls canonized as a part of it, would serve as a "portable homeland" for Jews of subsequent generations. But the Bible was not alone: post-biblical sages went on to develop Jewish culture in the oral medium. Yaakov Sussman's monumental study of the orality of the

Mishnah summarized here, analyzes the strategies used by the sages to redact in their non-scripted universe, an authoritative version of the sprawling oral law. The study also demonstrates the tremendous power of orality in developing and maintaining a foundational corpus that would shape Jewish law and life in future generations. The orality-literacy divide is also the core of Menahem Blondheim's chapter on the *Haggadah*, the text anchoring the most historically successful Jewish ritual: The Passover *seder*. It treats the fundamental tension between the ear and the eye in terms of memory and consciousness, and complicates that tension by adding print to the media equation.

In the next chapter, Doron Mendels and Arye Edrei locate the emergence of the Hebrew and Aramaic oral law in a broader geographical and historical context. They present here a comprehensive view of their revolutionary thesis on the role of communications in a dramatic turn of Jewish history in the Hellenistic age. It concerns the schism that developed between a Greek speaking "western" Jewry, and a Hebrew and Aramaic speaking "eastern" Jewry. Communications was thus the fundamental cause of estrangement between two branches of the Jewish people, and the historical consequences of this estrangement, as documented in the article, were dramatic. In a response to an earlier exposition of this thesis, Berachyhu Lifshitz presents an analysis of the estrangement of "western" Jewry that focuses on ideology, rather than on communications. He agrees with the depiction of a schism between Jews in the west and Jews in the east, but attributes it to fundamental disagreement about the authority of the oral law, not only ignorance of it due to its linguistic medium. His argument demonstrates surprising continuities between earlier schisms over the oral law and later conflicts subsequent to late antiquity.

Moving from antiquity towards modernity, two chapters address the Middle Ages. First and foremost is Haym Soloveitchik's landmark study of the foundational sources and cultural traditions underpinning the emergent Ashkenazi Jewry in the early Middle Ages. It highlights the remarkable mobility of Jewish traders and travelers in the era, who acquired and delivered Jewish texts along with other merchandise. This traffic enabled a variety of textual traditions to shape the Ashkenazi world of halakhic scholarship, not only the Jerusalem Talmud as previously assumed. Menahem Blondheim's study of communicative aspects of Cherem d'Rabenu Gershom, points in turn to local circumstances that conditioned this series of novel halakhic rulings in Ashkenaz in the turn of first millennium (CE). These rulings have had a major impact on Jewish life up to the present, and the chapter argues that the regulation of diasporic communications was the thematic focus of the corpus.

Oren Sofer's chapter delivers us into the heart of the modern era, and introduces the new media that Jews adopted and adapted in the time of the European enlightenment. Focusing on the periodical, he demonstrates how modern ideas could find appropriate media that would enable their sharing among Jewish elites across the European diaspora. Other Jewish social and ideological movements would adopt similar means for spreading their alternative ideas and agendas. A case in point is the Zionist movement. Our late colleague Tamar Liebes traces in one of the last articles she drafted (and edited by her colleagues after her untimely passing), the remarkably varied and creative strategies for diffusing and popularizing Zionism. Masterminded by the movement's prime-mover and former journalist Theodore Herzl, the imaginative media-mix of early political Zionism helped mobilize Jews throughout the diaspora to the cause of congregating in their ancient homeland, thus in effect using diasporic communications to eliminating the need for diasporic communications.

Paralleling the development of the Zionist movement, the United States competed with Palestine as the promised land for Jews experiencing economic and political as well as social and spiritual hardship in Easter Europe. In an article employing digital humanities techniques (in this case GIS), Zef Segal and Menahem Blondheim trace the pattern of religious communications that developed between the old world—considered the religious center of the western diaspora—and its newest offspring. Their technique yields the unintuitive but reasonable conclusion that while American *mitnagdim* tended to severe their ties with the rabbinic elite of western Europe, *chasidic* Jews maintained transatlantic contact with their religious leaders in the *alte heim*.

America is also the backdrop of the final chapter in the volume, by the late literary scholar Baruch Hochman, but it addresses the new home a generation later and on the basis of its English, rather than Hebrew texts. The language of the host society is indeed the core of the argument, that returns, as the volume closes, to the key issue of the languages of the Jewish diaspora. Embracing America's language, as well as its virtuoso use and demonstrations of its love, can indicate, according to Hochman's surprising conclusion, foreignness no less than integration or assimilation.

Concluding the volume, this chapter demonstrates how the languages of the Jews needs much broader and more extensive study in the project of understanding Jewish diasporic communications. In fact, the same can be said about the other articles and themes addressed in this volume: They demand much more attention and work, and present together an agenda that calls for pursuing. But as the sages of the Mishnah said—orally according to Yaakov Sussman in chapter 2—"it is not incumbent upon you to finish the task, but neither are you free to absolve yourself from it."

## Notes

1    John D. Peters, "Nomadism, Diaspora, Exile: The Stakes of Mobility within the Western Canon," in *Home, Exile, Homeland: Film, Media, and the Politics of Place,* ed. Hamid Nafisi (London & New York: Routledge, 1999), 20.

2    Yosef Hayim Yerushalmi, *Zakhor: Jewish History and Jewish Memory* (Seattle: University of Washington Press, 1996).

3    Menahem Blondheim, "The Jewish Communication Tradition and (the) New Media," in *Digital Judaism: Jewish Negotiations with Digital Media and Culture,* ed. Heidi A. Campbell (New York: Routledge, 2015).

4    See James W. Carey, "A Cultural Approach to Communication," in *Communication As Culture: Essays on Media and Society* (New York: Routledge, 1989). In Anderson's understanding, common media products bring into consciousness links connecting people in a given culture; however, according to Dewey, common media create and shape communities.

## Bibliography

Blondheim, Menahem. "The Jewish Communication Tradition and (the) New Media." In *Digital Judaism: Jewish Negotiations with Digital Media and Culture,* edited by Heidi A. Campbell, 16-39. New York: Routledge, 2015.

Carey, James W. "A Cultural Approach to Communication." In *Communication As Culture: Essays on Media and Society,* 13-36. New York: Routledge, 1989

Peters, John D. "Nomadism, Diaspora, Exile: The Stakes of Mobility within the Western Canon." In *Home, Exile, Homeland: Film, Media, and the Politics of Place,* edited by Hamid Nafisi, 17-41. London & New York: Routledge, 1998.

Yerushalmi, Yosef Hayim. *Zakhor: Jewish History and Jewish Memory.* Seattle: University of Washington Press, 1992.

CHAPTER ONE

# Diaspora Dreams
*Four Dreams, Five Scrolls*
ELIHU KATZ & MENAHEM BLONDHEIM[1]

From the perspective of the Jewish Diaspora, and most likely other Diasporas as well, it is reasonable to expect a variety of mind sets that may be summarized, tentatively, as Return, Remain, Revenge, and Take Over (Reign). While these strivings may also be enacted, their most accessible expressions are found in the arts – literature, the visual, theater, and cinema – in liturgy and in folklore. In the Jewish case, these sources obviously include scripture – that is, the Pentateuch, Prophets, and Writings. While we shall enlist portions of the Bible and other liturgical sources, the argument of this paper is anchored primarily in the Books of Ruth and Esther, as well as the more self-evident Book of Lamentations, and to a lesser extent, the Song of Songs and Ecclesiastes.[2] These texts that came to be known as the Five Scrolls (*megillot*, in Hebrew) are also the complete books of the Bible selected for inclusion in the central liturgies of the holidays that punctuate the Jewish calendar.

We wish to propose here that these five scrolls and the ceremonial occasions for reading them have special meaning for the Jewish Diaspora. First, we will review this proposed affinity of the Five Scrolls to the problem of Diaspora, a condition that defined the history of the Jews from its formative experience in Egypt, later in the aftermath of the destruction of the Temples, and to the present. Then, we shall consider the institutional ties linking the Five Scrolls—to each other, to the broader corpus of Writings, to the Jewish calendar, and to its rituals. The Five Scrolls, it will be suggested, highlight the four quintessential Diaspora dreams: Return, Remain, Revenge, and Reign.

I

The Five Scrolls were composed at different times. Three of them were assigned by ritual to the three pilgrimage holidays, likely because they refer to the seasons of the agricultural cycle to which each holiday corresponds – the Song of Songs sings of spring on Passover, the Book of Ruth alludes to the harvest season of *Shavuot* (Weeks), and the somber Ecclesiastes chanted on the Feast of Tabernacles (*Sukkot*) is thought to anticipate the darkness of fall and winter. These holidays also evoke the collective memory of historic occasions: Passover marks the deliverance from Egypt and Israel's return to the land of its fathers; Sukkoth, according to tradition, commemorates God's sheltering the Israelites in the scorching desert en route to the holy land;[3] The Feast of Weeks is associated with the giving of the Law, which many would subsequently consider the Jews' portable homeland; Purim, the holiday ordained by the Book of Esther, marks the deliverance from Haman; and the Ninth of Av, the memorial day on which Lamentations is read, marks the destruction of the Temple and exile.[4]

Thus, it seems apparent that the liturgical role assigned to each of these scrolls serves both calendaric and historical functions. There is reason to suggest, moreover, that these ties between Scrolls and holidays – especially those dated to post-exilic times – are explicitly intended to strengthen collective memory. Extending this thought, the present paper dares to propose that the Five Scrolls serve the added function of fomenting debate over Jewish attitudes towards Exile – or, in more recent times, when the choices may be more voluntary, toward Diaspora. Accordingly, we 'read' this group of scrolls as if they relate to the situation of a mostly powerless minority living amidst an often hostile 'host' who may be offering shelter, however temporary, and who may or may not also be responsible for their deportation. We decode these books as 'lessons' – albeit differing among (and even within) themselves – concerning types of accommodation of Jews to Exile and Diaspora. Sometimes explicit, sometimes latent, these lessons are not necessarily prescriptions for action. We call them Diaspora Dreams.

## *Return*

The first of these dreams is Return, the so-called longing for Zion that is explicit in the Jewish liturgy from the thrice daily prayer "Return in mercy to Jerusalem" and the benediction to "rebuild Jerusalem" in the grace after meals, to the petition of the three pilgrimage holidays "to gather our dispersed people from among the nations…to bring them to Zion in joy." The psalmist explicitly says "we are as dreamers…while contemplating how God will return us to Zion" (Psalms 126:1).

The Pentateuch is full of God's warnings to stay put in the Promised Land, never even to dream of the imagined plenty of Egypt. Famine in the Holy Land drove the patriarchs away many times but trouble usually followed, undermining a potential dream of Remain. Thus, the matriarchs Sarah, and then Rebecca, were abducted during Abraham and Isaac's respective sojourns in Egypt. Jacob got into a dangerous conflict with Avimelech, king of Philistines, when leaving Judea, not to mention his wranglings with Laban, as well as with his estranged brother, Esau. Most markedly, Pharaoh's invitation to Jacob's clan to remain in fertile Goshen, ended up in enslavement. This pattern is tragically illustrated by the death of Naomi's husband and her two sons for having crossed into Moab to escape the famine in Canaan. Only Naomi's bedraggled Return together with her loyal daughter-in-law, Ruth, is rewarded. Ruth, the Moabite, is to become the great-grandmother of David, the King.

The same message, but from the opposite perspective, permeates Lamentations. It describes the glory of Jerusalem when populated by Judeans, then the ignominy of the city and the humiliation of its people when in exile. For the glory of the past to be recaptured, namely to "renew our days as of old," the prescription is "return us Lord to thee"— perhaps spiritually, but certainly geographically — a return to "the Mount of Zion which is wasted" (Lamentations 5:17-21). The message of return can even be read into the Song of Songs: the beauty of the land, the vivid descriptions of its fauna and flora can launch nostalgic longings. Indeed, even the longing for the loved one is metaphorically equated with yearning for the land: "You are as beautiful as Tirza (=a royal city for the kings of Israel), gracious as Jerusalem" (Song of Songs 6:4). The story of the two lovers seeking each other can only culminate in their reunion in one place at the same time. In the lush, erotic text, arousal is a call for action: "For the fall has past, the rains have disappeared, the blossoms are everywhere in the land, the time of the nightingales has come, the voice of the turtledove is heard in our land, so arise my beautiful, my beloved, and come along" (Song of Songs 2:11-13). In both the simple and the allegorical reading of the Song of Songs, the place of reunion implies the Land of Israel.

## Remain

Alternatively, Song of Songs can be read as a subtle allusion to the dream of Remain. The romantic dictate, thrice repeated, "Do not awaken love until it so desires" (Song of Songs 2:7 and 3:5 are identical; 8:4; and cf. 5:8) is interpreted by the Midrash as a warning against premature action in the matter of Return until the right moment.[5] In other words, the message of Remain may be decoded as warranting a postponement until the Messiah gives the signal that the time has come. Consonant with the three pledges (and probably launching it in the first place), is the traditional reading of the Song of Songs as a hide-and-seek love affair between God and the Jewish people.[6] A reasonable conclusion is that staying put – rather than chasing each other – is the preferred plan of (non-) action. This, of course, is the message that the Zionists defied. Their ultra-Orthodox opponents have adopted the midrashic interpretation as the foundational text of their political ideology.[7]

The most explicit textual domain of Remain, however, is the Book of Esther, which stands in direct opposition to the Book of Ruth. The Jew, Mordecai, and his beautiful ward, Esther, were seemingly well-off in the Persian capital of Sousa, after being exiled there by Nebuchadnezzar, king of Babylon. Two unforeseen developments threatened their lives – both, incidentally, based on 'refusals'. The first was that Esther (yet unrevealed as a Jewess) won the beauty contest organized on the King's behalf to find a successor to Queen Vashti, who had been banished for refusing to exhibit herself at a State banquet. The other event was Mordecai's refusal to bow before Haman, the King's first minister, in response to which Haman planned to wipe out the entire Jewish community. But Esther and Mordecai – both, independently – found such favor in the King's eyes, that the tables were turned. When Esther revealed Haman's plot to the King and disclosed her true identity as a Jewess, the King was astounded. And just as Esther had been given Vashti's place, Mordecai was given Haman's. The Jews were allowed to defend themselves against the horde whom Haman had mobilized, and did unto Haman what he had readied himself to do to the Jews. The Jews seemed to have lived happily after that and there is no hint anywhere in the Book of Esther of anything but the dream of Remain. Only God absents himself from this dream.

Alone among the Five Scrolls, Ecclesiastes seems to have no dream. Befitting its somber mood and cynicism, one can hardly expect the book to advise – one way or another – for or against this place or that. The book is not only without place; it is also without community. It is addressed not to a people, but to individuals, by a world-weary writer who has seen everything, and found nothing – but "vanity" (Ecclesiastes 1:2) or, better yet, nothingness. True, there is a "time for all things" (Ecclesiastes 3:1), an acknowledgment of commitment, and priority, accompanied by a recommendation to enjoy life without being drawn into dreaming. Remain would seem to be its most likely message.

## Take Over (Reign)

The dénouement of the Esther story is also linked to the two remaining dreams, Revenge and Take Over. True, the Jews are allowed to retaliate and Mordecai is promoted to first minister. But we, the readers, know that there is trouble ahead not only in the act of Diaspora Jews having to arm themselves to fight off a threatening mob, but also in the very act of Taking Over. The dream of Reign implies a constant anxiety not only over violent confrontation but also over being accused as 'Elders of Zion'. There is need for an Anti-Defamation League and other weapons of defense.

The most canonic of Take Overs is that of Joseph's in Egypt, long before Mordecai's. At first, it looked like Joseph's banishment to Egypt would end very badly – for Joseph and for the brothers. But, like Mordecai, Joseph managed to impress the King and, ultimately, was appointed Minister in charge of stimulating the economy and, in effect, the King's first minister. Because of the famine, Joseph brought his father and brothers and all their possessions to Egypt, together with their sheep (which the Egyptians abhorred). Meanwhile, Joseph's patron died and his successor suspected the Jews, flourishing as they were, of conspiracy. He enslaved them, and then suspected that they might be dreaming of Return, or even worse, of Taking Over. "If war should break out, they [the Jews] may join our enemies," said Pharaoh, "They may do battle against us, and leave the country" (Exodus 1:8-9).

The parallelism of the Joseph and Mordecai stories has been much remarked on. And there are even passages in Esther that allude to Exodus.[8] The Take Over in the Joseph story leads to trouble until Moses rekindles the dream of Return, and more trouble. Indeed, the journey back is full of trouble, as was the journey of Naomi and Ruth.

## Revenge

The dream of Revenge is harder to place. In the book of Esther, it accompanies the dream of Remain and the dream of Take Over. In other words, Esther contains three of the four dreams. So, perhaps, does the Joseph story, even though Revenge in Exodus is better associated with Return than with Remain. But maybe not. The Jews pillage the Egyptians on their way out; they repaid their oppressors by destroying their property and their lives, as did the Jews of Sousa, at least to some extent.

Haman has become the focus of the dream of Revenge. His downfall is symbolized annually. Eastern European Jews added vindictive rituals of hate against their oppressive neighbors, often diverting their passion to native Hamans, as documented by Eliot Horowitz.[9] The ascension of a Jewish queen – a seductive Take Over – is also a well-known genre of Eastern European (non-Jewish) folklore and literature.[10]

There is a second dream of Revenge whose target is not the host country but the marauder who forces the Jews from their homeland, or who fought unfair wars such as Amalek. The Greeks and the Romans were well-remembered in this connection. Lamentations echoes the Amalek theme. The exiles in Babylon pray that all the wickedness of the oppressors "come before thee, and do unto them as thou has done unto me" (Lamentations 1:22). They plead with God to "give them their deserts, pursue them with passion, and destroy them" (Lamentations 3:66). In this case, Revenge accompanies the dream of Return, both in time ("renew our days as of old") and in space (from "the waters of Babylon, where we... remembered Zion"). "Renew our days as of old" alluding to times when the Israelites worshipped god in the Jerusalem Temple, could in fact allude to both—temporal and geographic Return.

## II

In the foregoing, the challenges of Diaspora and its paradigmatic dreams have led us to the Five Scrolls. Can the problematics of the Five Scrolls, severally and as a corpus, possibly lead us in the opposite direction, to Diaspora and its dreams? There are at least three major historical-philological problems with the Five Scrolls: they concern (1) the canonicity of individual scrolls—as it happens, the inclusion of each of these texts in the Bible is problematic; (2) their assembly as a sub-corpus of Writings, or in other words, finding what the Five Scrolls have in common or even to do with each other; and (3) their selection for incorporation in Jewish liturgy (in all five cases of the holidays). What made these texts, with their particular problem of canonicity, fit for liturgy?

The canonicity of three of the scrolls—the skeptical Ecclesiastes, the erotic Song of Songs, and the lively drama of Esther—was repeatedly questioned and contested in antiquity. The two others, Ruth and Lamentations, seemed to be dismembered elements of accepted books in Prophets: Ruth a stray part of Judges, Lamentations a particularly bleak appendage to Jeremiah, focused on a retrospective of the disaster rather than a prophetic projection of it. The debate over the canonicity of Ecclesiastes and the Song of Songs was particularly fierce, as evidenced by deliberations in the Mishnah and Talmud. Thus, their canonical status was extensively deliberated in the Diasporic era.[11] There was an obvious ground for doubting the inclusion of these scrolls in the Bible: God, the protagonist hero of the Pentateuch and Prophets, is not even mentioned by his name in these texts, nor in Esther.

The Five Scrolls can thus be seen as an odd assembly of misfits, and their contested status in the canon seems to be one of their only commonalities. Their themes and their authorship are attributed to very different historical times: Ruth to the era to the Judges, Ecclesiastes and the Song of Songs to Solomon's reign, Lamentations to the destruction of the first Temple, and Esther to the Persian era. Then too, each of the scrolls represents a distinct genre: the elegy, the love song, the courtesan drama, philosophical proverbs, and the folk romance.

Our notion that the Five Scrolls may be useful texts for contemplating Diaspora may help address these interrelated problems. The famous debate in Yavneh over the canonicity of the Song of Songs and Ecclesiastes, possibly also Esther, was what many consider a landmark conclave of the surviving rabbinic leadership searching for a post-Temple structure for Judaism.[12] With Diaspora looming, there was a need for texts fitting a religion no longer focused on a Temple, or for that matter, lacking a geographical, political, and spiritual center. There was need for a revised canon designed for a new socio-religious polity. The Song of Song's metaphorical reading could resonate well with the diasporic experience: it narrates God and his people desperately seeking each other. The thrice repeated promise that there would come an appropriate time for love to flourish, and metaphorically for God and his people to reunite, made sense as a Diaspora dream of Remain, until the time was right for Return. In the same vein, Ecclesiastes' focused pondering of the ways of everyman—divorced from considerations of time and space—could seem particularly appropriate for a socially, politically, and geographically scattered people. For a nation in exile, with no temple and no king, the scroll's individualistic and psychological turn could be sensed as most appropriate. Esther, the book of exile par excellence, would surely fit an exilic sub-canon.

We mentioned God's conspicuous absence or marginality in four of the Five Scrolls, in contrast to His centrality in most of the Bible. Could it be that the notion of exile was applied to the divinity itself: with His Temple abandoned and desecrated, and His people scattered, God's presence became abstract and inscrutable. Texts that didn't use his name, but merely documented the presumed deeds of his now invisible hand—such as Esther,[13] Ruth, and the Song of Songs—came into favor and were included in the canon. And of course, Lamentations, where god is portrayed as prime-mover of the earthly tragedy, became more relevant than ever.

As religious life in Diaspora passed from one generation to the next, extending well beyond the 70 year landmark of the first exile, merging those of the canonic texts that were made relevant by Diaspora into a sub-corpus became a reasonable course. If some arrangements of the emergent canon had appended Ruth to Judges, Ecclesiastes and the Song of Song to Kings, and Lamentations to Jeremiah, deep in the diasporic era they were made to share a sub-corpus of their own.[14] Other than by their joint relevance to Diasporic sensibilities, this development within the canon in late antiquity is practically inexplicable.[15]

The Five Scrolls' relevance to Diaspora dreams would likewise help explain the integration of all five scrolls into liturgy, early in the Middle Ages.[16] The Book of Esther and the Purim festival were associated from early on: indeed, the penetration of Purim into the holiday calendar may well have preceded the canonization of Esther—the successful reception of the holiday may well have been a factor in the canonization of its literary blueprint.[17] The fit between Lamentations and the liturgy of the all-purpose memorial day of the Ninth of Av was also a natural. But gradually, the Song of Song became associated with Passover, Ruth with the Feast of Weeks, and albeit less universally, Ecclesiastes with *Sukkot*. Thus, all five scrolls became elements of liturgy, and it is apparently for this reason that they came to share another three distinctions: like the Pentatuch that is read in the synagogue as part of liturgy, they became physically produced as texts penned on parchment; accordingly, they assumed the shared designation of 'scrolls', and a midrash was compiled on each of them.[18] This latter development of course underscores the high level of interest and contemplation that the Five Scrolls generated.

The incorporation of the Five Scrolls into liturgy, particularly for the holiday services, would fit well with their role as repositories of Diaspora dreams. The prayers of the Sabbath highlight liturgy's role as a substitute for the erstwhile temple offerings. This displacement would intensify on the holidays, when prayer was constructed as a substitute not only for the sacrifices in the Temple but also for the erstwhile pilgrimage to Jerusalem on the three biblical festivals. The textualized ritual of the Diaspora incorporated canonic texts about Diaspora in the new liturgy lamenting the elimination of Temple sacrifices, now that "because of our sins we are exiles from our contrary and distant from our land."[19]

## III

Elaborating the thesis that the rabbis packaged these texts and made them part of liturgy as a site for the broader project of deliberating Diaspora, our colleague Aryeh Edrei further suggests that this step heralded a major trend. He points out that the underlying tension between the pols of Return and Remain have characterized rabbinic writing ever since. He suggests that while Mishnah, framed after the destruction, chooses to document the already-irrelevant laws of the Land of Israel, the temple and the priestly codes anticipating return, the Babylonian Talmud faces up to the reality of Diaspora. In later developments, the tradition bifurcates between the Sephardic emphasis (culminating in the *Shulhan Aruch*) of framing a uniform *halakhah* for the entire Diapspora— in apparent preparation for Return—and the Ashkenazi tendency to celebrate local variation, recognizing Diaspora's entrenchment. In a further gesture of support, Edrei ventures that the cyclical revival of the mystical Kabbala—like other universalist ideologies—may be a manifestation of Take Over.

It will be noted that in casting the Five Scrolls as a communal *topos* for deliberating Diaspora, we have avoided reference to individuals and groups who took one or another position in these Diaspora debates. We might also have considered the state of the debate at different periods: even if we had limited ourselves to modernity, we might have analyzed the relative standing of Return vs. Remain at the time of the Zionist upsurge in Eastern Europe, or in pre-Holocaust Germany, for example, when real choice was still available. Instead, we have focused only on the perpetuity of these four dreams, and on their explicit and implicit presence—if we are correct—in the forum provided by the reading of the Five Scrolls during the great Jewish festivals.

But we cannot avoid confrontation with real people and groups when the major dream of Return has been realized. How has the reestablishment of a national homeland affected the restive status of these dreams? Is there any point, at the beginning of the 21st century, in continuing to talk about Dreams rather than Choices?

Consider the year 2018. The Dream of Return may still be alive—in the hearts of the communities of Zionist-Orthodox Jews in the Diaspora—but also in Israel—who feel more comfortable than ever before in the Holy Land, and also feel that the Messiah is on his way more or less immediately. Some secular Zionists—like Alan Dershowitz—are active supporters of the Dream. But beyond these dedicated stalwarts, there are large numbers of Diaspora Jews whose eyes still tear when they imagine Zion. Millions of Jews from the Arab Near East actually followed the dream and resettled in the land, and more recently, so did Jews from Ethiopia, as well as millions of Russian Jews, although more hesitatingly perhaps.

American Jews were all *de facto* Zionists for a while, but never abandoned the dream to Remain. Ironically, the affirmation of Diaspora has now attained the status of rationale for assuring the well-being of the Jewish State. Just as ironic, some of the ultra-Orthodox *Haredim* find themselves in the same *de facto* camp, although they claim to be guided not by real politics but by the three Midrashic pledges that have crystallized into a central tenet of their religious ideology. Thus, it would seem that if dreamt long enough, and if solidly enshrined in canon and ritual, dreams can prove more resilient than geo-political reality.

# *Notes*

1   This paper has its origin in a group project on diasporic communication carried out in the Israel Institute for Advanced Studies at the Hebrew University in 2005. Katz developed a thematic analysis of aspirations that arose during the course of the Jewish Diaspora. He proposed that these "dreams" may be inscribed in the canonic Five Scrolls associated with holiday liturgy. Blondheim joined in fleshing out this thesis and adding its relationship to our understanding of the historical process of the canonization of the Jewish Bible.

2   The Book of Jonah also seems related to this company, in consideration of both medium and message. The Book of Jonah focuses on a community outside the land of Israel, and details the eventful journey of Jonah the prophet to that community. Moreover, the Book of Jonah, like the Five Scrolls, is a relatively short text that was incorporated into holiday liturgy—in this case, appended to the reading from the Pentateuch as a *Haftarah* (a portion from the Prophets read along with the weekly Torah portion on Sabbaths, festivals, and fast days) in the afternoon services of the Day of Atonement.

3   R. Eliezer in *Babylonian Talmud, Sukkah*, 11b; Rashi and Ramban on Vayikra 23:43.

4   The Book of Jonah marks the deliverance of the prophet from the mouth of the whale and the deliverance of the repentant people of Nineveh from near destruction.

5   *Babylonian Talmud, Ktubot* 111; *Midrash Shir ha-Shirim* 2:18.

6   In recent years, with the increased separation between the sexes in the Orthodox world, the tension between the simple and allegorical readings seems to have increased (apparently as a response to liberalizing tendencies). A most significant reflection of this was the publication of the ArtScroll edition of the Song of Song, and the debate that ensued in its wake. In the ArtScroll edition, the love affair was translated only on the allegorical level, omitting the possibility of reading it as a human love story.

7   See: Yissachar Shlomo Teichtel, *Em ha-Banim Smecha* (Budapest: M.Z. Katzburg, 1943); Yoel Teitelbaum, Vayo'el Moshe (Brooklyn: Yerushalayim, 2006); Aviezer Ravitzki, "Exile in the Holyland: The Dilemma of Haredi Jewry," in *Studies in Contemporary Jewry: An Annual, vol. 5, Israel: State and Society, 1948-1988,* ed. Peter Medding (Oxford: Oxford University Press, 1990); Aviezer Ravitzki, *ha-Ketz ha-Meguleh u-Medinat ha-Yehudim* (Tel Aviv: Am Oved, 1993).

8   E.g. Adele Berlin, *Commentary on Esther* (Philadelphia: Jewish Publication Society, 2001).

9   Elliott Horowitz, *Reckless Rites: Purim and the Legacy of Jewish Violence* (Princeton: Princeton University Press, 2006).

10  Chone Shmeruk, "Ha'Magga'im Bein Ha'Sifrut Ha'Polanit Le'Vein Sifrut Yiddish al Sippur Esterke Ve'Kazimir Ha'Gadol Melekh Polin" ("Contacts between Polish and Yiddish Literature Concerning the Tale of Estherke and King Casimir the Great of Poland"), in *Sifrut Yiddish Be'Polin* (Jerusalem: Magnes Press, 1981); Ahuva Belkin, *The Purimshpil - Studies in Jewish Folk Theatre* (Jerusalem: The Bialik Institute, 2002).

11  Shnayer Z. Leiman, *The Canonization of Hebrew Scripture: The Talmudic and Midrashic Evidence* (Hamden, CT: Connecticut Academy of Arts and Sciences, 1976), 51-124, compiles and interprets the numerous references in the Mishnah and Talmud discussing—and questioning—the canonicity of four of the scrolls. He concludes that the canonization of Writings was completed long before the destruction of the Temple, and that the deliberations in the Mishnah and Talmud about the canonicity of the Five Scrolls and other books concerned not their addition to the Biblical canon but their elimination. Leiman's

proposition that texts sanctified for hundreds of years in a traditionalist society would become candidates for de-canonizing may appear far-fetched; on Lamentations see Shlomo Zeitlin, "An Historical Study of the Canonization of the Hebrew Scriptures," *Proceedings of the American Academy for Jewish Research* 3 (1931-1932): 134.

12   Mishnah, *Yadayim* 3, 5; considerable scholarly controversy surrounds the conclave and its proceedings with regard to Biblical canon. See, e.g., Jack P. Lewis, "What Do We Mean by Jabneh?" *Journal of Bible and Religion* 32 (1964): 125-132; Menahem Haran, *The Biblical Collection,* vol. 1 (Jerusalem: The Bialik Institute, 1996), 57-59 [Hebrew]; Leiman, *The Canonization of Hebrew Scripture,* 120-124.

13   The Midrash on Esther is replete with discussions of God's concealed role in the drama. Even Esther's name, phonetically reminiscent of *hester* (hiding), was used by the Midrash to anchor this idea.

14   The Talmud, in *Bava Batra* 14b, when providing the order of the books comprising Writings, does not group the Five Scrolls together, and in the Septuagint they are scattered among the books of the Prophets and Writings. This is also the case in the fourth-century Codex Vaticanus. However, in the two earliest extant manuscripts of the Bible-- *Keter Aram Tzova* (the Aleppo Codex) and the Leningrad Codex--they appear together, as a sub-corpus, in their supposed historical order. The designation of four, possibly all five as *megillot* is based on *Masechet Sofrim* 14:8, dating from late in the Gaonic period (ca. 700-1050).

15   According to Haran, *The Biblical Collection,* the small size of these five texts could be the reason for their grouping, as in the case of the twelve prophets.

16   The earliest comprehensive sources for the liturgical use of the scrolls are *Masechet Sofrim* 14:8 (mentioned above), and *Machzor Vitry.* For short summaries, see Yitzhak Moshe Albogen, *Hatfila be-Yisrael be-Hitpatchutah ha-Historit* (Tel Aviv: Dvir, 1972), 138-39; Ernst Daniel Goldschmidt, *Mechkerey Tfilah uPiyut* (Jerusalem: Magnes Press, 1979), 396-97; Hananel Mack, *Mavo le-Tfilot Yisrael* (Tel Aviv: Misrad ha-Bitachon, 2001), 124-26.

17   Zeitlin, An Historical Study, 132-34.

18   Samuel is the only Book of the Bible not read in synagogue that has a comprehensive Midrash compiled on it. Berachyahu Lifshitz, *Midrash Shmuel* (Jerusalem: Schechter Institute of Jewish Studies, 2009), iii-iv.

19   Quote is from the *Musaf* prayer during the Three Pilgrimage Festivals.

# Bibliography

Albogen, Yitzhak Moshe. *Hatfila be-Yisrael be-Hitpatchutah ha-Historit.* Tel Aviv: Dvir, 1972.

Belkin, Ahuva. *The Purimshpil - Studies in Jewish Folk Theatre.* Jerusalem: The Bialik Institute, 2002.

Berlin, Adele. *Commentary on Esther.* Philadelphia: Jewish Publication Society, 2001.

Goldschmidt, Ernst Daniel. *Mechkerey Tfilah uPiyut.* Jerusalem: Magnes Press, 1979.

Haran, Menahem. *The Biblical Collection.* Vol. 1. Jerusalem: The Bialik Institute, 1996.

Horowitz, Elliott. *Reckless Rites: Purim and the Legacy of Jewish Violence.* Princeton: Princeton University Press, 2006.

Leiman, Shnayer Z. *The Canonization of Hebrew Scripture: The Talmudic and Midrashic Evidence.* Hamden, CT: Connecticut Academy of Arts and Sciences, 1976.

Lewis, Jack P. "What Do We Mean by Jabneh?" *Journal of Bible and Religion* 32 (1964): 125-132.

Lifshitz, Berachyahu. *Midrash Shmuel.* Jerusalem: Schechter Institute of Jewish Studies, 2009.

Mack, Hananel. *Mavo le-Tfilot Yisrael.* Tel Aviv: Misrad ha-Bitachon, 2001.

Ravitzki, Aviezer. "Exile in the Holyland: The Dilemma of Haredi Jewry." In *Studies in Contemporary Jewry: An Annual.* Vol. 5, *Israel: State and Society, 1948-1988*, edited by Peter Medding. Oxford: Oxford University Press, 1990.

Ravitzki, Aviezer. *ha-Ketz ha-Meguleh u-Medinat ha-Yehudim.* Tel Aviv: Am Oved, 1993.

Shmeruk, Chone. "Ha'Magga'im Bein Ha'Sifrut Ha'Polanit Le'Vein Sifrut Yiddish al Sippur Esterke Ve'Kazimir Ha'Gadol Melekh Polin" ("Contacts between Polish and Yiddish Literature Concerning the Tale of Estherke and King Casimir the Great of Poland"). In *Sifrut Yiddish Be'Polin.* Jerusalem: Magnes Press, 1981.

Teichtel, Yissachar Shlomo. *Em ha-Banim Smecha.* Budapest: M.Z. Katzburg, 1943.

Teitelbaum, Yoel. *Vayo'el Moshe.* Brooklyn: Yerushalayim, 2006.

Zeitlin, Shlomo. "An Historical Study of the Canonization of the Hebrew Scriptures." *Proceedings of the American Academy for Jewish Research* 3 (1931-1932): 121-158.

CHAPTER TWO

# The Simple Meaning of 'Oral Law', or The Power of the Tip of a 'Yod'

YAAKOV SUSSMAN

## *'Oral Law' – A Dilemma*

The anachronistic term 'Oral Law' is a familiar generic term for rabbinic literature, even though this vast literature has been available to us in written form for centuries. The origin of the term dates back to yesteryear when the simple distinction between 'Written Law' and that transmitted orally still existed. The dilemma arises as to when did the major turning point occur and from when was this literature recorded in writing, thus ceasing to constitute a literal 'Oral Law'? Was it one clear, distinct crossroad, a decision made for some reason at some point in time by a particular group, or conversely, was it a slow, gradual process, developing naturally due to unperceivable reasons? Did the Sages discern between the various types of writings – such as personal records, random, and unofficial by nature – and planned, formal and, authoritative literatures? These fundamental questions regarding the very essence of the 'Oral Law' have pervaded the world of Jewish studies from the outset. Screeds of opinions, viewpoints, and considerations have been voiced on this issue, and numerous research studies have been written.[1]

Jewish scholars have been divided on the question of the recording in writing of the 'Oral Law' since the Geonic period (Between the eighth and eleventh centuries), through the medieval and until the contemporary scholars – declaring numerous opinions with a range of emphases and distinctions. These included the notions: (a) that every anthology, once finalized, was also written down; (b) that Sages wrote for themselves, but not in an official manner; (c) that oral study was continued even after the inception of written books; (d) that written compositions were not compiled until later generations. Lacking a clear conclusion, the matter remains unresolved and confusion reigns.

There is no doubting the importance of this issue in determining the fundamental cultural and historical reality of the Jewish world and, in addition, for understanding the development of the 'Oral Law' and the evolution of its literature. It is also important in gaining an understanding of the study methods in the Tannaic[2] and Amoraic intellectual world – be it an oral culture or a literary culture. In this respect, additional questions can be raised: When were the various compositions of the Sages' world first recorded in writing – around the time of their 'completion' and 'editing' or only much later? Did the editor complete the written Mishna and was he its real author or was the Mishna only subsequently recorded in writing, at some later period? These questions are pertinent for each and every composition in Tannaic and Amoraic literature, in *Halakha* (Jewish law) and in *Aggada* (Jewish folklore), and apparently also in liturgy and all other realms of Jewish creation. Are 'arranging' and writing, 'editing' and writing, 'formulation' and writing — all identical in rabbinic literature? Were the 'editors' of the Talmud also their final formulators and the ones to record them in writing, or did time elapse – perhaps a significant period of time – between the 'editing' and the writing, and between the 'completion' and the final formulation? Were there books present in the *Beit Midrash* (study hall) apart from the twenty-four holy books of the bible? In general, since when did any written manuscript exist? When was the first book in the world of the Sages written? These questions are clearly not without significance from a theological point of view.

The last comprehensive, balanced, and erudite study published on this sensitive topic is that of the late Professor J.N. Epstein in his 'Mavo le-Nusah Ha-Mishnah' (*Introduction to the Mishnaic Text*, 1948), in the chapter titled "Was the Mishna Written?"[3] In his study, Professor Epstein raised the central question which, formulated simply, is: In the academies of the *Amoraim*, in their different geographical locations and over the course of the generations of that period, during which the 'Oral Law' was studied intensively, was most of it or part of it written down, or rather, transmitted verbally in its entirety? Moreover, if the Mishna was indeed studied and transmitted orally, could the *Amoraim* consult a written book in case of need and clarify the wording of the Mishna by examining a question of the *Tanna* or by referring to the written Mishna? Furthermore, did any written books of the 'Oral Law' even exist during that time period?

Epstein summarizes all relevant sources and reaches the clear conclusion that "writing was prevalent in *Eretz Israel* (the Land of Israel) during the time periods of the *Tannaim* and the *Amoraim*." As proof of such writing during the

Amoraic period, Epstein presents ten examples of evidence from varied sources, according to which he concludes that "the Mishna edited by R. Yehuda HaNasi was also certainly written by his 'Tanna'," and was available to the *Amoraim* as a written composition. Most of the evidence, however, merely refers to the actual writing of a particular law, such as a story-like recording, writing on a private notebook of an anonymous Rabbi[4], the writing of a secret scroll, etc. None of these examples is of the planned, organized writing of a book of laws or the methodical recording of a sequential halakhic text. Epstein presents only two or three pieces of evidence supporting the existence of a real book of laws, that is to say, a written book in the possession of the *Amoraim*, which could have served them as a source for the laws determined by the *Tannaim*. The single seemingly clear and convincing proof – also according to Epstein himself – is a quote in the *Jerusalem Talmud* (Dem. 2:1) that supposedly alludes explicitly to a reference of written Tannaic material, apparently a book, from which a legal clarification can be learned.

We therefore return to our basic question as to 'The Written Mishna'. In other words, since when does this central work, the foundation of the entire 'Oral Law', exist as a written book? Was it a written composition open in front of the *Amoraim* who negotiated its meaning and were intimately familiar with all details of its syntax?

## *The Solutions*

It must first be established that from the seventeenth century until the mid-nineteenth century, the generally accepted consensus of opinion – almost without exception – among both rabbinical and 'enlightened' circles, was that of Rashi's (c. 1100) firm view: "During the period of the *Amoraim* there was not even one letter of written *halakha*."[5] Only when Samuel David Luzzatto ('Shadal', 1836)[6] decisively formulated this traditional standpoint with conservative zeal, did some scholars from the Enlightenment school set out to prove the validity of the rational 'Rambam Method', which challenges the Ashkenazi 'Rashi' by claiming that the editor not only completed the Mishna but also recorded it in writing.[7] Not long thereafter, this new standpoint was unequivocally adopted by the prominent figure in the new field of Talmudic research, R. Zacharias Frankel (1859), and subsequently by the comprehensive and impressive essay of R. Israel Moses Hazan (*Iyye ha-Yam*). From this point, the tables were turned. It was the rational method of the 'Rambam' that gained ascendency, thereby transforming the writing of the Mishna into an accepted axiom of research, to such an extent that not even the most prominent scholars challenged its verity.

Two main claims regarding the question of the written Mishna were set forth by Epstein: (a) Megillat Ta'anit[8] (The Scroll of Fasts) was definitely written down at an earlier time. Despite this fact, Megillat Ta'anit is quoted from in the same manner in which Tannaic sources are cited and in the same Talmudic style, such that the language of the Talmud therefore relates to written texts as oral sources. (b) 'Transmitters' orally studying and relating the laws of the Mishna also existed during the days of the *Geonim* even though they were in possession of written manuscripts of the Mishna.

Regarding Megillat Ta'anit, it is clear to all that it was written and available since its composition, and indeed the very name - *Megilla* (scroll) – bears evidence to this fact. During the days of the *Amoraim*, however, Megillat Ta'anit was also orally studied together with its commentaries, and is therefore occasionally cited in the Talmudic style of an oral source. The second claim is innovative, namely, in that during the Geonic period "when the Mishna and the *Baraita* (traditions in the 'Oral Law' not incorporated into the Mishna) were certainly already written [down]," oral 'transmitters' ('tannaim') were still being used. Indeed, despite the explicit and irrefutable evidence that written books of the 'Oral Law' existed during the Geonic period, efforts were made to continue the traditional, oral method of study using the 'transmitters'. Conversely, during the period of the *Amoraim*, for which we have no recorded trace of a written 'book', the exclusive use of the 'transmitters' can certainly point to the fact that the Mishna was as yet unwritten at that time.

⁜

The exclusive use of 'tannaim' ('transmitters') as the oral transmitters of the Mishna and its appended *Braita* during the entire Amoraic period, and the very existence of this unique and developed institution in the Land of Israel and in Babylon, certainly bear witness to a tradition of oral study. These anonymous 'tannaim', the overwhelming majority of whom apparently did not belong to the class of the Sages, were youngsters chosen for this role by virtue of their exceptional memory, and this despite the fact that they were not always renowned for their remarkable wisdom. They appear as 'tanna', 'The tannaim of Rabbi...' or wordings such as 'The one who ordered the Mishna before Rabbi Pappa', 'The old one/The blind one,' etc. Only a few of them are mentioned by name. Only occasionally do we hear of known Sages who also served as 'tannaim' and transmitters. These 'tannaim', holding 'packages of the Mishna' in their hands, were the sole substitute for written books, and it was their role to serve as a type of living book – "a basket full of books."[9] There were permanent 'tannaim' in each academy, and in close proximity to all the great *Amoraim* (apparently there were usually several professional 'tannaim' at every major academy), whose role it was to supply the 'Oral Law', and to whom those in the academy turned to when in need of an exact specific wording from the Mishna or from a halakhic ruling not ruled on in the Mishna. Searching for any Tannaic source, the solution was found not in the written book, but rather with the 'living book' – the 'tanna'. A classic example of this appears in the Talmudic story of R. Yohannan who arrives in the town of Parod. Seeking a source containing the teachings of Bar Kappara, he encounters them in the guise of the 'tanna', R. Tanhum, the faithful guardian of Bar Kappara's teachings. The 'tannaim' constitute the complete substitute for the book – from authenticating the wording of the text to editing and finalizing the final version.

The livelihood of these 'living books', who were already selected and trained from a young age, was paid out of the public treasury. It is known that at least during the Geonic period, blind children were especially chosen for this task, a fact referred to in the Talmud. It is also known that the attitude towards the 'tannaim' was not the most respectful, especially in Babylon where power of high intellect was preferred to a scholarly possession of profound knowledge. In addition, the *Amoraim* did not always rely on the 'tannaim' and often guided them in formulating the traditions they were familiar with. The attitude towards the 'tanna' as a silent book is expressed in the words of the Talmud, "a basket full of books," and as Rashi explains: "[The 'tanna'] is merely like a basket that has been filled with books but doesn't understand their contents." The Talmud further extends this notion, among others, by declaring: "The 'tannaim' are idlers of the universe", or "The 'tanna' spoke and did not understand what he said." Thus, the poorer in knowledge the 'tanna', the more reliable his version, and he was therefore suspected less of having made contributions of his own.

Having examined the professional 'tannaim' and their role, we will now focus on the study methods of the *Amoraim* and clarify the indications supporting the existence of books in the world of the Sages.

## The Study Regime of the Sages

The method of exclusive oral study and teaching was not the sole domain of the 'tannaim'. It was similarly common to all the illustrious *Amoraim* and their pupils. The 'tannaim' (transmitters) were responsible for the meticulous and precise preservation of the wording of the Tannaic sources,[10] while the main proficiency of the *Amoraim* was in the content of the Law, even if not always in its exact wording. Their scope of knowledge certainly varied individually as they were required to know and understand not only the Tannaic sources, but also the Amoraic tradition that had been handed down and developed over time. The extent of material transmitted and studied increased consistently from one generation to the next, and this immense accumulated body of knowledge was acquired through boundless effort, constant study, and endless repetition.

The degree of dedication is incomprehensible. It is difficult to exaggerate the uninterrupted intellectual pressure that the *Amoraim* endured. The Torah was their entire world and existence. The admiration and veneration evident in rabbinic literature when describing the total devotion of the Sages to Torah study, and the varied suggestions for 'acquiring ownership of the Torah', are no figment of the imagination, but rather a factual and realistic description of the daily life and world of the Oral Torah student. The 'Oral Law' is not acquired by reading a book, but rather by "attentive listening and verbal articulation," and the danger of forgetting is a constant threat. It therefore requires absolute devotion, endless repetition, and an ongoing personal connection. The majority of the *Amoraim* and their students personally and simply fulfilled the precept to "contemplate it day and night." Throughout their entire lives, from childhood[11] until old age,[12] the world of the Sages consisted solely of Torah – night and day,[13] not as an abstract principle or desired ideal, but rather as an accepted practice in the world of the Sages. Their speech and thoughts were devoted solely to

Torah.[14] Torah occupied their day, whether in prayer[15] or daily activities, and other pursuits were cancelled in favor of its study.[16] Rashi expounds on this by defining a *Talmid Hakham* (learned scholar) as being "used to constantly repeat his version." These scholars, whose whole world consisted of the four cubits of Torah, would travel from city to city and between countries in order to study,[17] and would leave their families for lengthy periods of time.[18] It was their prayer that "…[y]our Torah be our occupation all the days of our lives."[19]

The Sages frequently describe the great effort involved in studying the 'Oral Law'. The rabbis and their students were constantly 'striving and working' in the Torah, as the Midrash states: "The words of the Torah are hard to acquire … and easy to lose." They are acquired through "attentive listening,"[20] are safeguarded by constant repetition, and lost through forgetfulness. The sole means at the disposal of the students for acquiring and preserving their Torah was unending repetition, which in turn guaranteed the preservation of the 'Oral Law'. In the words of the Babylonian Talmud, the mouth of the Sage and his pupil "never stopped reciting" the Law, and new hearsay was committed to memory by even more repetition. Before entering into the presence of their rabbi, the students would prepare their Mishna and endless repetition was encouraged, for as the Babylonian Talmud explains: "The hundredth repetition is always different from the hundred and first review."[21] The fear of confusing the tradition was so great that anyone "switching from one Talmud to another," from the Babylonian tradition to the Jerusalem tradition, had no choice but to make sure that he "forgot the Babylonian Talmud so as not to be preoccupied with it in his new studies".

The objective of the incessant repetition was to acquire proficiency in the material and ensure its commitment to memory, even if this was achieved solely by repetition without gaining an understanding of its meaning: "One should always repeat [his studies] even if he does not understand what he is saying."[22] Various techniques were suggested for this initial learning process in order to absorb the studied material, to memorize it, and to prevent subsequent forgetfulness. The Sages proposed different ideas for the strengthening of the memory and implemented varied techniques in this mechanical process of repetition, such as incessant repetition, oral repetition, repetition of chapter headings, studying with a partner, studying next to a source of flowing water, grammatical precision, studying from a single Rabbi, different mnemonics, etc. This mechanical studying of varied fashions of constant repetition, such as multiple reviews of small sections ("hearsays") and frequent repetition of larger compositions (*sugiyot*), is characteristic of the manner in which the 'Oral Law' was studied in the time of the Sages, and served as a substitute for a written text.

Those studying the 'Oral Law' in the world of the Sages would "read" the 'Written Law' from a written text, "repeat" the teachings of the *Tannaim*, and verbally determine the hearsays of the *Amoraim*. The verb "read", in its range of variations, appears hundreds of times throughout rabbinic sources with reference to reading a written text, and not a single time regarding the 'Oral Law'. In the context of Torah study, it is used exclusively for the reading of holy texts, and the distinction between written Torah study and that of the 'Oral Law' is clearly maintained. An example of this appears in the *Tosefta* (a compilation of the 'Oral Law' supplementary to the Mishna) of the *Berakhot* (Benedictions) tractate: "…to read the Torah, the Prophets, and the Hagiographa, and to orally repeat the Mishna, the Midrash, the *Halakhot*, and the *Aggadot*." No procedures for study of the 'Oral Law' contain any reference to the reading of a single book, it is all conducted orally. No form of reading or writing in the context of the 'Oral Law' has been found – it is only acquired by common hearsay and constant repetition by the student. The student of the 'Oral Law' does not acquire his knowledge through seeing the texts, but rather by hearing them. And while preservation of the 'Written Law' is guaranteed by its being written down, the entire existence of the 'Oral Law' is dependent on its constant review.

This danger of forgetting Torah, lying in wait for the unwary student, leads to the many, repeated warnings that appear throughout the rabbinic literature from its origins and until the last of the *Amoraim*. Memory and forgetfulness are one of the predominant themes that control the world of the student of the 'Oral Law', as all the knowledge is dependent entirely on memory with no recourse for referring to a written book. Sages expound on the praiseworthy virtue of memory[23] and, conversely, on the fear of forgetfulness. The praises of memory are repeated throughout the generations of *Tannaim* and *Amoraim*, as in the case of R. Yohanan ben Zakkai's leading student who is likened to "a cemented cistern that never loses a drop."[24] The quality of a student was measured by his ability to listen and retain, and his test was to remember the passage he was studying. By contrast, rabbinic literature is full of ongoing expressions of concern of forgetting – both the Law, on an individual basis, and the Torah, in general, on a national level. Once the spoken material had been internalized, the listener is obligated to ensure its preservation by repetition and review, and to take care that it is not forgotten. In the world of the Torah scholar, the ultimate tragedy is the wise scholar who has forgotten his 'Talmud'. Naturally, some forgetting is unavoidable, however, the ideal is the student who "repeats a lot and forgets little." The great dream of Torah scholars throughout the generations was, and remains, to "study and not forget."

The fear that the "Torah will be forgotten from Israel," and the daily concern for the preservation of the Torah, runs as a 'scarlet thread' throughout rabbinic literature. This is not merely the concern of the individual student, but rather one on a general, national, even cosmic degree. Entire sections of laws have been lost to forgetfulness during past periods of crisis – from prehistory until the days of the Sages – only to be rescued by virtue of Divine Providence. For example, the Talmud describes how, close to the time of the receiving of the Torah, Moses admits that "[he] heard and forgot", and how also during the period of mourning for Moses laws were forgotten, a phenomenon that continued until the period of R. Yehuda HaNasi. The very evolution – initial formulating and editing – of the 'Oral Law' literature is explained by a similar fear: "When the Sages came together at Kerem B'Yavneh they said, 'A time will come when a person will seek a point of the Law and will not find it.' "[25] The solution was the designation of orally transmitted 'testimonies' and their ordering according to a mnemonic-like manner, while the option of recording them in writing for their long-term preservation was never considered. Eventually, at a period subsequent to that of the *Amoraim*, when faced with no hope and no other choice, the great revolution in which the 'Oral Law' was also recorded in writing took place. This occurred solely because of the fear of forgetting it: "It is better that one letter of the Torah is uprooted (referring to the prohibition of writing the 'Oral Law') than the whole Torah forgotten."[26] This fear of forgetting constantly accompanied the Sages throughout the generations until the last of the *Amoraim*. Lacking written books, the Sages themselves became the bearers of the Torah and the exclusive substitute for books. Indeed, in the world of the Sages, the wise man bearing the words of the 'Oral Law' considered himself as a 'book' without which the 'Oral Law' would cease to continue existing. When in time of distress, R. Eliezer, the abovementioned 'cemented cistern' of knowledge, was considered a "Torah scroll in distress," and after his passing was regarded as "the annulled Torah scroll," "the abolished Torah scroll," or "the rescinded Book of Wisdom."[27] Even a Sage who transgressed was likened to a 'book' whose content was removed.[28]

## Evidence from Talmudic Sources

The nature of the 'Oral Law' as an evolving Torah, transmitted and studied orally, is reflected throughout rabbinic literature. The living reality of the non-written creation and transmission of the 'Oral Law' is clearly evident from our acquaintance with the Sages' world. The entire way of life of the Torah scholar, the rabbi-student relationship, the attitude toward the sources and the approach to them, illustrate that it was all conducted orally. All manners of negotiation, critique of the sources, the study and discussion of the sources, and accordingly, the terminology of the *Beit Midrash* – all reveal a world in which everything depended on the utterance of the mouth and the discerning ear, on the accuracy of the transmitter and on the memory of the recipient. Any critical student of rabbinical sources will discern that the world of the Sages is never described in the context of written books. This fact is already expressed in the Talmudic terminology: the linguistics, expressions, and phrases commonly scattered throughout rabbinic literature. As previously mentioned, the allusion to Torah subjects, and the verbs used with reference to their study, already contain a clear distinction between the written Torah and that transmitted orally. On the one hand, there is the written, biblical verse, the 'Written Law' that is read from the book; on the other hand, there is the Tannaic Mishna and the Amoraic hearsay, which is verbally repeated and reviewed. Accordingly, we can observe the accepted terms of quotation, such as "It is written" as opposed to "We have learned," "It has been learned that…" etc. The most common terms in the world of the 'Oral Law' used to express study methods, the transmission and acquisition of new material, originate from the words "said", "heard",[29] "opined", and the like, but never from words such as "wrote", "read", "saw", etc., that are used in written books. In the world of the

Sages, the rabbi speaks and the student listens and draws a conclusion from his hearsay. In the study of the 'Oral Law' the mouth and the ear are employed, never the eye, for reading: Nowhere in rabbinic literature do we find examples of expressions of seeing in the physical sense with reference to halakhic texts in the 'Oral Law'. Although the Sages were keenly aware of the advantage of "he who studies from a book,"[30] and often preferred "that which my eyes saw" rather than "that which my ears heard"[31] – they deliberately refrained from writing. Oral Law is transmitted exclusively from the speaking mouth to the listening ear. In such a reality in which books are invisible, it is not the reading of letters that endows wisdom, but rather seeing the face of the rabbi from whose mouth the Torah is heard: "See the mouth of your rabbi."[32] This developed terminology is merely an external expression of the Sages' manner of study and transmission of the Law, one that faithfully reflects the reality of the Torah scholar's world.

᪥

One of the most striking characteristics of the Sages' halakhic compositions is its liveliness and flexibility in its flow, like a never-ending spring whose recent currents wash away their predecessors. This free flow is expressed, among others, in the flexibility of the wording, the interchange of linguistic terminologies, and those transmitting the tradition. Amendments in wording and interchanges of linguistic forms constitute a part of the Sages' Torah from its outset until its formulation – both consciously and unwittingly - from changes in names and linguistic terminology with the first *Tannaim* up to the late Amoraic issues, which were changed by their transmitters and later formulators. The Sages were aware of the fact that since the beginning of time various versions of those same *halakhot* had been passed down - often significant changes and sometimes just differing versions of texts bearing the same meaning. During the Amoraic period, there were different versions of the same Tannaic traditions and of the same Amoraic sayings. It was well known that the differing versions were melded by their transmitters like works of art, each according to his tradition and understanding. This duly led to the tendency towards a flexible Amoraic critique of these traditions and, when faced with no other choice, their discretion in considering an amendment, transformation, and reformulation of the sources in light of other parallel traditions. Several such prominent examples revealing the character of the Sages' Torah as an 'Oral Law' will be examined below.

We have seen that the preservation of the material from one generation to the next was deposited in the hands of the 'tannaim' (transmitters), who were the oral suppliers of the sources for the rabbis. The care taken in selecting reliable transmitters, and on the precise transmission of the exact wording and correct context, accompanied them at every step, with regards to both the Tannaic sources and the Amoraic traditions. However, the various mistakes, substitutions, and changes in any text passed on orally by the 'tannaim' (transmitters) were inevitable . The Sages were constantly aware of the danger inherent in forgetfulness and, consequently, also of the resultant amendments and interchanges of wording and content between different transmitters, *yeshivot* (academies), and geographical centers (Babylon vs. Israel). Indeed, Amoraic literature, both the Babylonian and that from *Eretz Israel*, contains constant encounters of disputed traditions and those in doubt regarding Tannaic sources[33] and Amoraic hearsays[34]. In some, it is their source, the originators' or transmitters' names, wording, meaning, and/or context which is in dispute. On some occasions, these disputes are explicitly mentioned in the Talmud, while on others, they are brought to light by a comparison of the parallel sources between the two versions of the Talmud, or between different discussions in the same one. These phenomena, common in rabbinic literature, once again depict a simple picture of a purely oral tradition, and constitute simple, natural, and easily understandable manifestations of the reality that was the free, oral dissemination of the Law.

Correspondingly, the methods of review of the wording employed by the *Amoraim* – of the Mishna, the *Baraitot*, and the wording of previous Amoraic sayings – also typified the flexible and fluid character of the wording of the 'Oral Law'. At each and every stage, the *Amoraim* meticulously checked their sources and the reliability of its bearers, especially the accuracy of the wording. Every text underwent a strict review with particular emphasis given to those wordings of Tannaic sources. The *Amoraim* were conscious of the different versions strewn throughout the traditions of the 'Oral Law'. As a result, they attempted to enlist every possible source and every relevant consideration in order to determine their correct rendition, primarily the accurate wording of 'our Mishna' – the Mishna of R. Yehuda HaNasi – that underwent an extremely pedantic review from the time of its arrangement until the period of the last *Amoraim*. Despite the immense effort involved, many doubts surrounded the wording of the Mishna, and a constant fear persisted regarding other Tannaic sources that were suspected of being inaccurate.

Lacking means with which to verify the original version, the *Amoraim* did not hesitate, when it was necessary, to garble and repair the sources in order to reconcile the differences. The *Amoraim* knew all too well that they were dealing with sources whose wording was 'flexible', sources transmitted orally in differing versions, and that it was entirely plausible that mistakes were made during this process. Therefore, it was to be assumed that any case of contradiction or difficulty should indeed be dealt with by amending the wording of the text. Just as traditions of interchanged versions had been passed down to them, and just as the sources of those transmitting the tradition were themselves mistakenly substituted (such as those 'tannaim' who garbled the material whose meaning they didn't understand), so too did the *Amoraim* deliberately reverse and substitute Tannaic and Amoraic sources when necessary.

However, not all the sources are equal in this respect. The wording of the Mishna was certainly preserved with special meticulousness, and much more caution was exercised towards it with regard to 'amendment' suggestions compared to the other Tannaic sources, and undoubtedly more than the Amoraic traditions. Though, in principle, the entire 'Oral Law' is subject to critique and amendment of its wording. This all bears evidence of a relatively liberal attitude toward the wording of the 'Oral Law' sources, that despite the abundant caution, would be fluid by nature and given to amendment. This is only because the Law was related orally rather than from a written book, a fact that naturally lends itself to a lesser degree of punctiliousness in language and style.

Consequently, lacking written books, when confronted with a halakhic problem, the *Amoraim* had no choice but to turn to the bearers of the oral tradition, be it a 'tanna' or other scholar in possession of halakhic knowledge and tradition. Whether in search for an unknown point of law or a clarification of the exact wording of a halakhic source, the person to be consulted was the one proficient in the oral traditions – but never a book. The suggestion to "consult the book" was never heard as it was in relation to the 'Written Law'. Of the thousands of halakhic inquiries in both versions of the Talmud – whether clarifying a problematic point of law or the correct version of the sources – the questions, doubts, and interchanges of traditions were only ever verified by oral transmitters, and any solution reached was always verbally delivered by the renowned rabbi, never from a written book of law.

## Did Books Exist?

This reality of oral study – and only oral study – in the world of the Sages, and the lack of 'Oral Law' books, is clearly confirmed by the picture emerging from the general literature. This vast ocean of literature yields a clear and full picture of all points of their material and spiritual life, of which the 'book' of the 'Oral Law' is conspicuously absent. We can learn not only about almost every detail of daily life of the various strata of society and of their immediate environment, but also, more specifically, about the way of life of the Sages themselves, their actions, beliefs, and opinions. Only in the most important realm of their world, the study of the 'Oral Law' in which they dealt day and night, do we lack evidence of any written source. This 'deafening silence' proclaims itself infinitely louder than any explicit statement.

The entirety of our classic literature, in all its layers and spheres, from Tannaic and Amoraic times – both in Israel and Babylonia, in law and legend, includes thousands of references to 'books', scrolls (*megillot*),[35] and various types of writings and renditions: the books of the Torah, the Prophets, and the Writings; external and heretical books; registries of accounts, notes, letters, talismans, and miscellaneous lists and also different book-related accessories (e.g. bags, chests of books, and writing materials such as skins, parchment, paper, quills, ink, inkwells, storage containers, et cetera). These objects appear with exclusive reference to the Holy Scriptures of the 'Written Law' or laymen's documents. Despite the abundant mention of scribes, authors, and readers, there is not even a single one referring to a book of the Sages' teachings of the Law. This exclusivity of the Holy Scriptures being the only books mentioned in the Rabbis' world is so extreme that they are often referred to merely as 'the Book'.

Furthermore, all expressions containing the root letters of the Hebrew word for 'book', such as 'scribe' or 'school', refer to occupations or places associated with the Bible. In those cases where the reference is to another book, its name is stated explicitly, e.g. 'Deutero-canonical books', 'the book of Ben Sira', 'Greek book', and others. There is no reference in the world of the Sages to any non-biblical book in the *Beit Midrash* except for "heretical books" attributed to "Elisha ben Abuya."[36]

Throughout the ages, the Sages proved to be profuse writers. They wrote social messages, public letters, and were even in contact via written correspondence with each other and with the authorities. Written questions were addressed to the rabbis and they, in turn, didn't refrain from replying in writing. Examples of such are the writing of letters containing rulings of law – both by means of visible and clear writing and occasionally in more implicit form. Furthermore, communication between the rabbis and the various centers of Torah study, specifically between those in Israel and Babylonia, was apparently commonly maintained by means of letters. In any case, there is no doubt that letters containing points of law were written in every generation, whether in Babylonia or in Israel. We have also seen that the *halakhot* were written not only in letters, but also in hints that the Sages wrote for themselves, by means of 'secret scrolls', 'notebooks', etc., and of succinct notes upon which they relied in times of need. There is, however, no mention in any source of any 'book' of law, and only in the *Aggada* are there occasional mentions of 'Aggadaic literature'.

It is clear that *Aggada* books existed at least from the time of the *Amoraim*, both in Israel and Babylonia, and there were those Sages who permitted themselves from time to time to peruse these books despite the vociferous objections of other rabbis. The very fact that these books are mentioned explicitly on more than one occasion in rabbinic literature, in spite of the objection they encountered, serves as further proof. Every instance in the world of the Sages wherein a book existed is borne witness to by a mention of that book. This holds true whether the book in question is an accepted and legitimate manuscript – such as the Holy Scriptures, Megillat Ta'anit, the Book of Ben Sira, mnemonic letters and lists – or conversely, more controversial works or those opposed by the Sages, such as translations of the Bible, Aggadaic books, blessings, or even Patrimonial works.

Had the *Amoraim* already been in possession of copies of the Mishna, it seems unreasonable that the *Geonim* would have ignored them and that so many generations would have continued clinging specifically to oral study. The *Geonim* themselves describe the course of events thus: In principle, the study of the 'Oral Law' must be specifically oral, as had been customary with the *Amoraim* and as is explained in the Talmud, "those who write the Law, burn the Torah." This state of affairs, however, had existed in previous generations and now, when according to them, "the heart has become weakened," the Law may be studied from a written text.

## Back to Epstein

The accepted assumption is that the majority of the transmission and development of the 'Oral Law' throughout the era of the Sages – *Tannaim* and *Amoraim* – was by word of mouth. The Early and Later scholars' presumptions that the 'Oral Law' was originally recorded in writing during the period of the Sages, did not usually include the Mishna of the *Tannaim* or the hearsay of the *Amoraim* until their last generations. It was also clear to J.N. Epstein that throughout the entire classical period of the Sages, the study of the rabbis and their students' was oral. The only question in doubt to him was in regards to the Mishna, that of R. Yehuda HaNasi: Did a written manuscript of the Mishna also exist during the period of the *Amoraim*, when their entire study was conducted orally? In other words, is it not reasonable to assume that after its final formulation and completion, and its acceptance as the foundation of the entire 'Oral Law', the Mishna was not also recorded in writing? And that from that point in time, the *Amoraim* possessed not only a unified, authoritative, and final Mishna studied and repeated orally by all, but also a written book of the Mishna?

Epstein's conclusion is clear: "The Mishna was certainly written down by his 'tanna'." This is a seemingly sound opinion, for without it, the fantastic unity of detail and wording of the Mishna throughout the Amoraic period in both Babylonia and Israel is incomprehensible. How could things that in their very foundation were exclusively oral remain so engrained in the memory of everyone? Indeed, it is sufficient to merely reflect on the many interchanges and significant alterations concerning the wording of the *Baraitot* and the Amoraic sayings when contrasted to the impressive unity of the wording of the Mishna. As propounded by his opponents, this wonderful phenomenon can apparently only be understood by the very reasonable assumption that at least the central text of the 'Oral Law' – the Mishna – was indeed recorded in writing. According to Epstein and the scholars who support his approach, the Mishna was indeed orally passed down by 'tannaim'. These 'transmitters', however, also possessed books and lists. Thus, alongside the main pipeline of verbal transmission there were books that were not read in public or at the *yeshiva* (academy), but rather served to safeguard the unified formula of the Mishna, and were available for consultation in times of need.

It is indeed true that the wording of R. Yehuda HaNasi's Mishna was generally fixed. This should not, however, be used as the basis for a conclusion that his Mishna was recorded in writing and that those 'tannaim' verbally transmitting the 'Oral Law' possessed books. There is no mention of the possibility of verifying the wording of the Mishna during the Amoraic period, and rabbinic literature reveals that the only books they did possess were those of the twenty-four books of the bible. The only recourse the *Amoraim* had in order to clarify their doubts was to turn to the 'tannaim'. We must accept the simple fact that the 'tannaim' in the *yeshivot* really served as the living books of the *yeshiva*, meticulously preserving the exact wording of the Mishna. That the accurate preservation of the wording of a text is definitely possible through oral transmission, and not necessarily by means of written books, has become an accepted tenet of the contemporary study of oral literature. The memory devices utilized by the Sages and the common techniques for preserving the exact wording of the text, were apparently sufficient in order to maintain a reasonably high level of accuracy. The Sages were especially meticulous in depending on reliable transmitters and took care to employ fastidious transmitters, scrupulous in their total precision. It is therefore no surprise that in at least the one limited corpus – the Mishna – more than any of the other traditions of the 'Oral Law', they took care, and to a large degree succeeded, in preserving a unanimous version. These 'tannaim', who constituted 'a basket full of books', served as a real substitute for written books, and there seems no reason not to accept things at face value – that this Torah, called the 'Oral Law', was indeed exclusively oral.

The discussion above deals solely with the Jewish sources. Interestingly enough, non-Jewish sources bear a similar message. The only exception is

Augustine, who lucidly asserts: "The Mishna was not written but rather transmitted orally, from person to person." Epstein rejected this allusion by saying: "Augustinus, a pagan living in Italy, knew nothing save what he heard from others."[37] But in truth, Augustine was particularly known for the interest he took in issues of memory—mnemonics-- and orality.

If this is so, and throughout the entire period of the Sages the 'Oral Law' was solely transmitted by word of mouth with no written halakhic composition, the question must of course be raised as to when did this state of affairs change and when did the Sages move from oral study to studying from written books? The transition from the ancient tradition of oral repetition to the new practice of study from written books, must have certainly not been a simple one and not without opposition. This was not merely a superficial issue of severance from an ancient tradition, but rather a fundamental and deep revolution in the very essence and character of the 'Oral Law': a progression from the free flow of the *halakha* to its affixation in a book, from a process of open give-and-take to a sealed and binding book. It can be assumed that significant factors were involved in the onset of this major development, probably the result of a time of crisis, one of real danger to the very existence of the 'Oral Law', lest the 'Torah be forgotten from Israel'. The question persists as to whether this was a sudden revolution — a clear cut decision by some authoritative body that reached the conclusion that circumstances dictate an extreme change and a desistance from the accepted tradition of oral transmission — or, was this perhaps the result of a gradual and maybe even natural evolution in which, alongside the changing circumstances, the sages slowly grew accustomed to a reality of written books of law until the custom became absolutely permitted. In any case, this was a major change, a true revolution, one that we would expect to leave some traces in the history of the 'Oral Law'. Throughout the generations, however, we find no significant evidence of a relevant discussion or debate until the period of the Karaites, who criticized the rabbis for daring to write down the 'Oral Law' that had been deliberately transmitted only in verbal fashion.

The accounts of the Tannaic and Amoraic periods reveal no allusion to such a revolution, and oral transmission is the norm - until the last of the *Amoraim* there is no reference to any book of law. It is therefore evident that the revolution did not occur during the classic stage, but rather at a later stage.

Then again, we have seen that books of the 'Oral Law' existed already during the classic Geonic period, when in the words of Natronai Ha-Gaon (853-858), "the Talmud was found by all." Even in this instance, however, it does not seem to be a revolutionary innovation, and books of the Mishna and Talmud are mentioned as known and generally accepted without any real debate. In a paradoxical fashion, the sources at our disposal provide evidence of two contrasting situations: on the one hand, until the end of the Amoraic period there is a complete absence of books of *halakha*, and on the other hand, during the Geonic period we are witness to the familiar and accepted reality of books of the Mishna and the Talmud. On the one hand, meticulous care is taken throughout centuries not to record the 'Oral Law' in writing, and even during trying times of real danger that the Torah would be forgotten, nobody dares to deviate from the accepted tradition of refraining from preserving it in writing. On the other hand, at some subsequent point in time, as if all this was forgotten or ignored, the 'Oral Law' becomes a written one and Torah students encounter a new reality wherein there is no obvious distinction between the 'Written Law' and that which is supposed to be oral, both being now recorded and distributed in written books. If so, when and how did this revolution occur? In other words, when did the Rabbinic Talmudic world transform from an oral culture to a written culture?

## Geonic Period

We are forced to conclude that the transition occurred during a time period of which we have sparse knowledge - that is, during the long and mysterious period between the classic time of the Sages and that of the classic Geonic era. There is a wide historical void between the two periods – between the last of the Babylonian *Amoraim* and the first of the great *Geonim*. Throughout this long period of time, between the fifth and eighth centuries, we have almost no knowledge of general Jewish history and, more specifically, of Torah scholars. According to the testimony of the *Geonim*, these were apparently periods of apostasy and forced conversions both in the Land of Israel and in Babylonia. It is reasonable to assume that during these trying times for the Jewish People, times of political and cultural upheavals, when a real danger threatened the existence of the Torah, the need arose to safeguard the preservation of the 'Oral Law' lest it be forgotten. Gradually, and faced with little choice, the Sages allowed themselves to record in writing that which had been protected fiercely through a long chain of transmission. This was done in accordance with the axiom that it was preferable to uproot one letter of the Torah rather than the Jewish People forget the whole Torah. The total lack of sources throughout the three hundred year period between the last of the Babylonian *Amoraim* and the first great *Geonim*, which actually featured some of the most fateful events in Jewish history and culture, means that no theory regarding this time can be discounted.

The first explicit reference regarding the existence of written books of Mishna and Talmud can be attributed to Pirkoi ben Bavoi (ninth century C.E.; the disciple of R. Yehudai Gaon), whose teachings reveal the existence, at least in his time, of written books of 'Oral Law', a fact he did not consider innovative. It can therefore be concluded that by the end of the eighth century, or beginning of the ninth century, books of the Mishna and Talmud were a feature familiar to the scholars of the time. The assumption is that the desire to disseminate the 'Oral Law' throughout the Diaspora, including those locations outside the centers of Torah study, was one of the important factors in its written recording.

## The Oral Culture of the Sages

There is no doubt that in practice, throughout the entire rabbinic era, the Sages resisted writing laws in a book format. The idea that "those who write the *halakha* are as those who burn the Torah" was widely accepted.

The Mishna was compiled, finalized, delivered, and thereafter studied for many generations exclusively in oral fashion. The Mishna gained a degree of consensus even prior to its writing, and its content, which was accepted by the majority of the schools of Sages both in Israel and Babylonia, was more or less constant. Nonetheless, despite the superb preservation of its wording, the Mishna underwent occasional amendments and substitutions.

If no written book of the Mishna existed — the exact wording of which was so meticulously safeguarded, never written down, and transmitted in an exclusively oral fashion throughout the entire Amoraic period — all the more so can the oral tradition be assumed from the other Tannaic and Amoraic halakhic traditions that were constantly being amended, and of which there is not a single written manuscript.

The success of the sages in preserving the formula of the Tannaic sources, and of the Amoraim in their oral transmission and creation, evokes a sense of wonder and astonishment. For us, as subjects of western culture and disciples of the written word, without which any intellectual work is inconceivable, the learned culture operating and creating without books and libraries is difficult to comprehend. Recent research by Lord and Parry and others have taught and convinced us that it is indeed feasible. It is now well known that widespread oral literary creation and transmission, without written books, was an accepted form in other ancient cultures as well. This was especially true of the Eastern civilizations during the period of the Sages.

If indeed this is the case, and the Pharisaic-rabbinic world of the 'People of the Book' was devoid of written books except for 'The Book' – i.e. the twenty four Books of the Bible – until much later generations, and all their religious study and creation was exclusively oral, we must reexamine the literature and culture of the Sages. This represents a unique cultural phenomenon: hundreds of wise men, of various degrees of esteem and recognition, operated for centuries – maybe close to a thousand years – both in Babylonia and in the Land of Israel, in completely different cultural environments, and created a vast body of literature solely by word of mouth. In contrast to the surrounding cultures, none of our sages composed a single work, just as none of the dozens of compositions in the Sages' literature have an author. In those pagan, Christian, and even Jewish cultures with which the Sages came into contact, hundreds of authors wrote books in nearly every realm of literature. This was also the case among Western civilization – Greek and Roman – where almost all the intellectual personalities wrote books, in stark contrast to the world of our Sages in which they wrote not a single one. They were responsible for the creation of a diverse body of literature – *halakha* and *Aggada*, jurisprudence and biblical commentary, religious and cultural philosophy – without any individual author. This immense and varied expanse of literature bequeathed to us by the Sages is entirely collective and anonymous – collective in its creation and anonymous in its consolidation. It developed in an almost autonomic, natural manner and flowed unfettered with only occasional 'completions', after which it continued its oral transmission, until being finally recorded in writing at a much later stage.

Indeed, literary-anthropological studies have shown the existence of similar phenomena in other cultures, such as Indian, Persian, and Arabian. However, the literature of the Sages remains seemingly unique as we are discussing a society that possesses 'books', venerates books, and is fully aware of the advantages of writing and studying from a book in contrast to oral study, and yet it consciously selects the oral route. Theirs was a wide ocean of literature in which the preservation of formula was of utmost importance, and which included texts that meticulously safeguarded each detail's exactness of wording. As formulated by the tenth century scholar Rav Sherira Gaon: "Talmud and Mishna shall not be written."[38] Indeed, many complete compositions from Tannaic and Amoraic literature that remained in oral form were lost and remain as mere references within the literature selected to be recorded in writing. Even after this change in custom, the Sages sought to continue, as much as possible, their ancient tradition of maintaining only oral study of the 'Oral Law'.

## Conclusion

The 'Oral Law' is indeed literally oral – one that that was not only originally given by word of mouth, but also passed down over the generations, studied, and developed throughout the rabbinic era by purely oral means. Transmitted from one mouth to the next rather than from a written book, the 'Oral Law' truly epitomized its name. Only upon reflection of the full significance of the fact that the world of the Sages – from the first pairs of rabbis until the last of the *Sevoraim*,[39] – was an exclusively oral world, one in which all literary works were created and transmitted orally, may we fully appreciate their literature and culture.

## Notes

1   See for example: Nachman Kohen Krochmal, Moreh Nebukhe ha-Zeman (Lemberg: Michael Wolf, 1851), Chap. 14; see also Samuel Löb Goldenberg, ed., Kerem Hemed 3 (1838): 47, and Samuel Löb Goldenberg, ed., Kerem Hemed 7 (1843): 158; See also: his letter to Samuel David Luzzatto (1831); See also: Leopold Zunz, HaDrashot beYisrael, trans. Hanoch Albeck (Jerusalem: The Bialik Institute, 1954), 162, 175; Zvi Hirsch Hayot, Torat Neviim (Zolkiew: Saul Meyerhoffer, 1836), 152, and Zvi Hirsch Hayot, Mevo HaTalmud (Lemberg: Saul Meyerhoffer, 1928), Chaps. 32-33.

2    The Tannaim were the rabbinic sages whose views are recorded in the Mishna (approximately 210-220 C.E.). In addition, the term 'Tanna' (from the Aramaic word for "repeat" or "learn") was also accorded to those scholars who specialized in memorizing and repeating particular sections of the 'Oral Law'.

3    Jacob Nahum Epstein, Mavo le-Nusah Ha-Mishnah ("Introduction to the Mishnaic Text") (Jerusalem: Magnes Press, 1948).

4    The sources clearly indicate that in general this was done in a simple notebook usually containing not more than a few plates, and even occasionally, when containing more, it was still far from constituting as a 'book', i.e. codex.

5    Rashi's systematic, impressive, and comprehensive standpoint should be expanded on, even within this limited framework. This is especially important as here too, as in most of the fields of historical Talmudic methodology, it was Rashi who determined the traditional standpoint that was adopted by the majority of his pupils and, in turn, their students, eventually becoming accepted in virtually the entire Diaspora as the dominant outlook until recent generations.

6    R. Samuel David Luzzatto (1800-1865) – an Italian Jewish scholar, poet, and Talmudist.

7    For example – the Rambam's terminology in his famous answer: 'And from where do we know how our Holy Rabbi wrote in the Mishna...'

8    Megillat Taanit (Hebrew: מגילת תענית) is a chronicle which enumerates 35 eventful days on which the Jewish nation either performed glorious deeds or witnessed joyful events.

9    Babylonian Talmud, Meg. 28b.

10   And indeed, it was to the 'tannaim' that they turned in order to determine the exact wording of the Mishna.

11   The rabbis were abundant in their praise of "he who learns as a child/teaches a child" (Avot 4:20, Avot D'Rabbi Natan Chap. 21, Babylonian Talmud, Ket. 103b, B.B. 21a, Shab. 21b, and many others).

12   Also: "Be occupied in the Torah even at the moment of death" (Babylonian Talmud, Shab. 83b). Even in the grave it is expected of a Torah scholar that "his lips will whisper words of Torah" (Jerusalem Talmud, Ber. 2:72 and others).

13   Not merely as an abstract tenet or legendary hyperbole, but rather as an accepted practice in the world of the Sages in which "Torah scholars wrinkle themselves (from lack of sleep) over the words of the Torah..." (Babylonian Talmud, Hag. 14a).

14   "A Torah scholar... cannot stand without pondering the Torah" (Babylonian Talmud, Ber. 24b; Babylonian Talmud, Ta. 20b).

15   Jerusalem Talmud, Ber. Chap. 1:3b, Babylonian Talmud, Shab. 11a, Ber. 8a, and others.

16   Jerusalem Talmud, M.Q. Chap. 3:83b, M. Avot. 4:9, Babylonian Talmud, Ber. 35b, Avot De-Rabbi Natan, end of Chap. 28 and others.

17   Babylonian Talmud, Erub. 54b, B.B. 8a, Ber. 63b, and others.

18   Babylonian Talmud, Ket. 62b, Erub. 22a and others.

19   Jerusalem Talmud, Ber. 4:7.

20   Mishna Avot. 6:5.

21 Babylonian Talmud. Hag. 9b.

22 Babylonian Talmud. A.Z. 19a.

23 Praise of memory is a theme repeated throughout the generations of the Tannaic and Amoraic periods: Mishna Avot 2:8, Jerusalem Talmud, Ket. 30a, Mishna Avot. 5:12, and others.

24 Mishna Avot. 2:8.

25 Tosefta, Ed. 1:1.

26 Babylonian Talmud, Tem. 14b.

27 Tosefta, Sot. 15:3.

28 Jerusalem Talmud, M.Q 3.

29 The wide variety of terms and expressions derived from the root of the verb 'hear' are overwhelmingly dominant in the world of 'Oral Law' study. They appear as a verb and noun in almost every possible form and conjugation, and they cover wide expanses of all realms of study: from comprehension and impartation (to learn and teach), by means of knowledge, inference, understanding, approval, etc.

30 Jerusalem Talmud, Ber. 86:10a.

31 Tosefta, Ah. 16:8.

32 Babylonian Talmud, Ker. 6a.

33 These doubts appear in many forms in the Jerusalem Talmud (M.S. 285; 55d, Yom. 81; 39d) and the Babylonian Talmud (Shab. 66a, Erub. 53b, Shab. 13b, and others).

34 In other words, the entire wide realm of traditions is comprised of extremely varied types.

35 Despite "all their books being made as a megilla" and "a megilla is to be regarded as a book" (Mishna Sot. 2:4, Babylonian Talmud, Erub. 97b, Meg. 8b), a mere 'megilla' in rabbinic literature refers to a small booklet while a mere 'book' is usually larger (Lev. Rab. 142). A megilla is smaller than a book (Deut. Rab 8:3) or part of a book, and occasionally was a small independent composition (such as 'Megillat Kinot', 'Megillat Ta'anit', 'Megillat Yochasin', 'Megillat Semamanim', 'Megillat Hassidim', 'Megillat Setarim', and others). A megilla generally refers to a relatively small written manuscript – smaller than a 'book' and larger than a 'letter'.

36 Babylonian Talmud, Hag. 15b.

37 Epstein, Mavo le-Nusah Ha-Mishnah, 698.

38 Benjamin M. Lewin, ed., Iggeret Rav Sherira Gaon (Haifa: Selbstverlag des Verfassers, 1921), 71.

39 The term used to signify the rabbis living from the end of the Amoraic period (around 500 C.E.) to the beginning of the Geonic period (around 750 C.E.).

## Bibliography

Albogen, Yitzhak Moshe. *Hatfila be-Yisrael be-Hitpatchutah ha-Historit.* Tel Aviv: Dvir, 1972.

Belkin, Ahuva. *The Purimshpil - Studies in Jewish Folk Theatre.* Jerusalem: The Bialik Institute, 2002.

Berlin, Adele. *Commentary on Esther.* Philadelphia: Jewish Publication Society, 2001.

Goldschmidt, Ernst Daniel. *Mechkerey Tfilah uPiyut*. Jerusalem: Magnes Press, 1979.

Haran, Menahem. *The Biblical Collection*. Vol. 1. Jerusalem: The Bialik Institute, 1996.

Horowitz, Elliott. *Reckless Rites: Purim and the Legacy of Jewish Violence*. Princeton: Princeton University Press, 2006.

Leiman, Shnayer Z. *The Canonization of Hebrew Scripture: The Talmudic and Midrashic Evidence*. Hamden, CT: Connecticut Academy of Arts and Sciences, 1976.

Lewis, Jack P. "What Do We Mean by Jabneh?" *Journal of Bible and Religion* 32 (1964): 125-132.

Lifshitz, Berachyahu. *Midrash Shmuel*. Jerusalem: Schechter Institute of Jewish Studies, 2009.

Mack, Hananel. *Mavo le-Tfilot Yisrael*. Tel Aviv: Misrad ha-Bitachon, 2001.

Ravitzki, Aviezer. "Exile in the Holyland: The Dilemma of Haredi Jewry." In *Studies in Contemporary Jewry: An Annual*. Vol. 5, *Israel: State and Society, 1948-1988*, edited by Peter Medding. Oxford: Oxford University Press, 1990.

Ravitzki, Aviezer. *ha-Ketz ha-Meguleh u-Medinat ha-Yehudim*. Tel Aviv: Am Oved, 1993.

Shmeruk, Chone. "Ha'Magga'im Bein Ha'Sifrut Ha'Polanit Le'Vein Sifrut Yiddish al Sippur Esterke Ve'Kazimir Ha'Gadol Melekh Polin" ("Contacts between Polish and Yiddish Literature Concerning the Tale of Estherke and King Casimir the Great of Poland"). In *Sifrut Yiddish Be'Polin*. Jerusalem: Magnes Press, 1981.

Teichtel, Yissachar Shlomo. *Em ha-Banim Smecha*. Budapest: M.Z. Katzburg, 1943.

Teitelbaum, Yoel. *Vayo'el Moshe*. Brooklyn: Yerushalayim, 2006.

Zeitlin, Shlomo. "An Historical Study of the Canonization of the Hebrew Scriptures." *Proceedings of the American Academy for Jewish Research* 3 (1931-1932): 121-158.

CHAPTER THREE

# Why is This Book Different From All Other Books?

## The Orality, the Literacy, and the Printing of the Passover *Haggadah*

MENAHEM BLONDHEIM

I

The *Haggadah* is the text that anchors the traditional Jewish Passover supper, the *seder*, in which families and friends festively observe the performative rituals of eating and drinking, reciting and talking.[1] The *seder,* as framed by the *Haggadah*, has proved the most popular Jewish ritual.[2] H*aggadah* literally mans "saying" or "telling," — and in the context of Passover it echoes the Biblical commandment "And thou shalt tell thy son on that day, saying — this is done for the sake of that which the Lord did unto me when I came forth out of Egypt" (Exodus 13, 8).[3] This biblical *haggadah*: telling things to one's children, is surely an oral process.[4]

Yet the Passover *Haggadah* holds a most prominent place in the universe of script and print. Many of the most exquisite illuminated manuscripts created by and for Jews were productions of the *Haggadah*, and it has been printed in far more editions than any other text on the Jewish book-shelf. Actually, it may even be the title published in more editions in its original language than any other in the world history of printing. Prior to 1960, no less than 4,715 editions of the *Haggadah* are known to have been printed, and many others went un-recorded. This number does not include the ca. 1,500 (!) titles of "Kibbutz *Haggadah*s" which represent variations on the traditional text. It is conservatively estimated that since 1960 the number of printed editions more than doubled, reaching far more than 10,000 editions,[5] and numerous other new and original editions have been posted on digital networks.[6]

The *Haggadah*'s popularity in the material world may be explained, at least partially, by some simple circumstances. An ancient text, it was available for publication since the earliest days of printing, and it has remained in robust demand ever since. It is also a short text, that can be easily and cheaply reproduced; but more importantly, the *Haggadah* structures a ritual that is not only the most widely observed among Jews, but also one that is performed at home. While in public religious events a single copy of a text read aloud is sufficient, at least one copy of the *Haggadah* is needed in each and every literate household. The gastronomic and spirituous elements of the *seder*, as celebrated in these households, would surely account for an unusually high rate of defacement and replacement of copies.

Yet great demand for copies of a work does not necessarily lead to the issuing of many editions. As in the case of Hebrew Bibles, prayer books, and of the basic texts of the oral law—particularly the limited repertoire of recital and study texts for women—large printings and reissues of the same editions usually sufficed. In the case of the *Haggadah*, however, a great number of separate editions, some very limited, were issued to satisfy the demand. Moreover, many of the numerous printed editions of the *Haggadah* reflect considerable editorial creativity, by way of novel typographical and graphic displays, original illuminations, the addition of translations, musical notations, and of either new commentaries on the text, or a selection of classical ones, or both.[7]

The outstanding expressiveness and creativity evinced in editions of the *Haggadah* over the ages underscores the central role of redaction in the development of a text that even in its earliest stages was the product of a project of editing. The *Haggadah* was not composed by a single author, nor through a collaborative effort by a group of authors. From its origins late in the first century AD in the generation after the destruction of the Second Temple, the *Haggadah* consisted of a collage of practical instructions for performing the *seder*, and of sayings by a variety of scholars who occasionally quoted Biblical verses as prooftexts.[8] As one generation passed into the next, consecutive editors added elements to the first century nucleus. These additions too had been authored by a variety of scholars, at different times and in diverse circumstances. A succession of editorial efforts thus yielded a text which, as stabilized and canonized in the high Middle Ages, became the most popular item on the bookshelf of the "People of the Book."

The *Haggadah* is thus an unusual cultural production not only in its printing history but also in the process of its composition. But further, even a cursory survey of its contents, such as that which follows, suggests that the canonized version of the text remains a conspicuously incomplete literary production. We shall suggest that the *Haggadah*'s composition and redaction was intentionally left unfinished, and further, that its conspicuous incompleteness and lack of closure paradoxically launched the dynamic of numerous printings.

## II.

From one important perspective the popularity of the *Haggadah* is perplexing. For notwithstanding the considerable efforts of so many editors and redactors—or precisely because of them—by any conventional literary standard the *Haggadah* is a deficient text. It intends to both structure the *seder* rituals and discuss the historical story of the exodus, but the two are not clearly differentiated and do not cohere well: the *Haggadah*'s structure and flow are quite baffling. Most disturbingly, the more contemplative parts of the text are hardly gratifying. They lack the compelling drama of Biblical stories, the typical sophistication and intellectual rigor of rabbinic homiletic discourse, and the grandeur of traditional Hebrew liturgy.[9] As a literary production, the *Haggadah* is simply not an engaging text.

The Biblical story of Exodus certainly is. As narrated in the books of *Genesis* and *Exodus* it is both action-packed and thought-provoking, featuring the sure-fire ingredients of any soap opera, as they reflect on the sociology of otherness and human striving for dignity and liberty.[10] The story begins with the complex psychodrama of the family of Jacob the Patriarch.[11] It progresses through Joseph's adventures in Egypt, featuring sexual harassment and seduction, then dense intrigue in the highest echelons of Pharaoh's court, and ultimately the meteoric rise of Joseph from prison rags to riches by concocting together with the ruling Pharaoh one of the greatest speculative stings in history: the cornering the Middle Eastern grain market. Joseph, the lost son, then arranges the migration of his family to Egypt. There the Hebrews gradually fall out of favor: a people apart, they become degraded and ultimately enslaved. Only a series of spectacularly gory acts of divine violence—the ten plagues—lead to their delivery from slavery. Led by Moses—Egyptian prince turned humble, unpresuming speech-impaired shepherd—the ultimate anti-hero brings the Hebrews' uprising to its climax: the exodus. The saga ends with the Red Sea closing in on the Egyptian cavalry as it pursues the escaping slaves on their way to self-determining their future in their promised land.

The *Haggadah* captures nothing of this compelling and colorful drama, nor of its profound sociological, philosophical and theological underpinnings. What we get instead is a perplexing literary hybrid: a to-do list intended to structure the *Seder* rituals, merged with scattered references to the Biblical story. The *Haggadah*'s literary deficiencies are most apparent when it comes to the latter. It doesn't tell the story of exodus in full, let alone in detail; Moses, for instance is mentioned only once, in passing. The *Haggadah*'s slackness in telling the exodus tale is highlighted in one of its opening accords. In our contemporary text, after the opening benedictions and several Aramaic introductory verses (apparently incorporated into the text in the tenth century),[12] the son is supposed to ask his father "why is this night different from all other nights," followed by four specified observations about the *Seder*'s unique procedures (known as "the four queries").[13] The father's response to his son[14] is the first substantive statement of the *Haggadah*: "Because we were slaves to Pharaoh in Egypt. And the Lord our God brought us out from there with a mighty hand and an outstretched arm." This would surely be an appropriate topical sentence by which to commence the narrative of the Biblical epic. But the *Haggadah*'s editors had no such sequel in mind. They have the father go on to say:

> And if the Holy One, blessed be He, had not brought our fathers out of Egypt, we, and our children, and our children's children would still be slaves to Pharaoh in Egypt. So, even were we all wise, all of us full of knowledge and understanding, all advanced in years and all versed in the Torah, it is nonetheless our duty to relate the going out from Egypt, and all the those who dwell on the story of the exodus are surely to be praised.[15]

The *Haggadah*'s editors simply decline responsibility for telling the story which is the raison d'etre of their text, and assign it, instead, to their readers. This of course would suggest that the *Haggadah* can not possibly be considered a literary failure, for it is not really a literary attempt. The *Haggadah*'s readers, required by its editors to "relate the going out from Egypt," were to be its authors. How editors conceived their own role vis a vis their reader-authors, remains to be seen.

Only one section of the *Haggadah* echoes a narration of the exodus. This section includes a scattering of Biblical verses from the Books of Genesis and

Exodus, interlaced with some shallow rabbinic teachings (described by a recent scholar as "primitive in comparison with Tanaitic halakhic midrash"[16]). Taken together, these fragments form a commentary on a Biblical passage, which abstracts the exodus story. Strangely, the passage is not from the original account in the Book of Exodus, but from Deuteronomy. It is the text the Bible prescribes for the pilgrims on the Feast of Weeks to recite upon offering their first fruits at the Temple in Jerusalem. The editors of the *Haggadah*, by choosing the Deuteronomy recitation as the centerpiece for the Seder's retelling of the exodus story, and particularly in their preferring it over the primary Biblical narrative of Genesis and Exodus, appear to have provided a key to their editorial rationale. The text they selected was a conscious retrospective, an exercise in retelling the exodus story in obedience with a Biblical commandment. Just as in their framing of the opening dialogic exchange between father and son, the *Haggadah*'s editors demonstrated here that their topical focus was not the exodus event but the process of recollecting it—not the historical experience but the experiencing of history.

The Deuteronomic text itself, the core of the *Haggadah*'s rendering of the exodus, is a minimalist, matter of fact synopsis of the Biblical story:

> A Syrian, wandering about, was my father [Jacob], and he went down into Egypt, and sojourned there with a family few in number, and he became there a nation, great, mighty, and numerous. And the Egyptians treated us ill, and afflicted us, and laid upon us hard labor. And then we cried unto the Eternal, the God of our fathers; and the Lord heard our voice, and looked on our affliction, and our trouble, and our oppression. And the Lord brought us forth out of Egypt with a mighty hand, and with an outstretched arm, and with great terror, and with signs and with wonders. [Deuteronomy, 26, 6-10]

The concluding verses of the recital in the Biblical text are: "And he brought us unto this place and gave unto us this land, a land flowing with milk and honey. And now, behold, I have brought the first of the fruits of the soil, which thou hast given me, O Lord." These verses were conspicuously omitted from the *Haggadah*.[17]

Deuteronomy's retrospective reflection on the exodus highlights a second important element of the *Haggadah*'s strategy: the forging of a link between the raconteur's contemporary experience and the historical event. The Deuteronomic synopsis of the exodus leads from the historical event to the time, place, and experiences of the individual bringing his Feast of Weeks offering, very much like the *Haggadah*'s "we were slaves" overture does ("we, and our children, and our children's children would still be slaves to Pharaoh in Egypt.") This affinity would appear hardly coincidental; rather, editors apparently intended to guide *Seder* participants on ways to update the exodus story and bring it to bear on their present. They launched an exercise in turning history into a surrogate personal memory, an imagined experience.[18] The final verses of the Deuteronomy retrospective were apparently omitted because they dated the updating of the story. They did not serve the future crystallization of what was ancient history into a living, usable, past.[19]

The earliest documented outline of the *Haggadah* provides a more comprehensive perspective on the editors' dual focus on foregrounding the process of recollection and on uncovering relevance of the exodus story. This outline appears in the *Mishnah*, the authoritative compilation of Jewish oral law (ca. 200 AD), in tractate *Pesachim* chapter 10. Representing the earliest layer of our contemporary *Haggadah*, the chapter provides a version of the abovementioned four questions to be asked by the son, but as in our contemporary text, it gives no answers. It includes Rabbi Gamliel's teaching that "Whoever has not said these three things on Passover, has not fulfilled his duty, namely: Passover, Matzah, and Bitter Herb." Notable here are both the negative voice and the minimal requirement: Rabbi Gamliel avoids positively ordaining what need be said, but establishes the minimum requirement for the performance of the *Haggadah*. What would supplement it was up to the participants of the *Seder* themselves.

The Mishnah also prescribes the reciting and interpreting of the passage from Deuteronomy discussed above, and it includes several other fragments which survive in our contemporary text, such as:

> In every generation, one ought to regard himself as though he had personally come out of Egypt. As it is said [Exodus 13,8]: "And thou shalt tell thy son on that day, saying. This is done for the sake of that which the Lord did unto me when I came forth out of Egypt."

This passage may be read as the editors' justification for the dual strategy of generating personalized recollection and relevant narration.

As noted, along with framing the verbal aspects of the *Seder*, the *Mishnah* prescribes the procedures for conducting its practical rituals. The text, however, does not differentiate between the practical instructions concerning benedictions, dietary and symbolic acts, and the layer of discourse that should be conducted as part of the *Seder*.[20] This symposium-style combination points to a third, and most significant aspect of the *Haggadah*'s strategy, which can serve as a key to understanding the entire composition. For the *Haggadah* essentially provides guidelines for the telling. Its core is sayings about the saying, in an effort to regulate the recital of the story, and not its substance. Taken together, the various elements incorporated in the *Mishnah*'s outline yield a unique textual being. The *Haggadah* is a toolbox that includes prescriptions for enhancing collective and individual memory. This apparatus includes performative symbolic acts and expert advice and examples for framing meaningful discourse to enhance the experience of remembering, internalizing the memory, sharing it, and teaching it.[21]

Subsequent layers of the *Haggadah* provide additional sayings and anecdotes attributed to second century scholars, which were not included in the relevant chapter in the *Mishnah*. These fragments too keep their distance from the story of the exodus, reflecting instead rabbinic traditions about the telling of the story. For instance:

> A tale is told of Rabbi Eliezer, and Rabbi Joshua, and Rabbi Elazar the son of Azariah, and Rabbi Akiba, and Rabbi Tarphon: They were reclining in Bnei Brak and were telling about the outgoing from Egypt during the whole of that Passover night, till their pupils came and said to them: Our teachers, the time has come for the recitation of the morning Sh'ma [chapter of the morning prayer].

Said Rabbi Elazar the son of Azariah: See, I am like one seventy years old, and have never been privileged to hear the story of the outgoing from Egypt told during the nights, until Ben Zoma expounded the Writ as follows: It is said "In order that you may remember the day of the going forth from the land of Egypt all the days of your life." [From which he inferred that, whereas the expression] 'the days of thy life' would indicate only the days. 'All the days of thy life' includes the nights as well.[22]

These passages argue when, how, and until when the story could and should be told. What the second century rabbis actually said or the moral of their story is not disclosed. Like the teachings in the *Mishnah* chapter, these fragments address the recital of the story, and carefully refrain from prescribing what to recall and remember, let alone what to say. The story was to be provided by the *Seder*'s participants.

A procession of subsequent editors in successive generations added elements and layers of text to the early compilations. These subsequent additions followed, in the main, the strategy of the first and second century editors. They did not provide the Biblical account of exodus in their texts. Nor did they chose the most significant among the meaningful, picturesque, and thought-provoking commentaries and homilies on the Biblical text, with which rabbinic literature is replete. Rather, they selected and collated a corpus of lore and sayings that focused on aspects of the telling of the exodus tale. Included in these additions are examples of how the story should and could be told in a meaningful way to four sons of varying attitudes and competencies: the wise son, the wicked son, the simple son and the son who does not even know how to ask. Other additions serve to demonstrate how far scholars could go in torturing every word in the Biblical story to yield fantastic implications (such as the Egyptians being afflicted by hundreds of plagues, not only ten), and how the redemption from Egypt could be cast as a typology providing morals for all subsequent generation: "For in every generation there are those who rise against us to destroy us, and the Holy One, blessed be He, delivers us out of their hands."[23]

The project of the *Haggadah*'s earliest editors was thus the shaping of a meta-text—a text framing a spontaneous, changing dialogue. Their intent was fully grasped by subsequent editors and emulated by them, mainly adding tools rather than finished literary products to the text. Yet nowhere did *Haggadah* editors elaborate on why they chose this unique editorial strategy: why they refrained from a comprehensive telling the story of exodus, leaving that task to their audiences. A recent historical study of the *Haggadah* in the context of the rabbinic encounter with Christianity could be construed to suggest that this strategy was shaped as a defensive move in response to the Christian appropriation of Judaism's scripted religious texts.[24] Yet the persistence of the *Haggadah*'s editorial approach over the ages, notwithstanding changes in Jewish-Christian relations (or even the advent of Islam), and the recurring emphasis on involvement rather than knowledge, point to a broader cause, one which relates to religious experience rather than to religious strife. This broader meaning appears to emerge from juxtaposing the unique characteristics of the *Haggadah* as a meta-text with its intended religious function, within the context of the media environment in which it evolved.

## III.

The *Haggadah* was created within a religious culture that was deeply conscious of the divide between the oral and the written. Whatever the oral underpinnings of the Hebrews' ancient heritage, this orality was effectively swamped by the dominance of the scripted book.[25] The written words of the Five Books of Moses reigned supreme in that religious culture as the expression of divine authority. But in what may be considered a surprising turn by conventional wisdom on the dynamics of orality and literacy, orality reentered the scene with gusto and established itself prominently in parallel to, and as distinct from, the literate tradition.[26]

From the middle of the first millennium BC there is evidence that a body of oral law had developed among the Jews alongside the scripted tradition, and moreover, that a clear distinction was made between the written text of the Pentateuch and this body of oral interpretations and supplements.[27] With the gradual canonization of the 24 books of the Hebrew Bible, the distinction between the scriptures and the oral tradition became sharper and more clearly defined.[28] Moreover, the oral law conferred on itself a divine authority. It was attributed to God, through a tradition that Moses received two bodies of law—one to be committed to writing (in the form of the Pentateuch), the other to remain unwritten. Ultimately, the distinction between the two bodies of the divine message would yield a theological theory of orality and literacy. God, according to this media theology, embraced the divide between the oral and the written by distinguishing two parts of his law by the medium of their conveyance.[29]

By sanctifying a duo-media religious universe this media theology provided religious leaders and scholars with tools that could promote both religious authority and flexibility—resilience in time and space but also adaptability to their forces of change. Scriptures, attributed to a divine source, would provide absolute, unchanging authority. The written text, if properly stabilized (through authoritative textual safeguards) and physically secured (most effectively through multiple copies), would carry on unchanging, absolutist authority across time.[30] Moreover, the oral law developed and matured in a culture well aware of the specter of exile and diasporic existence. The scripted law could serve as a centripetal anchor, a center of gravity unifying Jews scattered over international space just as it distinguished them from their gentile neighbors. Authoritative scriptures common to Jews throughout the diaspora could serve as a 'portable homeland'.

Yet vesting exclusive authority in stable and durable texts could not ensure the endurance of the message they carried. As material artifacts, texts exist outside the mind and are not necessarily part of experience and consciousness. A book can be marginalized, even neglected, and ultimately become an irrelevant historical relic. By stabilizing a supposedly divine text, it is inevitably frozen into a specific epoch, retaining the characteristic ideas and sensibilities, literary conventions and style, the language and even the graphic look and feel, of the temporal and spatial context in which it was canonized. Thus, paradoxically, precisely the stability and physical durability of scriptures, threaten their endurance as authoritative foundations for a vital culture, let alone a diasporic one.[31]

An oral tradition, in contrast, is refreshingly free from the specter of irrelevance, of becoming dated or foreign, then neglected and forgotten. Unlike the book that can be "laid in a corner"[32] and abandoned, oral knowledge cannot exist outside consciousness—'to have it is to know it.' Moreover, oral knowledge is homeostatic in nature. Since it can only be retained and developed through speech events in the course of the ongoing historical process, it inevitably takes on the hue and color of the time and place of its rendering, dynamically adjusting to contemporary circumstances and sensibilities and changing with them.[33] This sort of knowledge is also universally accessible: it does not require prerequisites such as mastery of the technique of reading, or the hermeneutic skills necessary for making sense of archaic wisdom.

Oral tradition is, however, deficient in stability and authority.[34] Its contingence on changing circumstances and on the social relations which plot its transmission, and the ephemerality bred of its homeostatic dynamic, raise the specter of anarchy and atrophy of the oral tradition. While its existence in the memories and minds of people gives it relevance and life, it also subjects it to corrosion and decay. And of course, the disasporic condition could lead to a decisive fragmentation of the formerly common oral tradition.

In the case of Jewish oral culture, a culture well versed in script, a possible solution to the peril of the oral law's atrophy could be the ongoing scripting of the oral tradition. But given that culture's media theology, such a solution could not be adopted: God had deliberately divided his message between the oral and the written medium; he expected the distinction to be respected, and ergo, the oral law would have to remain unwritten. The solution that scholars and religious leaders of antiquity arrived at was perfecting a procedure which scholar Saul Lieberman called "oral publishing." A definitive version of the oral law was shaped by recognized editors, and their compilations were committed to memory by specialists, and to an impressive extent, by general scholars too. In this way, the distinction between the oral and the written was preserved, but also a considerable degree of authority and stability of the oral law was achieved. This half-way publication scheme retained a significant measure of flexibility and dynamism: as the oral law developed and expanded, through applying the scriptures to changing spatial and temporal circumstances, new authoritative editions of the oral law were compiled and republished orally, by a succession of editors. In this way the duo-media system sustained a vital mix of fixity and flexibility.[35]

## IV.

Against the backdrop of this hybrid media environment, first century rabbis sought to reshape the celebration of Passover after the destruction of the Jerusalem Temple. Once the Biblically prescribed Passover precepts of pilgrimage and sacrifices could no longer be practiced, they had to search for substitutes. The most appropriate inspiration for a transformed ritual was going behind the letter of the Biblical precepts to what could be taken as their original intent. In the case of Passover observances, the Biblical rationale for the festival's rituals was apparent enough. The Bible had in fact articulated it explicitly and repeatedly.

The most complete explication of this rationale was provided in *Exodus* 13:3-10: that passage first explains that the Passover laws were instituted so as to "remember this day" of exodus, then that "thou shalt tell thy son on that day saying this is done for the sake of that which the Lord did unto me when I came forth out of Egypt." And finally, "And thou shalt keep this ordinance in its season from year to year." The rabbis decided to transform the didactic rationale the Bible gave for observing the Temple-focused Passover laws into a precept in its own right, shaping a ritual of telling.[36]

In streamlining this novel ritual of words, the rabbis apparently took their clue from a tension in the Biblical text. The two latter phrases just quoted appear to contradict: one ordains the recollection of the personal experience of exodus, the other calls for conveying this participatory legacy perpetually—inevitably to those and by those who had not, in fact, experienced it. The two verses, when taken together, were construed to imply that the telling, in generations after the exodus, should effect the transformation of historical knowledge into living memory and consciousness. The focus of the new post-destruction observances would thus be an exercise in fashioning an imagined experience. The Bible's explicit educational directive of passing on remembrance to one's progeny, together with the tradition of sacrificing the Passover offering in the framework of the family, pointed to the household as the appropriate venue for the transformed Passover ritual.

In their duo-media world, Jewish sages well knew that reading the contrived and dated Biblical text of Exodus, or hearing it read, was not equivalent to identifying with the narrated event nor to conveying it as a living memory to one's progeny. The Biblical text was history, not experience, and therefore, although they had prescribed Bible readings as part of ritual for other religious occasions, it was not appropriate for the Passover *seder* that was to covey an imagined personal experience. The alternative tool in the rabbis' media arsenal—orality—was admirably suited to the task. The homeostatic adjustment mechanism built into it would provide the necessary measure of relevance and experience, and its prescribed social setting was conducive to a didactic process.

The rabbis could, of course, establish an oral ritual of remembrance by transplanting the story of the exodus from the realm of the scriptures to the oral universe. They could compose an appropriate up-to-date text and publish it orally. With time, verses, anecdotes and sayings adjusting the original oral text to changing circumstances would be added and streamlined in successive oral publications. But, when it came to performing the Passover feast of remembrance, this method could not be followed—even more flexibility was necessary. For although a relevant, situationally sensitive, exegesis of the Book of Exodus, or a homily on Passover responsive to the here and now, could link past and the present and ensure relevance, one hegemonic voice could not possibly evoke, nor properly express, individual memory. A prescribed public telling of the Passover, even by the oral medium, could at best express collective memory and experience, but not properly represent or enhance personal consciousness. A polyphonic text was called for.

Moreover, the social situation conducive to generating and enhancing personal consciousness is dialogical. Indeed, the educational and didactic process prescribed by the Bible implied the adjustment of the exodus story to the personal capacities of each family member, be he wise, wicked, simple, or one who couldn't even ask.[37] And of course, by following the Temple-period tradition and prescribing the Passover ritual to the family circle, the rabbis practically precluded the possibility of prescribing a requisite oral text—the entire population could not be expected to commit to memory and repeat a comprehensive, orally published, rabbinic discourse. The most the public could be expected to memorize was the agenda for the feast of remembrance (later cast in a 16 word mnemonic), the three words stipulated by R. Gamliel and the short recital from Deuteronomy, discussed above as well as the four simple and quite obvious questions, to which parents were to improvise their own answers, as adjusted to the receptiveness of their own children and to the spirit of their times.[38] Thus, the editors of the *Haggadah* could not and would not determine what people were to say, but they could and did frame what people would talk about, and how, and when, and where. They articulated a rationale and structured a comprehensive framework for telling the story of the exodus in all future times and places, providing examples and offering recommendations for effective ways remembrance could be accomplished. They stopped short of telling the story: they left its narration, and making sense of it, to the actual performers—individuals and families in every home, in every age.

As the oral law expanded, and as Jewish life became increasingly destabilized, threats to the integrity, even to the mere retention, of the oral law mounted. Gradually, it was realized that scripting the orally published law was inevitable. Yet scruples about writing what God had wished should remain unwritten, persisted.[39] In the case of the Talmud, the scripted publication was cast in a dialogical, conversational form, underscoring its fundamental orality and thus distinguishing it from the writerly texts of the Bible. In the case of the *Haggadah*, no such contrivance was necessary. Its orally published, then scripted, elements were merely a shell, or a menu. Its true text had ever been, and was to remain, oral.

By the high Middle Ages, the scripted text of the *Haggadah* had been stabilized. Subsequently, print technology dramatically enhanced its fixity, broadening the gap between the prescribed and the spontaneous in the process.[40] The canonized *Haggadah* has remained generally unchanged, and lives on, in a productive tension between its stable, finite, script and the unwritten, open, and improvised discourse, which it implies and prescribes.

## V.

The *Haggadah*'s editors shaped a text, which occupies a unique enclave on the limen between the oral and the written. There are numerous scripted works that reflect oral foundations. Homer and the *Congressional Record*, the catechism and law reports, together with any number of other successfully scripted oral texts—including parts of the Bible itself—represent an oral foundation frozen into script. Yet the *Haggadah* works in the opposite direction—it was ever a deliberately "published" text, and ultimately a consciously scripted one, which rejects and subverts its own writerly medium and calls for an oral performance. Other textual genres—screenplays, scores, even cookbooks and restaurant menus—also call, implicitly, for their performance in a different medium. Yet they usually are designed to allow their performers only a limited degree of freedom in staging that which they prescribe in the alternative medium. The *Haggadah* is unique in its rejection of itself, in being a script imploring its readers to create and improvise their own oral text.

This fundamental tension built-in-to the *Haggadah* between the scripted and the oral text may account for its unsurpassed popularity in the worlds of script and print, as pointed out in the opening of this article. It may also explain the outstanding creative efforts invested by the numerous editors, publishers, and printers of the *Haggadah* over the past half-millennium. The text that editors prepared for print was an ancient one, yet its thrust was a plea for relevance, for a new and relevant rendering. Sensitive editors could not but respond to the tension between the text's closure and its underlying openness. They were led to respond to the *Haggadah*'s plea for relevance, or rather, to its meaninglessness without it. They dressed the ancient text with their most contemporary trappings: typefaces and graphics, illustrations, translations, scores, and commentaries. Since, as its earliest editors averred: "In every generation, one ought to regard himself as though he had personally come out of Egypt," editors of every generation and each Diaspora printed, as it were, their own story of exodus.

"Why do they print new *Haggadah*s every year?" a North American rabbi was asked early in the previous century. That was the time when millions of traditionalist Jewish immigrants from Eastern Europe were accommodating to an industrializing and modernizing secular America. Most did so by sloughing off their traditions and religious observances. "It is simple," answered the staunchly traditionalist American rabbi: The *Haggadah* tells of four sons: one of them is a wicked, sinful son. But since last year, lamented the rabbi, the spiritual condition of the community has deteriorated so badly, that last year's wicked son is a saint by this year's standards. We need new *Haggadah*s, concluded the rabbi, for the new and unfathomed wicked son of this year.[41] Following the logic, if not the sardonic stance, of the North American rabbi, the illustrations of the *Haggadah* demonstrate how the wicked son, together with the wise son, the simple son and the son doesn't even know how to ask, had changed over the generations and across the diaspora, as did the imaginations of *Haggadah* illustrators, from time to time and from place to place.

And indeed, as children grew up, their questions matured; and as parents aged, their worlds, their memories, and therefore their answers were reshaped. Since the *Haggadah* is a mere blueprint for a conversation between parent and child, between one generation and the next, and between man and history, every individual in every age and at every place was expected to edit and perform her own time- and space-sensitive *Haggadah*. The text's printers, by producing new editions, merely tried to keep pace with the dynamic transformation of history, people, and text.

## Epilogue

Editors, publishers, and printers mediate between texts and audiences. By transforming the text, they can redefine or create an intended audience. But redaction may do more than that: It may significantly affect 'conditions of reception'—the settings and circumstances in which the text is experienced by its audience.

Research on media-effects, from the era of the world wars to the present, has fluctuated between notions of the mass media having powerful effects on actions, opinions, and agendas, and notions of low media effects—of selectivity and autonomy on the receiving end. Over the past decades, with the increased focus on processes of reception and meaning construction, a weak media effects approach has prevailed. Recently, however, scholars studying the ways in which media determine the reception process itself, have proposed that by affecting conditions of reception, mediators exercise an important determining influence on the ways messages are experienced and decoded, internalized and acted on, by their audiences.[42]

The foregoing could be construed as a case demonstrating the significance of the communicators' power to shape reception conditions, in this case, the ways in which editors and printers may affect them. As we have argued, the *Haggadah*'s sequence of editors did not tell their audience what to think or say. They merely set an agenda for what to discourse about, and also, prescribed the time and place, the physical and social conditions, of the communicative process. Most significantly, they determined the medium to be used: by omission and by commission they prescribed a dialogic oral exchange as the medium through which history would be transformed into living memory.

To the extent that the story of exodus has survived as a personal and collective constitutive experience for Jews over past millennia, the *Haggadah*'s editors successfully delivered their message. The historical success of the *Haggadah* as the most popular Hebrew text, and of the *Seder* that it structures as the most widely observed Jewish ritual, would indicate that the *Haggadah*'s editors, by shaping conditions of reception, had conveyed a very powerful and effective message.

But in parallel to effecting their audiences, editors and publishers of the *Haggadah*, by consistently refraining from determining what people were to think and say about the exodus, also delivered an alternative, even conflicting message. This message was the celebration of the autonomy of readers, their freedom from the domination of authors, editors, and printers. No scripted message could be more relevant to the moral of the exodus and its message of cultural autonomy, intellectual liberty, and self-discovery.

## *Notes*

1   On the origins and significance of the term *"seder"* (lit. order) see David Henshke, *'Ma Nishtannah': The Passover Night in the Sages' Discourse* (Jerusalem: Magnes Press, 2016), 1, n. 1; Joseph Tabory, *Moadei Yisrael biTkufat haMishnah vehaTalmud* (Jerusalem: Magnes Press, 2000), 123 [Hebrew]. The nature of the social gathering of families and friends is predicated on the original nature of the Passover supper as a *"se'udat zevach"* (*Moadei Yisrael*, 115-116).

2   According to Shlomo Deshen, "Secular Israelis on Passover Eve: The Shadow of Family on Religious Symbols," *Megamot* 38 (1998): 528-546, the *seder* is observed by more than 80% of Israeli Jews, secular as well as religious. It is also the most commonly observed religious ritual among contemporary identifying Jews of the Diaspora: Shlomit Levy, Hanna Levinson, and Elihu Katz, *A Portrait of Israeli Jews: Beliefs, Observance of Tradition, and Values of Jews in Israel 2000* (Jerusalem: Israeli Democracy Institute, 2002), 7; and earlier: Shlomit Levy, Hanna Levinson, and Elihu Katz, *Beliefs, Observances, and Social Interactions Among Israeli Jews* (Jerusalem: Louis Guttman Institute of Applied Social Research, 1993), 9. Cf. poll on https://www.bjpa.org/content/upload/bjpa/beli/Beliefs%20 Among%20Israeli%20Jews.pdf. On reasons for the observance of the *Seder* by secular Jews see Yosef Hayim Yerushalmi, *Haggadah and History: A Panorama in Facsimile of Five Centuries of the Printed Haggadah from the Collections of Harvard University and the Jewish Theological Seminary of America* (Philadelphia: The Jewish Publication Society, 1997), 14-15.

3   For a variety of reasons, Biblical texts are quoted in Isaac Leeser's English translation.

4   This simple understanding of *'haggadah'* may also reflect the common contemporary—and apparently historical—practice of performing the *Haggadah* as oral conversational discourse. However, this understanding has been rejected by recent scholars of rabbinic literature. Berachyahu Lifshitz, for instance, argues that the use of *'haggadah'*, in the context of comprehensive compilations of Jewish oral law, denotes the free, legally unbinding,

public interpretations and homilies on the scriptures (in contrast to *"Aggadah"* which denotes 'secret' esoteric knowledge): Brachyahu Lifshitz, "Aggadah and its place in the development of oral law," *Shnaton Hamishpat Haivri* 22 (2001): 233-328; see also Yonah Frenkel's reservations and Lifshitz' rebuttal in *Netuim* 11-12 (2004): 63-79, 81-93. David Henshke appears to support this more technical terminology: Henshke, *'Ma Nishtannah'*, 17. This formal understanding of *"haggadah"* although it rejects the conversational dynamic of "telling," is compatible with the account below on the *"Arami oved avi"* recital.

5   Based on Isaac Yudlov, ed., *The Haggadah Thesaurus: Bibliography of Passover Haggadot From the Beginning of Hebrew Printing until 1960* (Jerusalem: The Magnes Press, 1997). The estimate is based on extrapolating from the 76 new editions published in 1960, and the increase in each year between 1955 and 1960 (e.g. 50% increase between 1959 and 1960). On "Kibbutz *Haggadahs*" see: Israel M. Ta-Shma, "Introduction," in *The Haggadah Thesaurus: Bibliography of Passover Haggadot From the Beginning of Hebrew Printing until 1960*, ed. Isaac Yudlov (Jerusalem: The Magnes Press, 1997).

6   The *Haggadah's* presence on the internet has included, since the latter 1990s, live broadcasts of public performances of the *Seder,* e.g. www.emanuelnyc.org/Seder, and cf.: http://jewmu.com/Seders.cfm. Playfulness as an attribute of cyberculture is evident in numerous internet *Haggadahs*. See, e.g.: http://www.ucalgary.ca/~elsegal/Uncle_Eli/Eli. html (hard copies available from author).

7   It even happened that the same author published more than one commentary on the *Haggadah*. Thus, in 1910 Gedeliah (George) Silverstone, Washington DC's leading Orthodox rabbi, published a *Haggadah* with a Hebrew commentary that represents a striking exposition of the state of Orthodox American Judaism in its formative phase. Thirty years later, in Palestine, he republished the *Haggadah* with his original commentary, and added a second commentary reflecting the tragic state of the Jewish world on the eve of the Second World War. These two commentaries, taken together, represent a revealing binocular perspective on the development of Orthodox Judaism in America, Europe, and Palestine in the 20th century, and on the *Haggadah* as a primary literary topos for working out the tensions between history and the ephemeral, as discussed below. Gedaliah Silverstone, *Seder Haggadah shel Pesach im Perush Korban Pesach* (New York: Hebrew Publishing Co., 1910); Gedaliah Silverstone, *Sefer Korban Pesach al Haggadah shel Pesach...bive'ur Hagigat Pesach* (Jerusalem: Dfus Ha'ivri, 1939).

8   The origins of the *Haggadah* are controversial; however, recent scholarship has established it as a post-Temple composition: see Henshke, *'Ma Nishtannah'* pp. 357-508; and earlier the standard work of Baruch M. Bokser, *The Origins of the Seder: The Passover Rite and Early Rabbinic Judaism* (Berkeley: University of California Press, 1989), and note 14 below. In constructing the history of the text I have mainly followed the critical edition of the *Haggadah* by Shmu'el Safrai and Ze'ev Safrai, *Haggadah of the Sages: The Passover Haggadah* (Jerusalem: Carta, 1998) [Hebrew], as well as two earlier critical editions: Menachem M. Kasher, *Haggadah Shlema: Seder Haggadah shel Pesach im Chilufey Nuscha'ot, He'arot Veztyunim Veyalkut Perushim* (Jerusalem: Torah Shlema, 1961) [Hebrew]; and E.D. Golschmidt, *The Passover Haggadah: Its Sources and History* (Jerusalem: the Bialik Institute, 1960) [Hebrew]. In the present case both Kasher and Goldschmidt predate the beginning of the *Haggadah* to the Second Temple period.

9   The *Haggadah* does incorporate the *Hallel*—"giving praise" a high-toned and impressive Psalms-based liturgy. Yet although *Hallel* includes Psalm 114 which refers to the exodus, it is not exclusive to the *Haggadah* and is integral to the liturgy of all holidays (in some of them in an abridged version).

10    See, for instance, Michael Walzer, *Exodus and Revolution* (New York: Basic Books, 1986).

11    The forerunner of the *Haggadah, Mishnah, Pesachim,* chap.10 (see below) prescribes (according to most interpretations) the telling of the Passover story beginning with Jacob's sojourn in Aram.

12    It begins with a reference to the *Matzah*—the unleavened bread—as *"lachma ania."* This phrase is commonly translated as "the bread of affliction" or "the bread of the poor," however, according to an opinion in the Talmud, it should be read as "bread of dialogue:" *Babylonian Talmud, Pesachim,* 36a, 116b—a reading consonant with our argument. Cf. Hayim Hirshensohn, *Luach Moadey Yisrael* (Jerusalem: Dfus Haivri, 1936).

13    Some commentaries consider the son's query as merely "in what way is this night different from all other nights," and the four observations about the *seder's* unique procedures are the preliminary answer: After all, the child is not supposed to know at the commencement of the *seder* what it's subsequent course will be.

14    This sexist formulation follows the traditional notion of gender roles. A short discussion of the role of women in the *Seder* is provided in Safrai & Safrai, *Haggadah of the Sages,* 46-47.

15    The *Haggadah* translations used here are by Abraham Regelson, *The Haggadah of Passover* (New York: Shulsinger Brothers, 1949).

16    Israel Jacob Yuval, *'Two Nations in Your Womb': Perceptions of Jews and Christians* (Tel Aviv: Am Oved Publishers, 2000), 93.

17    It is widely held that the first of these two verses, and possibly both, were originally part of the *Haggadah.* For a summary of these opinions see Joseph Tabory, "On the Text of the *Haggadah* in the Time of the Temple," *Sinai* 82 (1978): 97-108; and Joseph Tabory, "The History of the Order of the Passover Eve" (Ph.D. diss., Bar Ilan University, 1977), 238-249; Tabory, *Moadei Yisrael,* 120. Those who hold that an antecedent of the *Haggadah* existed in the time of the Temple quite reasonably relate the omission of these verses to the destruction of the Temple. However, it is still possible to hold that the *Haggadah* originated after the destruction, and the omission reflected the failure of the great revolt or the mass exile in its aftermath which made "gave us unto this land" inappropriate. See. Bokser, *Origins of the Seder,* 89-90.

18    Yuval explains the selection of the Deutronomic passage as a response to the Christian appropriation of the main text in Exodus. However, in other instances such as the focus on *Pesach, Matzah, and Maror,* Yuval proposes an opposite dynamic according to which the *Haggadah* emphasized precisely the elements that the Christians had appropriated, in an attempt at re-appropriation. This latter argument appears the more convincing: Yuval, *'Two Nations in Your Womb',* 83-93, as compared to pp. 94-103. See also Bokser, *Origins of the Seder,* 76-80.

19    An overview of the role of historical memory and consciousness in Jewish national-religious culture (although not historiography) is proposed in Yosef Hayim Yerushalmi, *Zakhor: Jewish history and Jewish memory* (Seattle: University of Washington Press, 1982). For related work on the role of cultural performances of historical construction in the service of nation building (focused on the American experience), see Jay Fliegelman, *Declaring Independence: Jefferson, Natural Language, and the Culture of Performance* (Stanford: Stanford University Press, 1993); Sandra Gustaphson, *Eloquence is Power: Oratory and Performance in Early America* (Chapel Hill: University of North Carolina Press, 2000).

20    The combination of these disparate elements has given rise to a long tradition of interpreting the *seder* on the model of the Hellenistic symposium. This approach has, however, been

rigorously criticized: see discussions in Tabory, "The History of the Order..." 251-259; Bokser, *The Origins of the Seder,* 50-66.

21 On the centrality of historical consciousness in Jewish history see: Yerushalmi, *Zakhor;* Yitzhak Baer, *Galut,* trans. Robert Warshow (Lanham, MD: University Press of America, 1988); Jacob Katz, "The Concept of Social History and its Possible Use in Jewish Historical Research," in *Studies in Economic and Social Sciences,* vol. 3, *Scripta Hierosolymitana,* ed. Roberto Bachi (Jerusalem: Magnes Press, 1956), 292-312.

22 On the sources for these sayings and the stage of their incorporation into the *Haggadah* see Safrai & Safrai, *Haggadah of the Sages,* 117-119.

23 On these additional layers see Ibid., 50-71.

24 Yuval, *'Two Nations in Your Womb',* 71-107, et passim.

25 Particularly lucid on this point is Martin S. Jaffee, "Writing and Rabbinic Oral Tradition: On Mishnaic Narrative, Lists and Mnemonics," *Journal of Jewish Thought and Philosophy* 4 (1994): 123-146; and see Martin S. Jaffee, *Torah in the Mouth: Writing and Oral Tradition in Palestinian Judaism 200 BCE-400 CE* (New York: Oxford University Press, 2001).

26 For a summary of the communicative significance of this process see: Menahem Blondheim and Shoshana Blum-Kulka, "Literacy, Orality, Television: Mediation and Authenticity in Jewish Conversational Arguing, 1-2000 C.E.," *The Communication Review* 4 (2001): 511-540.

27 The Sadducees, however, who as priests guarded the authoritative copies of the written law archived in the Temple, may have incorporated oral law teachings into the text, in contrast to the Pharisees who upheld the differentiation between the two bodies of law. See Lifshitz, *"Aggadah"*; Yaacov S. Spiegel, Pages from the *History of the Hebrew Book: Proofs and Proofreading* (Ramat Gan: Bar Ilan University Press, 1996); A. Rosenthal, "Tora Shebe'al Pe Vetorah MiSinai: Halakhah Uma'aseh," in *Mechkarey Talmud,* vol. 2 (Jerusalem: Magnes Press, 1993) [Hebrew].

28 A useful introduction to this process of canonization is Herbert Edward Ryle, *The Canon of the Old Testament: An Essay on the Gradual Growth and Formation of the Hebrew Canon of Scripture* (London: Macmillan and Co., Limited, 1909); but see Sid Z. Leiman, *Canonization of Hebrew Scripture: The Talmudic and Midrashic Evidence* (New Haven: The Connecticut Academy of Arts and Sciences, 1991); and the somewhat divergent perspective in Jacob Neusner, *Canon and Connection: Intertextuality in Judaism* (Lanham, MD: University Press of America, 1987).

29 Here and in the following the masculine was used. No disrespect for either women or God is intended. The literature on this issue is extensive. For an introduction see Jacob Neusner, *Oral Tradition in Judaism: The Case of the Mishnah* (New York: Garland Publishing, Inc., 1987). The literature features differing opinions as to the relative importance of the tradition as opposed to the derivation aspect of the oral law. For a recent discussion placing a strong emphasis on derivation see Jay M. Harris, *How do we Know This? Midrash and the Fragmentation of Modern Judaism* (Albany: SUNY Press, 1995); for a more balanced analysis see Yohanan D. Silman, *The Voice Heard at Sinai: Once or Ongoing?* (Jerusalem: Magnes Press, 1999).

30 An overview of the process of stabilizing the scriptures and subsequently the texts of the oral law is Spiegel, *Pages from the History.*

31 This analysis is based on Harold Adams Innis's approach, which emerges from the various essays in Harold Adams Innis, *The Bias of Communication* (Toronto: University of Toronto Press, 1951). Innis's approach is discussed in Menahem Blondheim, "Harold Adams Innis

and his Bias of Communication," in *Canonic Texts in Communication Research*, eds. Elihu Katz, Tamar Liebes and John Peters (London: Polity Press, 2003).

32 *Babylonian Talmud, Kiddushin*, 66a. Yet the original intent of the phrase was probably that a text is accessible to all while oral knowledge is under the willful control of those who possess it.

33 Convenient and accessible introductions to the psychodynamics of orality and literacy are: Walter J. Ong, *Orality and Literacy: The Technologizing of the Word* (London & New York: Routledge, 1982; heavily influenced by Jack Goody's seminal works) and Ruth Finnegan, "Sociological and Anthropological Issues in Literacy," in *Literacy: An International Handbook,* eds. D. A. Wagner, R. L. Venezky & B. V. Street (Boulder, CO: Westview Press, 2000), 89-94.

34 Notwithstanding the assumed Godly origins of both bodies of law, the role of human agency was acknowledged as much greater in the case of the oral law. This agency had two aspects: one was the transmission of the divine teachings not committed to writing from one generation to the next by word of mouth. The other was the derivation of the oral law from the text of the Testament by means of supposedly God-given exegetical tools. According to both aspects, God's original intent became subject to the human mind—to its powers of memory in transmitting oral edicts in the first case, to its intellectual powers to divine the 'true' meaning of the texts in the second, and in both cases to man's competence in applying the principles of the law to changing circumstances. Either way, an important implication of an oral law was the notion of accommodation—of God empowering the products of human intellectual processes. See, e.g., Gershom Scholem, *The Messianic Idea in Judaism* (New York: Schoken Books Scholem, 1995), 284-291; Amos Funkenstein, *Perceptions of Jewish History* (Berkeley: University of California Press, 1993), 88-121.

35 Saul Lieberman, *Hellenism in Jewish Palestine* (New York: Jewish Theological Seminary of America, 1950), 20-46; and see Sussman's article in this volume.

36 Cf. Bokser, *The Origins of the Seder*, 1-13.

37 I have previously argued that the dialogic structure of oral speech acts, in contrast to the hegemonic one-way structure of literacy, could serve to symbolize dimensions of equality and liberty, associated with Passover: Menahem Blondheim, "The *Haggadah* as a Story without an End," *Amudim* (Spring 1994): 168-170 [Hebrew].

38 Not surprisingly, mnemonics are prominent in the early layers of the *Haggadah*. Thus, the entire structure of the *Seder* is shorthanded into a list of 15 items (most pairs of items rhyme), and Rabbi Yehudah's arrangement of the ten plagues in three acronyms. Safrai and Safrai suggest that anchoring the exodus story on the Deuteronomy passage was due to the ease of recalling it from memory due to its brevity: Safrai & Safrai, *Haggadah of the Sages,* 33-35, 128-131.

39 It may even be that the names of the tractates of the Mishnah and their acronymic arrangement yielding the words *"zman nekat"*—lit. time to hold/seize reflect an apologetic stance and allude to the text commonly used to justify the scripting of the oral law: *Psalms* 119, 126 (e.g. Bavli, Gittin, 60a; Tmurah, 14b).

40 The degree to which print affected cultural closure and uniformity remains highly controversial. For a summary of the opposing positions see: Elizabeth L. Eisenstein, "An Unacknowledged Revolution Revisited," *American Historical Review* 107, no. 1 (February 2002): 87-105; and Adrian Jones, "How to Acknowledge a Revolution," *American Historical Review* 107, no. 1 (February 2002): 106-125.

41  Yehuda Leib Graubart, *Dvarim Kikhtavam: Drushim* (St. Louis: Salz & Galman Publishing Co., Chicago: 1931/2), 27. The title of this sermonic work is of particular relevance to the issues discussed in the foregoing: *Sayings as Written: Sermons.*

42  Research on media effects is vast. For a convenient summary see: Denis McQuail, *Mass Communication Theory: An Introduction* (London: Sage Publications, 1994), 325-372 (on reception studies alluded to above see pp. 283-324). Investigation into conditions of receptions is associated with the work of Elihu Katz and Daniel Dayan: e.g. Daniel Dayan and Elihu Katz, *Media Events: The Live Broadcasting of History* (Cambridge: Harvard University Press, 1992); Elihu Katz and Michaela Popescu: "Supplementation: On Communicator Control of the Conditions of Reception," in *European Culture and the Media,* eds. P. Golding and I. Bondjberg (Bristol: Intellect Press, 2005).

## *Bibliography*

Baer, Yitzhak. *Galut.* Translated by Robert Warshow. Lanham, MD: University Press of America, 1988.

Blondheim, Menahem. "The *Haggadah* as a Story without an End." *Amudim* (Spring 1994): 168-170 [Hebrew].

Blondheim, Menahem and Shoshana Blum-Kulka. "Literacy, Orality, Television: Mediation and Authenticity in Jewish Conversational Arguing, 1-2000 C.E." *The Communication Review* 4 (2001): 511-540.

Blondheim, Menahem. "Harold Adams Innis and his Bias of Communication." In *Canonic Texts in Communication Research,* edited by Elihu Katz, Tamar Liebes, and John Peters. London: Polity Press, 2003.

Bokser, Baruch M. *The Origins of the Seder: The Passover Rite and Early Rabbinic Judaism.* Berkeley: University of California Press, 1989.

Dayan, Daniel, and Elihu Katz. *Media Events: The Live Broadcasting of History.* Cambridge: Harvard University Press, 1992.

Deshen, Shlomo. "Secular Israelis on Passover Eve: The Shadow of Family on Religious Symbols." *Megamot* 38 (1998): 528-546.

Eisenstein, Elizabeth L. "An Unacknowledged Revolution Revisited." *American Historical Review* 107, no. 1 (February 2002): 87-105.

Finnegan, Ruth. "Sociological and Anthropological Issues in Literacy." In *Literacy: An International Handbook,* edited by D. A. Wagner, R. L. Venezky and B. V. Street, 89-94. Boulder, CO: Westview Press, 2000.

Fliegelman, Jay. *Declaring Independence: Jefferson, Natural Language, and the Culture of Performance.* Stanford: Stanford University Press, 1993.

Frenkel, Yonah. "HaAgaddah Besifrut HaTalmudit - Nachzor Al Rishonot." *Netuim* 11-12 (2004): 63-79 [Hebrew].

Funkenstein, Amos. *Perceptions of Jewish History.* Berkeley: University of California Press, 1993.

Golschmidt, E.D. *The Passover Haggadah: Its Sources and History.* Jerusalem: the Bialik Institute, 1960 [Hebrew].

Graubart, Yehuda Leib. *Dvarim Kikhtavam: Drushim.* St. Louis: Salz & Galman Publishing Co., Chicago, 1931/2.

Gustaphson, Sandra. *Eloquence is Power: Oratory and Performance in Early America.* Chapel Hill: University of North Carolina Press, 2000.

Harris, Jay M. *How do we Know This? Midrash and the Fragmentation of Modern Judaism.* Albany: SUNY Press, 1995.

Henshke, David. *'Ma Nishtannah': The Passover Night in the Sages' Discourse.* Jerusalem: Magnes Press, 2016.

Hirshensohn, Hayim. *Luach Moadey Yisrael.* Jerusalem: Dfus Haivri, 1936 [Hebrew].

Innis, Harold Adams. *The Bias of Communication.* Toronto: University of Toronto Press, 1951.

Jaffee, Martin S. "Writing and Rabbinic Oral Tradition: On Mishnaic Narrative, Lists and Mnemonics." *Journal of Jewish Thought and Philosophy* 4 (1994): 123-46.

Jaffee, Martin S. *Torah in the Mouth: Writing and Oral Tradition in Palestinian Judaism 200 BCE-400 CE.* New York: Oxford University Press, 2001.

Jones, Adrian. "How to Acknowledge a Revolution." *American Historical Review* 107, no. 1 (February 2002): 106-125.

Kasher, Menachem M. *Haggadah Shlema: Seder Haggadah shel Pesach im Chilufey Nuscha'ot, He'arot Veztyunim Veyalkut Perushim.* Jerusalem: Torah Shlema, 1961 [Hebrew].

Katz, Elihu, and Michaela Popescu. "Supplementation: On Communicator Control of the Conditions of Reception." In *European Culture and the Media*, edited by P. Golding and I. Bondjberg, 19-40. Bristol: Intellect Press, 2005.

Katz, Jacob. "The Concept of Social History and its Possible Use in Jewish Historical Research." In *Studies in Economic and Social Sciences.* Vol. 3, *Scripta Hierosolymitana*, edited by Roberto Bachi, 292-312. Jerusalem: Magnes Press, 1956.

Leiman, Sid Z. *Canonization of Hebrew Scripture: The Talmudic and Midrashic Evidence.* New Haven: The Connecticut Academy of Arts and Sciences, 1991.

Levy, Shlomit, Hanna Levinson, and Elihu Katz. *Beliefs, Observances, and Social Interactions Among Israeli Jews.* Jerusalem: Louis Guttman Institute of Applied Social Research, 1993.

Levy, Shlomit, Hanna Levinson, and Elihu Katz. *A Portrait of Israeli Jews: Beliefs, Observance of Tradition, and Values of Jews in Israel 2000.* Jerusalem: Israeli Democracy Institute, 2002.

Lieberman, Saul. *Hellenism in Jewish Palestine.* New York: Jewish Theological Seminary of America, 1950.

Lifshitz, Brachyahu. "Aggadah and its place in the development of oral law." *Shnaton Hamishpat Haivri* 22 (2001): 233-328.

Lifshitz, Brachyahu. "Al Rishonot Anu Mitztaarim - A Response to Prof. Yonah Frenkel." *Netuim* 11-12 (2004): 81-93 [Hebrew].

McQuail, Denis. *Mass Communication Theory: An Introduction.* London: Sage Publications, 1994.

Neusner, Jacob. *Canon and Connection: Intertextuality in Judaism.* Lanham, MD: University Press of America, 1987.

Neusner, Jacob. *Oral Tradition in Judaism: The Case of the Mishnah.* New York: Garland Publishing, Inc., 1987.

Ong, Walter J. *Orality and Literacy: The Technologizing of the Word.* London & New York: Routledge, 1982.

Regelson, Abraham. *The Haggadah of Passover.* New York: Shulsinger Brothers, 1949.

Rosenthal, A. "Tora Shebe'al Pe Vetorah Misinai: Halakhah Uma'aseh." In *Mechkarey Talmud.* Vol. 2. Jerusalem: Magnes Press, 1993 [Hebrew].

Ryle, Herbert Edward. *The Canon of the Old Testament: An Essay on the Gradual Growth and Formation of the Hebrew Canon of Scripture.* London: Macmillan and Co., Limited, 1909.

Safrai, Shmu'el, and Ze'ev Safrai. *Haggadah of the Sages: The Passover Haggadah.* Jerusalem: Carta, 1998 [Hebrew].

Scholem, Gershom. *The Messianic Idea in Judaism.* New York: Schoken Books Scholem, 1995.

Silman, Yohanan D. *The Voice Heard at Sinai: Once or Ongoing?* Jerusalem: Magnes Press, 1999.

Silverstone, Gedaliah. *Seder Haggadah shel Pesach im Perush Korban Pesach.* New York: Hebrew Publishing Co., 1910.

Silverstone, Gedaliah. *Sefer Korban Pesach al Haggadah shel Pesach...bive'ur Hagigat Pesach.* Jerusalem: Dfus Ha'ivri, 1939.

Spiegel, Yaacov S. *Pages from the History of the Hebrew Book: Proofs and Proofreading.* Ramat Gan: Bar Ilan University Press, 1996.

Tabory, Joseph. "The History of the Order of the Passover Eve." Ph.D. diss., Bar Ilan University, 1977.

Tabory, Joseph. "On the Text of the *Haggadah* in the Time of the Temple." *Sinai* 82 (1978): 97-108.

Tabory, Joseph. *Moadei Yisrael biTkufat haMishnah vehaTalmud.* Jerusalem: Magnes Press, 2000 [Hebrew].

Ta-Shma, Israel M. "Introduction." In *The Haggadah Thesaurus: Bibliography of Passover Haggadot From the Beginning of Hebrew Printing until 1960,* edited by Isaac Yudlov. Jerusalem: The Magnes Press, 1997.

Walzer, Michael. *Exodus and Revolution.* New York: Basic Books, 1986.

Yerushalmi, Yosef Hayim. *Zakhor: Jewish history and Jewish memory.* Seattle: University of Washington Press, 1982.

Yerushalmi, Yosef Hayim. *Haggadah and History: A Panorama in Facsimile of Five Centuries of the Printed Haggadah from the Collections of Harvard University and the Jewish Theological Seminary of America.* Philadelphia: The Jewish Publication Society, 1997.

Yudlov, Isaac, ed. *The Haggadah Thesaurus: Bibliography of Passover Haggadot From the Beginning of Hebrew Printing until 1960.* Jerusalem: The Magnes Press, 1997.

Yuval, Israel Jacob. *'Two Nations in Your Womb': Perceptions of Jews and Christians.* Tel Aviv: Am Oved Publishers, 2000.

CHAPTER FOUR

# Orality, Language, & Segregation
## The Split Jewish Diaspora Revisited
### ARYE EDREI AND DORON MENDELS

## Two Languages - Two Worlds of Knowledge

The Jewish world during the Hellenistic period was noticeably dispersed.[1] In addition to the center in the Land of Israel, there were diaspora communities in both the East and the West.[2] The eastern diaspora extended from Trans-Jordan to Babylonia, and the western diaspora included Asia Minor, Greece, Italy, and the Mediterranean islands. Most scholars in the past who have dealt with the Jewish diaspora during this period have blurred the distinction between the eastern and western diasporas, explicitly or implicitly assuming that knowledge about one diaspora could inform the other.[3] Hesitations about this assumption have emerged in recent years, as for example in Tessa Rajak's article and, in particular, in an article by Martin Goodman.[4] In this study, we wish to re-examine this topic, and to suggest that the distinction between the two diasporas was not only geographic, but actually reflected a much more substantive split. The centrality of Jerusalem and the Land of Israel as a unifying force was a significant factor in the Jewish world prior to the destruction of the Temple. This was not so after the destruction. Our study will focus on the period *following* the destruction and the split that grew in its wake. The Jewish world had already been divided with regard to language in the early Greek period. In the West, Jews wrote and spoke only Greek, while in the East, Hebrew and Aramaic prevailed. The Land of Israel served as the border between the two diasporas. Even there, there were communities that wrote and spoke Greek. Our argument is that the language gap between the two diasporas led to a much deeper cultural gap than we tend to think, and also led in practice to a division from a normative perspective. Later in our discussion, we will challenge the accepted scholarly assumption that the rabbis in the center, that is the Land of Israel, maintained contact with the entire Jewish diaspora and affected practice related to religious and cultural life. We will see that there are clear and unequivocal proofs that this connection existed with the eastern diaspora, but with regard to the western diaspora, there is a deafening silence on this issue in Jewish sources. We will explain this gap against the background of the widening abyss between the eastern and western diasporas. This fact must be taken into account when considering not only the relationship between the diasporas, but also on a deeper level, the similarities and differences between the Judaisms of each diaspora.

Diaspora communities vacillate between the desire to preserve both their unique identity and their connection to their cultural center and a desire to integrate into the broader cultural context in which they live.[5] The destruction of the Temple by its very nature upset the balance between these two aspirations,[6] as the connection to the center became an unclear, and even irrelevant, concept. The loss of the center has far reaching implications for communication, which is enhanced by a strong center that controls a defined system of communication. As we know, the Temple constituted a clear and unequivocal center for the entire Jewish world. Its status derived from both its imposing physical symbolism and its recognized functions, well known for many generations and accepted by the entire Jewish world, as well as from a long supportive tradition.[7] As we will argue, the rabbinic literature and world of knowledge, that emerged after the Temple disappeared in 70 C.E. and subsequently became the new "center," was inaccessible to the Greek Jewish diaspora. The messages that emanated from this center were essentially different from those that emanated from the previous center, and could not be deciphered by the Hellenistic Jewish diaspora. Our discussion in this study does not review the differences that developed between the motherland and Hellenistic Judaism, nor the distinction between the syncretistic Judaism that developed in the diaspora and the less-syncretistic Judaism in the Land of Israel. Rather, our focus is on the loss of communication and the clear gap in Jewish practice that developed in the aftermath of the destruction of the Temple.

Our argument might be better understood when contrasted with the situation in the Middle Ages in which the *Mishnah* and the *Talmud*, which had already been committed to writing, served as the basis for both a common learning curriculum and a common normative practice. These works were both accessible and studied extensively during this time period. Scholars throughout the Middle Ages wrote about the *Talmud*. Their works were written exclusively in Hebrew, with some intermittent Aramaic, the language of the *Talmud* that everyone knew.[8] As a result, in spite of the development of different academic approaches and different customs, everything flowed from community to community because there was no language barrier.[9] This was not the case in the period that we are discussing. We claim that during the period after the destruction of the Temple, a hierarchical system of communication emerged in the eastern Jewish diaspora that included leadership, institutions, a bureaucracy, and a clear message. On the other hand, the western diaspora itself developed a flat system of communication, lacking both institutions that paralleled those in the Land of Israel and a leadership that spoke their language.

The distinction between the eastern and western diasporas is reflected in the Jewish literature that prevailed in each community. The Bible was the common literature of the entire Jewish community, with each separate community maintaining access to it in their own language. Yet, in the Land of Israel, a new Jewish literature developed during this period, the tannaitic literature (*Mishnah* and *Midrash)*, and subsequently the amoraic literature (the *Talmud*). This literature spread eastward, and the Babylonian community became full partners in its development. It could not, however, reach the West because the Jews of the western diaspora were unable to decode it. Simultaneously, the western diaspora adopted a very different collection of literature – the apocrypha and pseudepigrapha – which was rejected by the sages of the East.

A comparison of the two different and separate corpuses preserved in the two diasporas will illuminate and strengthen our theory regarding the isolation of the western diaspora. The halakhic and aggadic corpus built upon Hebrew and Aramaic was preserved as an oral tradition in the eastern diaspora.[10] In contrast, the corpus preserved in the West was a written tradition. Whereas the Hebrew Bible was translated into Greek early on, the Rabbinic corpus was not translated, and to the best of our knowledge, there was no attempt to translate it into Greek or Latin. This fact strengthens the hypothesis that the vast majority of Jews in the western diaspora had no access to this literature. In contrast, certain books of the apocrypha and pseudepigrapha, which developed in the early Hellenistic period, were fundamentally different from the eastern literature in both content and genre. Some of this literature was originally written in Greek (such as 2 Maccabees), while some others were written in Hebrew and subsequently translated into Greek (such as 1 Maccabees[11]), and distributed among the Greek speaking community.[12] Just as the halakhic and aggadic literature preserved in the East was not made accessible by translation in the West, most of the apocrypha and pseudepigrapha did not continue to be preserved in the Hebrew-Aramaic speaking eastern diaspora (some exceptions are the Aramaic Testament of Levi, Tobit, Ben Sira, and Jubilees in Hebrew, but most of them were not accepted by the rabbis). It is thus clear that in Babylonia they were similarly unable to access the literature written in Greek and Latin. This literature is practically not mentioned in the rabbinic literature, and when it is mentioned, it is referred to as "external" literature in order to distinguish it from the Biblical canon.[13] One thus gets the sense of two very different communities on either side of the Mediterranean Sea, serviced by two diverse bodies of literature that were distinct in terms of content, genre, language, worldview, and normative practice.[14] On one side, the Bible and rabbinic literature that was still transmitted orally, and on the other side, the Greek translation of the Bible and part of the Pseudepigrapha and Apocrypha, the so called "external" literature. This created a reality characterized by two distinct universes of discourse, two different systems of communication, and the different ideologies that developed as a result.

Even before the destruction of the Temple, the normative system that was in force in the western diaspora differed from the practices that prevailed in the Land of Israel. For example, there were areas of practice that were relevant to Jewish life in the Land of Israel but were irrelevant in the diaspora, such as laws relating to agriculture and working the land (*Seder Zeraim*), or laws relating to purity and impurity and the Temple service. There is no doubt that prior to the destruction of the Temple, these laws constituted a majority of the normative Jewish legal system. This fact accentuates the gap between the Land of Israel and the diaspora, and the benefit that the sages saw in living in the Land of Israel – the opportunity to fulfill the entire Torah. This gap should have narrowed after the destruction of the Temple, but in reality, the opposite occurred – many normative areas that had previously been identical became different. Prior to the destruction of the Temple, we can detect the influence of early rabbinic tradition in the Jewish community of Rome, a phenomenon that was probably facilitated by extensive pilgrimages of Jews from Rome to Jerusalem. After 70 C.E., however, rabbinic influence faded away.[15] Thus, for example, laws relating to the holidays and to prayer were transformed following the destruction because of the circumstances of the period. We claim that specifically this area of the normative system, which was eventually adopted in the eastern diaspora as in the Land of Israel, could not reach the western diaspora because of the communication and language barrier. After the destruction, when the leaders of the Jewish community in the Land of Israel struggled for their future survival, the normative gap between the community in the Land of Israel and the community in the western Greek-speaking diaspora represented a significant cultural and religious gap.[16]

Sanders has already demonstrated at length that during the second Temple period, the Jews of the diaspora did not passively obey instructions from the Pharisaic leadership in Israel, even though they attributed great importance to Jewish law and wished to observe it. He believes that the view held by many scholars that the rabbis held sway over the entire diaspora is a baseless illusion. Sanders bases his opinion primarily on sources that preceded the destruction of the Temple, and it is logical to conclude that this would be even more accurate after the destruction when diaspora Jews traveled less often to Israel and the connection weakened. Thus, for example, Sanders claims that Jews who made pilgrimages to Israel for the festivals certainly purified themselves before entering the Temple and were familiar with the ritual baths of Israel. Nevertheless, we have no evidence of the existence of ritual baths in the diaspora at that time. This would certainly be the case as well in areas of Jewish law that were not noticeable from visits to Israel. The Jews of the Greek diaspora read the Bible and followed its commandments, as they understood them according to the tradition that they had received. It is therefore obvious that these Jews observed the laws of *kashrut* (Jewish religious dietary laws), an area of Jewish law that is quite clear from the Biblical injunctions themselves, as is confirmed in Jewish and non-Jewish sources:[17]

> The diaspora Jews, left entirely to their own devices, without Pharisees whizzing around the Mediterranean telling them what to do, read the Bible and did what they thought was appropriate.... Diaspora Jews too loved the law and wanted to obey it, and they did not depend on Pharisees to tell them to do so.[18]

Prior to the destruction of the Temple, pilgrimages and the donation of funds to the Temple were instrumental in maintaining a strong connection with the national and spiritual center in the Land of Israel. In the wake of the destruction, the Jews of the diaspora sent contributions to support the institution of the *Nasi* (title of the highest-ranking member and president of the *Sanhedrin*, or Assembly).[19] However, two Roman laws dated to the years 363 and 399 C.E. deal with the cancellation of this tax.[20] In the law from 363 C.E., the emperor stated explicitly as follows:

> That which is termed by you the tax of the emissaries is nullified. In the future, no one will be able to harm your multitudes by exacting these taxes. You are thus freed from worry....[21]

The law, from 399 states:

> It is a matter of shameful superstition that the Archsynagoges, the presbyters of the Jews, and those they call apostles, who are sent by the patriarch on a certain date to demand gold and silver, exact and receive a sum from each synagogue, and deliver it to him. Therefore everything that we are confident has been collected when the period of time is considered, shall be faithfully transferred to our Treasury, and we decree that henceforth nothing shall be sent to the aforesaid.[22]

It is clear from these laws that until that point, the Jews had sent money to the *Nasi* administration. The fact that the Romans believed that it was possible to break the bonds between the diaspora and the *Nasi* in the Land of Israel might indicate that they viewed the connection as purely bureaucratic. Moreover, the harsh terminology used by both emperors may allude to the fact that they believed that this tax was seen by the Jews as an unnecessary and disturbing obligation. This supports the argument that the connection between the western diaspora and the Land of Israel became progressively weaker. The emperor intervened because he understood the reality. He was not working against the Jews, but was rather working on their behalf. The gap between the two normative worlds widened, and the strength of the bond between them correspondingly weakened. There is nothing in these laws to suggest that there were spiritual or religious connections between the *Nasi* and the Jews in the western diaspora beyond the financial sphere.[23]

We base ourselves on the assumption that is accepted by most scholars that the Jews of the West did not know Hebrew or Aramaic, and that their religious lives, including the reading of the Torah and prayer, were conducted only in Greek.[24] The Torah was translated into Greek in the third century B.C.E., and in subsequent centuries the rest of the Bible was translated as well. It should be pointed out that in certain rabbinic circles, the translation to Greek was viewed as a necessity of the reality of the times. The sages recognized that there were entire diaspora communities that spoke only Greek, and that they would be lost to the Jewish people in the absence of an authentic translation. While the sages struggled for the preservation of Hebrew as the sole language for religious activity, that is, prayer and Torah study, they simultaneously provided for an authorized translation of scripture for the Greek speaking communities. A conspicuous example is the Biblical translation of Aqilas,[25] the student of R. Akiva, who modified the Septuagint according to the unique approach of R. Akiva that attributed importance to every letter and word.[26] The sages generally approved of this translation. Nevertheless, the rabbinic literature of the time, namely, the *Midrash* and the *Mishnah*, whether preserved orally or in written form, was not translated. Therefore, as the years progressed, these works remained obscured from the Greek speaking Jews.[27] We wish to emphasize that although scholars agree that the sages in Israel knew Greek to varying degrees,[28] one cannot conclude from this that Jews in the Greek diaspora knew Hebrew. We will return to the issue of translation later on.

Research regarding inscriptions found in synagogues in Israel and in the Greek diaspora lends support to our contention. These discoveries lead to dramatic conclusions about the differences between the Jewish communities of Israel and the diaspora, differences that can primarily be assumed to be the result of a language barrier. Approximately 100 synagogue inscriptions were found in the Greek diaspora. These finds have greatly enriched our knowledge about the Greek diaspora, largely because of the discovery of communities that had previously been unknown. All of the inscriptions are in Greek, in contrast to the findings in synagogues in the Land of Israel that included inscriptions in Greek, Aramaic, and Hebrew. Of greater significance, however, are the differences in the content of the inscriptions found in the Land of Israel and those found in the Greek diaspora, as pointed out convincingly by Lea Roth-Gerson.[29] She adduces some examples, such as that the Greek concept "soteria" (salvation) is found notably in the inscriptions of the Greek diaspora and at times in the Greek inscriptions in the Land of Israel, but never in Hebrew and Aramaic inscriptions. Similarly, the Greek inscriptions tend to emphasize the Hellenistic focus on the individual donor, while the Aramaic and Hebrew inscriptions reflect the rabbinic worldview that places the community at the center. Roth-Gerson also points out that contributors are praised differently in the eastern inscriptions than they are in the inscriptions in the Greek diaspora. For example, the Greek inscriptions in the Land of Israel state that: "He should be remembered for good and for blessing," which is a direct translation of the Hebrew and Aramaic terminology. In contrast, the Greek diaspora inscriptions utilize the term "eulogia" (blessing), but not in the context that it is used in Israel. On this point, Roth-Gerson comments as follows: "While in Israel they related to the contributor with words of good wishes and blessing, they are honored in the inscriptions in the diaspora in another style."[30] These three examples indicate three facts. First, that there was a difference between the character of the synagogues of the Land of Israel and those of the Greek speaking diaspora as expressed in the synagogue inscriptions. Second, and even more important, in the Land of Israel there was a strong presence of the Rabbinic worldview, while the western diaspora reflects more of Hellenistic culture. Moreover, we see that the synagogue in the Land of Israel was actually influenced by both cultures, drawing from both the Hebrew and Greek concepts. The western synagogue, however, did not draw at all from the eastern synagogue model. This astonishing fact indicates that in the Greek Jewish world, influence went from west to east and not vice versa. The Greek inscriptions in the Land of Israel reflect motifs from the inscriptions in the western diaspora, but the Greek inscriptions in the western diaspora are not reminiscent of the Greek inscriptions in the Land of Israel. Thus, components of the Greek inscriptions in the Land of Israel that were clearly translations from the Hebrew and Aramaic inscriptions did not find their way to the West. Greek inscriptions from the West, however, did influence Greek inscriptions in the Land of Israel.

## Did the Rabbis Communicate with the Western Diaspora?

Henceforward we will make an attempt to demonstrate that rabbinic literature indicates the fact that the rabbis themselves did not view the western diaspora as an integral part of their turf.

First, one of the most important rabbinic innovations is the creation of centers of Torah study (*yeshivot*), where the Oral Law emerged and developed. Whereas those institutions are apparent in the Land of Israel and the Babylonian diaspora, none can be found in the western diaspora. Moreover, there are practically no laws or teachings attributed to sages from the western diaspora in the entire corpus of the Oral Law (*Mishnah, Tosefta,* both versions of the *Talmud,* and the *Midrash*). Of the hundreds of rabbis who participated in the creation of the corpus of Oral Law, a collective and multi-generation production by eastern rabbis, there are only a few questionable exceptions. We think that scholars have underestimated the significance of this decisive evidence. Many have ignored the phenomenon altogether, while some have claimed that western rabbis did take part in the rabbinic discourse. Yet, we believe that a careful examination will confirm that there is hardly any western voice to be found in rabbinic literature.

In fact, rabbinic scholars from the West are hardly mentioned in the *Talmud,* and when they are, the references to them are so minimal that it actually points to an acknowledgment of an almost complete absence of rabbinic teaching in the West. One of them is Todos ish Romi ("the Roman"), yet the fact that this is the only ruling attributed to him throughout rabbinic literature, reveals his obscure position. The *Tosefta* records that his instruction to take a lamb on the night of Passover was "close to feeding people sanctified meat outside of the confines [of Jerusalem]."[31] Similarly, there is only one homiletical teaching in his name in rabbinic literature. We really know nothing about this sage, to the point that scholarly estimations of the time that he lived span 200 years, ranging from the first century B.C.E. through the first century C.E.[32] How might we explain that we know hardly anything about a well-known scholar in Rome? Is there a significant *tanna* or *amora* about whom we do not know the generation in which he taught, his activities, his teachers, and his students? Furthermore, how is it possible that an important scholar has only one law and one homiletical teaching recorded in the *Talmud,* and these in an off-handed manner? Indeed, there was apparently a Jewish religious leader in Rome named Todos (or Tavdas), but the fact that he is practically not mentioned in the *Talmud* itself proves that there was a lack of contact between the sages in Palestine and the Jewish community in Rome.

Similarly, with regard to Rav Matya ben Heresh. We are told that he migrated from the Land of Israel to Rome to establish a *yeshivah*,[33] but interestingly in the final analysis, nothing is known about his activity in Rome. We do not know if he succeeded in establishing a *yeshivah*, and, if so, what was taught there. There is no record in all of the rabbinic literature of a new idea that emanated from there. Apparently, he did not foster protégés, and we know nothing about the proceedings of his academy or its fate. We also know nothing about his students or about sayings that he delivered while serving in Rome.

Likewise, a third century *amora,* known as R. Abba the Cartheginian, is mentioned approximately ten times in the *Jerusalem Talmud.* Another sage from the third century, known as R. Shmuel Kapadocia, is mentioned three or four times in the *Jerusalem Talmud.* R. Yudan Kapadocia, a fourth century *amora* who studied under R. Yosi, is also mentioned. We have no information regarding these sages, but we can assume that they were from Cappadocia in Asia Minor. There are a number of similar sages who were mentioned once in the *Jerusalem Talmud.* In all instances, it is clear that we are talking about sages of marginal importance, who are rarely mentioned and about whom we know very little. Apparently, we are talking about individuals who came from the diaspora, or whose families came from the diaspora, but who clearly learned their Torah in the Land of Israel.[34] In this context, it is also worth mentioning R. Shimon ben Yosi ben Lakonia who is mentioned several times in Talmudic literature, and about whom it is claimed that his family may have originated in Sparta.[35] Even if this claim is correct, it supports our thesis: The only scholars of western origin mentioned in the *Talmud* are those who had immigrated to Palestine, or whose ancestors had immigrated to Palestine, and who studied Torah there. There are, however, no proofs of scholars from the Land of Israel who went to the West to teach Torah, and certainly not to learn Torah.

Illuminating is the following legend told by the Rabbis:

> The government sent two agents and told them to disguise themselves as Jews and observe the nature of their Torah. They went to Rabban Gamliel in Usha and studied the Bible, the *Mishnah*, the *Midrash*, the laws, and the *Aggadah* (lore). When they left, they [the agents] said to them: "All of the Torah is pleasant and praiseworthy except

for one thing – that you say that something stolen from a non-Jew is permissible, but not something stolen from a Jew. But we will not inform the government of this."[36]

The rabbis imagine a situation from the standpoint of the Roman authority. They wish to explore the Torah, but the only way to do so was to travel to Usha, the rabbinic center in the Galilee. In other words, one can imagine that the rabbis had an interest to tell us about the diffusion of their oral lore into the entire Jewish world in the Roman Empire, yet they emphasize that the only place for rabbinic learning is in the Land of Israel.[37]

Furthermore, against the background of the tension regarding the authority to sanctify and announce the new month, a major issue in rabbinic thought, the absence of any of the western Jews in this debate is remarkable. Even more astonishing is the fact that the rabbis do not inform the western diaspora about the declaration of the new month. The information about the sanctification of the new moon that was decided by the court in the Land of Israel was important for the diaspora as well, and was publicized by means of a system of fire signals or by emissaries. In all of the sources that deal with this issue, we find no reference to the western diaspora. One gets the impression from these sources that only the eastern diaspora was within the rabbinic communication network. This is demonstrated, for example, in the following source:

> There are two matters that constitutes *prima facie* evidence that a person is a member of the priesthood in the Land of Israel: raising one's hands [during the priestly benediction], and receiving [heave-offerings] at the threshing floor. In Syria up to the place where the messenger who reports about the new moon reaches: raising one's hands [during the priestly benediction], but they do not receive the [heave-offerings] at the threshing floor. And Babylonia is like Syria. R. Shimon ben Elazar says: "Also Alexandria [was like Syria] in the early days when there was a court there."[38]

In a different context, mention is made of a letter that the sages sent from Jerusalem to the diaspora that dealt with a number of issues, including the intercalation of the month. Here too, it is evident that the western diaspora was not included in the system of distribution. In addition, the letter was written in Aramaic which implies that it was directed to the eastern diaspora:

> There was an incident in which Rabban Gamliel and the sages were in session on the steps of the Temple, and Yohanan the scribe was before them. He said to them, "Write: To our brethren, residents of the Upper Galilee and residents of the Lower Galilee, may your peace increase. I inform you that the time of the removal has come, to separate the tithes from the olive vats. To our brethren, residents of the Upper South and residents of the Lower South, may your peace increase. We inform you that the time of the removal has come, to separate the tithes from the sheaves of grain. To our brethren, residents of the Exile of Babylonia, and residents of the Exile of Media and of all the other Exiles of Israel, may your peace increase. We inform you that the pigeons are still tender, the lambs are thin, and the spring tide has yet not come. So it is proper in my view and the view of my colleagues, and we have added thirty days to this year.[39]

The above supports the finding of Abraham Wasserstein that western Jews adhered to a different calendar.[40] The possibility of a split calendar within the Jewish people cannot be underestimated.

There is, however, another source from which we can apparently deduce that the Jews in the West did follow the calendar established by the rabbis:

> There was an event in which R. Meir went to Asia to intercalate the year, and he did not find a Scroll of Esther written in Hebrew, so he wrote one from memory and read from it.[41]

Beyond the fact that this source is the only one of its kind in contrast to the other sources that we have discussed, its credibility is also questionable from a number of standpoints. From a technical perspective, it is not clear why the calendar would be intercalated in Asia, when the practice was for the Rabbinic Court in Israel to declare a leap year and then to inform the communities in the diaspora.[42] From a geographical standpoint, scholars disagree as to the location of "Asia" mentioned in this source.[43] In any case, the source refers to the intercalation of the calendar – i.e. adding a month to the calendar in order to synchronize it with the solar calendar, and not to informing the diaspora communities about *kiddush ha-hodesh* (the declaration of the new month), a topic that is totally ignored in Talmudic literature vis-à-vis the western diaspora even though the process is discussed quite a bit as it relates to the eastern diaspora.

A third indication relates to the separation of tithes outside of the Land of Israel. Safrai[44] and others claim that the Jews of the diaspora were accustomed to sending tithes and *terumot* (donations), even during the time of the Temple. Sanders disagrees and contends, based on his understanding of the source, that there is no proof for this argument. On the contrary, he claims that the opposite is the case. It is possible that they sent voluntary monetary contributions, and it is certain that they paid a Temple tax, but they did not send tithes and *terumot*. There is a relevant source in rabbinic literature relating to the borders of the Land of Israel that discusses whether Syria is or is not part of Israel. This discussion clearly demonstrates that the obligation of giving *terumot* was in force only in areas that were considered part of the Land of Israel. Similarly, there are no Greek sources that indicate conclusively that members of the Greek diaspora were obligated to give *terumot*. The following *Mishnah* from tractate *Yadayim* discusses a controversy between the sages regarding the giving of tithes in the sabbatical year outside of the borders of the Land of Israel. The seventh year – the Sabbatical year – did not obligate Jews living outside of the borders of the Land of Israel. These Jews, therefore, in contrast to the Jews in the Land of Israel, gave *terumot* and tithes also in the seventh year. The controversy in the *Mishnah* is whether the appropriate tithe in the seventh year was the second tithe that was given to the priest or the tithe given to the poor.

> On that day they said: "What of Ammon and Moav in the seventh year?" R. Tarfon decreed: "They must give the poor man's tithe." And R. Elazar ben Azaryah decreed: "They must give the second tithe." R. Yishmael said to him: "Elazar ben Azaryah, you must bring proof since you issued the more stringent ruling, and the one who gives a more stringent ruling must bring proof." R. Elazar ben Azaryah said to him: "Yishmael my brother, it is not I who has changed the order of the years, but Tarfon my brother has changed it, and he must bring proof." R. Tarfon responded: "Egypt is outside the Land of Israel, and Ammon and Moav are outside of the Land of Israel. Therefore, just as in Egypt the poor man's tithe must be given in the seventh year, so too in Ammon and Moav poor man's tithe must be given in the seventh

year." R. Elazar ben Azaryah answered: "Behold, you are as one who would bestow on them worldly gain, but you suffer souls to perish, you rob the heavens so they send down neither rain nor dew, as it is written: 'Will a man rob God? Yet you rob me. But you say, wherein have we robbed you? In tithes and heave offerings.'"[45]

R. Yehoshua said: "Behold, I am as one who will answer on behalf of Tarfon my brother, but not according to the subject of his words. [The rule relating to] Egypt is a new work, and [the rule relating to] Babylonia is an old work. Let us argue concerning a new work from a new work, but let us not argue concerning a new work from an old work. [The rule relating to] Egypt is the work of the elders, and [the rule relating to] Babylonia is the work of the prophets, and the argument before us is the work of the elders. Let us argue concerning the work of the elders from the work of the elders, but let us not argue concerning the work of the elders from the work of the prophets." They voted and decided that Ammon and Moav should give poor man's tithe in the seventh year. And when R. Yosi ben Dormaskit came to R. Eliezer in Lod, he said to him: "What new thing was learned in the house of study today?" He responded: "They voted and decided that Ammon and Moav should give poor man's tithe in the seventh year." R. Eliezer wept and said: "'The secret of the Lord is with them that fear him, and he will show them his covenant.' Go and tell them: 'Be not anxious by reason of your voting, for I have received a tradition from Rabban Yohanan ben Zakkai, who heard it from his teacher, and his teacher from his teacher, as a law given to Moses on Sinai that Ammon and Moav should give poor man's tax in the seventh year.'"[46]

Whether we see this source as a reflection of a reality in which tithes were sent to Israel from the far reaches of the diaspora or as a "romantic" portrayal of the ideal,[47] the *Mishnah* clearly mentions each part of the eastern diaspora – Ammon, Moav, Egypt, and Babylonia – while locations in the western diaspora were apparently not on the halakhic horizon of the author of the *Mishnah*.

Another source that supports this view is the *Mishnah* in tractate *Ta'anit*. The *Mishnah* deals with public prayers for rain that were held in the Land of Israel at the beginning of the winter. The *Mishnah* raises the question when should those prayers begin, and answers as follows:

On the third day of [the month of] *Marheshvan* they request the rains. Rabban Gamliel says: On the seventh therein, fifteen days after the Festival, so that the last one [of the pilgrims from Babylonia] in Israel may reach the Euphrates River.[48]

This means that they had to wait two weeks after the festival of Tabernacles *(Sukkot)* so the pilgrims could reach their home and not encounter rain. We see again that from the author of the *Mishnah*'s perspective, pilgrims came from the Euphrates River, from Babylonia in the East, yet there is no mention of the pilgrims that came from the West.

A fifth indication relates to the manner in which the western diaspora is referred to in rabbinic sources. At the beginning of this study, we mentioned the fact that scholars generally equate the relationship between the rabbis and the two diasporas. This equation is based on the fact that the western diaspora is mentioned in rabbinic literature. From both a qualitative and quantitative perspective, however, there is no comparison between the references to the eastern diaspora and the western one. In fact, the rabbinic sources that mention the western diaspora actually demonstrate the weakness of the connection between the center in Israel and the Greek diaspora. We will examine a number of these sources below. Before doing so, however, we bring a quote from Safrai, one of the experts on the Jewish diaspora, who ascribes to the reading of the sources that equates the two diasporas. In his article, entitled "The Land of Israel and the Jewish Diaspora," Safrai deals with the connection between the leadership in Israel and the diaspora communities following the destruction of the Temple, a period of significant growth in the diaspora both because of emigration from Israel and a wave of conversion:

The Oral Law did not coalesce and was not recorded in books of *halakhah*, *Midrash*, and *aggadah* until the end of the tannaitic and the amoraic periods. The prayer book and the regular reading of the Torah were set during the period of the *tannaim*, while the Hebrew calendar was set during the amoraic period. There are many similar phenomena. The matters that were innovated in the Land of Israel, particularly in the council chambers or the High Court when it was located in Yavneh, and subsequently in the cities of the Galilee, were transmitted and accepted in the Jewish diaspora. The *Mishnah*, that was redacted in the end of the second century and the beginning of the third century, became the foundation of the Oral Law and of Jewish law both in the Land of Israel and the Babylonian diaspora. Similarly, the approach of Midrash Halachah that were formulated in the academies of R. Yishmael and R. Akiva became the basis for Midrashic study for generations in Israel and Babylonia. The life style that was established after the destruction in Israel, such as the holidays, fasts, and the remembrance of the siege of Jerusalem and the destruction of the Temple, and the laws in general that were formulated in Israel, became the law for all of Israel to the far reaches of the diaspora. Most of the sources on this matter are from Babylonian Jewry, but one can assume that this was the reality, at least in principle, in the other diasporas.[49]

Thus, "we know" for certain with regard to the Babylonian community, while "we can assume" with regard to the western diaspora. We question whether this is really so. Is there any basis in the sources to support Safrai's conjecture that the knowledge that we have about Babylonia is true of the western diaspora as well? Scholars today justifiably raise doubts about the viewpoint of Safrai and his contemporaries regarding the nature of the influence of rabbinic literature on diaspora Jewry and the effectiveness of its distribution.[50] Nevertheless, even they have not noted the significant gap demonstrated in rabbinic literature itself between the influence of the sages on the eastern diaspora in contrast to their influence on the western diaspora.

Let us examine the sources upon which the scholars base their opinions on this matter.

1. There are a number of sources in which Rabban Gamliel of Yavneh travelled to other communities in order to answer Jewish legal questions:[51]

> R. Yehudah said: "There was an event in which Savion, the head of the synagogue in Achziv, purchased a vineyard in its fourth year of growth from a gentile in Syria, and he gave him payment. Then he came and asked Rabban Gamliel who was passing from place to place [whether the produce of that field is liable to the

restriction of the fourth year]. He said to him: "Wait until we can dwell upon the law."[52]

R. Yehudah said: "Even though both of its witnesses are Samaritans, it is valid." R. Yehudah said: "There was an incident in which they brought before Rabban Gamliel in Kfar Otenai the writ of divorce of a woman, and its witnesses were Samaritans, and he declared it valid." R. Akiva declares it valid in the case of all [documents], and the sages declare it invalid ...[53]

There are also sources in which we find Rabban Gamliel in Tiberias and Lod. Yet, we do not see from these sources that Rabban Gamliel travelled overseas.[54] In fact, the opposite is the case. All of the locations mentioned are either in the Land of Israel or in close proximity (Kfar Otenai and Achziv), and there is no indication that Rabban Gamliel traveled outside of Israel for halakhic consultations with communities.

2. It has also been argued that halakhic inquiries were sent to Rabban Gamliel from overseas.[55] This claim is based on the following passage in the Babylonian Talmud, *Gittin* 34b:

R. Yehudah said in the name of Shmuel: "The Jews from overseas[56] sent to Rabban Gamliel the following inquiry: If a man comes to the Land of Israel whose name is Yoseph but is known as Yohanan, or whose name is Yohanan but who is known as Yoseph, how is he to divorce his wife?" Rabban Gamliel thereupon made a regulation that they should write in the writ of divorce "The man so-and-so or by whatever names he is known, the woman so-and-so or by whatever names she is known" in order to prevent abuses.

It should be noted, however, that this source is a Babylonian source from a period much later than Rabban Gamliel, and that there is no parallel source in rabbinic literature in Israel or from the time of Rabban Gamliel. It seems that we can say with some certainty that the Talmudic scholar Shmuel did not intend here to convey a historical tale, and that this source does not constitute, therefore, an historical document. Rather, it is a didactic explanation of the decree of Rabban Gamliel discussed in the *Mishnah*.

3. It has also been argued that when the *Sanhedrin* was housed in Yavneh, halakhic inquiries were sent from all of the far reaches of the dispersion to Yavneh.[57] An orderly examination of the sources, however, reveals that all of the locations mentioned are within the borders of the Land of Israel or in close proximity (Tiv'on, Gennosar, Sidon, Sepphoris, Hamat Gader). There is only one source that appears in three places with the following wording:

Concerning this law, the men of Asia went up for three successive festivals to Yavneh, and on the third festival, they [the authorities of Yavneh] declared it valid for them.[58]

This is apparently an important source that indicates that residents of Asia went to Yavneh to ask halakhic questions. This same expression appears in two other places in the *Tosefta*, in relation to the law of the red heifer and the regulations of ritual baths.

Concerning this law, the men of Asia went up for three successive festivals to Yavneh, and on the third festival, they [the authorities of Yavneh] declared it valid for them as a special dispensation [based on a temporary need]. R. Yosi said: "Not for this [law] did they give dispensation, but for…"[59]

A reservoir that distributes water among the villages, if it was perforated by a hole the size of the stopper of a water skin, it does not spoil the immersion pool, and if not, it spoils the immersion pool. Concerning this law, the men of Asia went up for three successive festivals to Yavneh, and on the third festival, they [the authorities of Yavneh] declared it fit even if it was perforated by a hole the size of a needle.[60]

It appears that these sources are dealing with practical halakhic questions. Yet, how could the red heifer have been relevant to the diaspora when it relates to issues of purity and impurity that were practiced only in Land of Israel and in the

Temple. This idiosyncrasy supports the conclusion of Alon which we discussed above that Asia actually refers to Ezion Gaver,[61] which was in close proximity to the border of Israel, and was considered from a Jewish legal standpoint to be part of the Land of Israel. It is clear that the diaspora with which they were in contact was close to Israel, and in any case, was not the western diaspora. This leaves us with no rabbinic sources that indicate that halakhic inquiries were sent from the western diaspora to the academy in Yavneh.

4. One of the well-known arguments is that the sages from the Land of Israel traveled throughout the diaspora in order to teach *halakhah.*[62] Here too, however, a thorough examination of the sources available to us indicates that a majority of the places to which the sages traveled were across the Jordan, on the Mediterranean coast just north of Israel up to Tyre and Sidon, in Syria, or in Egypt. Testimony regarding a connection with the diaspora overseas is practically non-existent:

> R. Akiva expounded when he came from Ziprin [apparently a place in Syria]…[63]

> R. Yehoshua ben Levi once visited Gabla where he saw vines laden with clusters of ripe grapes that appeared like calves. He remarked: "Calves among the vines!"[64]

Gabla, in eastern Trans-Jordan, is mentioned as well in a source relating to R. Hiyya bar Abba:

> R. Hiyya bar Abba once came to Gabla where he observed Jewish women who conceived from proselytes who had been circumcised but had not performed the required ritual immersion. He also noticed that idolaters were serving Jewish wine and Israelites were drinking it, and that idolaters were cooking lupins and Israelites were eating them. Nevertheless, he did not speak to them on the matter. He called, however, on R. Yohanan who instructed him: "Go and announce that their children are bastards, that their wine is forbidden as wine of libation, and that their food is forbidden as food cooked by idolaters because they are ignorant of Torah.[65]

This source demonstrates that in these places the law was very different.

> R. Yehoshua ben Levi was in Laodecia and R. Yudan said to him: "Wait while we immerse this female convert tomorrow." The next day, R. Zira asked R. Yitzhak bar Nahman: "Why? Was it because of the honor due to an elder, or was it because they did not immerse a female convert at night?" He said to him: "It is because they did not immerse a female convert at night."[66]

Laodecia is located on the Mediterranean coast south of Antiochia and north of Tyre-Sidon. We see again that the places on the itineraries and halakhic dealings of the sages were close to the Land of Israel.

Not a few scholars also built their arguments on sources like the *Tosefta Terumot* 2:13, quoted above, which indicates that Rabban Gamliel visited in Achziv, north of Israel, while travelling 'from place to place', but in reality, all that we know is that he arrived at Achziv which is north of Israel.

There are many sources about sages from Israel that were in places such as Tyre and other locations around Syria. Here too, the sources prove that the reach was particularly to places that were close to the Land of Israel, as we stated above, but that there was either no contact or little contact with more remote overseas communities.[67]

In this context, it is important to distinguish also between Egypt and the rest of the Greek diaspora. It is clear that during the time of the Temple, there was a long-standing and strong connection between the Greek speaking Jewish community of Egypt and the center in the Land of Israel.[68] Yet, the nature of the connection after the destruction of the Temple and during the Rabbinic period is unclear. Although we cannot rule out the possibility that there was communication and symbiotic influence between rabbinic scholarship in the Land of Israel and Egypt, we cannot escape the fact that there is practically very little evidence to support this assumption in all of rabbinic literature, and even less evidence of a substantive contribution to rabbinic scholarship on the part of Egyptian Jewry.[69]

The most interesting sources in this regard are the stories of sages who visited Rome. We hold that a study of these stories actually reveals a clear recognition on the part of the sages that a clear connection and bond between them and the Jews of Rome is lacking. We do not view these stories as historical sources, but rather as sources that reveal the perspective of the rabbis on Rome and on the nature of their relationship with the Jews there. The following two stories appear in different parts of the *Tosefta*:

> There was an episode wherein R. Joshua went to Rome and they said to him: "There is a child here – a Jerusalemite, with beautiful eyes and face, and standing in *kalon*." And R. Joshua went to examine him. When he reached the doorway, he said this verse: "Who gave Jacob for a spoil and Israel to the robbers?" (Isaiah 42) The child answered: "Is it not the Lord, He against whom we have sinned and in whose ways they would not walk" (*Ibid.*) At that moment, R. Joshua said: "As heaven and earth are my witness, I will not budge from here until I ransom him." He ransomed him at a high figure and dispatched him to the Land of Israel. And about him they said: "The precious children of Zion, comparable to gold." (Lamentations 4)[70]

> He took the blood from the one stirring it, entered the place where he entered and stood in the place where he stood, and sprinkled from it on the curtain against the two Ark-poles -one up and seven down. And he didn't intend to sprinkle upward nor downward, but rather like he was whipping ... R. Judah said in the name of R. Eliezer: Thus he would count: "One, one and one, two and one, three and one, four and one, five and one, six and one, seven and one." He would walk with his left to the curtain and would not reach the curtain; if he reached, he reached. Said R. Lazar b. R. Yose: "I saw it in Rome, there were upon it drops of blood. And they said to me: 'These are from the blood of the day of atonement.' "[71]

These two stories essentially communicate the same message. In the eyes of the rabbis, Rome was a place of captivity and oppression, reflected in a captive child and captive utensils from the Temple. Rome was not from their perspective a place of Jewish life, and certainly not a source of Jewish creativity. It is important to note that in both stories, the visit to Rome is for the purpose of returning stolen items to the Jewish people, not for an encounter with a vital Jewish community.[72]

In another source from the *Tosefta*, sages tell about the following visit and discourse during a visit to Rome:

> Philosophers asked the elders in Rome: "If idol worship is against His
> will, why does He not destroy it?" They said to them: "Would that
> they would worship something the world does not need, for He would
> destroy it; lo, they worship the sun and the moon and the stars. Should
> he destroy his world because of the fools? Rather, leave them to act
> as their wont and the fools that corrupted will come and they will
> give judgment. One who steals seeds to plant, they are not destined to
> sprout. One who beds a married woman; she is not destined to give
> birth. Rather, leave them all to act as is their wont, and the fools that
> corrupted will come and they will give judgment."[73]

Here the sages tell about a meeting and the associated discussion, but the discussion
is not with Jews, but rather with "philosophers" who mock them regarding Jewish
theological positions. Here too the sages go to Rome to vanquish the non-Jews, in
this case in a theological debate. In this source, as well, they do not go to Rome
in order to meet the Jewish community, nor to teach or learn.[74] Even within the
context of the theological debate, there is no mention of a meeting with the Jews
or the involvement of any local Jews in the controversy.

In another rabbinic source, we find the sages apparently sermonizing in Rome:

> Rabban Gamliel, R. Joshua, R. Eliezer b. Azariah, and R. Akiba that
> they went to Rome and taught there: The ways of God differ from
> those of man - whereas man directs others to do a thing whilst he
> does nothing; God is not so. There happened to be a heretic there
> who accosted them as they were going out with the taunt: "Your
> words are only falsehood. Did you not say that God says a thing and
> fulfils it? Then why does He not observe the Sabbath?" They replied:
> "Wretch! Is not a man permitted to carry on the Sabbath in his own
> courtyard?" He replied: "Yes." Whereupon they said to him: "Both
> the higher and lower spheres are the courtyard of God."[75]

However, if we study it carefully, we will find that the credibility of this
source is highly questionable, both in terms of its content and in terms of the
source in which it appears. Firstly, this story is very similar to the stories that
we saw previously, which implies that the narrative is a clear typology – all

of the sages vs. the emperor, and they win. The sages go to Rome to vanquish the Roman approach in its own capital. According to the Roman doctrine, the king is not subject to the rule of law, and as such, God is better than the Roman emperor and the Torah is preferable to Roman law. God's stance is more moral and just since he subordinates himself to the law. Lieberman already asserted that this source reflects a fundamental argument against the Greek principle *"Para basileus ho nomos agraphos"* – "the law is not written before the king" – which was in force in Rome.[76] Scholars hypothesize that the story recounts a sermon delivered in a synagogue,[77] but it should be noted that the source does not mention where the sermon takes place and to whom. In contrast, the only member of the audience who is identified is a "heretic" who argues with the sages.[78]

If we view this in the context of sources known to us in which sages travel to Rome for political missions and the aforementioned fact that we know of no scholars who lived in Rome, we get a clear general picture that Rome was, in the perception of the rabbis, not a place of Torah nor a place where Jews who were in contact with them resided. Rome, the capital of the empire, was simply a place where one would go to vanquish the non-Romans, be it in a theological debate or to redeem Jews and holy objects from captivity.

৻৶

In addition to the previous sources cited, there are a very limited number of sources that apparently testify to a rabbinic link with the western diaspora. It appears from the following two sources that the sages in the generation of Yavneh and which followed went to a variety of places throughout the Jewish diaspora, including the Greek diaspora, to deal with a number of matters including halakhic issues:

> R. Akiva said: "When I was travelling on the sea, I saw a ship struggling in the waves, and I was saddened at the fate of a disciple of sages who was on board. And when I came to Caesarea-Mazaca in Cappodocia, I saw him, sitting and asking questions of law before me. I said to him: 'My son, how did you escape from the ocean?' He said to me: 'One wave tossed me to the next, and the next to the next, until

> I came up on dry land.' I said: 'How great are the words of the sages, for they have said: "If it is within the sight of the shore, his wife is permitted [to remarry]. If it is not in sight of the shore, his wife is not permitted."[79]

This story is brought to support the law that is mentioned that if a boat sinks in the open ocean, we must consider that the man was saved and reached shore securely. This leads to the conclusion that we cannot allow his wife to remarry solely based on the fact that ship has sunk. It is important to note that even when the sages imagine themselves in this story in Cappodocia, they meet each other as survivors of the rough seas, but do not encounter any local Jews. The Jew who takes interest in the activities of R. Akiva in Cappodocia is one who himself arrived there by sea, presumably from the Land of Israel. Another aggadic source regarding the travels of R. Akiva and other sages appears in a *Braita* in the *Babylonian Talmud*.

Yet, we must question whether these sources are reliable from a historical perspective. It should be noted that both of these texts contain legendary stories that cannot be accepted as historical sources. Moreover, they do not intend to be historical in nature.

Another source that seems doubtful is the following:

> Come and hear what Ben Yasyan related: "When I went to the coastal towns, I came across a certain proselyte who had married the wife of his maternal brother. I said to him: 'Who, my son, permitted [this marriage] for you?' He replied: 'Behold the woman and her seven children.' On this bench sat R. Akiva when he made two statements: 'A proselyte may marry the wife of his maternal brother' and 'And the Lord came to Yonah a second time, saying' – only a second time did the Divine Presence speak to him, but a third time the Divine Presence did not speak to him.[80]

There is no parallel to this source in the rest of rabbinic literature, and we do not even know who Ben Yasyan, the narrator of the story, is. The story relates to second hand testimony, and the *Talmud* itself questions whether the witness is reliable since he is affected by the decision. Nevertheless, in contrast to the two sources mentioned above, this source may have a historical kernel which documents a visit of R. Akiva to the western diaspora in which he deals with the laws of conversion, an issue of relevance to them given the large number of converts at that time.[81] Another source that seems more credible is the story in the *Tosefta* regarding R. Natan who was in "*mizgat shel kapotkiyah*" and issued a ruling there relating to circumcision.[82]

As we have stated, these sources in general are somewhat suspicious, but even if we accept their historical validity, their paucity in contrast to the large number of sources that deal with visits to Babylonia, Egypt, and locations in close proximity to northern Israel support the argument that there was a significant disconnect between the center in Israel and the western diaspora.

In addition, it should be noted that although we are aware of the existence of many synagogues throughout the Hellenistic diaspora, we have almost no documentation of sages who spoke or taught Torah in any of them. In contrast, we do have a good amount of documentation of visits to Rome for political purposes, and of meetings with the leaders of the empire. It is possible that at the same time, the rabbis met with the Jewish community there.[83] It is also possible that emissaries were sent to these communities for the purpose of fundraising.[84]

In summary, we can say that even if we assume that the above sources relate to locations in the western diaspora and that they recount the visit of a particular sage, we can draw the following conclusions:

1. Sources relating to a rabbinic visit to the western diaspora are sparse and questionable, particularly in contrast to the number of sources that deal with the connection between the center in Israel and the eastern diaspora.

2. The number of places in the western diaspora mentioned in rabbinic literature is severely limited. Rabbinic literature almost entirely ignores the vast western diaspora that existed at the time. This is particularly noticeable when compared with the relatively large number of places mentioned in chapter 2 of Acts, and in the chapters describing the journeys of Paul (Acts 13ff), as well as the Pauline epistles which give a comprehensive picture of the geography of the western Jewish diaspora.[85]

3. It is our contention that the significance of these points is that during the period under discussion, two Judaisms arose with an ever-growing gap developing between them. As a generalization, we could label these Judaisms

the western "Written Torah Judaism" and the eastern "Oral Law Judaism." While in the East, a new normative standard, the Oral Law, developed, and in the West, the Jewish communities remained Biblical, maintaining the tradition as it existed before the rise of the rabbis and their teachings. In fact, the rabbinic corpus testifies that the western diaspora was not consistently connected to the system of communication or the rabbinic authority in the East. This dichotomy sharpened after the destruction of the Temple. The sages admit and mention this.

## Jewish Presence in Europe

Our claim that the linguistic barrier was the grounds for the emerging gap between East and West should be examined against the background of epigraphic remnants found in the areas under discussion. Jewish gravestones have been found in southern Europe, providing evidence of the existence of Jewish communities there.[86] We believe it doubtful that these Jews had significant contact with eastern Jewish communities and with the spiritual world of the rabbis. We draw the reader's attention to the following facts and claims:

a. A vast majority of the inscriptions on Jewish grave stones from western Europe are in Greek or Latin. This fact demonstrates that these languages were the primary languages, if not the exclusive languages, for both interpersonal communication and public expression in the spiritual and intellectual lives of these Jews.

b. Indeed, on a significant percentage of the gravestones, there is also some Hebrew writing. The Hebrew inscriptions indicate that even though Hebrew was not the language of these Jews, they viewed it as an important symbol of their identity. They also indicate that these Jews wished to preserve their separate Jewish identity. However, in examining the inscriptions themselves, it becomes clear that their knowledge of Hebrew as a living language was quite weak. Furthermore, the content of the inscriptions does not show any knowledge of the innovations of the rabbis. It is interesting to note that along with the Hebrew inscriptions, or in their place, the monuments often include drawings of Jewish symbols such as a *shofar* (ram's horn) or a *menorah* (candelabrum).[87] We will comment on this iconography later on.

c. It should be noted that a large percentage of the Hebrew inscriptions consist of isolated words that are found repetitively on many monuments, such as *"shalom"* ("peace"), or phrases such as *"shalom al yisrael"* ("peace on Israel") or *"shalom al menuhato"* ("rest in peace"). These words and phrases are repeated frequently and were apparently copied in a mechanical fashion. It is therefore correct, in our opinion, to view these inscriptions as accepted cultural symbols, and not as a proof of the use of Hebrew as a vernacular, and certainly not as an indication of familiarity with rabbinic Hebrew and lore.

d. There are a number of inscriptions on monuments that demonstrate a somewhat more sophisticated Hebrew,[88] and there are similarly a number of Biblical quotes in Hebrew, at times accompanied by a Greek or Latin translation.[89] It is our impression that in ritual occasions, Jewish and Christian, Hebrew was probably used at times, comparable to the use of Latin in the Church in non-Latin speaking communities. At any rate, such references were most probably literary topoi, and therefore do not alter the overall picture of the lack of Hebrew knowledge by western Jews.[90] In this context, we would suggest that while Hebrew served at times as a cultural symbol, only later — i.e. with the proliferation of rabbinic literature in the ninth century — did it become a vernacular.[91]

e. Shaye Cohen[92] proved that the title "Rabbi" that appears on inscriptions in Italy (and in other places) does not refer to the title as used in the *Mishnah* and *Talmud*. Rather, it is used in a popular fashion to refer to a person that has a respected standing in the community. Therefore, the appearance of the title in inscriptions does not give evidence of a leadership position that is parallel to the position accepted in Rabbinic Judaism.

All of these points, in addition to the fact that the inscriptions found were located in a confined geographic area, mainly southern Europe, indicate that epigraphy does not support the conclusion that Jews in the West had a significant knowledge of Hebrew, or that they were influenced in any way by Rabbinic Judaism in the East. But they do testify to a Jewish existence in southern Europe. Also, an examination of the three volumes of Jewish inscriptions from the Balkan, Greece, the Greek islands, Crete, Asia Minor, and Cyprus, among other regions, strengthens what we claim here, i.e. that Jewish presence was manifest in the first centuries C.E. and that its language was certainly Greek and Latin. Hebrew is rarely found in these inscriptions.[93]

In addition to gravestones, there are other archaeological finds of interest, including the remains of synagogues in Byzantine Europe,[94] in which we find Jewish symbols such as the *menorah*, the *shofar*, and the *lulav* (palm branch). For example, on the gravestone of Claudia Maximilla and a Jewish family from Panonia (today number 62.70.1 in the Archaeological Museum in Budapest), there is a Latin and Greek inscription accompanied by the picture of a *menorah*. The inscription is from the fourth century of the common era. Be that as it may, these symbols are all of Biblical origin and served as (iconographic) symbols prior to the Second Temple period.

However, we differ somewhat from the well-known position of Goodenough that the art from the period and location under discussion reflects a Judaism that is certainly not rabbinic.[95] While we do not see ourselves as having the expertise to discuss art, we would like to point out that Biblical Jewish symbols were not antithetical to rabbinic practice, as they continued to be accepted and authorized in all generations and across all geographical boundaries (from Dura Europus, to Palestine, to Europe). These symbols represent an agreed upon and accessible common denominator between the Jewish communities of the East and the West. In reality, because of the language gap that we described above, the visual arts served as a common and accessible language of communication for all of Judaism. In addition, it is important to note that even in later periods, particularly rabbinic Jewish symbols did not develop. The ancient symbols that we have mentioned, with additional motifs from pagan and Christian art, continued to serve the needs of Jewish iconography well into the Middle Ages. A Jew who was committed to Rabbinic Judaism and a western Hellenistic Jew could both accept the Jewish iconography discussed without any dissonance with the form of Judaism that they adopted.[96] Iconography can provide a unifying symbolism that bridges language differences, and even sectarianism. Even a Jew who does not know Hebrew can remain connected to iconographic symbols.

ᴄᴚ

## On Prayer and Festivals

We will now try to concretize the gap that developed in the Jewish lifestyle as a result of the language barrier described above through a demonstration of two aspects of Jewish daily life – the festivals and prayer.

### A. Passover

Rabbinic innovations with regard to the ritual world after the destruction of the Temple come to full expression in the new character awarded to Passover. Let us briefly mention what we know about the activities of the rabbis in this regard during the first generations following the destruction. The significant question relating to our deliberation is whether the rabbinic innovations were accepted in the Hellenistic diaspora overseas.

The Biblical Passover consists of the prohibition of *hametz* (leavened products) and the injunction to eat *matzah* (unleavened bread), as well as of the sacrificing the Passover offering (*korban pessach*). The pilgrimage to Jerusalem and the public offering of the sacrifice were central events in the celebration of the festival in the time of the Temple that were considered important by the entire people. Clearly, the focal point of the Passover celebration at that time was Jerusalem.[97] This connection obviously ended after the destruction of the Temple, and the rabbinic leadership intervened to try and reformulate the holiday in its absence.

Many sources indicate that the festival meal consisted of two elements – the eating of the sacrifice and the singing of songs. Thus for example, with regard to the "last supper," which was a Passover meal, it states that "after they sang songs of praise, they went out to the Mount of Olives."[98] Similarly, in describing the festive meal on Passover night, Philo indicates that the significance of the occasion was the addition of "prayers and songs of praise (*hallel*)."[99] We can assume that this description relates not only to the Passover meal in Jerusalem, but also to all other places where the holiday was celebrated without the sacrifice but with meal and songs. We ought to remember that despite the large number of pilgrims, those who arrived were a small percentage of the total number of Jews living in the Land of Israel, and certainly a very small percentage of the number of Jews in the diaspora.[100]

In the wake of the destruction, the rabbis were not satisfied only with continuing the traditional meal, but decreed many injunctions that reformulated the festive meal. There were two central elements of this newly designed celebration – the text of the *haggadah* and the various symbols designed to retain the memory of both the exodus from Egypt and the celebration of the festival in the Temple.[101] The *haggadah* focused on the idea of "retelling the story of the exodus" (*sippur yetsiat mitsrayim*), a practice that is not known to us from the period in which the Temple existed.[102] It is very difficult to believe that the *haggadah* found its way to the Greek and Latin speaking communities.

The *haggadah* was created during the first generations of *tannaim* after the destruction of the Temple as a substitute for the Passover offering and the celebration surrounding it. The text, telling the story of exodus, is composed mainly by Tannaitic *midrashim*.[103] It seems clear that we have no evidence that the commandment of *sippur yetsiat mitsrayim*, the story telling of exodus, was part of the Passover ritual, and certainly no evidence regarding the existence of a text for Passover night, prior to the destruction of the Temple. In fact, on the contrary, most of the evidence supports the fact that the holiday was celebrated only with the sacrifice and songs of praise, as we noted above.[104] Since we have no evidence of a change in the manner that Passover was celebrated in the western diaspora, it is logical to assume that it was celebrated after the destruction in the same way that it was celebrated before – according to the Greek translations of the Bible. It apparently involved a meal in which *matzah* was eaten, and, as indicated by Philo, songs of praise were sung.[105] Even if we assume that there were scholars or intellectuals in these communities who knew Hebrew, this would not impact the Passover celebration, which was a family based celebration and not a synagogue based event, such as prayer or the reading of the Torah. There was certainly not a Hebrew speaker in every family. We must assume, therefore, that the *haggadah* and the commandment of *sippur yetsiat mitsrayim* were not central components of the Passover celebration in the western diaspora.[106]

The uniqueness of the text of the *haggadah* goes well beyond the ritual compensation that it effected – i.e. prayer in place of the sacrifice that could no longer be offered. It also compensated for the center that was lost. Prior to its destruction, the Temple served as the national center for the entire nation.[107] Even those who were not able to physically go to Temple fixed their gaze toward Jerusalem. There the national events took place. This was the place that defined and directed the community. The liturgy created by the sages sought not only to substitute new rituals, but also to create a new way of defining the community. A person in any location who sat on that day and read that text defined himself as a member of the community. This new method of defining community, and connection to the community, was particularly well-suited for dispersed communities. Even though there was a diaspora during the time of the Temple, the big change after its destruction was the disappearance of the center. The text was the substitute for the center that had defined the community. It is therefore clear that one who could not read the text could not be part of a community of readers for whom the text was the means of connecting to the community.

Thus, our claim is not only that the western diaspora lacked the means to remain connected to the center after the destruction of the Temple, but that the newly created center gave rise to an entirely new medium for connectedness – i.e. a common text. If, however, the text was to serve, among other functions, as the new medium for defining community, it was incumbent on everyone in the community to recite it in a common language. Ironically, the Greek-speaking, Hellenistic diaspora, which was so much in need of connectedness to the center, was essentially cut off from the community as a result of this new medium because of their inability to read Hebrew and the lack of translations into Latin or Greek in ancient times. This same phenomenon relates to the development of Jewish prayer, as we will discuss below.

To conclude, prior to the destruction of the Temple, connectedness to the community was achieved through an emotional identification with the Temple through an ongoing awareness of what transpired there and an anticipation of traveling there on pilgrimages. Following the destruction, the *haggadah* became one of the primary means of identification with the community. Since it was not translated, the Greek-speaking communities were left dangling, and their level of connectedness weakened progressively. They lost the old method of bonding with the center, but were unable to adapt to the new method.

## B. Prayer

The institution of a set prayer service was quite revolutionary. We do not find such a practice in Biblical sources or in other ancient cultures.[108] The concept of prayer is of course well known throughout the Bible, but not as an obligatory structured commandment that included fixed texts and set times.[109] In the time of the Temple, we are aware of prayers that accompanied the sacrifices that were comprised of verses from the Bible, primarily from the *Book of Psalms*. The concept of prayer as a form of Divine worship in itself was an innovation of the rabbinic leadership in the generations following the destruction of the Temple. The magnitude of this innovation was not just in the recognition of the value of prayer independent of the Temple ritual, but also in that it became obligatory and structured. The establishment of an obligatory prayer service with set times and a predetermined and closed liturgy was implemented in place of spontaneous prayer that flowed from the emotions of the individual and his internal spiritual need to communicate with his God. Obligatory and set prayer is not mentioned in sources from the time of the Temple, in the apocrypha and pseudepigrapha, in the writings of Philo or Josephus, or in the New Testament.[110] Research also indicates that ancient synagogues during the time of the Temple were not places of worship through prayers, but were primarily places of group gatherings for the purpose of reading, listening to, and studying the Scriptures, an aspect that is emphasized by Philo and Josephus.[111] Fleischer demonstrated that the New Testament includes numerous references in which Jesus appears in a synagogue where he teaches, answers questions, and reads from the Torah, but never prays. The same is true of the visits of Paul and the Apostles to diaspora synagogues. The recurring theme is that the synagogue was a place for reading the Torah and for delivering sermons, but not for prayer.[112] Prayer in the New Testament appears in a very individualized and intimate format, rather than in an institutionalized context. The new format of set prayer thus represented a significant shift in religious life. The formulation and organization of the prayer service was part of a larger attempt by the rabbis to construct an orderly and structured form of Divine worship to replace the Temple service. Order was also needed as a means of creating structure for the people. Set ritual helps to create an organized community around it. Just as the worship in the Temple was not spontaneous, the new form of worship was similarly designed in a structured format. We have clear information from the first tannaitic generation of Yavneh (first to second centuries C.E.) that the sages worked intently to formulate and establish structured prayer.[113] Their efforts were part of a reformulation of Jewish identity and the fashioning of a new form of Divine worship to compensate for the loss of the Temple.[114] In prayer, as in other areas, the powerful innovations of the generation of Yavneh saved Judaism by refashioning its world anew. It is possible that they did not create this world *ex nihilo*. The degree to which the prayers established by the rabbis were based on pre-Temple antecedents is a point of controversy in scholarly literature. It seems to us, however, that this very argument was contained in the deliberations in the study halls of Yavneh. The preponderance of evidence that the issue of prayer engaged so much of the attention of the sages indicates that they viewed it as a significant innovation from recognized practice.[115]

Let us additionally emphasize two important points regarding prayer:

1. The prayers adopted by the rabbis represent the ultimate text in terms of the triumph of the Hebrew language. There is a recognizable Greek influence in rabbinic literature, indicating that the sages were aware of the Greek language and that some were proficient in it. Nevertheless, this does not find expression in the prayer service, as we find practically no Greek expressions or words in Jewish prayer.[116]

2. The prayers are essentially part of the Oral Law in that they were transmitted orally and were not committed to writing until the Oral Law itself was committed to writing. The first evidence of a written prayer book appears in tractate *Sofrim*, which was written in the seventh or eighth century. We also have clear proofs that the sages opposed the publication of the prayers in written form, as reflected in the following *Tosefta*:

> If they were written in paint, red ink, gum ink, or calcanthum, they save them and store them away. As to the scrolls containing blessings, even though they include the Divine Name and many citations from the Torah, they do not save them, but they are allowed to burn where they are. On this basis, they have stated that those who write blessings are as if they burn the Torah. A certain person would write blessings and they told R. Yishmael about him. R. Yishmael went to examine him. When he climbed the ladder, he [the writer] sensed that he was

coming. He took the sheaf of blessings and put it in a dish of water. And in accord with the following statement did R. Yishmael address him: "The punishment for the latter deed is harder than for the former."[117]

We see that the rabbis took dramatic steps to create a new prayer service. This form of prayer took shape during the period of the *tannaim* and became a set ritual for Jews in the Land of Israel and the eastern diaspora. As such, it also served as the glue that bonded people to the community. The rabbis insisted on the use of pure Hebrew in the prayers, and that they not be committed to writing, and certainly not translated. (This latter stance is comparable to the reluctance of the Catholic Church to replace the Latin liturgy with different vernaculars.) These facts lead to the unequivocal conclusion that these prayers could not penetrate into the synagogues in the Greek speaking diaspora. This means that the dramatic development of the liturgy that took place in the first generations following the destruction of the Temple and that became a significant component in the definition of Jewish identity from both a religious and a social perspective was essentially inaccessible to the Jews of the western diaspora. Apparently, the western diaspora remained with non-institutional prayer, and without a clear liturgical structure. The gap between the diasporas, caused by the deep language barrier, left the western diaspora beyond the reach of the new prayer structure developed by the rabbis. It seems clear that there was no parallel liturgical development in the Greek speaking diaspora because there was no recognized body that had the authority to create such a structure. We find support for this thesis from sources emanating from the western diaspora:

1) We find no reference to the *amidah* ("standing") prayer in the apocrypha and pseudepigrapha literature.[118]

2) Evidence from a Christian author for the knowledge of the *amidah* prayer that was recited on the Sabbath can be detected in the Christian Apostolic Constitution from the fourth century C.E. (Book 7, Chapters 33-38). This work is preserved in Greek, and recent studies have clarified that the source of these chapters of the Apostolic Constitution derives from the Syrian Church, and that it was originally written in Syriac and translated later into Greek. The proximity of Syria to the rabbinic centers, and the fact that these chapters were originally written in Syriac, may have been the

cause for this Christian acquaintance with the Jewish prayer. We can therefore assume that the prayer that was known to the author came to his awareness from Hebrew communities in the East.[119] The fact that the author of the Apostolic Constitution mentions only the *amidah* of the Sabbath relates to the reality that he is writing for a Christian population that meets for prayer only on the Sabbath.

There is no need to further elaborate on the impact of the ever widening gap between the nature of prayer and of the synagogue in the eastern and western diasporas, and the deepening bifurcation into two distinct Judaisms that resulted.

⚬

## Five More Proofs for the Rift between Eastern & Western Judaism

1. The most recent research on Jewish nationalism by David Goodblatt is very interesting from our perspective.[120] Goodblatt rightly contends that Jewish nationalism during the Second Temple period and afterwards was based on the vernacular – i.e. on Hebrew. Goodblatt therefore, strengthens our claim, since the process of dichotomization between the East and the West thus coincided with the twilight of nationalism among the Jews of the West who did not know Hebrew. This dichotomy, in addition to the dichotomy created by the estrangement of these western Jews from the rabbinic revolution, led to their feelings of dissimilarity and their disengagement from the Jews of the East. Those who claim that the destruction of the Temple did not bring about the end of Jewish nationalism are correct.[121] According to Goodblatt, however, the nationalism was based on Hebrew language, and was thus minimal in the West. In addition, one has to emphasize that the fact that eastern Jews produced an enormous literary heritage in the vernacular whereas the western Jews did not create anything (even in Greek and Latin), points to a wider cultural issue: is it possible to preserve one's culture without vernacular?

2. In *Antiquities of the Jews*, Josephus Flavius makes numerous references to Jewish Law, mainly Biblical.[122] The lack of references to rabbinic law in the writings of Josephus is not surprising since it is the product of Second

Temple Judaism that preceded the dramatic innovations introduced by the rabbis.[123] Additionally, it might be that the fact that Josephus wrote in Greek and resided in Rome might have influenced the Jews of Rome who learned from him.

In addition, the writings of Philo Judaeus demonstrate that he relied strongly on the Septuagint, rather than on the Hebrew Bible. There is also no indication of early rabbinic laws that were known to Philo.[124] The fact that he used to write down everything in the Greek language signifies how far he was from the rabbinic world, since they kept everything oral and in Hebrew and Aramaic. Moreover, the fact that Philo was acquainted with Palestinian *aggadah*, but does not refer to the *halakhah*, may indicate that early Palestinian *halakhah* did not penetrate Egyptian Hellenistic Judaism. Needless to say, the rabbis in turn did not use Philo,[125] which means that from their point of view they did not see him as a legitimate source. On the other hand, we should emphasize that aggadic influences on Philo may point to the fact that in the Greek Diaspora bordering the Land of the Israel, there may have been certain rabbinic influences. By and large Philo was a victim of the language barrier.

3. A law enacted by Justinian on February 8, 553 C.E. may supports our claim that the Jewish world was divided between Greek and Hebrew based communities.[126] The reality reflected in this law has far reaching implications regarding the duality of the community. As indicated by the law, Justinian was intervening in an internal Jewish matter at the behest of the community. The emperor states explicitly that the Jews presented him with a petition requesting his involvement: "However we could not bear to leave them with an unresolved controversy. We have learned from their petitions…"

We emphasize this point to negate the interpretation that this represented a Jewish-Christian conflict. It is logical to assume that the unresolved controversy was between the Jews of Israel and the Greek speaking diaspora. This is indicated by the fact that the legislation that permits reading in Greek and other languages gives preference to the Septuagint translation over that of Aqilas, and negates the Oral Law:

".... Those who read in Greek shall use the Septuagint tradition, which is more accurate than all the others, and is preferable to the others particularly in reason of what happened while the translation was made....we give permission to use also Aqilas' translation, although he was a gentile and in some readings differs not a little from the Septuagint. What they call *Mishnah*....we prohibit entirely, for it is not included among the Holy Books, nor was it handed down from above by the prophets, but it is an invention of men in their chatter, exclusively of earthly origin and having in it nothing of the divine."[127]

The document reflects the tension between the two diasporas and the conflict over issues of language and acceptable translations. Later in the article we will elaborate upon how we interpret Justinian Novella in line with our theory.

4. The portrayal of the Jew in Greek and Latin Pagan literature is of one who lives according to the laws of the Torah, but not the Oral Law. For example, in the writings of Tacitus and others up until the sixth century, Jews are described according to the model known to us in the Bible. The characteristics of the Jew found in this literature include Sabbath observance, celebration of Passover, the prohibition of statues, circumcision, and separation with regard to marriage and eating. These are classical Biblical motifs. Through them, we also find a shallow encounter with certain Biblical characters such as Abraham and Moses. For example, the laws are referred to as the 'Mosaic Law'. On the other hand, we do not find in the literature of Tacitus or other Pagan literature references to innovations that took place in rabbinic academies, including new practices such as prayer or novel holiday observances. Their descriptions could not rely on anything other than the Bible because the Oral Law was not written and was not translated to Latin or Greek. The Pagan writers usually relied on their surface knowledge of local Jews. Thus, their use of the term 'Mosaic Law' reflects the fact that they did not know of the existence of any other literature beyond the Bible.[128] The fact that the rabbis highlighted Moses as a prophet, the first and most prominent prophet in history, stands in complete opposition to the centrality of Moses as legislator in Greek and Roman literature.

Additional support for the Biblical image of Jews and Judaism in the first centuries of the common era also comes to the fore in the writings of the Greek and Latin Church fathers. Their polemics with Jews and Judaism were based on their common text, the Old Testament. This holds true of the Church fathers from different places in different times, such as Ambrossius (Milan, fourth century), Augustinus (Africa, fifth century), Eusebius (Palestine, third to fourth century) and John Chrisostomus (Syria, fourth century). As a rule, the Church fathers ignored the rabbinic laws and lore. This does not surprise us since for the Greek and Latin fathers who did not know Hebrew, the latter was not accessible, and for the ones who knew Hebrew and Aramaic, one can assume that they suspected rabbinic literature inter alia because it was not written down.[129] This perhaps is yet another facet of the dichotomy that existed between Judaism and Christianity in this respect: Whereas the Jews remained oral during the first centuries, the Christians developed a tendency to write down almost everything, which accounts in part for the success of their diffusion. We may speculate that the oral rabbinic lore and laws seemed to many Christians to be lacking the authority often attributed to written material by literate societies. This may be the reason that both Origines and Eusebius as well as Hieronymus, who lived in Palestine not too far from the academies of the rabbis, do not show any real acquaintance with the world of knowledge of the latter.[130] Also, the rabbis, according to certain *midrahsim*, were reluctant to spread their knowledge to foreigners, which might explain the oral nature of their literature and the fact that they did not get through to their competitors, the Church fathers. Be that as it may, most of the Church fathers primarily encountered western Jews who were not at all acquainted with rabbinic literature.

5. The Jewish Rebellion (115-117 C.E.) might also support our argument. It is a surprising fact that the Jews were divided in their participation in the revolt. While the eastern diaspora from Mesopotamia to Egypt actively participated in the rebellion (doubts regarding the participation of the community in the Land of Israel as to the "war of Kitos" are unjustified), the western diaspora was completely passive, except for Cyprus and Libya, which were anyway in close proximity to the East.[131] The enclosed

map shows that whereas the yellow colored regions were what we call here typical western Jewish communities, and the white were eastern Hebrew-Aramaic ones, some of the in-between regions (off yellow) may have included spots where rabbinic lore infiltrated.

⤶

## A Secret Literature: Why Were the Rabbis Reluctant to Translate the Oral Law?

The reader might wonder why the rabbis simply did not make an effort to translate their new corpus into Greek and Latin in order to expose the western communities to their world of knowledge, and thus preserve the unity of the Jewish world. We suggest a two-fold answer that is based on the essence of rabbinic thought. First, the fact that their corpus of knowledge remained oral made it almost impossible to translate. Secondly, and most importantly, they were reluctant to expose their world of knowledge and beliefs in the Greek and Latin languages, for fear that they become accessible to the non-Jewish world.

This thesis is supported by *Midrash Tanhuma*, which cites R. Yehudah bar Shalom, a scholar in the Land of Israel from approximately the middle of the fourth century C.E., who prohibited the writing of the Oral Law so that it would not be possible to translate it.

> R. Yehudah bar Shalom said: "When God said to Moses (Exodus 34:27): 'Write for yourself', Moses requested that the *Mishnah* be written. But God anticipated that the nations of the world would in the future translate the Torah and read it in Greek, and they would claim 'I am Israel', and until now the scales would be balanced. God said to the nations: 'You claim that you are my children. I do not know, but the ones who have my secret are my children.' And what is it? It is the *Mishnah* that was transmitted orally."[132]

As long as we are talking only about the Written Law, the "scales are balanced," there is equality, as it were, between Israel and the nations. In contrast, the Oral Law is unique to Israel – it is the secret between God and Israel. **The means of preventing the nations from gaining access to the secret is by preventing**

**its translation into Greek, which is achieved by maintaining it as an oral tradition.** It seems that this *Midrash* is responding to the claim of the Church that saw itself as the true heir of Israel. The canon, the Book of Books, is no longer the sole property of Israel. According to the *Midrash*, it is the *Mishnah* that separates Israel from the nations and expresses their uniqueness as the ones who have access to the secret conferred by God. It is therefore important to make every effort to preserve the Oral Law as the exclusive possession of the Jews so that what happened with the Torah not happen with it – i.e. that the nations not adopt it and claim to be Jews. In reaction to the Christian desire to strengthen the level of holiness of their sources by connecting them to the older sources and publishing them together, the Jews wished to strengthen the mysterious nature of their sources, secret sources that were given to them by God to preserve.

The *Jerusalem Talmud* records the following:

> R. Zeira said in the name of R. Elazar: "'I will write for him so many things of my Torah' (Hosea 8:12): Is a majority of the Torah written? Rather, more things are learned from the written Torah than those things learned orally. Yes and no. More beloved are the things learned orally than those learned from the written Torah [...] What is the difference between them and the nations of the world — these produce their books, and these produce their books; these produce their interpretations, and these produce their interpretations?" R. Hagai said in the name of Shmuel bar Nachman: "Things were stated in writing and orally, and we do not know which are more beloved. However, from what is written (Exodus 34:27) — 'For after the tenor of these words I have made a covenant with thee and with Israel' — it implies that those learned orally are more beloved." R. Yohanan and R. Yudan ben R. Shimon: One said "If you preserve what is stated orally and what is stated in writing, I will make a covenant with you, and if not I will not." The other said: "If you preserve what is stated orally and fulfill what is written, you will receive a reward, and if not, you will not receive a reward."[133]

Various interpreters make efforts to emphasize the importance and belovedness of the Oral Law, even more than the Written law, and the fact that it is unique to

Israel. The controversy with Christianity is clearly reflected in their respective canons – "These produce their books, and these produce their books" – and the Oral Law is thus the work that uniquely characterizes the Jews, leading to the strengthening of its position in comparison to the Written Law.[134] The *Midrash* cited above takes an additional and significant step, prohibiting the translation of the Oral Law into Greek so that it does not fall into the hands of the nations. It is the translation to Greek that is likely to lead to the exposure of the Oral Law and to the rupture of the uniqueness of Judaism. The *Midrash* encourages the preservation of the Oral Law as an oral tradition in order to prevent its translation.

Talmudic sources reflect a positive relationship of the sages toward the translation of the Torah in Greek. The *Mishnah* states:

> There is no differences between Torah scrolls, *tefillin*, and *mezuzot* except that Torah scrolls can be written in any language, while *tefillin* and *mezuzot* can only be written in *Ashurit*. Rabban Shimon ben Gamliel said: "For Torah scrolls too it is only permitted in Greek."[135]

The *Babylonian Talmud* provides the reasoning behind the permit to write the Torah in Greek: "Because of the episode of King Ptolemy (the writing of the Septuagint translation)."[136]

In other words, the Septuagint translation was perceived as a miracle and as a successful outcome. This is reflected in the continuation of the *Talmud* as well:

> R. Yohanan said: "What is the reasoning of Rabban Gamliel? – Because the verse states (Genesis 9:27): 'God enlarge Yefet, and he shall dwell in the tents of Shem' - The words of Yefet will be in the tents of Shem … The beauty of Yefet will be in the tents of Shem."[137]

The same sentiment is expressed in the *Jerusalem Talmud*:

> The rabbis learned: Rabban Shimon ben Gamliel said: "For Torah scrolls too it is only permitted in Greek." They examined it and found that the Torah could only be translated properly in Greek.…
> R. Yirmiyah said in the name of R. Hiyya bar Abba: "Akilas the

proselyte translated the Torah in the presence of R. Eliezer and R. Yehoshua, and they praised him and said to him: 'You are more beautiful than the children of Man' (Psalms 45:3)."[138]

The concern regarding translation was that it would not be sufficiently precise, i.e. that it would not be able to be translated properly – but in Greek there was no concern that it could not be translated properly because of its beauty and glory – "the beauty of Yefet." The special relationship of the sages to Greek comes through clearly here. Even though they preferred the translation of Akilas to the Septuagint, the Septuagint was also viewed as suitable. "The episode of King Ptolemy," described in the *Babylonian Talmud* as a miracle, was understandably construed even more so in early Greek Jewish sources as a miracle, and as an important and positive event. So it is in the letter of Aristeias and in the writings of Philo, who tells that a holiday was even established to commemorate this event.[139]

In later sources, however, a completely opposite picture emerges. In *Massekhet Sofrim*,[140] a post-Talmudic work from approximately the eighth century, the episode of Ptolemy is described as follows: "That day was as difficult for Israel as the day on which the golden calf was made, for it was impossible to properly translate the Torah." The same sentiment is found in lists of fast days from a variety of post-Talmudic sources. One of the most well-known texts with such a list is a work entitled *Megillat Ta'anit Batra*, which is integrated into the ninth century Babylonian code *Halakhot Gedolot* of R. Shimon Kayara. It includes a list of fasts related to events in different periods from Biblical times until after the destruction of the Second Temple, which served as a source for lists in later halakhic works. The following is the description of the writing of the Septuagint in *Megillat Taanit Batra*:

> "The following are days on which we fast as a Torah injunction: ...
> The 8th day of Tevet, the day on which the Torah was written in the
> times of the Greek king, Ptolemy, and darkness encompassed the
> world for three days."[141]

The source for this list of fast days was apparently composed in the Land of Israel, as it appears in liturgical poems of Israeli origin. For example, in a liturgical poem for the month of Tevet, R. Pinchas ben Yaakov Ha-Kohen, an eighth century poet from the Land of Israel, wrote: "The fast for the writing [of the Torah] in Greek falls on the 18[142] of the month."[142] The author of this text does not give a reason why the translation of the Torah into Greek should be a source of mourning. He apparently felt that it was self-evident. Shulamit Elitzur, who has studied these lists in depth, claims that the Greek translation of the Torah was perceived as unsuitable and damaging when it was adopted by the Christians.[143] Elitzur points out an ancient manuscript with the following formulation: "For the Torah should have only been translated for Israel alone." This formulation is surprising in light of the words of the *Tanhuma*, with which we opened this discussion, which only related in this way to the Oral Law.[144]

The conclusion that we might draw from these sources is that the sages perceived that the translation of the Torah to Greek resulted essentially in the loss of the Torah as an exclusive Jewish possession by its transformation into a universal source. The original sense of joy associated with the translation of the Torah and its resulting accessibility to Jews who did not know Hebrew, turned into mourning several centuries later when it was perceived to be a loss of Jewish exclusivity, allowing the Christians to claim: "I am Israel." This would explain the fierce opposition of the rabbis to the translation of the Oral Law. In light of the transformation of the Torah to a universal document, it became increasingly important to preserve the Oral Law as the secret and exclusive heritage of the Jewish people. The price of making the Torah accessible to the Greek speaking Jews had already been paid, but should not be paid twice. The *Midrash Tanhuma* draws an even more radical conclusion – that the transmission of the Oral Law remain oral so that it cannot be translated.

⚬

## Was the Split between East and West a Result of Sectarianism in Judaism?

Might it be that the sectarian distinctions familiar to us in Jerusalem before the destruction of the Temple continued after the destruction as a division between the two Judaisms on opposite banks of the Mediterranean Sea? Was the eastern Jewish community Pharisaic and the western community Sadducean? We believe that this was not the case. In addition to the fact that we find no evidence of Sadducean Judaism in the West, we would like to raise other points that make this thesis improbable in our eyes.[145]

1. There is a controversy as to what motivated and initiated the sectarian divisions in Jerusalem during the Second Temple period. Some place its beginnings as early as the third century B.C.E. and some as late as the middle of the second century B.C.E. Nevertheless, everyone agrees that the phenomenon disappeared when the Temple was destroyed. Our primary source of information about the sects is from the writings of Josephus Flavius. Josephus wrote in Rome and described the Jewish sects during the time of the Second Temple period,[146] but he writes about them as a phenomenon that occurred in historical times. From Josephus's writings it becomes apparent that sectarianism was a matter of the past.

2. We must keep in mind that although the appearance of sectarian movements during the Second Temple period was an important phenomenon, it was relatively marginal in its scope. Although much of the information about the sects is inaccessible, there are some points that are clear and agreed upon, such as the fact that it was centered primarily in Jerusalem, and that it involved maximally 10% of the total Jewish population of Israel.[147] There is a debate as to whether there were sects in the Galilee region, but there is certainly no evidence that the sects existed in the diaspora. Thus, the remaining 90% of the Jews in Palestine and all of the Jews of the diaspora at that time were simply Jews – not Pharisees or Sadducees, or members of any other sect. Let us cite one of the important scholars of the period on this point: "The question has been raised, what characterized the others – 90% of the population – who were not members of the various sects. We might say that the silent majority were dedicated to the Temple, which was the central institution in the life of the nation. They did not identify with any particular group, and the controversy between the sects did not interest them. He who was connected to the mass of the people accepted the traditions received from his parents and grandparents as self-evident, and fulfilled the commandments of the Torah with the assumption that whatever was good for them, was correct for him as well."[148]

3. We must ask how it could happen that the position of one group took hold in one region, while the other dominated in another region. It is clear that at the outset, both had followings in all areas. A historian would have to explain how this pluralism ended and was replaced by a dichotomy.

4. The essence of the Sadducean laws as we know them, and the essence of the polemic between the Sadducees and the rabbis, revolved around the administration of the Temple. The Pharisees were the ones who transferred the focal point of the Jewish religious experience from the Temple to daily life, an approach that was continued by the rabbis. A significant portion of the extant halakhic controversies between the Pharisees and the Sadducees relate to the stringencies of the Sadducees regarding the Temple ritual and regarding purity and impurity. The religious experience of the Sadducees focused on the Temple, where they waged their religious struggles and sought to strengthen the standing of the priesthood. In light of these facts, it is logical to assume that Jews who were geographically distant from the Temple would also be distant from the Sadducean approach. It would be hard to explain why a community that was so far removed from the world of the Temple, and that was integrated to some degree in a non-Jewish daily life, would adopt an ideology that was primarily concerned with the administration of the Temple. While the Qumran sect was known to be very involved with Temple ritual in spite of their distance from Jerusalem, they existed in isolation, unlike the western Jews who were integrated in the life of the surrounding society.

Thus, even if we accept Berachyahu Lifschitz's claim regarding the continued existence of the Sadducees in the first centuries of the common era, there is no relationship between his claim and the dichotomy that we have posited. The question of the disappearance of the Sadducees is a completely different question than the one that we are addressing. Turning the gap between the eastern and western diasporas into a Jewish ideological issue is simply a reduction of the central question that we have raised.

⸙

## *Networks of Knowledge*

A short comment on the impact of the emerging rift in Judaism on early Christianity is in order. In spite of the fact that the New Testament can be taken as evidence just for the first century C.E., it does provide some support for our claim. We believe that Paul and the first Apostles, and subsequently the Church fathers, took advantage of the developing vacuum in the western diaspora resulting from the fact that it was cut off from the main Hebrew-Aramaic network of the eastern Jewish community. They worked toward spreading their beliefs in the western Jewish diaspora. It is a fact that Paul never considered going eastward, and that the only population that he thought might possibly accept his teachings were the Jews of the Greek speaking diaspora.[149] Greek speaking Jews who became part of the western diaspora could easily have perceived Paul, who was a student of R. Gamliel I, as a rabbi who came to teach the Oral Law. The big advantage for Paul, and consequently the Church fathers, was that they taught in Greek. Paul's ability to enter the public sphere of the Jewish community via the synagogue was related to the fact that these Jews were spiritually cut off from the center in the Land of Israel and from Babylonia.

> "Now Paul and his company set sail from Paphos, and came to Perga in Pamphylia [....] but they passed on from Perga and came to Antioch of Pisidia. And on the Sabbath day they went into the synagogue and sat down. After the reading of the law and the prophets, the rulers of the synagogue sent to them, saying, 'Brethern, if you have any word of exhortation for the people, say it.' So Paul stood up, and motioning with his hand said: 'Men of Israel, and you that fear God [....]' As they went out, the people begged that these things might be told them the next Sabbath. And when the meeting of the synagogue broke up, many Jews and devout converts to Judaism followed Paul and Barnabas, who spoke to them and urged them to continue in the grace of God."[150]

The same is true of the later Church fathers who could have been perceived by some Jews as rabbinic authorities.[151] Here we would like to emphasize that Jews living in Syria and Lebanon and even Palestine, which were Greek speaking communities, can be considered as 'western Jews' if they could not decode rabbinic messages. On the other hand, it is clear that in communities closer to the Land of Israel, the Jews had some degree of Hebrew facility and could therefore decode the developing rabbinic legal corpus.[152] The lack of hierarchical and structured communication within the western diaspora, and its isolation from the East, created a place for early Christianity to establish a foothold, and to build a structured Christian hierarchy. The people who attached themselves to this hierarchy were Jews who were estranged from their brethren in the East.[153] Thus, "religious commodities," such as the epistle of James, were sent from the Land of Israel to the West, demonstrating that a connection between the Jews of Palestine and the western diaspora did exist in the first century C.E. This fact, nevertheless, strengthens our thesis regarding the deep significance of language in the creation of the split between the diasporas. The New Testament and the sermons delivered by Paul in synagogues in the western diaspora, as described in the New Testament, could be understood by the Jews of the West, even by the Jews who knew Greek but not Hebrew. If so, we might see Paul and the first apostles as agents who brokered between the two worlds. Paul, a Jew from the western diaspora (Tarsus), is an excellent example, for he had one leg in Palestine, planted in the Hebrew-Aramaic world, but also traveled to the West and was fluent in Greek. He thus carried in his bag a "religious commodity" from the Land of Israel that he could transmit in Greek. If this claim is correct, then Paul and the first apostles were insightful enough to understand the deepening gap that was developing between the western diaspora and the Jews of the East, and the benefits of bridging between the worlds by maintaining a dialogue with the Greek-speaking diaspora. In this way, Paul and the apostles contributed to widening the schism between the rabbinic Jews of the East and the Biblical Jews of the West. In terms of modern research on networks of knowledge, Christianity benefited from being a network of knowledge inter alia because it was capable of transferring knowledge. Thus it "became more productive than organizations that are less capable of knowledge transfer."[154] In other words, Paul and the apostles capitalized on their knowledge of Greek to create a network for transferring knowledge from the Land of Israel to the West while rabbinic messages were not transferred by them and could not, or would not, be transferred by the rabbis themselves. Many of the western Jews, who probably lacked any spiritual leaders, grasped the opportunity that was presented by the Greek speaking Christian apostles, who became their new leaders. These Jews are apparently the ones referred to in Acts 21.20-21, Galatians 2.8-9 (and elsewhere, the so-called "Judaizantes"). Moreover, the insistence of the rabbis on oral knowledge on the one hand, and its devastating effect on Judaism on the other, may explain why the oral phase of Christianity was so short (from Jesus to circa 70 C.E. when the Gospel of Mark was written down). The Christian leadership understood early on that in order to gain ground in the population, both pagan and Jewish, their new ideas should be written down as quickly as possible. This explains why Christians, as opposed to the Jews, were so vehement about publishing and from the outset put an emphasis on mission, a concept that was not inherent in Judaism.[155] Let us now elaborate a bit on the New Testament as evidence for our thesis.

## The New Testament as Evidence for the Jewish Split Diaspora

As already mentioned above, Paul was familiar with both worlds which emerged in the Judaism of his day, East and West. The evidence from the New Testament strengthens this assumption by showing that he, in a masterful manner, designed a strategy that exploited this gap, so it seems, and accomplished the following:

1. It granted "ammunition" to communities of Jesus's followers in the Greek west who obviously entertained a lively – not always too friendly – dialogue with their Jewish neighbors.[156] That Jews and Jesus's followers mingled, and the fact that Jews and Jesus's Jewish followers alike adhered to the Torah, or parts of it, is very clearly understood from Galatians 2.1-10, and 2. 16ff, 4.8-11, 21 (and elsewhere). From some of Paul's epistles we can learn about the voices of both sides of the dialogue, those of Jesus's Jewish followers and those of the so called western Jews. In fact, we have here an interesting case of a dialogue where one speaker addresses another through a third party (which apparently was already quite convinced by what the speaker wished to transmit to the third party). For instance, the Jewish voice comes to the fore clearly from Paul's polemics in Romans chapters 1-4.

2. Paul entered the authority vacuum that ensued in western Judaism by posing as a kind of rabbi who,[157] so exceptionally, spoke Greek with his Jewish addressees (with great personal authority, in synagogues and through

vociferous clashes with pagans in the public sphere, showing his persistence and charisma; he thus publicized his ideas quite effectively). That an authority vacuum existed in the western Diaspora we can learn easily from the Book of Acts read with some of Paul's epistles. In Palestine, Paul was confronted, like Jesus and Peter before him, by the Pharisees (namely the rabbis) and their formal central institutions (such as the Sanhedrin), whereas in the Jewish diaspora, except for some local leaders (such as heads of synagogues), who were confrontational, no rabbis seem to go against his mission, and no central Jewish institution was involved. At any rate, by following the ancient rules of rhetoric (namely, that one has to know his addressee very well in order to convince him[158]), when speaking to Jews (as said, via his addressees) Paul on the one hand did not deny the importance of the Old Testament – where this was useful for his purpose (as he himself says explicitly in 1 Corinthians 9.19-21 and when he appeases the Jews, as in Galatians 5.3 where he argues that if one keeps circumcision he has to fulfill the whole Torah; probably having in mind those Jews who were circumcised but neglected to adhere to the whole Torah, Galatians 6.13), and on the other hand occasionally intertwined rabbinic material (in Greek, of course, in order to show that he was not alien to this new oral lore; see also his mention of the rabbinic custom of blessing over the wine and bread, 1 Corinthians 11. 23-28).[159] It is not accidental that Paul was quite attentive to the role of languages in the process of diffusing a religion. For instance, in 1 Corinthians chapter 14 he so beautifully says that many languages can be an obstacle for common belief, and suggests a unifying method as prophecy, namely enthusiastic prophecy like the one the king elected by God, Saul, experienced in the Old Testament (see also Acts 2, and 10.46). If, then, Jews in the West got a taste of the Oral Law of the rabbis, it was ironically Paul who provided a channel for such information to "leak out" from the Hebrew and Aramaic "mysterious" Jewish lore created in Palestine (*torat ha'mistorin*).

3. He, as opposed to the "oral" rabbis who consequentially at the end of the day lost contact with their fellow Jews in the West, cared to *write down* his message. We would repeat here what Mendels said in his recent book, *Why Did Paul Go West?*:[160] "The religious leadership of Jesus's followers (Gentile and Jewish) from the first century to the fourth was probably aware of the difficulties in diffusion of oral material. This leadership could

simply observe its devastating results in the Jewish world, and elsewhere. These opposite strategies of preserving religious material, oral and written, became evident at that juncture of the history of the rise of Christianity against the background of Judaism." In short, in contradistinction to their Jewish brethren, who kept everything oral, the religious leaders of Jesus's followers (including the Church fathers of the first centuries C.E.) took care to write down everything important from the outset. This may be also the reason why the history of the early church was so quickly written down, namely not too long after the occurrences took place (in the form of Gospels and the Book of Acts).

4. It seems quite likely that Paul exploited the situation of the religious and authority gap between East and West, and grasped the opportunity to persuade many of the vulnerable Jews in the West to follow Jesus's teaching in the sense of Acts 24.5.[161] We will not open here the complex issue with all of its implications or deal with the ad nauseam discussion of the meaning of conversion, but only emphasize what we can learn from the available Christian sources about the split diaspora, and in fact get a glimpse of the Jewish western side of it. The Book of Acts in fact adduces the first steps of what Mendels called the "media revolution of early Christianity" and has, as in other matters concerning the Jews mentioned here, a well-designed strategy. We will not discuss this subject here, but will only mention that Paul went west because he saw from his own vantage point what we saw just some years ago. He understood that many of his addressees would henceforward remain diaspora Biblical Jews who spoke Greek and that he would not have to confront the "difficult" Pharisees (rabbis) of the eastern Jewish sphere in order to achieve his goals. Unless one understands the existence of the schism in Judaism at that time, it is difficult to explain the reasons why Paul went west. This approach freed him from a dialogue with the "rabbis" of Palestine and enabled him to speak to western Jews in a language that they would understand, from both a linguistic and a spiritual-religious perspective. Although written by someone (Luke) from a later perspective, it should be mentioned that we learn from Acts chapters 13-18 (and elsewhere) that Paul went to speak to Jews in synagogues. This is one of our proofs that he spoke to western Jews. (If we are not mistaken, we cannot find him speaking to Jews in gatherings in the Land of Israel;[162] the participants in the synagogue of the libertines and other diaspora synagogues in Jerusalem were mainly for Jews

who arrived from the diaspora and were visiting Jerusalem.[163]) In fact, Paul and the apostles were quite well received by many Jews in the western diaspora, for instance in Ephesus, Acts 18.18-21. In other synagogues they were received nicely by some and not just rejected.[164] One has to take into consideration that "simple" Jews who probably did not yet know the Gospel stories could really see him as a sort of rabbi. It is also clear from Acts that Paul and the apostles spoke in synagogues having the Torah as their basic text (17.2, and 18.28, where Apollos "confuted the Jews in public, showing by the scriptures that the Christ was Jesus"). "Scriptures" ("graphon") here refers to the Old Testament, since the New Testament did not exist yet as Scripture, a matter Luke knew quite well. As we all know that this is the beginning of a long tradition in Christian hermeneutics, i.e. to prove from the Old Testament that it foresaw many things that are connected to the rise of Jesus. Be that as it may, all of the above point to Paul's special position between eastern and western Judaism. Moreover, it seems that his dealings with Palestinian Pharisees ("rabbis") were tense and he was reluctant to speak to them (as he did with his fellow Jews in the West; for instance, Acts 13.13-52) unless he was forced to do so. He speaks out only when arrested in Palestine (Acts 21.27-26.32), whereas in the western Diaspora he approaches the Jews in synagogues freely.

Let us elaborate a bit on this issue. Paul's dissociation from the eastern Judaism of his day enabled him to limit his dialogue with the western Jews to a common text shared at that time by Jews and Jesus's Jewish followers, the Old Testament in Greek, without the eastern baggage of the Pharisees (and their Hebrew Bible). The Old Testament in Greek was the only binding religious text of Jews in the western Diaspora – no other text as yet existed for Jewish and Gentile followers of Jesus as well – if you accept our thesis of the split Jewish diaspora. Thus, Paul accommodates to this particular audience – as he so emphatically says himself in 1 Corinth 9.20-21 – and does not use *Midrash*, rabbinic speculation, or halakhic deliberations, with which he was no doubt familiar having been a student of Gamliel I. This is the reason for instance why Paul, while addressing the Jewish followers of Jesus in the Greek speaking world and the Jews and "Judaizers" of this particular world, mentions historical figures from the Old Testament (not in an aggadic manner so typical of the Palestinian Pharisees) that could be commonly accepted by Jesus's Jewish followers, Jews, and "Judaizers" alike, without arousing too much antagonism from either group. Figures like Abraham prior to his circumcision are well suited for this purpose (for instance Galatians chapter 3, Romans 4.13ff, appeasing Jews and Jesus's followers alike). This is a well-known issue, and we do not need to elaborate on this point. Moreover, having the western Jews in mind, he not only refrains from rabbinic material (with minor exceptions pointed to by Menahem Kister[165]), but also does not refer back to the narratives later to be adduced in the Gospels. He no doubt knew the stories of Jesus and Peter – still in their oral form – from his own experience and many of the stories that were circulating after the crucifixion of Jesus and his ascension. Paul does mention the Messiah frequently, but is quite cautious not to mention in detail the recent linear history of the first followers of Jesus.[166] His, as it were, non-historic position concerning recent Christian "Palestinian" history also comes to the fore in the narrative of Acts 7 when he, still as a Jew, killed the author of a "Christian" interpretation of a linear Jewish history taken from the Old Testament. This is a symbolic act on his behalf. Thus, on the one hand, Paul mentions "convenient" figures from the Bible familiar and holy to the Jews, and on the other, does not adduce the recent history of Jesus and his followers (with only very minor exceptions).

Why is that so? We would suggest that this stance of Paul towards "Christian" history shows that he operates within a western Jewish environment. It is probable that western Jews, already at this early point in the history of the relationship between Jews and Jesus's followers, could and perhaps *did* dissociate from the (oral) gospel narratives where the conflict between Jesus's followers and the Jews was with *rabbis* (Pharisees, eastern Jews). When the Gospels were published in their written form a couple of decades later in the century and became popular, this dissociative mood of western Jews may have increased. *The Book of Acts*, written by Luke, one of the Gospel authors, strengthens our impression here: The first section of the book dealing with the aftermath of Jesus's death shows a clash between Peter and the first Christians of the Land with the Pharisees of the Land of Israel and their institutions. This is also the impression gained from the last chapters of the book where clashes between Paul and the Pharisees of Palestine take place. Moreover, already earlier in his career he has a fierce conflict (9.29) even with western Diaspora Jews, who probably like himself came to study rabbinic lore in Palestine and symbolically decided to move back to the western Diaspora, to his birth town of Tarsus (see also his conflict with Jewish pilgrims from Asia

Minor who were apparently among his opponents there, but the setting of this conflict is Palestine, Acts 21.27 and 24.12, 18-21). Paul's rift with Palestine and its emerging Rabbinic Judaism – echoed so well in 1 Thessalonians 2.14-20 – was continued by the Church fathers, even those who lived near rabbinic centers (who, as the *Midrash Tanchuma* actually views it, "hijacked" the Old Testament for their own demonstrative purposes). They wrote in Greek and Latin, arguing from the Old Testament which remained their central text (the rabbis in any case could not follow what the Church fathers wrote in Greek and Latin, and the Church fathers never really used the oral traditions of the sages; we have of course Eusebius's Dem. Evan and Praep. Evan, in mind). Thus, toning down of a recent history of the clash between the first followers of Jesus and Jews was one of the persuasion techniques adopted by Paul in order to attract Jews who still had not "joined" the communities of the followers of Jesus, or those who did and were suspected of being "spies" (Galatians 2.4). In short, since the Pharisees and their painful conflict with Jesus and his disciples do not figure prominently in Paul's letters, and since many of Paul's addressees are western Jews, the latter (and one would imagine, Paul as well) could have had a more relaxed dialogue with each other because according to the Gospels it was the Pharisees "of the east" who clashed with the new movement of Jesus and his followers. The narrative, known to Paul from personal experience and the oral traditions which developed after Jesus's crucifixion, was a narrative of conflict with *rabbis*; in contradistinction to Biblical Jews who were "exempt" from the influence of the eastern emerging rabbis and who probably saw themselves as quite distanced and not really involved with this new history of Christian origins.

We can surmise that Paul's restrained approach to the Palestinian history of Jesus and his successors in his epistles may have enabled him to more tranquilly address the western Jews in their own spiritual and religious language. For instance, he claims that the one who adheres to the Torah can keep it, and that those who were circumcised could carry on living with Jews or Jesus's followers. He exploited the fact that western Jews were so different from their brethren in the East since many of them partially adhered to the Torah and mingled with adherents of Jesus's teaching when they were discussing the Torah or visiting each other on the Jewish holidays.[167] As a consequence, some remained Jews to a degree or became in some way followers of Jesus, whatever that meant at the time. The fact that the western Jews were not rabbinic, made it easier for them to mingle with Jesus's followers even in later centuries when Christianity became more defined and the rabbis more erudite in their hostility towards gentiles which became more sophisticated and more clearly expressed in their literature, as we can learn from decisions of synods, Roman laws, etc.

This point is of great importance. Rabbinic Jews in Palestine in fact challenged the Roman authorities by creating their own code of laws, thus defining their own sovereignty within the greater authority sphere of the Roman Empire (their strategy to keep it oral may have also been the reason for hiding it from the authorities; see the story about the "sardiotot"). We have devoted a separate article to this issue which was published several years ago.[168] We would not, therefore, be surprised if this very tension between the two systems of law (i.e. sovereignties) brought about the clash of the Romans with the Jews in Palestine as early as the first century C.E. (in contradistinction to the Jews in Parthia who until the third century C.E. were free to create their own "state within a state," a matter which probably increased the migration from Palestine, which was under Roman rule, to Sura, Pumbadita, and to Neharde'a). Hence, according to the "split diaspora" thesis, the Jews in the western diaspora did not create their own sovereign code and also did not participate in the code that was created in the East by the rabbis there. We have shown above that only three or four rabbis out of hundreds migrated from the western diaspora and probably settled in Palestine, but their contribution was minor. For Paul, who thought in terms of submission to the sovereign state (Romans 13, other variants were also adduced by him) in what we call civil and criminal law, the dialogue with the western Jews could have been easy. Neither he nor the western Jews were happy with the idea of a "state within a state," to use modern terminology (Francis Fukuyama and others).[169] Moreover, and here we come to a crucial issue, it is common knowledge that even the most observant Biblical Jews in the western diaspora did not, and could not, follow all the ordinances of the Torah (perhaps they fulfilled 60% of them). And even when they did, they were not up-to-date with rabbinic law. Thus, for instance, they could celebrate the Passover ritual (but even prior the destruction of the Temple in Jerusalem could not sacrifice there, unless they made a pilgrimage). Yet, as we have mentioned above, in the second century, after the destruction of the Temple, they had no *haggadah* for the service at home (an invention of the rabbis as a substitute to the sacrifice in the Temple). Furthermore, they could not fulfill the many agricultural and political ordinances linked to residence in the Land of Israel (as for instance the Sabbatical Year [*shemitah*] and the Rule of the King, which the rabbis "corrected" to suit the new circumstances; see the *Mishnah*). Similarly, many of the severe sanctions of the "criminal" code in the Bible could not be performed in the diaspora, as for instance capital punishment, etc. (even Tacitus, who is not favorable toward the Jews, does not mention exceptional behavior on their part which goes against Roman Law). Biblical laws that were practiced in the western diaspora were not in conflict with the Roman state. On the other hand, they could and did fulfill the personal ordinances such as circumcision which apparently did not clash with the law of the sovereign. This **partial** fulfillment by Jews of the laws of the Torah, probably became a trigger for Paul to crystallize his own views concerning the **incomplete** fulfillment of the Torah by his addressees. Hence it is no wonder that Paul refers quite a bit to circumcision and tolerates it (he even circumcises Timothy, Acts 16.1-3; and see Galatians 2.1-3 [Titus], and 5.1-6), and feels free to state several times that the ordinances of the Bible are superfluous in other matters. This shows quite clearly that Paul – perhaps more than scholars would admit – in some ways reflects a superb acquaintance with the day to day behavior of western Jews who could not and did not adhere to the *whole* of their Torah. Yet in some instances Paul moves some steps further from this Jewish pattern. While for his Jewish audience he never expresses an "abolitionist" stance (if to use American civil war terminology) of the Torah or part of it, he as well tolerates people who relinquish the Torah as a whole and are just great believers in ethical and spiritual values (for instance Romans chapters 2 and 3). Hence, "loving your neighbor as yourself" means for him the sum total of all the Torah. In other words, by living in the western diaspora in a host-state, the western Jews had no other choice but to relinquish some of the ordinances of the Torah, some of which could in any case not be fulfilled there, as they had neither Pharisaic lore to provide the new interpretations, nor authoritarian rabbis to inspect and fight them when they did not strictly fulfill them. As stated, Paul reflected this very mood, but goes much further and says that the Torah can be used in an even more relaxed manner, similar to what his fellow western Jews had been doing all along. Judging from some of his epistles, Paul differentiates between three Jewish western diaspora types: (a) those who are strict adherents of the Torah (but as stated above, even they could not fulfill all the laws appearing in the Torah), (b) Jews who were relaxed about their Torah and in some cases did not even circumcise their children, and (c) Jews who became followers of Jesus to a certain degree, even if they were circumcised – some of whom were suspected of being Jewish "spies" while others probably enjoyed a good relationship. It is not our purpose here to discuss the other main groups to whom he spoke, such as the gentile Greeks and "proper" adherents of Jesus (Philippians), etc., because this has no bearing on our split diaspora thesis. That there were some kind of "borders" already then between Jesus's Jewish followers and Jews we can deduct from the famous passage in Galatians 2. 1-21.

To sum up: Paul's epistles and even more so the Book of Acts, reflect a receptive and lively western Jewish diaspora, which on the one hand is "exempt" from the beginnings of rabbinic lore and law, and on the other is unable to fulfill its biblical ordinances as an entity. Paul, judging from his epistles and his history narrated in the Book of Acts, exploited this situation in order to find supporters from among the Jews in the western diaspora. This happened in the fifties of the first century C.E. against the background of his fierce conflict with the Jewish leadership in Palestine. Not all of the Jews in the western diaspora were supportive of him, but according to the Book of Acts, his epistles were effective there since some of the western Jews supported his message (it seems that in a Pharisaic environment in Palestine this would not have been the case). In the above, we have drawn a picture of the Jews in the West living without "rabbinic" lore while challenged by Paul and his new message. Of one thing we can be sure: the gap that we are discussing here existed as early as the first century C.E., widened in later centuries, and, from a Jewish point of view, became a disaster.[170]

࿇

## Repercussions of the Rift in Judaism
## Throughout the Early Middle Ages

The gap between the eastern and western communities discussed above, which began even before the first century of the Common Era, continued to exist well into following centuries. The gap between the Jewish and non-Jewish sources regarding European Jewish history in the early Middle Ages is vast. Historians who attempt to write the history of European Jews are confused. There are essentially no contemporary Jewish sources that enable us to learn about Jewish history in Christian Europe between the second and ninth centuries.[171] Surprisingly, however, particularly in this period, we find a good deal of information from Christian sources about the local Jews.[172] One of the results of the lacuna in Jewish sources is that Jewish communities in Christian Europe that were well established by the tenth century developed legends that dealt with the origins of their communities.[173] This reality raises the question of how to explain the gap between Christian and Jewish sources during this period. Additionally, we might ask why, during the very same period, we find an unusual surge in literary creativity in the eastern Jewish communities, Palestinian and Babylonian, that does not acknowledge the Jews of the West. As we indicated above, practically no scholars from the West are mentioned in the entire *Talmud*. Also, the allusions concerning communications of the *Geonim,* the sixth to ninth century leaders of the academies in Babylon, with Jewish communities in the West before the ninth century are very scarce.[174] It thus seems that the Jews of Christian Europe had no contact with those centers until possibly the mid-ninth century.[175]

From the second century on, the sources available to us relating to the Jews in Europe become increasingly sparse. From this period until approximately the ninth century, practically the only sources available are the laws issued by local authorities, Church synods, and the opinions of individual Christians about the Jews. There are scholars who claim that the legal sources reflect a repetitive nature – e.g. that the new laws repeat the wording of older ones – that brings into question the degree to which they relate to real Jewish communities in the legislators' locales. In the view of these researchers, this explains the lack of parallel Jewish sources.[176] We will demonstrate further on that this conclusion is not inevitable, and will try to explain the dearth of Jewish sources in a manner that is consistent with the thesis of this study.

It is worth emphasizing the extent of the lack of contemporary Jewish sources during this period by pointing out that the Jewish book-shelf, or alternatively the Jewish cultural tradition, contains practically nothing that was created in Christian Europe during the first millennium. As stated previously, we know from religious and secular legal sources, as well as from Christian theological writings, of the presence of Jews in a variety of locales. These sources clearly testify that Jews observed circumcision, the Sabbath, the festivals, and dietary laws. However, as previously mentioned, none of this information has been preserved in Jewish sources. One possible explanation would be that the Church completely destroyed existing Jewish literary works. This explanation does not seem plausible to us. In later periods, as is well known, the tremendous efforts of the Church to burn and completely destroy Jewish manuscripts were only partially successful. Why would we assume a much greater degree of success in the period under discussion, in which the relationship of the Church to the Jews was much more favorable, as we will discuss later. Suffice it to say that the hostility toward the Jews in this period paled by comparison to the persecutions in the late Middle Ages. It is more logical to assume that during this period the Jews did not produce significant literary works. The reason, we suggest, is twofold: First and foremost, Vico already hinted in his *La Scienza Nuova*, published in 1744, that after the fifth century C.E., Europe was not a civilization of the written word (1051):

> "…from the fifth century onward, when so many barbarous nations began to inundate Europe…it came about from the barbarism of the enemies of the Catholic religion that in those iron times we can find no contemporary documents in the vulgar tongues, whether Italian, French, Spanish, or even German…Among all the aforesaid nations we find documents only in barbarous Latin, understood only by a very few nobles, who were also ecclesiastics. Hence we may assume that in all those unhappy centuries the nations had reverted to communicating with each other in the mute language…"[177]

This is no doubt an exaggeration, but can account for the fact that Jews lived in a non-literary society and behaved accordingly. Second, if we examine the relatively few scholars that produced writings in the 400 years from the fifth century to the beginning of the ninth century, we can say that most authors were either themselves in a position of authority, persons such as Gregory of Tours, Gregory the Great, and Isidore of Seville, who were powerful bishops, or people who were invited by princes and kings to write at the centers of political power (Cassiodorus and Boethius). We can also detect literary activity in monasteries, in particular the copying of manuscripts.[178] The Jews who in any case lacked significant spiritual leaders did not acquire similar positions as did some Christian intellectuals, gained no authority, and thus produced nothing during all these centuries.

Since there is some evidence that there were Jews in Europe during the period under discussion, we believe that the aforementioned points strengthen our claim that throughout the period, Jews in Latin and Greek (Byzantine) Europe were either almost completely cut off from the rabbinic tradition and from an ongoing connection to the Jews in the East and their literature, or had left Judaism altogether. In our opinion, this fact explains the gap between information found in Jewish and Christian sources in Europe. The Jew who was the subject of Jewish literature in the East (Palestinian and Babylonian), and for whom it was written, was a Jew already committed to the rabbinic tradition to some degree. This Jew knew the Hebrew and Aramaic languages in which he studied, prayed, and read the Torah. In contrast, the European Jew was cut off from this, and was thus understandably not referred to in later medieval Jewish sources. The Jews of the East and the West were unable to communicate with each other, from the perspectives of both the language and content of their traditions. On the other hand, the Christian literature in that period viewed the Jews of the West as the preservers of the Biblical tradition in every way. The Christians viewed them as being faithful to the Old Testament, and therefore mentioned them in that context in their literature.

A study of Christian laws from this period reveals a well-known trend that the Church tried vigorously to create legal barriers between Christians and Jews. Various approaches have been suggested to explain the motivation for this separation,[179] which is not the subject of this article. One can, however, conclude, based on the efforts of the Church to create barriers, that such barriers did not naturally exist in practice. The prohibitions imposed by the Church imply that Jews and Christians actually did business with each other, ate together, celebrated together, mingled socially, and even married each other.[180] The Church tried to alter this reality and create a separation between Christians and Jews. Yet, as far as we know, there were not serious persecutions of the Jews in Europe during this period as part of a broad policy, with the exception of some unusual incidents, which we will discuss soon.[181]

Be that as it may, a close look at these laws continuously raises the image of the Jew as one who lives basically according to the guidelines of the Bible. Thus, for example, references to the synagogue relate to the reading of the Torah

(*Novella of Justinian*, 553 C.E.), to the recitation of Psalms,[182] and, one can infer, to assembly for prayer on the Sabbath and festivals.[183] Yet, we do not find references, for example, to two paradigmatic rabbinic innovations – organized prayer on weekdays in the morning or evening, and regular Torah study. It is fascinating to take note, in this context, of the Jewish holidays mentioned in the Christian laws. *Pessach* (Passover), *Shavuot* (Pentecost), *Sukkot* (Tabernacles), and *Yom Kippur* (the Day of Atonement), which are all Biblically ordained holidays, are mentioned. Purim, a holiday cited in the Writings, is also mentioned in the early Christian laws, and naturally offended the Christians.[184] To the best of our knowledge, *Hanukkah* is not mentioned at all, probably, we can assume, because the western Jews did not celebrate it, since it was a rabbinic innovation. It is worth pointing out in this context that also in anti-Jewish laws, such as can be found in Visigoth Spain, Jewish rituals that are prohibited include only circumcision, the Sabbath, the festivals, and the dietary laws, and not rituals that are characteristically rabbinic. This corresponds to the image of the Jew we have already detected in the pagan authors of the Greco-Roman world.[185] Let us give an example.

The Christian laws relating to Jews deal significantly with issues associated with Christian slaves serving Jews. Toch claims that it is difficult to assume that there were Jewish slave merchants dealing with Christian non-Jewish slaves, since the Jews were religiously observant and according to halakhic law would have to convert the slaves in their possession.[186] He concludes that the Christian law forbidding ownership bore no resemblance to the reality. However, the prohibition of retaining in one's possession uncircumcised slaves is not a Biblical one, but a later halakhic one.[187] It is thus probable that the western Jews, who relied solely on Biblical tradition, were not familiar with the halakhic innovation of converting slaves in their possession. In fact, the Talmudic law of converting slaves deals with the owners of slaves who work in their houses and on their property, and not with merchants who buy and sell slaves in the market. Thus, even if Toch is correct, Urbach already demonstrated that the law requiring a non-Jewish slave to undergo circumcision, essentially rendering him a Jew, is an early rabbinic law from the Hasmonean era, and was practically not observed after the destruction of the Temple.[188] In addition, after the decrees of Adrianus, which prohibited circumcision, R. Yishmael, in opposition to R. Akiva, explicitly ruled that it is permissible to keep a non-Jewish slave who is not circumcised.[189] In a *braita* (a tradition in the Jewish Oral Law not incorporated in the *Mishnah*) there, we also find the explicit opinion of R. Yehoshua ben Levi who permits one to keep an uncircumcised slave for up to twelve months, and to subsequently sell him if he refuses circumcision. It is thus very questionable to expect pious Jews to follow the Talmudic law, since the degree to which that very law was in force varied dramatically. Beyond that, making assumptions about common practice among the Jews of the West based on Talmudic law is ludicrous according to Urbach's position. The prohibition of selling non-Jewish slaves is not found in the Bible, and is a much later development. It is thus probable that the western Jews, who relied solely on Biblical tradition, were not familiar with the Talmudic law. We could, therefore, assume that the Christian law had some basis in reality.

In his excellent article regarding the Jewish diaspora during the period under discussion, Toch claims that a majority of the Jews disappeared from Europe during this time. As such, he suggests that Christian legislation relating to Jews was not based on contemporary reality, but was at times a rehash of earlier laws that the legislator utilized. This position, however, is not universally accepted by scholars. Some claim that there were significant pockets of Jewish population in Europe during this period.[190] We believe that regarding the issue as to whether or not there were Jews in Europe at the time, we must consider the possibility that the gap between what is implied by Christian and Jewish sources is not the result of a gap between the legislation and the reality, but rather reflects a gap between **two** types of Jews. According to this suggestion, the Christian legislator describes the Jew in his locale as a Biblical Jew who refused to accept Jesus and who continued to observe a number of Biblical commandments. In contrast, sources from the East and tenth century European Jewish sources deal with a normative rabbinic Jew. These sources, therefore, do not refer to European Jews during the period under discussion. In addition, Christian laws and Church synods often refer to apostate Jews who ostensibly accepted Christianity, but whose allegiance was suspect. The sources suggest that this phenomenon was widespread. There is also evidence of apostate Jews, or crypto-Jews, in historical sources that include stories, in our opinion aetiological, which explain why so many Jews living in the cradle of Christianity disappeared.[191] These points all strengthen our conclusion that many Jews in Christian areas disappeared, and that the rest remained Biblical Jews.

## The Penetration of Rabbinic Law into Non-Rabbinic Western European Jewry and the increase in Anti-Semitism

We can set a terminus ad quem for the indifference of the Jews of Latin Europe to rabbinic law. Agobard of Lyons, writing to Emperor Louis the Pious in Aachen in the third decade of the ninth century, portrays the Jews as abiding by minutia of the rabbinic laws of kosher food. They also possess the *Shiur Qomah* (a mystical work on the dimensions of the Godhead), some of the mystical *Hekhalot* literature, and traditions about God's abode taken either from the Talmudic tractate of *Hagigah* or from works sharing this tradition.[192] We may assume that these religious practices and traditions were characteristic of the Jews around Lyon and, probably, also of those in Lotharingia where the Carolingian capital was located. However, this may not be true for all Jews in the Carolingian Empire. The transformation both in practice and in outlook may not have been completed until the mid-tenth century or so.

In this regard, we believe that trends in Christian anti-Semitism in Medieval Europe also reflect the late arrival of rabbinic literature to European Jewish communities. Without seeking to enter the complex question of the reasons behind the transformation of European anti-Semitism in the course of the twelfth and thirteenth centuries,[193] we would like simply to make the following observation. Cohen and others have observed that in the course of the late twelfth and early thirteenth century Europe, Christians discovered that the Jews did not live by Biblical law but by a different code of religious conduct known as the Oral Law. This discovery placed under heavy question the long standing Augustinian doctrine of tolerance of the Jews. Thus, we wish to note that it may not simply be a question of Christian discovery but also of Jewish re-making, by adopting the Oral Law which was unknown to them. The Jews themselves discovered the Oral Law and undertook to live by its light only in the late eighth and early ninth centuries, at the earliest, or by a later estimate possibly only in the course of the tenth century. As long as Jews in Europe were faithful only to the Biblical tradition and viewed only the Bible as canon, the Christians viewed them as a people that preserved the ancient faith that preceded Christianity. While they might have viewed them as stubborn, misguided, and perhaps even dangerous because they did not accept the new revelation, they also saw them as proof of the New Testament that was built upon the old. Once rabbinic literature became known in Europe, however, the Jews constituted a more blatant challenge to the Christian interpretation of their common roots. From a Christian perspective, a Biblical Jew was "stuck" in the past, anachronistic, but still a "member of the family."[194] A rabbinic Jew, in contrast, was one who had chosen an interpretation of the Old Testament that diverges from the Christian interpretation, and is thus more foreign, more different, and more of a threat. Such a Jew can no longer be considered a "member of the family" who lends credence to the New Testament. It may be worthwhile to integrate this new perspective on the belated rabbinism of the Jews of Latin Europe with the recent studies of the transformation of medieval anti-Semitism and see if there are any significant connections between these two far-reaching mutations.

It is possible to find the initial stages of this metamorphosis already in seventh century Spain. Scholars have wondered why in the decisions of the Councils of Toledo in 638 C.E.[195] the Christians adopted an increasingly aggressive tone toward the Jews in contrast to the relatively moderate tone that characterizes this era.[196] Perhaps we can find the answer in the formulation of the legislation itself. In the oath to be taken by Jews who converted to Christianity, they had to declare, among other things, that:

> We undertake to present to your inspection all the Scriptures that
> are customarily held by our nation in the synagogues for the sake
> of the doctrine, those which are authoritative as well as those they
> call *deuteras*; and those they name *apocrypha* in order that...[197]

In other words, there is a hint here that the appearance of the *Mishnah* (*dueteras*), and perhaps the Oral Law in general in Spain, albeit as a non-binding text,[198] caused an increase in the harshness of the Christian tone toward the Jews as early as the beginning of the seventh century. By the time rabbinic literature was in force among the Jews of Europe in the tenth century, this harshness was at its height. As such, we can point to the Councils of Toledo as a harbinger of future developments in Europe several centuries later. We would not attribute the change of approach solely to the aggressive anti-Jewish stance of Isidore Bishop of Seville (560-636).[199] We emphasize that the events in Toledo apparently corresponded to the first appearance of rabbinic literature there, a phenomenon which, according to Jewish sources, occurred much earlier in Spain than in Germany.[200] It is possible to see the first signs of the arrival of rabbinic literature in Europe in the aforementioned writings of Agobard on the Jews. It appears that he had some familiarity with this literature, if not from reading it himself, then at least from his discussions from local Jews or from hearsay.[201] An even earlier reference to the *Mishnah* is found in the *Novella of Justinian* in 553, which was written in Greek-speaking Byzantium several decades prior to the Councils of Toledo. These two references are like a drop in the bucket in comparison to the activity in the same locations several centuries later, corresponding to the appearance and proliferation of rabbinic literature in Europe, apparently arriving with waves of immigration from the East.

Let us focus for a while on the *Novella of Justinian*, mentioned above, in order to clarify our point here. We wish to analyze the following citation:

> Furthermore, those who read Greek shall use the Septuagint tradition, which is more accurate than all others, and is preferable to the others particularly in reason of what happened while the translation was made. [...] Let all use mainly this translation, but in order that we shall not appear to prohibit them all the other translations, we give permission to use also Aqilas' translation, although he was a gentile and in some readings differs not a little from the Septuagint. What they call *Mishnah*, on the other hand, we prohibit entirely, for it is not included among the Holy Books, nor was it handed down from above by the prophets, but it is an invention of men in their chatter, exclusively of earthly origin and having in it nothing of the divine.

Scholars have wondered about the identity of those mentioned by Justinian. It should be emphasized here that we do not view the Novella as a proof of our theory, but rather, we believe that it is explained well by our theory. This interpretation completes the picture regarding the gap between the diasporas that we described. It is important to keep in mind that Justinian ruled in Palestine as well, and that he thus ruled over different types of Jews – on the one hand, Aramaic-speaking Jews in Israel who were committed to the rabbinic tradition, and on the other hand, Greek-speaking western Jews who were not connected to this tradition (Greek speaking 'western Jews' also settled in certain parts of the eastern Mediterranean coast, as we demonstrated above). It is thus reasonable to posit that the *Novella* suggests an attempt by Hebrew-Aramaic Jews of the East in the sixth century to bridge the gap by bringing rabbinic literature to the attention of the western Jews. It reflects a conflict between the Jews of the East and the West. The western Jews, who were already cut off from these developments for centuries, were apparently opposed to accepting the Oral Law as binding and authoritative. This in itself is interesting, i.e. that after hundreds of years that the *Mishnah* had been an authoritative text and that the two Talmuds had granted it sanctity and legitimacy, the western Jews still questioned its authority. Be that as it may, Justinian was called upon to mediate between them, and he did indeed come to a compromise of sorts. On the one hand, he allowed the use of the translation of Aqilas in the synagogue, a move that might have appeased the rabbis who preferred this translation to the Septuagint. On the other hand, he probably appeased the western Jews by opposing the Oral Law. The rabbis tried – at least at a later stage – to bring them into the fold of rabbinic law, but they were rebuffed. In our opinion, a similar attempt is reflected in the rulings of the Councils of Toledo several decades later. This latter attempt succeeded to the degree that the Jews of the West accepted rabbinic law as a non-binding text. We see at the end of the first section of the *Novella* that Justinian warns the rabbis of Israel not to meddle any more in matters relating to the Jews of the West, and not to try to impose the Oral Law upon them. Here the Emperor probably expresses the aspiration of the Christians that the Jews remain dedicated solely to the Old Testament, and their severe opposition to the Oral Law. The Jew as a witness was certainly preferable.

An alternative explanation that we might suggest to the *Novella* (which does not negate our theory regarding the split in the diaspora) is that the internal conflict that it reveals was within the Jewish community in Palestine, and that the community turned to the Emperor for a decisive ruling. The *Novella* mentions the 'Archipherekitae'. This probably refers to the "*reish pirka*" (lit: "beginning of the chapter"), an expression that was well known in the Land of Israel. Thus, it could be that the *Novella* responds to a controversy over the language for the reading of the Torah between the Greek-speaking and Hebrew-speaking Jewish communities in the Land of Israel itself. While addressing this issue, Justinian, as a Christian Emperor, takes the opportunity to prohibit the reading of the *Mishnah* which he views as a human creation that is "not included among the Holy Books, nor was it handed down from above by the prophets, but it is an invention of men in their chatter." If this interpretation is correct, then the *Novella of Justinian* does not suggest an attempt by the rabbis to disseminate the *Mishnah* among the Jews of the West. This would be consistent with our claim above that the rabbis did not initiate attempts to connect the western diaspora to rabbinic law.

What happened to the Jews in Greek-speaking Europe (the Byzantine Empire)? The evidence in the early Middle Ages is even more dismal. Indeed, fragments found in the Cairo *genizah* (a place where Jews store sacred documents when they fall out of use) written in Judeo-Greek (Greek written in Hebrew letters) were published by De Lange.[202] This collection includes, among other things, a translation of *Ecclesiastes* to Judeo-Greek, and fragments of the Passover *haggadah* also in Judeo-Greek. The *genizah* also includes two Hebrew-Greek glossaries for the language of the *Mishnah*.[203] This fact only gives evidence that the *Mishnah* and the Passover *haggadah* were known in Europe by the tenth century,[204] as the Cairo *genizah* only includes material from the ninth to tenth centuries onward. There are scholars who claim that these fragments testify to the existence of a Greek Jewish community that represents a direct and natural continuation of Judaism during the Roman-Hellenistic period.[205] In our opinion, this theory is built upon unfounded assumptions. In addition, De Lange published the translation of a section of *Ecclesiastes* in Judeo-Greek that appears to be very close to the translation of Aqilas.[206] As is known, the rabbis supported the translation of Aqilas.[207] To the best of our knowledge, the Aqilas translation was a precise literal translation.[208] If, however, it included rabbinic influences, it would prove that the rabbis knew that they could only influence the western community through the Bible and Greek language! They understood that the Bible was considered by this Jewish community to be the authentic religious literary creation, and that it would be impossible to impose any other literature.[209]

With regard to our claim, it is clear beyond doubt that the Jews in both Greek and Latin Europe who did not convert to Christianity, and had difficulties in communicating with each other, remained Biblical Jews until the ninth to tenth centuries. If there are still scholars who believe that rabbinic literature was known in Europe before the ninth century, they are certainly not supported by either the Church laws and synods, or by the writings of Christian theologians. On the contrary, these sources clearly prove that the

Christians in these areas were not familiar with rabbinic literature, and that the Christian reactions when they did appear were substantively different than their earlier reactions, to the fact that the Jews were merely seen as the testimony of the Old Testament.

As stated, there is hardly any internal Jewish information until approximately the ninth century regarding the presence of Jews in Europe and their history.[210] It is interesting to consider at what point Jewish sources begin to provide systematic information, and why? The simple fact is that the appearance of internal Jewish information and inscribed fragments of a collective memory regarding the Jews of Europe parallels, in terms of both time and location, the beginning of rabbinic writing in Europe, or in other words Torah study, in the ninth to tenth centuries. From the time that we have rabbinic writings that are preserved in the rabbinic tradition, we also have the preservation of information that allows for the initial writing of history. As mentioned previously, from the first centuries through the ninth century, the only information available to us is through Christian sources. It is quite certain that a Jewish presence all over Europe was apparent, albeit a significant minority, and that those Jews were not connected to the tradition of rabbinic writing and thought. It is, therefore, no wonder that this tradition does not mention them. In contrast, the literature of the Christians, who maintained a dialogue with them, does mention them.

✍

To summarize: The Jewish world during the period under discussion began to separate into two worlds with an ever-widening gap between them. This gap was the result of a language barrier of Hebrew and Aramaic vs. Greek and Latin which was primarily caused by geographical divide. The common assumption of an ongoing connection between the Greek-speaking diaspora in the West and the centers in the Land of Israel and Babylonia has been challenged in this work. To prove our claim, we drew on Jewish sources, as well as pagan and Christians ones.

In the course of time, two different knowledge bases and two distinct literatures were created: In the West, the Bible in its Greek translations along with some of the Apocrypha and Pseudepigrapha, and in the East, mainly rabbinic literature (e.g. *Mishnah, Tosefta,* both versions of the *Talmud,* and the *Midrash*). Thus, a divide was created that naturally led to a normative gap of distinct diasporas. While the Hebrew-Aramaic speaking East developed a normative standard presented by the rabbis, the Greek-Latin west maintained a Biblical normative system based on the translations.

An Oral Law did not develop in the western diaspora, and western Jews contributed nothing to the development of the Oral Law in the east. The codex of Roman laws and synods of the Church dealing with Jews confirm in a variety of places the gap between the eastern and western diasporas. Pagan literature paints a picture of Jews who live according to the Torah, and not according to the Oral Law.

Archeological findings also demonstrate that such a gap existed in a number of areas of life. The gap was not just a language barrier, but was also theological and cultural. This reality is contrary to the reality of later diasporas in which all of the diaspora communities were based on the Oral Law, and the "official" Jewish language was Hebrew.

Sources that discuss rabbinic travels to western diaspora communities point to the fact that these visits were chance occurrences. The Church tried to create a communication network, bureaucratic unity, and a church law in order to impose standards in every place. Even the early apostles traveled to many places to preach. Such an approach did not exist among the Jews in the West, there was no bureaucratic system that imposed, or even transmitted information about the *halahkah*. There were no emissaries who went out to preach.[211] In contrast, it is clear that the eastern diaspora did create a communication system that transmitted laws systematically. The *Mishnah* itself was transferred from Palestine to Babylonia and there became the corner stone for the creation of the *Babylonian Talmud*. The *Talmud* is filled with stories of sages who travel between the Land of Israel and Babylonia, carrying with them laws and traditions. The comments of well-known scholars from Israel are quoted frequently in the *Babylonian Talmud*, and vice versa. No such thing is recorded in the western diaspora. The few sources that do exist demonstrate that the connection was sporadic. The Jewish communities that were isolated from the rabbinic network, served as a receptive basis for the development of an alternative Christian network by Paul, which enabled it to spread throughout the Mediterranean basin.

In this study, we have described a phenomenon that challenges the accepted scholarly view of the Jewish diaspora in the period following the destruction of the Temple in 70 C.E. We did not address a number of critical questions that flow from our analysis: Why did the rabbinic leadership allow this fissure to develop and grow? Did they relinquish the western diaspora intentionally, and if so, why? Perhaps they could not manage the enormous diaspora that was created to their west. On the other hand, why did the western Jews forfeit their connection with the center in Israel? Perhaps the language barrier that we described was not a cause but a symptom, reflecting a cultural divide that severed the relationship between the two communities. Or, perhaps the divide simply became so large in reality that it could not be bridged. It is possible that future scholars will choose to see this divide as part of a larger context of similar schisms that occurred throughout the generations in Jewish history. It is not unlikely that the potential forces which drove the Jewish nation to such a rift, were imminent in Judaism all along from Biblical times. Rifts in Judaism were of social, political, religious, and halakhic nature and became a driving force in the trial and error processes of Jewish history. In contradistinction with rifts in Israel described in the Bible, the rift that we describe here did not get any explicit coverage in Jewish literature (even where we would have expected it, e.g. the Apocrypha, Pseudepigrapha, and rabbinic literature). The loss of such a large portion of the Jewish people is a tragedy in itself, yet our main concern in this study was its disappearance from the collective memory of Judaism. The enormous part lost to the Jewish people during the Greco-Roman period and the early Middle Ages was simply forgotten. In the Hebrew Bible, rifts of various kinds occurred, and were formulated into pervasive memories and fragments of memories. There are sections that became foundation narratives that express the fear of the loss of parts of the nation (e.g. Joshua 22; 1 Kings 12 about the creation of the ten tribes that were later lost; see 2 Kings 17). Yet, in many instances the Jews express their reluctance to come to terms with loss of the ten tribes. For instance, the constant mention of the twelve tribes in context that the ten are already lost comes to the fore.[212] In rabbinic literature, we can detect an awareness of the loss of the ten tribes, but ironically not of the loss described in this book. The phenomenon that we describe here is not just the physical disappearance of a large part of the Jews, but also its disappearance from the national consciousness forever. We hope that our analysis will serve as a catalyst for further research, and will ultimately lead us to a deeper understanding of Jewish history and sociology.

# *Notes*

1   This study was a result of our work in 2005 at the Institute for Advanced Studies at the Hebrew University of Jerusalem, in the group on communication and the Jewish Diaspora. Our work was published in various publications. See: Arye Edrei and Doron Mendels, "A Split Jewish Diaspora: Its Dramatic Consequences," *Journal for the Study of the Pseudepigrapha* 16, no. 2 (2007): 91-137; Arye Edrei and Doron Mendels, "A Split Jewish Diaspora: Its Dramatic Consequences II," *Journal for the Study of the Pseudepigrapha* 17, no. 3 (2008): 163-187; Arye Edrei and Doron Mendels, "A Split Jewish Diaspora Again — A Response to Fergus Millar," *Journal for the Study of the Pseudepigrapha* 21, no. 3 (2012): 305-311; Arye Edrei and Doron Mendels, "Reaction to Fergus Millar's article 'A Rural Community in Late Roman Mesopotamia, and the Question of a 'Split' Jewish Diaspora'," *Journal for the Study of Judaism* 43, no. 1 (January 2012): 78-79. See also Arye Edrei and Doron Mendels, *Zweierlei Diaspora: Zur Spaltung der antiken Juedichen Welt* (Goettingen: Vandenhoeck & Ruprecht, 2010); Arye Edrei and Doron Mendels, "Why Did Paul Succeed Where the Rabbis Failed?" in *Jesus Research: New Methodologies and Perceptions (The Second Princeton-Prague Symposium on Jesus Research)*, vol. II, ed. James H. Charlesworth (Grand Rapids, Michigan: William B. Eerdmans Publishing Company, 2014), 361-399. In this article, we have taken the opportunity to respond to various reactions to our previously published articles.

2   For evidence of Jews in the East and the West at that time and later, see Paul R. Trebilco, *Jewish Communities in Asia Minor* (Cambridge: Cambridge University Press, 1991); Steven T. Katz, ed., *The Cambridge History of Judaism, Volume IV: The Late Roman-Rabbinic Period* (Cambridge: Cambridge University Press, 2006), especially chapters 2, 19.

3   For a good summary of various approaches regarding the nature of the relationship between the diasporas and the center in the Land of Israel, see Lee I. Levine, "Unity and Diversity in Ancient Judaism: The Case of the Diaspora Synagogue," in *The Jews in the Hellenistic-Roman World: Studies in Memory of Menahem Stern*, eds. Isaiah Gafni et al. (Jerusalem: The Zalman Shazar Center for Jewish History, 1996), 379-392 [Hebrew]. Other scholars dealing with the Jewish diaspora did not tackle this problem. See for instance John M. G. Barclay, *Jews in the Mediterranean Diaspora: From Alexander to Trajan (323 BCE-117 CE)* (Edinburgh: T. & T. Clark, 1996); Isaiah M. Gafni, *Land Center and Diaspora: Jewish Constructs in Late Antiquity* (Sheffield: Sheffield Academic Press, 1997); Leonard V. Rutgers, *The Hidden Heritage of Diaspora Judaism*, 2nd. ed. (Peeters: Leuven, 1998) (but see his comment on page 94); and Erich S. Gruen, *Diaspora: Jews amidst Greeks and Romans* (Cambridge, MA: Harvard University Press, 2002). Tessa Rajak, "The Jewish Community and its Boundaries," in *The Jewish Dialogue with Greece and Rome* (Leiden: Brill, 2001), 335-354, discusses the connection between the Greek Jewish diaspora and the rabbinic community in the Land of Israel (and see there much of the older bibliography). She claims that we do not have enough evidence to make a determination regarding this subject. See also Martin Goodman, "Jews and Judaism in the Mediterranean Diaspora in the Late Roman Period: Limitations of Evidence," in *Judaism in the Roman World, collected Essays*, ed. Martin Goodman (Leiden: Brill, 2007), 233-259, who says: "my own preference is for skepticism about the applicability of rabbinic evidence outside the immediate circles for which it was composed" (p. 234). We have gone a step further and argue that a dichotomy developed between the two diasporas.

4   Rajak, "The Jewish Community and its Boundaries"; Goodman, "Jews and Judaism in the Mediterranean Diaspora in the Late Roman Period".

5   Barclay, *Jews in the Mediterranean Diaspora;* and his edited book, John M. G. Barclary, ed., *Negotiating Diaspora: Jewish Strategies in the Roman Empire* (London: T. & T. Clark International, 2004).

6   Shmuel Safrai, *In Times of Temple and Mishnah: Studies in Jewish History,* vols. 1-2 (Jerusalem: Magnes Press, 1994) [Hebrew]. Later on, however, he claims that the connection with the diaspora was renewed in the time of Rabban Gamliel. Below we will discuss the sources that he tackles.

7   On the centrality of the Temple in the relationship with the diaspora and in the national consciousness before the destruction, see Aryeh Kasher, "Jerusalem as a 'Metropolis' in Philo's National Consciousness," *Cathedra* 11 (1980): 45-56 [Hebrew]; Uriel Rappaport, "The Jews of Eretz-Israel and the Jews of the Diaspora During the Hellenistic and Hasmonean Periods," *Te'uda* 12 (1996): 1-9 [Hebrew]; Doron Mendels, *The Rise and Fall of Jewish Nationalism,* 2nd. ed. (Grand Rapids: Eerdmans, 1997).

8   In Christian Europe, all rabbinic literature was written exclusively in Hebrew. This was true of the commentaries on the *Talmud,* Biblical commentaries, and halakhic literature – Israel M. Ta-Shma, *Talmudic Commentary in Europe and North Africa,* vol. 1 (Jerusalem: Magnes Press, 1999), 25 [Hebrew]. This fact remained constant until the onset of the enlightenment. There were, however, different levels of writing. Some of the literature, halakhic writing in particular, was written in "Rabbinic Hebrew" that integrated Hebrew and Aramaic. The critical factor was not only that they were written in Hebrew, but perhaps more importantly, that this cannon was not translated into any other languages. Thus, the Bible, *Talmud,* and prayer book were published only in their original languages throughout the Middle Ages in Christian Europe. In reality, Hebrew was also the dominant language of writing and creativity in all disciplines in Moslem Spain, even if at the beginning of the eleventh century we can detect influences of Babylonian writings in Arabic. The first Spanish scholars, such as R. Shmuel Ha-Nagid and Ritz Ge'ut, wrote a mixture of Hebrew and Arabic (Ibid., *Talmudic Commentary in Europe and North Africa,* 157-159). It is perhaps for this reason that these works were lost to a great degree and had less influence. This is true as well of Babylonian Geonic literature that was composed in Judeo-Arabic (Arabic written in Hebrew characters with some Hebrew words included), particularly the halakhic monographs of the *Geonim* that were written in Judeo-Arabic and undeniably had little influence on the halakhic discourse. This phenomenon can be attributed to the fact that they were written in Arabic, a language that lost its importance in the Jewish world from the beginning of the twelfth century – Simha Assaf, *Tekufat ha-Geonim ve-Sifrutah* (Jerusalem: Harav Kook Institute, 1955), 188 [Hebrew]; Robert Brody, *The Geonim of Babylonia and the Shaping of Medieval Jewish Culture* (New Haven: Yale University Press, 1998), 222. R. Sa'adia Gaon, in the tenth century, was the first scholar to write a book of Jewish law in Arabic in Babylonia. This phenomenon continued throughout the Geonic period also in Spain throughout the eleventh century, as stated. Yet, those who wrote in Arabic utilized Hebrew characters. This clearly indicates that the target population, Jews whose primary language was Arabic, were able to read Hebrew letters and, therefore, able to read the Torah in Hebrew and pray from a Hebrew prayer book, even if they didn't fully understand what they were reading. In the area of philosophy, a number of important works were written in Arabic until the middle of the twelfth century (*Emunot Ve-Deot of Sa'adia Gaon; Hovot Ha-Levavot* of Rabeinu Bahya ibn Pakuda, *The Kuzari* of R. Yehuda Halevi, and *The Guide for the Perplexed of Maimonides*), but all of them were translated into Hebrew soon after they were written. Works that were not translated into Hebrew became marginal and less important (for example, *Mekor Haim* of Shlomo ibn Gabirol). Maimonides wrote his early halakhic works, *The Commentary on*

*the Mishnah and The Book of Commandments,* in Arabic, and only made the transition to Hebrew in the writing of the *Mishneh Torah.* In a responsum that Maimonides wrote to a scholar in Tyre, he related to his *Book of the Commandments* as follows: "I regret that I wrote in Arabic since everyone should read it, and I am waiting to translate it into the holy tongue, with God's help." – Maimonides, *Responsa,* ed. Joshua Blau, vol. 2 (Jerusalem: Sumptibus Societatis Mekize Nirdamin, 1986), responsum 447, 725 [Hebrew]. Maimonides continued to write in Arabic only in works that were designed for an Arabic speaking population. Rabbi Menachem Ha-Meiri of the thirteenth century wrote in a clear Hebrew, and not in the mixture of Hebrew and Aramaic that was accepted in rabbinic literature, apparently because of the influence of Maimonides's *Mishneh Torah.*

9   The transition to a common language during the late Middle Ages is comparable to what happened in the Roman Church that used Latin as its common language. The concept of a unified academic Jewish language was a new phenomenon from the eleventh century onwards. In the ancient Jewish world, there was Jewish literature in Aramaic, Greek, Latin, and other translations. In addition, in Babylonia and Moslem Spain, a considerable number of the *Geonim* and rabbis wrote in Arabic. The transition to national languages during the course of the Middle Ages and the period of the Renaissance caused a crisis in the Catholic Church as reflected in the movements of Wyclif – Christopher Allmand, ed., *The New Cambridge Medieval History,* vol. 7, c.1415–c.1500 (Cambridge: Cambridge University Press, 1998), 23; Malcolm Lambert, *Medieval Heresy: Popular Movements from the Gregorian Reform to the Reformation,* 3rd. ed. (Oxford: Blackwell, 2002), 247-322; Hus – Allmand, *The New Cambridge Medieval History,* 23, 377; Lambert, *Medieval Heresy,* 323-349); and later Luther – Robert Scribner, "Germany," in *The Reformation in National Context,* eds. Robert Scribner et al. (Cambridge: Cambridge University Press, 1994), 4-29, in particular, p. 13.

10   Yaakov Sussmann, "Torah she-Beal Peh Peshutah ke-Mashma," in *Mehqerei Talmud: Talmudic Studies Dedicated to the Memory of Professor Ephraim E. Urbach,* vol. 3, eds. David Rosenthal and Yaakov Sussmann (Jerusalem: Magnes Press, 1993), 209-305 [Hebrew].

11   On the centrality of Greek and the almost complete disappearance of Hebrew from Jewish life in the Greek diaspora, see Nicholas De Lange, "The Hebrew Language in the European Diaspora," *Te'uda* 12 (1996a): 111-137.

12   See in general M. D. Herr, "The End of Jewish Hellenistic Literature: When and Why," in *The Jews in the Hellenistic-Roman World: Studies in Memory of Menachem Stern,* eds. Isaiah Gafni et al. (Jerusalem: The Zalman Shazar Center for Jewish History and The Historical Society of Israel, 1996), 361-375 [Hebrew].

13   Jacob Shalom Licht, "Hitsonim u-Genuzim," Encyclopaedia Biblica 5 (1978): 1104-1105 [Hebrew]. For rabbinic sources that oppose the use of external literature, see: *Mishnah Sanhedrin* 10:1; *Babylonian Talmud, Sanhedrin* 90a, 100b; *Jerusalem Talmud, Pe'ah* 1:1, 16b [col. 85]; *Jerusalem Talmud, Sanhedrin* 10:1, 28a [col. 1317]; *Bamidbar Rabbah* 14:4, 15:22. See also Saul Lieberman, *Greek and Hellenism in Jewish Palestine* (Jerusalem: Bialik Institute, 1962), 1 [Hebrew].

14   See also Goodman, "Jews and Judaism in the Mediterranean Diaspora in the Late Roman Period."

15   See Ranon Katzoff, "The Laws of Rabbi Eliezer in Ancient Rome," in *Torah Lishma: Essays in Jewish Studies in Honor of Professor Shamma Friedman,* eds. David Golinkin et al. (Ramat Gan: Bar Ilan University Press; The Jewish Theological Seminary of America and the Schechter Institute of Jewish Studies, 2007), 344-357 [Hebrew]. In his article,

Katzoff attempts to compare articles written by W. M. Clarke with that of the known Talmudic scholar, Yitzhak D. Gilat. Clarke deals with several sections from the *Satyricon* written by Petronius in Latin. He cites three sections that all have to do with peculiar rituals involving hand washing. Clarke found very similar parallels to these customs in Talmudic literature, all of them attributed to the tradition of Eliezer ben Hyrcanus. In a different article, Gilat relates to a custom mentioned in five Roman novels indicating that Jews fasted on the Sabbath. Gilat claims that there is one source in the *Jerusalem Talmud* that indicates that this was the position of Eliezer ben Hyrcanus – that the Sabbath was designed for purification of the body and the soul. When viewed together, these two articles suggest that the opinions of Eliezer ben Hyrcanus were known in Rome and are mentioned in Roman literature as the customs of the Jews.

Eliezer ben Hyrcanus serves throughout the *Talmud* as a paradigm of the conservative Sage who demanded the transmission of the tradition without any innovation or exegesis. He stated about himself: "I never taught anything that I didn't hear from my teachers" (Babylonian Talmud, *Sukah* 28a). Similarly, his teacher, Rabban Yohanan ben Zakkai, described him as "a pit that does not lose a drop." Eliezer ben Hyrcanus, who was also referred to in the *Talmud* as "Shamuti" because he followed the tradition of the conservative Bet Shammai, serves in the literature of Talmudic research as the penultimate conservative sage from whose teachings one can learn about more ancient laws, and from whose controversies with other sages one can learn about the developments in Jewish law that took place in the first century C.E. This status was established by Gilat himself in his book – Yitzhak D. Gilat, *R. Eliezer Ben Hyrcanus – A Scholar Outcast* (Ramat-Gan: Bar-Ilan University Press, 1984).

If Katzoff is indeed correct, and the studies of Clarke and Gilat are accurate, then his conclusions provide significant support for our thesis. We find that Roman literature, even in later periods, attributed customs to the Jews that went beyond Biblical law, customs that are known to us from the literature as ancient halakhic traditions, and therefore were probably transmitted to the West during the period that Jews still made pilgrimages to Jerusalem. Alternatively, they were brought to the West by Jews who were exiled after the destruction. In contrast, the subsequent changes and developments that occurred in the rabbinic world and found expression in rabbinic literature are not found in Rome. As time progressed, the bond weakened – the Roman Jews did not know Hebrew and the rabbis did not translate their teachings, leading to an ever-widening gap.

16  It is possible that some rabbinic anti-diaspora concepts derived from their knowledge that western Jews did not fulfill the laws. See, for example, the rabbinic opinion claiming that the fulfillment of the commandments of the Torah outside of the Land of Israel has no inherent value, but serves only as a method of remembering the commandments for the eventual return to Zion: "Place markers for yourself." See *Sifre Devarim* 43, Finkelstein edition, p. 102: "Although I am banishing you from the land and sending you into exile, keep yourselves identified with the *mitzvot,* such that when you return they will not be new to you. It is similar to a human king who got angry with his wife and banished her to her father's home. He said to her: 'Bedeck yourself with your jewelry so that they will not be new to you when you return.' So too, God said to Israel: 'My son, excel in the performance of the *mitzvot,* such that when you return they will not be new to you.' As Jeremiah said (Jer. 31:20) 'Place markers for yourself' – these are the commandments in which Israel excels; 'make for yourself road-signs' – this is the destruction of the Temple. ..." This perspective was adopted by Nachmanides in his *Commentary on the Torah* (Leviticus 18:25). See in general Aviezer Ravitzky, " 'Way Marks to Zion': The History of an Idea," in *The Land of Israel in Medieval*

*Jewish Thought,* eds. Moshe Hallamish and Aviezer Ravitzky (Jerusalem: Yad Izhak Ben-Zvi, 1991), 1-39 [Hebrew]. From this perspective, the Torah was given only to be fulfilled in the Land of Israel, and its performance in the diaspora was only to prevent it from being forgotten in the interim before returning to Israel

Another example is the concept of "the impurity of foreign lands" developed in rabbinic literature in the middle of the second century C.E. and formulated as a law, relegating Jewish life in the diaspora in principle to an inferior status. See *Mishnah Nazir* 7:3; *Tosefta Ohalot* 18:1-5; *Tosefta Parah* 3:5. This law is not mentioned at all in the Bible. Although the rabbis derived this law from verses in the *Prophets* (such as "and you shall die in foreign land" in *Amos* when he spoke to the exiled king of Babylonia), it is clear that it is tannaitic in origin. Numerous references in both Talmuds indicate that this enactment was attributed to R. Yosi ben Yoezer and R. Yosi ben Yohanan (first century B.C.E.). This impurity was considered to be very severe, similar to the impurity caused by a dead body. It is mentioned several times by Philo and Josephus. The formal reason given for this impurity is that outside the Land of Israel, bodies were buried everywhere. Gedaliah Alon, however, contends that the law is based on the perception that all of the nations were impure from worshipping idols, and that their land was thus also impure. This law grants a special status to the Land of Israel as the only place that a person can live a complete Jewish life without being influenced by idolatry. A person who returns to the Land of Israel from the diaspora must therefore purify himself from the impurity that he contracted there. See also Hanoch Albeck, *Mishnah*, vol. VI, Order Tohorot (Jerusalem: The Bialik Institute; Tel Aviv: Dvir, 1958), 536 [Hebrew]; Safrai, *In Times of Temple and Mishnah*, 632-634; Y. Neeman, "Tumat Eretz ha-Amim: Hebet Histori," *Sinai* 2 (1997): 56-61 [Hebrew]; Saul Lieberman, *Tosefta Ki-Fshutah: A Comprehensive Commentary on the Tosefta,* Part VII, Order Nashim, Tractate Nezirut (New York: Jewish Theological Seminary in America, 1955-1988), 510, n. 34 [Hebrew].

17    Ed Parish Sanders, *Jewish Law from Jesus to the Mishnah: Five Studies* (London: SCM Press; Philadelphia: Trinity Press International, 1990), in particular chapters I and III.

18    Ibid., 298-299.

19    Funds collected in the diaspora were called *dmei klila,* or the collection of the sages. See Gedaliah Alon, *The Jews in their Land in the Talmudic Age, 70-640 C.E.,* vol. 1 (Jerusalem: Magnes Press, 1977), 156-159. There he also cites sources from after the destruction of the Temple. See also: Ben Zion Rosenfeld, "The Crisis of the Patriarchate in Eretz Israel in the Fourth Century," *Zion* 53 (1988): 239-257 [Hebrew]. The best survey of the Institution of the Nasi remains Martin Jacobs, *Die Institution des Juedischen Patriarchen* (Tuebingen: Mohr- Siebeck, 1995).

20    Amnon Linder, *The Jews in Roman Imperial Legislation* (Detroit: Wayne State University Press; Jerusalem: Israel Academy of Sciences and Humanities, 1987), Laws no. 13 and 30.

21    Ibid., Law no. 13.

22    Ibid., Law no. 30.

23    Against this background one can also explain the Stobi Inscription (Jacobs, *Die Institution des Juedischen Patriarchen,* 244-247). In general, for the lack of evidence concerning the influence and/or authority of the Nasi over the diaspora see Ibid., 346-348.

24    See Emanuel Tov, "The Text of the Hebrew/Aramaic and Greek Bible Used in the Ancient Synagogue," in *The Ancient Synagogue from its Origin until 200 C.E.: Papers Presented at an International Conference at Lund University, October 14-17, 2001,* eds. Birger Olsson and Magnus Zetterholm (Stockholm: Almqvist & Wiksell, 2003), 237-259, who argues that

there is ample literary evidence for the notion that Scripture was read in Greek in religious gatherings of the Greek speaking communities in the diaspora from the first century onward. Yet, some scholars argue that the Greek translation of the Torah and the *Psalms* were read along with the Hebrew original – see Albert I. Baumgarten, "Bilingual Jews and the Greek Bible," in *Shem in the Tents of Japhet: Essays on the Encounter of Judaism and Hellenism,* ed. James L. Kugel (Leiden: Brill, 2002), 13-20. The fact that we do not have any Hebrew manuscript of the Old Testament from the western diaspora of before the ninth century C.E. perhaps supports our view.

25  *Jerusalem Talmud, Megillah* 1:8, 71c [col. 749]: "Aqilas the convert translated the Bible before R. Eliezer and R. Yehoshua, and they praised him, saying: 'You are the most beautiful among men.'" See also: Leopold Zunz, *Ha'drashot Be'Yisrael ve'Hishtalshelutan Ha'historit* (Jerusalem: Bialik Institute, 1954), 41 [Hebrew]; Lieberman, *Greek and Hellenism in Jewish Palestine,* 14-15.

26  Emanuel Tov, *The Textual Criticism of the Bible: An Introduction,* 2nd. ed. (Jerusalem: Bialik Institute, 1997b), 116 [Hebrew]. In general, see Emanuel Tov, *The Text-Critical use of the Septuagint in Biblical Research,* 2nd. ed. (Jerusalem: Simor, 1997a), *passim.*

27  The question of the influence of rabbinic law on the Septuagint has been raised frequently. It is clear that the controversy flows primarily from the fact that there are very few proofs of such influence. See, for example, Lester L. Grabbe, "Aquila's Translation and Rabbinic Exegesis," *JJS* 33 (1982): 527-536; Karen H. Jobes and Moises Silva, *Invitation to the Septuagint* (Grand Rapids: Baker Academic, 2001), 294-296.

28  Lieberman, *Greek and Hellenism in Jewish Palestine,* 1-21.

29  Lea Roth-Gerson, "Similarities and Differences in Greek Synagogue Inscriptions of Eretz–Israel and the Diaspora," in *Synagogues in Antiquity,* eds. A. Kasher et al. (Jerusalem: Yad Izhak Ben-Zvi, 1987), 133-146 [Hebrew].

30  Ibid., 142.

31  *Tosefta Yom Tov* 2:15. Lieberman, *Greek and Hellenism in Jewish Palestine,* claims that those who roasted a lamb in the Land of Israel on Passover eve did not call it a Paschal lamb because they made a distinction between a sacrifice and plain meat, while in Rome they did not make that distinction and referred to the roasted lamb as the Paschal lamb. In other words, the rabbis vigorously opposed it because it was seen as the Paschal lamb. This example teaches us very little about a particular scholar in Rome, but it demonstrates how estranged the Roman community was from rabbinic opinion. See Baruch M. Bokser, "Todos and Rabbinic Authority in Rome," in *New Perspectives in Ancient Judaism, Vol. I,* eds. Jacob Neusner et al. (Lanham, MD: University Press of America, 1987), 117-129.

32  The *Babylonian Talmud* wonders who this man was: "They asked him, 'Was Todos the Roman a great man or a sycophant?'" (Berakhot 19a). The *Jerusalem Talmud* also raises the question: "What is Todos", meaning who is Todos? In both Talmuds, the response is that he supported scholars: "Who is Todos? R. Hananya said, 'He sent support to the scholars'" (*Jerusalem Talmud* 7:1, 34a [col. 536]). And in the *Babylonian Talmud,* "R. Yosi bar Avin said, 'He filled up the pockets of the scholars" (*Berakhot* 53a, and parallels). The contention that he supported scholars is not cited in either Talmuds as a historical assertion, but rather as an explanation of his name. Nevertheless, the fact that each *Talmud* asks about his name indirectly implies that they did not know of him or his activities. The reference to the transference of money may point yet again to the fact that the rabbis thought of the western diaspora in financial terms.

33  The legend that appears in *Yalkut Shimoni* (Exodus [vayera], 182) is certainly from a relatively very late date and can thus certainly not serve as a historical source for the ancient world.

34  This might hint to the fact that there was a degree of immigration to the Land of Israel from the diaspora at the end of the second century and in the third century. See Safrai, *In Times of Temple and Mishnah,* 305.

35  Ory Amitay, "Some Ioudaio-Lakonia Rabbis," *Scripta Classica Israelica* 26 (2007): 131-134.

36  *Sifre Devarim* 344, Finkelstein edition, 400-401. See Catherine Hezser, *Form, Function, and Historical Significance of the Rabbinic Story in Yerushalmi Neziqin* (Tübingen: Mohr-Siebeck, 1993), 15-24.

37  Indeed, it is logical to assume that the sages visited the Roman Jewish community during their stay in Rome for political purposes (see our discussion below). Nevertheless, the important and fascinating fact is that there is no evidence in the literature of even one halakhic question that was addressed to the rabbis by the Roman Jewish community during their visit there. In contrast, the *Mishnah (Avodah Zarah* 4:7) cites a question that was addressed by the non-Jewish scholars in Rome: "They asked the Elders (*zekenim*) in Rome: 'If he does not wish to perform idolatry, why does he not nullify it?' " Parallel sources in the *Tosefta* and in the *Baraita* in the *Gemara (Tosefta Avodah Zarah* 6:7; *Babylonian Talmud Avodah Zarah* 54b) state: "The philosophers asked the Elders in Rome." This question, in terms of its content, is the question of an idol worshipping pagan addressed to the sages of Israel who opposed idolatry. Tal Ilan, "Die Juden im antiken Rom und ihr kulturelles Erbe," in *"Wie schön sind deine Zelte Jacob, deine Wohnungen Israel!" (Num* 24,5): *Beiträge zur Geschichte jüdisch-europäischer Kultur,* ed. Rainer Kampling (Frankfurt/Main: Peter Lang, 2009), 47-78, suggests that the text refers to the Elders who were in Rome, i.e. the Jewish sages who lived and worked in Rome. This claim does not stand up to critical evaluation. The term "Elder" is found in at least three places in the *Mishnah* and the *Tosefta* in reference to scholars who traveled with Rabban Gamliel to Rome on a ship. ("It happened that Rabban Gamliel and the Elders were traveling to Rome on a ship…" [*Mishnah Ma'aser Sheni* 5:9]; "It happened that Rabban Gamliel and the Elders were coming on a ship, and a non-Jew made a ramp, and they descended on it…" [*Mishnah Shabbat* 16:8]; "It happened that Rabban Gamliel and the Elders were coming on a ship, and the sanctity of the day descended upon them. They said to Rabban Gamliel …" [*Tosefta Shabbat* 13:14]. There is a parallel to the law mentioned in the *Tosefta* in the *Mishnah,* but in the *Mishnah,* the names of specific scholars are mentioned in the place of the term "Elders": R. Elazar ben Azariah, R. Yehoshua, and R. Akiva – i.e. the greatest scholars from the Land of Israel at that time. We also find a similar reference in the *Midrash [Torat Kohanim* 16]: "It happened that Rabban Gamliel and the Elders were coming on a ship, and they did not have a *lulav.*" In addition, we also find a reference in the *Mishnah* to the visit of "Rabban Gamliel and the Elders" to Tiberias in the Land of Israel.) On the other hand, we find no references in rabbinic literature to "the Elders in Rome" or any other expression alluding to the scholars of Rome. From these sources, it seems clear that the story mentioned in *Mishnah Avodah Zarah* regarding the question that the scholars of Rome asked, to the degree that it has a basis in history, refers to a question that the sages of the Land of Israel were asked during a visit to Rome. It is important to point out that the expression "Elders" is used many times throughout rabbinic literature in reference to the scholars of the Land of Israel, in the Temple and the like. (See, for example: *Yoma* 1:3; *Sukkah* 2:1; *Sukkah* 4:4; *Ta'anit* 3:6; etc.) It does not seem to us that the fact that this expression appears in Ps. Philo teaches us anything about the geographical location of these sages.

38 *Tosefta Pe'ah* 4:6 (and parallel sources in *Tosefta Ketubot* 3:1; *Babylonian Talmud, Ketubot* 25a). For a description of the fire signals and emissaries, see also *Mishnah Rosh Hashanah,* 2:2-4, which clearly indicates that the fire signals were directed only toward the eastern diaspora. See also Saul Lieberman, *Tosefta Ki-Fshutah: A Comprehensive Commentary on the Tosefta,* Part V, Order Mo'ed, Tractate Rosh Hashanah (New York: Jewish Theological Seminary in America, 1955-1988), 1028-1030. Lieberman cites the opinion of the Raavad (died 1198) that the fire signals were only directed toward the east, but that the messengers went out to the entire diaspora, but he rejects his claim, arguing that according to the order of the fires, it seems they were directed to the north and the east: "And it is also difficult to understand why they discriminated against the rest of the diaspora." See also: Joseph Tabory, *Jewish Festivals in The Time of the Mishnah and Talmud* (Jerusalem: Magnes Press, 1995), 30-34 [Hebrew], which includes a map of the fires on page 31. See also Alon, *The Jews in their Land in the Talmudic Age, 70-640 C.E.,* 149-156. On the importance of communication in the sanctification of the month, see: Safrai, *In Times of Temple and Mishnah,* 460 [298]: "The emissaries were often Torah scholars, and they created a strong bond, regular contact, and supervision…"

39 *Tosefta Sanhedrin* 2:6. See Samuel Klein, *Eretz Yehuda* (Tel Aviv: Dvir, 1939), 210ff [Hebrew]. In the *Jerusalem Talmud, Ma'aser Sheni* 5:8, 56c [col. 308]), after the "Median exile" the "Greek exile" was added. Yet, it appears that this wording is less genuine than that of the *Tosefta.*

40 See Abraham Wasserstein, "Calendaric Implications of a Fourth – Century Jewish Inscription from Sicily," *Scripta Classica Israelica* 11 (1991-1992): 162-165.

41 *Tosefta Megillah* 2:5. In a later Babylonian *aggadah,* the story is reiterated but is attributed to two different sages who are apparently imaginary, who go to intercalate the calendar. Nevertheless, it is clear from the literary style that it is a late Babylonian source. See *Babyloninan Talmud, Sanhedrin* 26. See also Aaron Amit, "On the Contribution of the Comparison of the Babylonian Talmud and the Palestinian Talmud to Lexicography אגיסטון and האסטו," *Lĕšonénu: A Journal for the Study of the Hebrew Language and Cognate Subjects* 72, no. 1-2 (2010): 135-154; we wish to thank Orit Malka for sharing with us her unpublished draft on that story.

42 Indeed, see the *Jerusalem Talmud, Megillah* 74:4, which states not that R. Meir went to Asia to intercalate the calendar, but that R. Meir was in Asia (with no reference to the intercalation of the calendar).

43 Gedaliah Alon has argued that this source refers to Etzion Gaver, a place that was very close to southern Israel and was considered to be part of the Land of Israel because of its proximity. See Alon, *The Jews in their Land in the Talmudic Age, 70-640 C.E.,* 144-146; Aharon Oppenheimer, " 'Love of Mordechai or Hatred of Haman'? Purim in the Days of the Second Temple and Afterwards," *Zion* 62 (1997): 411-413 [Hebrew], supports this view, as did many others. Bezalel Bar-Kochva, "On the Festival of Purim and some of the Succot Practices in the Period of the Second Temple and Afterwards," *Zion* 62 (1997): 395-402 [Hebrew], argues that in contradistinction with other passages where this term is used, it may refer to Asia-Minor. Since in other instances where the term Asia is mentioned it does not refer to Asia-Minor, we have doubts about Bar-Kochva's hypothesis concerning this particular reference. Bar-Kochva himself holds the opinion that in the other instances where Asia is mentioned, the reference is to a place in the Land of Israel. Moreover, even if we would accept Bar-Kochva's opinion, it should be noted that it is the sole account of one single rabbi going to one particular place in the West in order to intercalate the month

within the whole corpus of rabbinic literature. See also, Aaron Amit, "Agiston and Haesto in Harmony," *Lĕšonénu: A Journal for the Study of the Hebrew Language and Cognate Subjects* 73, no. 3-4 (2011): 479-490, and especially p. 481, note 6. If we accept the version that our *baraita* mentions the word "Hebrew" then this source supports the argument that the rabbis were aware of the absence of Hebrew Bible in the West.

44  Safrai, *In Times of Temple and Mishnah: Studies in Jewish History,* 632 [Hebrew].

45  *Malachi* 3:8

46  *Mishnah Yadayim* 4:3

47  Safrai, *In Times of Temple and Mishnah: Studies in Jewish History,* derived historical lessons from the *Mishnah.* He saw in it a certain proof that in Egypt tithes were gathered and sent to the Temple in Jerusalem. Sanders, *Jewish Law from Jesus to the Mishnah,* 301, disagreed with him, demonstrating in detail that this thesis has no basis. Sanders agrees that perhaps in the sabbatical year Jews sent more donations to Israel in order to support the farmers that could not work the land. However, it is logical to assume that this *Mishnah* presents only a romantic description of the nature of the relationship with the diaspora. In light of his comments, the sense is strengthened that even in this "romantic" picture, the western diaspora does not appear as a potential source of support for the community in the Land of Israel.

48  *Mishnah Ta'anit* 1:3.

49  Safrai, *In Times of Temple and Mishnah,* 294, bold emphasis added; Safrai's article was written in 1982, but it appears that he later softened his position on this matter. He wrote the following in a 1996 article: "While during the Temple period until the Jewish war in the days of Trajan in 115-117 C.E., the primary contact was with the Hellenistic diaspora, after that time, the primary contact was with the eastern diaspora, the Jewish community of Babylonia." – Shmuel Safrai, "Contacts between the Leadership of the Land of Israel and the Hellenistic and Eastern Diasporas in the First and Second Centuries," *Te'uda* 12 (1996): 26 [Hebrew].

50  See Seth Schwartz, *Imperialism and Jewish Society: 200 BCE to 640 CE* (Princeton, NJ: Princeton University Press, 2001).

51  See Alon, *The Jews in their Land in the Talmudic Age, 70-640 C.E.,* 146-147; Hugo D. Mantel, *Studies in The History of The Sanhedrin (Mehkarim be-Toldot ha-Sanhedrin)* (Tel Aviv: Dvir, 1969), 214 [Hebrew]; in general, Safrai, *In Times of Temple and Mishnah,* 294-310. For Rabban Gamliel's circuits in the Land of Israel, see: Aharon Oppenheimer, "Rabban Gamliel of Yavneh and his Circuits of Eretz Israel," in *Between Rome and Babylon: Studies in Jewish leadership and society* (Tübingen: Mohr Siebeck, 2005), 145-155.

52  *Tosefta Terumot* 2:13. According to tradition, the returning Jews from Babylonia in the sixth century B.C.E. occupied the land almost to Achziv in the north, and it is therefore beyond the borders of the Land of Israel, just north of the border. See *Mishnah Shevi'it* 6:1; *Demai* 1:3.

53  *Tosefta Gittin* 1:4. Kfar Otenai is situated near Megiddo.

54  See Oppenhiemer, "Rabban Gamliel of Yavneh and his Circuits of Eretz Israel," 145-155.

55  Mantel, *Studies in The History of The Sanhedrin,* 215.

56  See David Goodblatt, *"Medinat Hayam"* ("The Coastal District"), *Tarbiz* 64 (1994-1995): 13-37 [Hebrew]. Goodblatt holds that the meaning of the phrase *"medinat ha-yam"* is the coast of the Land of Israel. If so, this story does not refer at all to the Greek diaspora.

57 Mantel, Studies in *The History of The Sanhedrin,* 214-215 and n. 101; Safrai, *In Times of Temple and Mishnah,* 298.

58 *Tosefta Hullin* 3:10.

59 *Tosefta Parah* 7:4.

60 *Tosefta Mikvaot* 4:6. The continuation of the *Tosefta* reads: "R. Elazar the son of R. Yosi said: 'I taught this law in Rome, deeming it pure, and when I came to my colleagues, they said: you have ruled well.'" The main purpose of R. Elazar's trip was apparently for political purposes. See *Babylonian Talmud, Me'illa* 17a-b. The relevance of this question in Rome requires clarification, as we have not found that there was a pure immersion pool in the diaspora.

61 See n. 42 above. It should be noted that according to Bar-Kochva, "On the Festival of Purim…", the reference here is to a place in the Land of Israel with the name Asia or 'Asia.

62 Alon, *The Jews in their Land in the Talmudic Age, 70-640 C.E.,* 147-149; Mantel, *Studies in The History of The Sanhedrin,* 217-222.

63 *Tosefta Baba Kama* 10:17.

64 *Babylonian Talmud, Ketubot* 112a.

65 *Babylonian Talmud Yevamot* 46a; see also a parallel source in *Babylonian Talmud, Avodah Zarah* 59a. The law here, however, is quite different.

66 *Jerusalem Talmud, Yevamot* 8:1, 8d [Col. 865].

67 See Arye Edrei and Doron Mendels, "A Split Jewish Diaspora Again – A Response to Fergus Millar."

68 For example: 2 Macc. 2 opens with a letter from the Jews of Jerusalem and Judea to the Jews of Egypt – see Daniel R. Schwartz, *The Second Book of Maccabees* (Jerusalem: Yad Izhak Ben-Zvi, 2004), in the same place [Hebrew]; We find high priests during the time of Herod who came from Alexandria (see Mendels, *The Rise and Fall of Jewish Nationalism,* chapter 10); *Tosefta Megillah* 2:17 – Saul Lieberman, ed., *The Tosefta: According to Codex Vienna with Variants and a Brief Commentary, Mo'ed* (New York and Jerusalem: The Jewish Theological Seminary of America, 1970), 352 [Hebrew], mentions a synagogue of Alexandrians in Jerusalem; and *Babylonian Talmud, Niddah* 69b discusses questions that were asked of R. Yehoshua ben Hananya by the Jews of Alexandria. In the last example, it is possible that the questions were still from the time of the Temple, as R. Yehoshua was a recognized scholar at that time (see *Tosefta Eduyot* 3:3). This situation changed after the destruction of the Temple. The close relationship was the result of geographical proximity and the existence of a land route between the communities, as well as the fact that Alexandria was a very old community with a long-standing history of contacts with the community in the Land of Israel. This is true in spite of the fact that the Jews in Egypt spoke Greek.

69 Menahem Stern cites from *Damascius* a story from the sixth century in Alexandria about a rebellious Jew who rode on a white donkey on the Sabbath – See Menahem Stern, *Greek and Latin Authors on Jews and Judaism,* vol. 2 (Jerusalem: Israel Academy of Science and Humanities, 1976-1980), 678. A reminiscent motif appears in the *Talmud* (TP *Haggigah* 2:77b). It is logical to assume that this motif derived from Jewish sources. Sporadic penetration of rabbinic lore and motifs to Egypt is very logical and does not represent any systematic comprehensive knowledge of the core of the literature. Tanhum bar Papa, *Jerusalem Talmud, Kiddushin* 64:4; R. Zakai, *Jerusalem Talmud, Yebamot* 8:2, *Avodah Zarah* 42:1. A renowned scholar who came to Egypt was R. Yohanan Ha-Sandlar, a resident

of the Land of Israel and a student of R. Akiva. Also, R. Hanan the Egyptian lived in the Land of Israel, but came to the area of Alexandria. We learn from the *Jerusalem Talmud, Eruvin* 21:3 that a more significant scholar, R. Abahu, visited in Egypt, but we also see there that this visit did not represent a continuous and set relationship, as it is clear from his dialogue with the local residents that he was cognizant of the fact that this visit was incidental and that he would not be there the following year.

70   *Tosefta Horayot* 2:5. In the Erfurt manuscript, it does not say "Rome." However, see the *Jerusalem Talmud* here and the *Babylonian Talmud, Gittin* 58a. See also *Eikhah Rabbah* 4. Yehuda A. Kurtzer, "What Shall the Alexandrians Do? Rabbinic Judaism and the Mediterranean Diaspora" (PhD diss., Harvard University, 2008), sees this lad as a typology of Esav the Adomi (red). However, it seems to us to be an illusion to King David who was "ruddy, and withal of a fair countenance." (Samuel I, 17:42) The metaphor is a sage who redeems the Messiah.

71   *Tosefta Kippurim* 2:16.

72   For additional sources, see *Babylonian Talmud, Avodah Zarah* 18a; *Avot de-Rebbe Natan*, version 2, chapter 7.

73   *Tosefta Avodah Zarah* 6:7. The term "philosophers" does not appear in the *Mishnah*. It simply states: "they asked the Elders in Rome.

74   Kurtzer, "What Shall the Alexandrians Do?" 105ff, explains this *Mishnah* as a discussion about tactics in the polemic against idolatry ("know what to respond") between the sages and people who are not idolaters. In our opinion, however, this story tries to show that the sages have the upper hand in their controversy with gentiles and even idolaters. According to Kurtzer's interpretation, the story should be viewed as a historical account. As such, he contradicts himself on the methodological level. According to his approach, why should we not identify these people as Jews, these as rabbis, etc. Furthermore, and primarily, it is important to pay attention to the formulation of the *Tosefta*, which says: "The philosophers asked."

75   *Exodus Rabbah, Mishpatim* 30.

76   See *Jerusalem Talmud, Rosh Hashanah* 1:3: "R. Lezer said: 'the law is not written before the king.' The practice in the world is that when a human king makes a decree, he can fulfil it if he wants, and others must fulfil it if he wants. God, however, is not so – rather, when he makes a decree, he fulfils it first..." See also *Vayikra Rabbah, Behukhotai* 35:3. See Alexander Kohut, *Aruch Completum (Arukh ha-Shalem)*, vol. 1 (Wien-Berlin: Selbstverlag, 1926), 30 [agraphos]. See also Moshe Silberg, *Talmudic Law and the Modern State*, trans. Ben Zion Bokser (New York: Burning Bush Press, 1973), 63; Lieberman, *Greek and Hellenism in Jewish Palestine*, 28-29.

77   See Yitzhak D. Gilat, "The Drasha and the Reading of the Torah in the Synagogue on the Sabbath," in *Jews and Judaism in the Second Temple, Mishna and Talmud Period (in Honor of Shmuel Safrai)*, eds. Isaiah Gafni and Aharon Oppenheimer (Jerusalem: Yad Izhak Ben Zvi, 1993), 266-278 [Hebrew].

78   This source appears in *Shemot Rabbah*, a part of *Midrashei Tanhuma*, which is difficult to date precisely. Yet, it is clear that this is a late *midrash*, estimated by scholars to be from between the fifth and ninth centuries. Nevertheless, a parallel story published by Schechter appears to be a much earlier source, see Ayelet Lazarovsky, "Midrash Shemot Rabbah, Parshat Mishpatim, Scientific Edition and Discussion of Stories" (Master's thesis, The

Hebrew University of Jerusalem, 2005, 62). The essential legal argument that compares the Roman and Torah positions appears in other sources, but without reference to a visit in Rome. Here the staging of the debate and the attack against the Roman approach, and the victory of the sages, take place in the capital of the empire itself.

79   *Tosefta Yevamot* 14:5.

80   *Babylonian Talmud, Yevamot* 98a.

81   On conversion at that time, see Ephraim E. Urbach, *The Sages: Their Concepts and Beliefs* (Jerusalem: Magnes Press, 1978), chapter 15.

82   *Tosefta Shabbat* 15:8 – Saul Lieberman, ed., *The Tosefta, Mo'ed*, 70-71 [Hebrew], and parallels.

83   See our discussion in note 36 above. See also Safrai, *In Times of Temple and Mishnah*, vol. 2, 365-381. Safrai deals with trips to Rome by the sages of Yavneh, but it is clear that rabbis also traveled to Rome in later periods for political purposes. See, for example, *Babylonian Talmud, Me'illah* 17b. It is important to note that a number of sources that mention Rome are referring to Kfar Roma located in the Galilee, as mentioned in Josephus Flavius, BJ 3.233. See the commentary of Yehudah Felix, *Talmud Yerushalmi Masechet Shevi'it*, vol. 1 (Jerusalem: Rubin Mass, 1980), 233 [Hebrew]; Saul Lieberman, *Tosefta Ki-Fshutah: A Comprehensive Commentary on the Tosefta,* Part V, Order Mo'ed, Tractate Erubin (New York: Jewish Theological Seminary in America, 1955-1988), 360, n. 80.

84   Thus, for example, it is recorded: "There was an incident in which R. Eliezer, R. Yehoshua and R. Akiva went up to Hulat Antiochia for the purpose of raising funds for the sages" (*Jerusalem Talmud, Horayot* 3:6, 48a [col. 1427]). This source also refers to Syria and not to the overseas Greek diaspora. In this context, see also the Roman laws cited above.

85   That there was a Jewish population in the West, does not indicate that they were rabbinic Jews. In his article, Aron C. Sterk, *"Latino Romaniotes:* The Continuity of Jewish Communities in the Western Diaspora, 400-700 CE," *Melilah, Manchester Journal of Jewish Studies* 9 (2012): 21-49, attempts to refute our thesis. However, ביקש לקלל ונמצא מברך ("wished to curse, but instead found himself blessing") since those arguments that he based on sensible evidence support our main ideas. We have argued indeed that there were Jewish communities in western Europe during the first eight centuries. We have built our thesis on this assumption. Concerning Sterk's claim that rabbinic Judaism can be traced in the western Diaspora, he has not added any substantial evidence to refute or support our claims. On the other hand, his efforts to argue that Hebrew was used more by Jews towards the eighth century are welcome in line with what we have argued in our two articles and a German book. As to the case of Rabbi Meir in Asia Minor see our discussion above (note 43). Be that as it may, the bigger picture of the gap between the eastern Aramaic speaking Jews as against the Greek and Latin speaking ones in the West and its dramatic consequences for the Judaism of the day have not yet been discarded by any of the scholars who were eager to do so.

86   David Noy, *Jewish Inscriptions of Western Europe,* Vol.1, Italy (excluding the City of Rome), Spain and Gaul (Cambridge: Cambridge University Press, 1993).

87   Erwin R. Goodenough, *Jewish Symbols in the Greco-Roman Period,* vol. 12 (New York: Pantheon Books, 1965); Noy, *Jewish Inscriptions of Western Europe.* See Anna Collar, *Religious Networks in the Roman Empire: The Spread of New Ideas* (Cambridge: Cambridge University Press, 2014), and van der Horst's justified criticism of her theses – Pieter W. van der Horst, *Saxa judaica loquuntur, Lessons from Early Jewish Inscriptions* (Leiden: Brill, 2014).

88  Noy, *Jewish Inscriptions of Western Europe,* 151, 157, 169, 207. These inscriptions are relatively late.

89  Noy, *Jewish Inscriptions of Western Europe,* 154-160. Only 6 out 600 gravestones from the first centuries C.E. that were found in Rome had any Hebrew or Aramaic inscription whereas all the others were in Greek or Latin.

90  For example, Gregory of Tours, *History of the Franks,* Book 8:1 describes the entry of king Guntran into Orleans, in 585 C.E., in which it is written: "a huge throng of people came to meet him with standards and banners, singing praises. And here the Syrian language, there that of the Latins, and again that even of the Jews, sounded together strangely in varied praises, saying: "Long live the king; may his reign over the people last unnumbered years." And the Jews who were to be seen taking part in these praises said: "May all the nations honor you and bend the knee and be subject to you." And so it happened that when the king was seated at dinner after mass he said: "Woe to the Jewish tribe, wicked, treacherous, and always living by cunning. Here's what they were after," said he, "when they cried out their flattering praises today, that all the nations were to honor me as master. [They wish me] to order their synagogue, long ago torn down by the Christians, to be built at the public cost; but by the Lord's command I will never do it." In the funeral of Hilary of Arles (449), it is said: "...Hebraeam concinentium linguam in exsequiis honorandis audisse merecolo..." (Patrologia Latina 50, 1242-3). Michael Toch, "Mehr Licht: Eine Engegnung zu Friedrich Lotter," *Zeitschrift fuer Geschichte und Kultur der Juden* 11 (2001): 470-474, argues that these events and others of that kind mentioned in Christian sources are literary inventions and that Jews did not use Hebrew. Yet, if we take such references at face value, then we may assume that Jews recited Hebrew phrases in public events when they wanted to emphasize their unique communal identity.

91  In addition, in the Carolingian law of the ninth century, it is mentioned that when a Jew swears, "He must have in his right hand Moses's five books according to his law, and if he could not have it in Hebrew he shall have it Latin." From: Merovingian and Carolingian Capitularies in Amnon Linder, *The Jews in the Legal Sources of the Early Middle Ages* (Detroit: Wayne State University Press; Jerusalem: The Israel Academy of Sciences and Humanities, 1997), 346.

92  Shaye J.D. Cohen, "Epigraphical Rabbis," *Jewish Quarterly Review* 72, no. 1 (1981): 1-17.

93  Shlomo Simonsohn, "The Hebrew Revival Among Early Medieval European Jews," *American Academy for Jewish Research II*, Salo Baron Jubilee Volume (1974): 831-858; Shlomo Simonsohn, *The Jews of Italy: Antiquity* (Leiden: Brill, 2014); Noy, *Jewish Inscriptions of Western Europe,* 247 (Tortosa, fifth to sixth centuries; Taranto, seventh to eighth centuries). In western Europe, as of the ninth to tenth centuries we find evidence of the appearance of more sophisticated Jewish literature in Hebrew, such as *Josippon* and various *Midrashim* – see Amos Geula, "Lost Aggadic Works Known only from Ashkenaz" (PhD diss., The Hebrew University of Jerusalem, 2006) [Hebrew], Ahima"az, etc. For the inscriptions of the Greek side in the first centuries C.E. Compare also David Noy, Alexander Panayotov, and Hanswulf Bloedhorn, *Inscriptiones Judaicae Orientis I. Eastern Europe* (Tuebingen: Mohr Siebeck, 2004); Walter Ameling, *Inscriptiones Judaicae Orientis. II Kleinasien* (Tuebingen: Mohr Siebeck, 2004); David Noy and Hanswulf Bloedhorn, *Inscriptiones Judaicae Orientis III.* Syria and Cyprus (Tuebingen: Mohr Siebeck, 2004).

94  Lee I. Levine, *The Ancient Synagogue: The First Thousand Years* (New Haven: Yale University Press, 2000), 232-237.

95  In his monumental work, *Jewish Symbols in the Greco-Roman Period,* Goodenough stated the following: "But it seems to me overwhelmingly probable that the actual artifacts in Rome and

Dura are more reliable evidence for Jewish thought in Rome and Dura than are the *Mishnah* and early *Midrashim* of the rabbis in Palestine" (Ibid., 185). Scholars have suggested that the replacement of the tablets received by Moses by a scroll in representations found in Italy of the fourth and fifth centuries C.E. were influenced by a *Midrash* on *Song of Songs* 5:14 (Song of Songs Rabbah 5:14). But Noga-Banai has convincingly shown that no midrashic influence should be adduced in order to explain this shift in representations. See Galit Noga-Banai, *The Trophies of the Martyrs* (Oxford: Oxford University Press, 2008a), 21-24. We should also mention that Bezalel Narkis, "Pharaoh is Dead and Living at the Gates of Hell," Jewish Art 10 (1984): 6-13, has claimed that "the salvation of Pharoah motif was known both to Jews and to Christians since the fourth century C.E. *The Mekhilta de Rabbi Ishmael* on *Exodus* 14:28 conveyed a shortened version of the story. It is therefore not surprising that this detail found its artistic expression in the wall mosaics of the church of Santa Maria Maggiore in Rome, c. 432-440." Narkis himself admits that there is no way to prove in a satisfactory manner that there was a direct connection between Jewish Midrash and the Pharaoh mosaic in the Santa Maria Maggiore. We would add that the above mentioned motif may have been an aggadic version that circulated in Christian circles. Christians, as well as Jews, could have toyed with the motif of saved and repenting pagan kings while drawing on such models found in the Greek (and Latin) Bible (the Nebuchadnezzar of *Daniel* 2 [4], Antiochus IV of 2 *Maccabees* 9, Ptolemy in 3 *Maccabees*, etc.). At any rate, even if a Jewish midrashic motif can be detected here and there in the Jewish western diaspora in the first centuries C.E., it is quite clear that the *Halakhah,* as well as *Aggadah,* as complete corpora, penetrated Jewish life in western Europe only late during the eighth to ninth centuries.

96    For a specific example concerning the Menorah see Galit Noga-Banai, "Between the Menorot: new Lights on a Fourth-Century Jewish Representative Composition," *Viator* 39, no. 2 (2008b): 21-48. We should like to add that we do not necessarily agree with Goodenough regarding the sources from which the art sprouted – i.e. Hellenistic literature, and primarily the works of Philo of Alexandria. See Goodenough, *Jewish Symbols in the Greco-Roman Period,* 3-21. For an academic digest of research on this topic, see Steven Fine, *Art and Judaism in the Greco-Roman World, Toward a New Jewish Archaeology* (Cambridge: Cambridge University Press, 2005).

97    Shmuel Safrai, *Pilgrimage at the Time of the Second Temple* (Tel-Aviv: Am Ha'ssefer Publishing, 1965) [Hebrew]; Joachim Jeremias, *Jerusalem in the Times of Jesus* (London: SCM Press, 1969).

98    Matthew 26:30.

99    *The Special Laws* II, 144-149. The Greek source refers to "prayers and hymns" ("euchon te kai humnon"). See Philo, *The Special Laws,* 2.148; see in general Tabory, *Jewish Festivals in The Time of the Mishnah and Talmud,* 84-95. The *haggada* or any ritual of storytelling do not appear in any of the second temple literature. See Baruch M. Bokser, *The Origins of the Seder* (Berkeley: University of California, 1984); Solomon Zeitlin, "The Liturgy of the First Night of Passover," *JQR* 38 (1948): 431-460; David Henshke, *'Mah Nishtannah': The Passover Night in the Sages Discourse* (Jerusalem: Magnes Press, 2016), 17-35. The eating of the sacrifice accompanied by songs of praise is also indicated in tannaitic sources, see *Mishnah Pesahim* 10:6-7; *Tosefta Sukkah* 3:2; *Tosefta Pesahim* 3:11.

100   Safrai, *Pilgrimage at the Time of the Second Temple,* 71-74.

101   Some of the new symbols instituted included the eating of bitter herbs in the absence of the Passover offering, drinking four cups of wine, dipping, and other rituals representing the process of redemption.

102 There is no mention of the *haggadah* or of the commandment of *sippur yetsiat mitsrayim* in any of the early or non-rabbinic sources. See: Shmuel Safrai and Ze'ev Safrai, *Haggadah of the Sages* (Jerusalem: Carta, 1998) 13-18 [Hebrew]; see in general Joseph Tabory, *The Passover Ritual Throughout the Generations* (Tel-Aviv: Hakkibutz Hame'uchad Publishing House, 1996), 350 [Hebrew]. It is very interesting to pay attention to the fact that in paintings of the fourteenth and fifteenth century of the last supper, the *haggadah* never appears. It is certain that artists were aware of the fact that their Jewish neighbours had a special text to recite during this evening, and yet they eliminated it from their paintings. We would suggest, that the artist want to draw a clear distinction between the Christian Jewish heritage and the Rabbinic Judaism that they observed around them.

103 Daniel Goldschmidt, *The Passover Haggadah: Its Sources and History* (Jerusalem: Bialik Institute, 1960), 30 [Hebrew]. The *Mishnah,* in the tenth chapter of tractate *Pesahim,* parallels the *haggadah,* and all of the *tannaim* mentioned there are from the generation of Yavneh, the first tannaitic generation after the destruction of 70 C.E. (Rabban Gamliel, R. Akiva, R. Tarfon, R. Elazar b'R. Zadok). While Finkelstein suggested that the *haggadah* is a more ancient text that existed already during the time of the Maccabees, all of his proofs have been negated by other scholars.

104 It is worth noting, as well, that the literature of the apocrypha and pseudepigrapha from the Land of Israel and the western diaspora make no mention of the *haggadah* or of the commandment of the telling of the exodus, *sippur yetsiat mitsrayim,* on the night of Passover.

105 Philo, in his description of the Passover celebration, utilizes the term "symposium" which refers in the apocryphal literature to a meal with wine.

106 For the medieval *haggadot* found in the Cairo Genizzah, written in Judeo Greek, see Nicholas De Lange, *Greek Jewish Texts from the Cairo Genizah* (Tuebingen: Mohr-Siebeck, 1996b); Nicholas De Lange, "Jewish Use of Greek in the Middle Ages: Evidence from Passover *Haggadoth* from the Cairo Genizah," *The Jewish Quarterly Review* 96, no. 4 (Fall 2006): 490-497.

107 Mendels, *The Rise and Fall of Jewish Nationalism*, chapters 5, 10.

108 Joseph Heinemann, *Prayer in the Period of the Tanna'im and the Amora'im: Its Nature and its Patterns* (Jerusalem: Magnes Press, 1966), 17-28 [Hebrew].

109 See Moshe Greenberg, "Tefilah," in *Encyclopaedia Biblica,* vol. 8 (Jerusalem: Bialik Institute, 1982), 896-922 [Hebrew]. An anticipation to some aspects of fixed times and certain fixed prayers can already be found in early Judaism (*Daniel* 6:10; in Qumran [4Q503, in ed. Charlesworth Vol. 4A pp. 235-286]). See in general on prayer in Qumran, Bilha Nitzan, *Qumran Prayer and Religious Poetry* (Lieden: Brill, 1994). This fact emphasizes even more the lack of institutionalized prayer in western Judaism, where there are no signs of a beginning of such prayers.

110 Ezra Fleischer, "On the Beginnings of Obligatory Jewish Prayer," *Tarbiz* 59 (1989-1990): 402 [Hebrew].

111 Lee I. Levine, ed., *The Synagogue in the Late Antiquity* (Philadelphia: American Schools of Oriental Research, 1987); Carsten Claußen, *Versammlung, Gemeinde, Synagoge: Das hellenistisch-jüdische Umfeld der frühchristlichen Gemeinden* (Göttingen: Vandenhoeck & Ruprecht, 2002); James C. VanderKam, *Introduction to Early Judaism* (Grand Rapids: William B. Eerdmans Publishing Company, 2001), 212.

112 Fleischer, "On the Beginnings of Obligatory Jewish Prayer," 402-411.

113 There are scholars who claim that the process of formulating set prayer was unrelated to the Temple service, but they admit that we have no sources from the Temple period that prove that there was prayer outside of the Temple. See Heinemann, *Prayer in the Period of the Tanna'im and the Amora'im: Its Nature and its Patterns,* 22. There are many rabbinic sources that claim that the origin of the adopted prayer service was ancient, pre-dating the Temple period (see for example *Babylonian Talmud Megillah* 18a; *Babylonian Talmud, Brakhot* 33a; *Jerusalem Talmud, Megillah* 3:7, 74c [col.767]). These sources prove that the sages wished to attribute an ancient character to the prayers, but they do not prove that they actually existed prior to their time.

114 See in general: Stefan C. Reif, *Judaism and Hebrew Prayer* (Cambridge: Cambridge University Press, 1993).

115 See *Mishnah Brakhot* 4:3-4. It appears in this source that Rabban Gamliel is strongly advocating that a newly formulated prayer be adopted as a set prayer. His colleagues, R. Yehoshua and R. Akiva, take a softer and somewhat equivocal stand. On the other hand, R. Eliezer, the conservative *tanna,* challenges the very concept of set prayer and wishes to preserve prayer as an intimate personal prayer that was known from the time of the Temple (see also The *Babylonian Talmud, Berakhot* 29b). See also the *Baraita* in *Babylonian Talmud, Berakhot* 28a: "Shimon Happakuli in Yavneh laid out the eighteen benedictions before Rabban Gamaliel in proper order," which supports the contention that this prayer was created during the time of Rabban Gamliel (See Fleischer, "On the Beginnings of Obligatory Jewish Prayer," 425-433. See also Reif, Judaism and Hebrew Prayer, 60). See also *Mishnah, Berakhot* 1:4-5; *Babylonian Talmud, Berakhot* 27b; and many other sources that indicate that in the beginning of Tannaitic period, a big effort was devoted to decisions about organizing the prayers.

116 In fact, with regard to the *shema* prayer, we find that in Caesaria, it was recited in Greek: "Rabbi said: 'I say that *kriat shema* should only be recited in the holy language (Hebrew). What is the reason? For it states: And these words shall be …' R. Levi bar Hayta went to Caesaria and heard them reciting the *shema* in Greek. He wanted to stop them. R. Yosi heard and was adamant, saying: 'I say that a person who cannot read *ashurit* should not read it, but should say it in any language that he knows.' R. Berachya responded: 'With regard to the Scroll of Esther, if he reads in *ashurit* and in the vernacular, he only fulfils the requirement in *ashurit.*' Rabbi said: 'How do we know that if he knows how to read the Scroll of Esther in *ashurit* and in the vernacular, he only fulfils the requirement in *ashurit*? Rather, if he reads the vernacular, he fulfils the obligation in the vernacular. Similarly, he prays in any language that he knows so that he can request his needs and make the blessing over food. So he knows who he is blessing, we make him swear an oath of testimony or an oath on a deposit in his language…' " (*Jerusalem Talmud, Sotah* 7:1, 21b [col. 933]). It should be noted that this source is talking about *kriat shema* that is comprised of a number of Biblical sections that had certainly been translated into Greek hundreds of years earlier. What interests us in this study are those prayers that were formulated and written by the sages, particularly during the generation of Yavneh.

117 *Tosefta Shabbat* 13:4.

118 Randall D. Chesnutt and Judith Newman, "Prayers in the Apocrypha and Pseudepigrapha," in *Prayer from Alexander to Constantine: A critical Anthology,* ed. Mark Christopher Kiley (London and New York: Routledge, 1997), 38-42. They speak rightfully about the "scripturization of prayer" in the Pseudepigrapha and Apocrypha.

119 Gerard Rouwhorst, "Jewish liturgical Traditions in early Syriac Christianity," *Vigiliae Christianae* 51 (1997): 36-93; David A. Fiensy, "Prayers, Hellenistic Synagogal," in Anchor Bible Dictionary, ed. David N. Freedman, 5 vols. (Garden City, NJ: Doubleday, 1992), 450-451.

120 David Goodblatt, *Elements of Ancient Jewish Nationalism* (New York: Cambridge University Press, 2006).

121 Mendels, *The Rise and Fall of Jewish Nationalism*; Goodblatt, *Elements of Ancient Jewish Nationalism.*

122 See Abraham Shalit, *Kadmoniot Ha'yehudim*, vol. 1 (Jerusalem and Tel-Aviv: Bialik Institute, 1967), XXXVI-XLIX [Hebrew]. Regarding laws in *The Antiquities,* see several laws cited in David Goldenberg, "The Halakhah in Josephus and Tannaitic Literature: A Comparative Study," *JQR* 67 (1976): 30-43.

123 Though there are at times obscure references to older *halakhot.*

124 See in general on this issue David Rokeah, "A New Onomasticon Fragment from Oxyrhynchus and Philo's Etymologies," *Journal of Theological Studies* 19 (1968): 70-82; David Rokeah, *Philonis Alexandrini De Providentia-De Decalogo Hypothetica* (Jerusalem: Magnes Press, 1976), 13-16 [Hebrew].

125 David T. Runia, *Philo in Early Christian Literature, A Survey* (Assen and Minneapolis: Van Gorcum and Fortress Press, 1993).

126 Linder, *The Jews in Roman Imperial Legislation,* Law no. 66. For Justinian and the Jews in general, see: Alfredo Mordechai Rabello, "Justinian and the Revision of Jewish Legal Status," in *The Cambridge History of Judaism* IV, ed. Steven T. Katz (Cambridge: Cambridge University Press, 2006), 1073-1076.

127 Linder, *The Jews in Roman Imperial Legislation,* 409, and see his commentary on pp. 402-405, concerning the term *Mishnah.*

128 Stern, *Greek and Latin Authors on Jews and Judaism, passim.*

129 Compare for the incredible output of written material in Christianity: Harry Y. Gamble, *Books and Readers in the Early Church: A History of Early Christian Texts* (New Haven and London: Yale University Press, 1995); Doron Mendels, *The Media Revolution of Early Christianity* (Grand Rapids: Eerdmans, 1999).

130 That they knew of its existence can be seen in several instances that are dealt with in Jacobs, *Die Institution des Juedischen Patriarchen,* especially pp. 248-272 (including Libanius). Also, we know from the "Hexapla" that Origines knew of Aquiles's translation to the Bible (which was supported by the rabbis).

131 Regarding the Jewish rebellion of 115-117 C.E., see: Mendels, *The Rise and Fall of Jewish Nationalism,* 385-386; Miriam Pucci Ben-Zeev, "The Uprising in the Jewish Diaspora, 116-17," in *The Cambridge History of Judaism* IV, ed. Steven T. Katz (Cambridge: Cambridge University Press, 2006), 93-104.

132 *Midrash Tanhuma* (Warsaw), *Parshat Ki Tissa* 34. In *Pesikta Rabbati* (Ish Shalom), Ch. 5, *Yelamdenu [Rabbeinu]Mahu:* "R. Yehudah said in the name of R. Shalom: Moses requested that the *Mishnah* be recorded in writing, and God anticipated that *the nations of the world would in the future translate the Torah in order to read it in Greek, and they would claim: 'You are not Israel.'* God said to Moses: 'In the future, the nations of the world will say: 'We are Israel, we are the sons of Israel, we are the sons of God.' And now the scales are balanced. God said to the nations: 'That which you claim to be my children, I do not know. But they who have my secret in their hands are my children.' They said to him: 'What is your secret?' He responded: 'It is the *Mishnah.*'" See Lieberman, *Greek and Hellenism in Jewish Palestine*; See also Urbach, *The Sages,* 305; Francois Dreyfus, "The Scales Are Even," *Tarbitz* 52, no. 1 (1982): 139 [Hebrew]; A. A. Hallevy, "The Scales Are Even," *Tarbitz* 52, no. 3 (1983): 514 [Hebrew].: Mordechai A. Friedman, "And So Far, the Scales are Balanced," *Tarbitz* 54, no. 1 (1984): 147 [Hebrew].

133 *Pe'ah* 2:6,17a, [Col. 89].

134 See Urbach, *The Sages,* 286-314, and especially 305-310; Abraham Rosenthal, "Torah She'al Peh Ve-Torah Mi-Sinai – Halakhah U-Ma'aseh," in *Mehqerei Talmud: Talmudic Studies Dedicated to the Memory of Professor Eliezer Shimshon Rosenthal,* vol. 2, eds. Moshe Bar-Asher and David Rosenthal (Jerusalem: Magnes Press, 1993), 448 [Hebrew].

135 *Megillah* 1:8.

136 *Megillah* 9a.

137 *Babylonian Talmud, Megillah* 9a.

138 *Megillah* 8:1, 71c [Col. 749]; See Lieberman, *Greek and Hellenism in Jewish Palestine,* 13-15; Gedaliah Alon, *Mehkarim Be-Toldot Yisrael* ("Studies in the History of Israel"), vol. 2 (Tel-Aviv: Ha-Kibbutz Ha-Me'uhad, 1970), 241-248 [Hebrew].

139 See Philo, *Moses,* 25-43 (pages 277-281 in the Daniel-Nataf Hebrew edition).

140 *Masekhet Sofrim* 1:7.

141 Shulamit Elitzur, *Wherefore Have We Fasted? 'Megilat Taanit Batra' and Similar Lists of Fasts* (Jerusalem: World Union of Jewish Studies, 2007), 65, 70 [Hebrew]. For other somewhat different formulations that express the same idea, see Ibid., 75, 77, 86, 94, 111, 121.

142 Ibid., 31. An earlier liturgical poem by Kalir is the only one that includes a list of fast days and does not include a fast on the translation of the Torah into Greek. See Ibid., 18.

143 Ibid., 197.

144 The manuscript is Vatican, Apostolic Library Cod. Ebr. 171. In the wake of the adoption of the Torah by the Christians, we find the following statement of R. Yohanan: "A non-Jew who studies the Torah is punishable by death, as it says (Deuteronomy 33:4): 'Moses commanded us the law, an inheritance of the congregation of Jacob.' – an inheritance for us and not for them" (*Babylonian Talmud, Sanhedrin* 59a). See Urbach, *The Sages,* 550.

145 Professor Berachyahu Lifschitz from the Faculty of Law at the Hebrew University suggested (in a conversion with the authors) that the split that we described was not between eastern and western Judaism, and was not the linguistic barrier, but rather an ideological one, along religious lines, regardless of geographical dispersion. This was a natural continuation of the phenomenon of sectarianism, which characterized Jewish society prior to 70 C.E., which did not disappear as historians have claimed. According to this idea, the Jews that emigrated or were dispersed to the West brought with them the multifaceted character of the Jewish community in Israel, and thus in both locations, the Jews were divided into sects, Pharisees and Sadducees. Sadducees were the ones who wanted no part of Rabbinic Judaism, which was the continuation of Pharisaic Judaism, without relation to language or to geography – east or west. The problem with this proposal, in our opinion, is that it is difficult to claim, in light of the proofs discussed above, that there were Pharisees in the West who relied on the tradition of the rabbis and accepted their authority.

146 Jewish War 2.8; *Antiquities* 18.11-25.

147 Albert I. Baumgarten, *The Flourishing of Jewish Sects in the Maccabean Era: An Interpretation* (Leiden-Koeln: Brill, 1997).

148 Albert I. Baumgarten, *Second Temple Sectarianism: à Social and Religious Historical Essay* (Tel-Aviv: Ministry of Defense, 2001), 16 [Hebrew].

149 Doron Mendels, "Pagan or Jewish? The Presentation of Paul's Mission in the Book of Acts," in *Identity, Religion and Historigoraphy* (Sheffield: Sheffield Academic Press, 1998b), 394-419.

150 *Acts* 13:13-43.

151 With regard to stories in the New Testament about the emissaries, the Christian emissaries were called "apostles." Jewish emissaries send by the *Nasi* were referred to as "apostles" by Roman law. However, it should be noted that contrary to the spiritual mission of the Christian "apostles," the Jewish ones were but collectors of money to support the *Nasi* in the Land of Israel.

152 See Fergus Millar, "A Rural Jewish Community in Late Roman Mesopotamia, and the Question of a 'split' Jewish Diaspora," *Journal for the study of Judaism* 42 (2011): 351-374. A careful examination of *The Lives of the Eastern Saints* by John of Ephesus leads Millar to the conclusion that some Hebrew was known in Syria, particularly in areas where dialects of Syriac and Aramaic were known. This conclusion is supported by our thesis and by evidence from rabbinic literature. The closer we get to areas in which the spoken languages were Aramaic and Syriac, the more we see evidence of rabbinic visits, a familiarity with rabbinic ideas, etc. In contrast, much less rabbinic influence is found in Greek speaking areas. For the Jewish-Greek presence in this region, see: *The Cambridge History of Judaism* IV (2006).

153 Regarding the development of a Christian system of communication at that time, see Mendels, *The Media Revolution of Early Christianity*.

154 Andrew C. Inkpen and Eric W.K. Tsang, "Social Capital, Networks and Knowledge Transfer," *Academy of Management Review* 30, no. 1 (2005): 149.

155 Mendels, "Pagan or Jewish…"; The saying in Mt.23.15: "Woe to you, scribes and Pharisees, hypocrites! for you traverse sea and land to make a single proselyte" is of course a rhetorical exaggeration, and can be seen as a Christian missionary interpretation.

156 For a friendly dialogue, see *Acts* 18.24-28, and for a less friendly one see *Acts* 18.12-17. We are not referring to the inner conflicts within the communities of Jesus's followers (1 Corinth 1.10-31 and elsewhere).

157 According to *Acts* 22.3-5, and 23.6, he himself says that he is a Pharisee.

158 Aristotle, Rhetoric.

159 For the rabbinic material in Paul, see Menahem Kister, "Romans 5:12-21 against the background of Torah-Theology and the Hebrew usage," Harvard Theological Review 100, no. 4 (2007): 391-424.

160 Doron Mendels, *Why Did Paul Go West? Jewish Historical Narrative and Thought* (London: Bloomsbury Publishing, 2013).

161 The question of "borders" between what we term "Christianity" and Judaism will not be discussed here.

162 He himself says to Felix in *Acts* 24.12 that he did not stir up a crowd "either in the Temple or in synagogues or in the city." Although he refers to the recent twelve days of his stay in Palestine, this points to his strategy concerning Palestine all along.

163 *Acts* 6.9. Some of those Jews who came from Asia were the ones who chased him during his last visit to Jerusalem. See *Acts* 2.9 with 21.27.

164 As in *Acts* 17.1-4, where in Thessalonica he speaks for three consecutive Sabbaths, and appears as well in Ikanion (14.1-3) and in Antiochia (13.43).

165  Kister, "Romans 5:12-21..."

166  From our point of view this is a significant observation since the difference between Paul of Luke-Acts and Paul of the epistles is not just a result of the presentation by two authors at two different points in time. The *Book of Acts* blames the Jews constantly – with some interesting exceptions – for the crucifixion of Jesus. (One such exception is *Acts* 17.2-3 where the narrator grants the Jews a positive role in the history of Christianity, stating that "... Paul went in, as was his custom, and for three weeks he argued with them from the scriptures, explaining and proving that it was necessary for the Christ to suffer and to rise from the dead...") In contradistinction, Paul in his epistles written between 50 and 60 C.E. is somewhat milder in this respect and does not blame the Jews as explicitly as does Luke in *Acts*. This toning down of Jewish guilt can be seen as yet another part of a strategy designed by him to attract Jews in The Greek West. Interestingly, in 1 Thessalonians (2.14-20), his first epistle written around 51 C.E., Paul is probably still not aware of his future strategy and harshly blames the Jews for the crucifixion.

167  See for the centrality of the Torah in both communities – physical and spiritual – as a topic in the dialogues between Jesus's followers and Jews, see *Romans* chapter 7, and 1 *Corinthians* 5.7-13, 9.8-9, and 10.1-9.

168  See Arye Edrei and Doron Mendels, "Preliminary Thoughts on Structures of 'Sovereignty' and the Deepening Gap between Judaism and Christianity in the First Centuries C.E.," *Journal for the Study of the Pseudepigraph* 23, no. 3 (2014), 215-238.

169  When Paul does not behave like a Jew who adheres to the Torah, he ironically is accused of acting against the Roman law (*Acts* 16.20-21): "These men are Jews [typical misunderstanding of the gentiles who do not differentiate between Jews and Christians] and they are disturbing our city. They advocate customs which it is not lawful for us Romans to accept or practice." On the other hand, Gallio the governor of Achaia does not see any clash of Roman law with that of the Jews either through their own interpretation or that of Paul (*Acts* 18.12-17). At any rate, these two references indicate that the legal clash between the Torah and Roman law was an issue. In theory, Paul promoted the idea of refraining from any clash. See Edrei and Mendels, "Preliminary Thoughts on Structures of 'Sovereignty'..."

170  Thanks to the participants in the conferences in Munich (January 2015) and Tel Aviv (November 2015) for their discussion on this section of our article. Thanks also to Professor Peter van der Osten-Sacken for reading an earlier version of the above and giving some good advice. In particular we wish to thank Serge Ruger who read this section and offered some useful comments.

171  For a brilliant summary of research on the history of the Jews in Europe during this period, see Michael Toch, "The Jews in Europe 500-1050," in *The New Cambridge Medieval History,* vol. 1, ed. P. Fouracre (Cambridge: Cambridge University Press, 2005), 547-570. For the latest Jewish compositions in Rome in Antiquity see Rutgers, *The Hidden Heritage of Diaspora Judaism,* 235-284. If the attempts made by Tal Ilan, "Die Juden im antiken Rom und ihr kulturelles Erbe," to argue that *the Biblical Antiquities of Ps.* Philo was composed in Rome are justified (which we doubt), then she supports our claim that the western Jews created their own book-shelf. For the first century, Palestinian provenance of the book, see Doron Mendels, *Identity, Religion and Historiography* (Sheffield: Sheffield Academic Press, 1998a), 294-313.

172  See, for example, sources collected from legislation in Linder, *The Jews in Roman Imperial Legislation*; Linder, *The Jews in the Legal Sources of the Early Middle Ages*; and Heinz

Schreckenberg, *Die Christlichen Adversus-Judaeos-Texte und ihr Literarisches und Historisches Umfeld* (1.-11. Jh.), 2nd. ed. (Frankfurt am Main: P. Lang, 1990).

173 See, for example, Sara Zfatman, *The Jewish Tale in the Middle Ages: Between Ashkenaz and Sepharad* (Jerusalem: Magnes Press, 1993) [Hebrew], which relates the rise of the communities of Spain and Germany vis-à-vis the decline of the Babylonian domination. Regarding the Jews of Italy, see *the Scroll of Ahima'atz* and Reuven Bonfil, "Between Eretz Israel and Babylonia," *Shalem: Studies in the History of the Jews in Eretz Israel* 5 (1987): 1-30 [Hebrew]. Nevertheless, tales are problematic as historical documents. See Avraham Grossman, *The Early Sages of Ashkenaz: Their Lives, Leadership and Works* (900-1096) (Jerusalem: Magnes Press, 1982), 1-8 [Hebrew].

174 Brody, *The Geonim of Babylonia and the Shaping of Medieval Jewish Culture,* 123-134.

175 In general, it might be worthwhile to relate to the thesis proposed by some scholars that Rabbinic Judaism constituted only a small percentage of the eastern Jewish diaspora (Schwartz, *Imperialism and Jewish Society*; but see Yaron Eliav, "The Matrix of Ancient Judaism: A Review Essay of Seth Schwartz's Imperialism and Jewish Society 200 BCE to 640 CE," *Prooftexts* 24 (2004): 116-128; and Yaron Eliav, "Jews and Judaism 70-429," in *A Companion to the Roman Empire,* ed. David S. Potter (Oxford: Blackwell, 2006), 565-586). The question that we raise in this study is completely different than questions regarding the degree to which the rabbis were accepted in the Hebrew and Aramaic speaking communities. Our basic theory regarding the gap between the two diasporas relates primarily to the fact that Rabbinic Judaism did not proliferate in the West because of the language gap that existed between the two communities, regardless of the degree to which it was accepted in the east. Thus, the claim that the acceptance of Rabbinic Judaism was limited in the East does not negate our claim regarding the dichotomy between the East and the West.

176 See, for example, Friedrich Lotter, "Die Grabinschriften des lateinischen Westens als Zeugnisse jüdischen Lebens im Übergang von der Antike zum Mittelalter (4.-9. Jahrhundert)," in *Jüdische Gemeinden und ihr christlicher Kontext in Kulturraeumlich vergleichender Betrachtung,* Christoph Cluse et al. (Hannover: Verlag Hahnsche Buchhandlung, 2003), 87-147, in contrast to Toch, "The Jews in Europe 500-1050." See Asher Frishman, *The Early Ashkenzi Jews: Since their Settlement in North-West Europe to the First Crusade* (Tel-Aviv: Hakibbutz Hameuchad, 2008), 25-110, for more details on the apparent existence of Jews in Europe in the early Middle Ages.

177 Giambattista Vico, *La Scienza Nuova* ("The New Science"), trans. of 1744 edition Thomas Goddard Bergin and Max Harold Fisch (Ithaca, New York: Cornell University Press, 1948).

178 Jacques Fontaine, "Education and Learning," in *The New Cambridge Medieval History,* vol. 1, ed. Paul Fouracre (Cambridge: Cambridge University Press, 2005), 735-759.

179 Shaye J.D. Cohen, *The Beginnings of Jewishness: Boundaries, Varieties, Uncertainties* (Berkeley: University of California Press, 1999); Kenneth Stow, *Jewish Dogs: An Image and its Interpreters: Continuity in the Catholic-Jewish Encounter* (Stanford: Stanford University Press, 2006).

180 Toch, "The Jews in Europe 500-1050."

181 See, for example, for the moderate tone, Linder, *The Jews in the Legal Sources of the Early Middle Ages,* 465-466 (Gaul, the Vannes Synod in 465 C.E.).

182  See Linder, *The Jews in the Legal Sources of the Early Middle Ages,* 477, on the Synod of Narbonne in 589 C.E., which prohibited the Jews from reciting psalms during a funeral.

183  It appears from various documents that the Jews would gather on holidays in order to conduct communal celebrations. Nevertheless, the implication is that the place that they gathered was not necessarily a synagogue. See, for example, the letter of Gregory I to Peter, the Bishop of Terracina in March 591 which is found in Linder, *The Jews in the Legal Sources of the Early Middle Ages,* 417-418.

184  See, for example, Ibid., 27 (Passover, fast – apparently Yom Kippur, and presents – apparently Purim), 48 (Sabbath, Purim, and other festivals), 64 (Sabbath and other holidays), 68 (festive gifts), 80, 83, 86, 138 (Sabbath and other holidays), 184-185 (festivals and Passover), 220 (Sabbath and other festivals), 240 (festivals), 263 (Sabbath, Passover, and other festivals), 285 (Sabbath, Passover, and other festivals), 294 (Sabbath, the New Month, Sukkot and other holidays), 322 (Sabbath and other festivals), 324 (Sabbath and other holidays), 418, 443 (festivals), 463 (Passover, acceptance of gifts, other festivals), etc. Concerning Purim see the Law of Theodosius II with Honorius from 29.5.408 (Linder, *The Jews in Roman Imperial Legislation,* 236-238).

With regard to Passover, we find in several laws a reference to the 14th of Nissan as the date that the Jews celebrated the holiday. See, for example, the Visigoth law (Linder, *The Jews in the Legal Sources of the Early Middle Ages,* 263) which was codified in the seventh century. The 14th of Nissan is the biblical holiday of *Pessach* (Passover) when the Passover lamb was sacrificed, while the rabbinic holiday is celebrated on the 15th. Is it possible that the 14th of Nissan is mentioned instead of the 15th because the Jews continued to celebrate according to the Biblical calendar, and perhaps even by roasting a lamb on the afternoon before Passover, a practice that was unequivocally prohibited by the rabbis. The *Tosefta* (*Yom Tov* 2:15) records that Todos the Roman would roast a lamb on Passover, which incurred the wrath of the rabbis.

185  Linder, *The Jews in the Legal Sources of the Early Middle Ages,* 517-521. It is an interesting fact that formal documents from the period that deal with the Jewish holidays do not, to our knowledge, mention Hanukkah (a passage in the Canons of the Apostles [Ibid., 27] definitely does not refer to Hanukkah). This too might be because it is a holiday that was initiated by the rabbis and which was not adopted in the West.

186  Toch, "The Jews in Europe 500-1050," 563.

187  Ephraim E. Urbach, *The World of the Sages: Collected Studies* (Jerusalem: Magnes Press, 1998), 142-189 [Hebrew].

188  Ibid., 167.

189  *Babylonian Talmud, Yebamot* 48b.

190  See Toch, "The Jews in Europe 500-1050"; Lotter, 2003.

191  Socrates, EH, Book 7:38 (The Jews of Crete); Severus of Minorca (Schwartz, *Imperialism and Jewish Society,* 197); Gregory of Tours, *The History of the Franks,* Book 5, chapter 11 (mass conversion of the Jews in Clermont-Ferrand).

192  CC CM, 52, 189-195.

193  Amos Funkenstein, "Changes in the Patterns of Christian Anti-Jewish Polemics in the 12th Century," *Zion* 33, no. 3-4 (1968): 125-144 [Hebrew]; Amos Funkenstein, "Basic types of Christian anti-Jewish polemics in the later Middle Ages," *Viator* 2 (1971): 373-382; Merhaviah, 1970; Cohen, *The Beginnings of Jewishness,* 147-166.

194 It is possible to argue that before the ninth century, prior to the arrival of rabbinic literature, the Jews received informal Christian education, a practice that was presumably minimized with the introduction of formal Jewish education in Hebrew-Aramaic. With regard to education in the Middle Ages, see Ron B. Begley and Joseph W. Koterski s.j., *Medieval Education* (New York: Fordham University Press, 2005), and Fontaine, "Education and Learning." We might also assume that the introduction of rabbinic literature and of formal, institutionalized Jewish education, distanced the Jews from gentile education and widened the gap between Christians and Jews. The importance of mandatory education in the Jewish tradition to the preservation of Jews and Judaism was recently emphasized by Hillel Rapoport and Avi Weiss "In-group Cooperation in a Hostile Environment: An Economic Perspective on Some Aspects of Jewish Life in (Pre-modern) Diaspora," in *Jewish Society and Culture: An Economic Perspective,* eds. Carmel U. Chiswick, Tikva Lecker, and Nava Kahana (Bar-Ilan University Press, 2007), 103-128. It must be remembered in this context that mandatory education was one of the most important rabbinic innovations, and therefore happened in communities that became familiar with rabbinic innovations.

195 Linder, *The Jews in the Legal Sources of the Early Middle Ages,* 494-500 [Toledo 6].

196 Toch, "The Jews in Europe 500-1050," 551; Cohen, *The Beginnings of Jewishness,* 103-105; Scott Bradbury, "The Jews of Spain, c. 235-638," in *The Cambridge History of Judaism* IV, ed. Steven T. Katz (Cambridge: Cambridge University Press, 2006), 508-516.

197 Linder, *The Jews in the Legal Sources of the Early Middle Ages,* 499.

198 It is interesting to note that there is a clear distinction here between three categories of literature: the Old Testament, the Oral law, and the Apocrypha.

199 Cohen, *The Beginnings of Jewishness,* 100-115.

200 See David J. Wasserstein, "Langues et frontieres entre Juifs et musulmans en al-Andalus," in *Judios y musulmanes en al-Andalus y el Magreb. Contacos intelectuales,* ed. M. Fierro (Madrid, 2002), 1-11; and the response of Carlos Del Valle, "Sobre las lenguas de los judios en la Espana visigoda y al-Andalus," *Sefarad* 63, no. 1 (2003): 183-193.

201 Chen Merchavia, *The Church Versus Talmudic and Midrashic Literature [500-1248]* (Jerusalem: Bialik Institute, 1970), 71-84 [Hebrew]; Cohen, *The Beginnings of Jewishness,* 130.

202 De Lange, *Greek Jewish Texts from the Cairo Genizah;* See, among others, the criticism of D. Jacoby, "Greek Jewish Texts from The Cairo-Genizah – Lange, 1996," *Byzantinische Zeitschrift* 91 (1998): 110-112; Johannes Niehoff-Panagiotidis, "Review of Nicholas de Lange, Greek-Jewish Texts from the Cairo Genizah," *Suedost-Forschungen* 58 (1999): 474-480; and Israel M. Ta-Shma, "Hebrew-Byzantine Bible Exegesis ca. 1000 from the Cairo Geniza," *Tarbiz* 49, no. 2 (2000): 247-256 [Hebrew]; For a comprehensive bibliography, see Shifra Sznol, "Medieval Judeo-Greek Bibliography: Texts and Vocabularies," *Jewish Studies* 39 (1999): 107-132.

203 De Lange, "The Hebrew Language in the European Diaspora," 295ff; Shifra Sznol, "A Comparative Lexical Study of Greek and Latin Words in Late *Midrashim* and Judeo-Greek Vocabularies from Biblical Translations and Glossaries," *Erytheia* 26 (2005): 87-103; Shifra Sznol, "A Mishnaic Hebrew Glossary in Judeo-Greek from Cairo Gniza," *Massorot: Studies in Languages Traditions and Jewish Languages* 8-9 (2006): 225-252 [Hebrew].

204 It is important to note that the Greek *Haggadah* found in the *genizah* includes the opening section *"Ha Lahma Anya"* ("This is the bread of affliction"). This section, the only section of the *Haggadah* written in the original Aramaic rather than in Hebrew, dates from the

period of the *Geonim* in Babylonia, as opposed to the rest of the *Haggadah* that originated in the Land of Israel. In other words, it is certain that the Greek *Haggadah* in the *genizah* is a later text that originated in Babylonia and does not give evidence to the continuity of the Byzantine Jewish community. See Safrai and Safrai, *Haggadah of the Sages*, 109-112.

205  Niehoff-Panagiotidis, "Review of Nicholas de Lange…"

206  De Lange, "The Hebrew Language in the European Diaspora," 71-78.

207  *Jerusalem Talmud Megilah* 1:11, 73c [col.749]; Lieberman, *Greek and Hellenism in Jewish Palestine,* 12-14.

208  See, for example, the recent work of Moshe Zipor, *The Septuagint Version of the Book of Genesis* (Ramat-Gan: Bar Ilan University Press, 2005), 33-35 [Hebrew].

209  Shifra Sznol, "Medieval Judeo-Greek Bibliography: Texts and Vocabularies," *Jewish Studies* 39 (1999): 107-132; Shifra Sznol, "A Mishnaic Hebrew Glossary in Judeo-Greek from Cairo Gniza," *Massorot: Studies in Languages Traditions and Jewish Languages* 8-9 (2006): 225-252 [Hebrew].

210  For an interesting attempt to prove the twilight of Judaism in Europe in this period in the literature of the later period, see Bonfil, "Between Eretz Israel and Babylonia."

211  With regard to the Church, see Mendels, *The Media Revolution of Early Christianity.*

212  See the Testament of the Twelve Patriarchs, *Matthew* 10:1; Letter of Aristeias, etc.


# Bibliography

Albeck, Hanoch. *Mishnah.* Vol. VI, *Order Tohorot.* Jerusalem: The Bialik Institute; Tel Aviv: Dvir, 1958 [Hebrew].

Allmand, Christopher, ed. *The New Cambridge Medieval History.* Vol. 7, *c.1415–c.1500.* Cambridge: Cambridge University Press, 1998.

Alon, Gedaliah. *Mehkarim Be-Toldot Yisrael* ("Studies in the History of Israel"). Vol. 2. Tel-Aviv: Ha-Kibbutz Ha-Me'uhad, 1970 [Hebrew].

Alon, Gedaliah. *The Jews in their Land in the Talmudic Age, 70-640 C.E.* 2 vols. Jerusalem: Magnes Press, 1977.

Ameling, Walter. *Inscriptiones Judaicae Orientis. II Kleinasien.* Tuebingen: Mohr Siebeck, 2004.

Amit, Aaron. "On the Contribution of the Comparison of the BT and the PT to Lexicography אגיסטון and האסטו." *Lěšonénu: A Journal for the Study of the Hebrew Language and Cognate Subjects 72, no. 1-2* (2010): 135-154.

Amit, Aaron. "Agiston and Haesto in Harmony." *Lěšonénu: A Journal for the Study of the Hebrew Language and Cognate Subjects 73, no. 3-4 (2011):* 479-490.

Amitay, Ory. "Some Ioudaio-Lakonia Rabbis." *Scripta Classica Israelica* 26 (2007): 131-134.

Assaf, Simha. *Tekufat ha-Geonim ve-Sifrutah.* Jerusalem: Harav Kook Institute, 1955 [Hebrew].

Bar-Kochva, Bezalel. "On the Festival of Purim and some of the Succot Practices in the Period of the Second Temple and Afterwards." *Zion* 62 (1997): 387-407 [Hebrew].

Barclay, John M. G. *Jews in the Mediterranean Diaspora: From Alexander to Trajan (323 BCE-117 CE)*. Edinburgh: T. & T. Clark, 1996.

Barclary, John M. G., ed. *Negotiating Diaspora. Jewish Strategies in the Roman Empire*. London: T&T Clark International, 2004.

Baumgarten, Albert I. *The Flourishing of Jewish Sects in the Maccabean Era: An Interpretation*. Leiden-Koeln: Brill, 1997.

Baumgarten, Albert I. *Second Temple Sectarianism: A Social and Religious Historical Essay*. Tel-Aviv: Ministry of Defense, 2001 [Hebrew].

Baumgarten, Albert I. "Bilingual Jews and the Greek Bible." In *Shem in the Tents of Japhet: Essays on the Encounter of Judaism and Hellenism*, edited by James L. Kugel, 13-20. Leiden: Brill, 2002.

Begley, Ron B., and Joseph W. Koterski s.j. *Medieval Education*. New York: Fordham University Press, 2005.

Bokser, Baruch M. *The Origins of the Seder*. Berkeley: University of California, 1984.

Bokser, Baruch M. "Todos and Rabbinic Authority in Rome." In *New Perspectives in Ancient Judaism*. Vol. I, edited by Jacob Neusner et al., 117-129. Lanham, MD: University Press of America, 1987.

Bonfil, Reuven. "Between Eretz Israel and Babylonia." *Shalem: Studies in the History of the Jews in Eretz Israel* 5 (1987): 1-30 [Hebrew].

Bradbury, Scott. "The Jews of Spain, c. 235-638." In *The Cambridge History of Judaism* IV, edited by Steven T. Katz, 508-516. Cambridge: Cambridge University Press, 2006.

Brody, Robert. *The Geonim of Babylonia and the Shaping of Medieval Jewish Culture*. New Haven: Yale University Press, 1998.

Chesnutt, Randall D., and Judith Newman. "Prayers in the Apocrypha and Pseudepigrapha." In *Prayer from Alexander to Constantine: A critical Anthology*, edited by Mark Christopher Kiley, 38-42. London and New York: Routledge, 1997.

Claussen, Carsten. *Versammlung, Gemeinde, Synagoge: Das hellenistisch-jüdische Umfeld der frühchristlichen Gemeinden*. Göttingen: Vandenhoeck & Ruprecht, 2002.

Cohen, Shaye J.D. "Epigraphical Rabbis." *Jewish Quarterly Review* 72, no. 1 (1981): 1-17.

Cohen, Shaye J.D. *The Beginnings of Jewishness: Boundaries, Varieties, Uncertainties*. Berkeley: University of California Press, 1999.

Collar, Anna. *Religious Networks in the Roman Empire: The Spread of New Ideas*. Cambridge: Cambridge University Press, 2014.

De Lange, Nicholas. "The Hebrew Language in the European Diaspora." *Te'uda* 12 (1996a): 111-137.

De Lange, Nicholas. *Greek Jewish Texts from the Cairo Genizah*. Tuebingen: Mohr-Siebeck, 1996b.

De Lange, Nicholas. "Jewish Use of Greek in the Middle Ages: Evidence from Passover Haggadoth from the Cairo Genizah." *The Jewish quarterly Review* 96, no. 4 (Fall 2006): 490-497.

Del Valle, Carlos. "Sobre las lenguas de los judios en la Espana visigoda y al-Andalus." *Sefarad* 63, no. 1 (2003): 183-193.

Dreyfus, Francois. "The Scales Are Even." *Tarbitz* 52, no. 1 (1982): 139 [Hebrew].

Edrei, Arye, and Doron Mendels. "A Split Jewish Diaspora: Its Dramatic Consequences." *Journal for the Study of the Pseudepigrapha* 16, no. 2 (2007): 91-137.

Edrei, Arye, and Doron Mendels. "A Split Jewish Diaspora: Its Dramatic Consequences II." *Journal for the Study of the Pseudepigrapha* 17, no. 3 (2008): 163-187.

Edrei, Arye, and Doron Mendels. *Zweierlei Diaspora: Zur Spaltung der antiken Juedichen Welt.* Goettingen: Vandenhoeck & Ruprecht, 2010.

Edrei, Arye, and Doron Mendels. "A Split Jewish Diaspora Again – A Response to Fergus Millar." *Journal for the Study of the Pseudepigrapha* 21, no. 3 (2012): 305-311.

Edrei, Arye, and Doron Mendels. "Reaction to Fergus Millar's article 'A Rural Community in Late Roman Mesopotamia, and the Question of a 'Split' Jewish Diaspora'." *Journal for the Study of Judaism* 43, no. 1 (January 2012): 78-79.

Edrei, Arye, and Doron Mendels. "Why Did Paul Succeed Where the Rabbis Failed?" In *Jesus Research: New Methodologies and Perceptions (The Second Princeton-Prague Symposium on Jesus Research).* Vol. II, edited by James H. Charlesworth, 361-399. Grand Rapids, Michigan: William B. Eerdmans Publishing Company, 2014.

Edrei, Arye, and Doron Mendels. "Preliminary Thoughts on Structures of 'Sovereignty' and the Deepening Gap between Judaism and Christianity in the First Centuries C.E." *Journal for the Study of the Pseudepigraph* 23, no. 3 (2014)" 215-238.

Eliav, Yaron. "The Matrix of Ancient Judaism: A Review Essay of Seth Schwartz's *Imperialism and Jewish Society 200 BCE to 640 CE.*" *Prooftexts* 24 (2004): 116-128.

Eliav, Yaron. "Jews and Judaism 70-429." In *A Companion to the Roman Empire,* edited by David S. Potter, 565-586. Oxford: Blackwell, 2006.

Elitzur, Shulamit. *Wherefore Have We Fasted? 'Megilat Taanit Batra' and Similar Lists of Fasts.* Jerusalem: World Union of Jewish Studies, 2007 [Hebrew].

Felix, Yehudah. *Talmud Yerushalmi Masechet Shevi'it.* 2 vols. Jerusalem: Rubin Mass, 1980 [Hebrew].

Fine, Steven. *Art and Judaism in the Greco-Roman World, Toward a New Jewish Archaeology.* Cambridge: Cambridge University Press, 2005.

Fiensy, David A. "Prayers, Hellenistic Synagogal." In *Anchor Bible Dictionary*, edited by David N. Freedman, 5 vols., 450-451. Garden City, NJ: Doubleday, 1992.

Fleischer, Ezra. "On the Beginnings of Obligatory Jewish Prayer." *Tarbiz* 59 (1989-1990): 397-441 [Hebrew].

Fontaine, Jacques. "Education and Learning." In *The New Cambridge Medieval History.* Vol. 1, edited by Paul Fouracre, 735-759. Cambridge: Cambridge University Press, 2005.

Freidman, Mordechai A. "And So Far, the Scales are Balanced." *Tarbitz* 54, no. 1 (1984): 147 [Hebrew].

Frishman, Asher. *The Early Ashkenzi Jews: Since their Settlement in North-West Europe to the First Crusade.* Tel-Aviv: Hakibbutz Hameuchad, 2008.

Funkenstein, Amos. "Changes in the Patterns of Christian Anti-Jewish Polemics in the 12th Century." *Zion* 33, no. 3-4 (1968): 125-144 [Hebrew].

Funkenstein, Amos. "Basic types of Christian anti-Jewish polemics in the later Middle Ages." *Viator* 2 (1971): 373-382.

Gafni, Isaiah M. *Land Center and Diaspora: Jewish Constructs in Late Antiquity.* Sheffield: Sheffield Academic Press, 1997.

Gamble, Harry Y. *Books and Readers in the Early Church: A History of Early Christian Texts.* New Haven and London: Yale University Press, 1995.

Geula, Amos. "Lost Aggadic Works Known only from Ashkenaz." PhD diss., The Hebrew University of Jerusalem, 2006 [Hebrew].

Gilat, Yitzhak D. *R. Eliezer Ben Hyrcanus – A Scholar Outcast.* Ramat-Gan: Bar-Ilan University Press, 1984.

Gilat, Yitzhak D. "The Drasha and the Reading of the Torah in the Synagogue on the Sabbath." In *Jews and Judaism in the Second Temple, Mishna and Talmud Period (in Honor of Shmuel Safrai)*, edited by Isaiah Gafni and Aharon Oppenheimer, 266-278. Jerusalem: Yad Izhak Ben Zvi, 1993 [Hebrew].

Goldenberg, David. "The Halakhah in Josephus and Tannaitic Literature: A Comparative Study." *Jewish Quarterly Review* 67 (1976): 30-43.

Goldschmidt, Daniel. *The Passover Haggadah: Its Sources and History.* Jerusalem: Bialik Institute, 1960 [Hebrew].

Goodblatt, David. *"Medinat Hayam"* ("The Coastal District"). *Tarbiz* 64 (1994-1995): 13-37 [Hebrew].

Goodblatt, David. *Elements of Ancient Jewish Nationalism.* New York: Cambridge University Press, 2006.

Goodman, Martin. "Jews and Judaism in the Mediterranean Diaspora in the Late Roman Period: Limitations of Evidence." In *Judaism in the Roman World, collected Essays*, edited by Martin Goodman, 233-259. Leiden: Brill, 2007.

Goodenough, Erwin R. *Jewish Symbols in the Greco-Roman Period.* 12. New York: Pantheon Books, 1965.

Grabbe, Lester L. "Aquila's Translation and Rabbinic Exegesis." *Journal of Jewish Studies* 33 (1982): 527-536.

Greenberg, Moshe. "Tefilah." In *Encyclopaedia Biblica.* Vol. 8, 896-922. Jerusalem: Bialik Institute, 1982 [Hebrew].

Grossman, Avraham. *The Early Sages of Ashkenaz: Their Lives, Leadership and Works (900-1096).* Jerusalem: Magnes Press, 1982 [Hebrew].

Gruen, Erich S. *Diaspora: Jews amidst Greeks and Romans.* Cambridge, MA: Harvard University Press, 2002.

Hallevy, A.A. "The Scales Are Even." *Tarbitz* 52, no. 3 (1983): 514 [Hebrew].

Heinemann, Joseph. *Prayer in the Period of the Tanna'im and the Amora'im: Its Nature and its Patterns.* Jerusalem: Magnes Press, 1966 [Hebrew].

Henshke, David. *'Mah Nishtannah': The Passover Night in the Sages Discourse.* Jerusalem: Magnes Press, 2016.

Herr, Moshe David "The End of Jewish Hellenistic Literature: When and Why." In *The Jews in the Hellenistic-Roman World Studies in Memory of Menachem Stern*, edited by Isaiah Gafni et al., 361-375. Jerusalem: The Zalman Shazar Center for Jewish History and The Historical Society of Israel, 1996 [Hebrew].

Hezser, Catherine. *Form, Function, and Historical Significance of the Rabbinic Story in Yerushalmi Neziqin.* Tübingen: Mohr-Siebeck, 1993.

Ilan, Tal. "Die Juden im antiken Rom und ihr kulturelles Erbe." In *"Wie schön sind deine Zelte Jacob, deine Wohnungen Israel!" (Num 24,5): Beiträge zur Geschichte jüdisch-europäischer Kultur,* edited by Rainer Kampling, 47-78. Frankfurt/Main, Peter Lang, 2009.

Inkpen, Andrew C. and Eric W.K. Tsang. "Social Capital, Networks and Knowledge Transfer." *Academy of Management Review* 30, no. 1 (2005): 146-165.

Jacobs, Martin. *Die Institution des Juedischen Patriarchen.* Tuebingen: Mohr- Siebeck, 1995.

Jacoby, D. "Greek Jewish Texts from The Cairo-Genizah – Lange, 1996." *Byzantinische Zeitschrift* 91 (1998): 110-112.

Jeremias, Joachim. *Jerusalem in the Times of Jesus.* London: SCM Press, 1969.

Jobes, Karen H., and Moises Silva. *Invitation to the Septuagint.* Grand Rapids: Baker Academic, 2001.

Kasher, Aryeh. "Jerusalem as a 'Metropolis' in Philo's National Consciousness." *Cathedra* 11 (1980): 45-56 [Hebrew].

Katz, Steven T., ed. *The Cambridge History of Judaism* IV. Cambridge: Cambridge University Press, 2006.

Katzoff, Ranon. "The Laws of Rabbi Eliezer in Ancient Rome." In *Torah Lishma: Essays in Jewish Studies in Honor of Professor Shamma Friedman,* edited by David Golinkin, Daniel Sperber, Menahem Schmelzer, Mordechai Akiva Friedman, and Moshe Benovitz, 344-357. Ramat Gan: Bar Ilan University Press; The Jewish Theological Seminary of America and the Schechter Institute of Jewish Studies, 2007 [Hebrew].

Kister, Menahem. "Romans 5:12-21 against the background of Torah-Theology and the Hebrew usage." *Harvard Theological Review* 100, no. 4 (2007): 391-424.

Klein, Samuel. *Eretz Yehuda.* Tel Aviv: Dvir, 1939 [Hebrew].

Kohut, Alexander. *Aruch Completum (Arukh ha-Shalem).* Vol. 1. Wien-Berlin: Selbstverlag, 1926 [Agraphos].

Kurtzer, Yehuda A. "What Shall the Alexandrians Do? Rabbinic Judaism and the Mediterranean Diaspora." PhD dissertation, Harvard University, 2008.

Lambert, Malcolm. *Medieval Heresy: Popular Movements from the Gregorian Reform to the Reformation.* 3rd. ed. Oxford: Blackwell, 2002.

Lazarovsky, Ayelet. "*Midrash Shemot Rabbah, Parshat Mishpatim,* Scientific Edition and Discussion of Stories." Master's thesis, The Hebrew University of Jerusalem, 2005.

Levine, Lee I., ed. *The Synagogue in the Late Antiquity.* Philadelphia: American Schools of Oriental Research, 1987.

Levine, Lee I. "Unity and Diversity in Ancient Judaism: The Case of the Diaspora Synagogue." In *The Jews in the Hellenistic-Roman World: Studies in Memory of Menahem Stern,* edited by Isaiah Gafni, Aharon Oppenheimer, and Daniel R. Schwartz, 379-392. Jerusalem: The Zalman Shazar Center for Jewish History, 1996 [Hebrew].

Levine, Lee I. *The Ancient Synagogue: The First Thousand Years.* New Haven: Yale University Press, 2000.

Licht, Jacob Shalom. "Hitsonim u-Genuzim." *Encyclopaedia Biblica* 5 (1978): 1104-1105 [Hebrew].

Lieberman, Saul. *Greek and Hellenism in Jewish Palestine.* Jerusalem: Bialik Institute, 1962 [Hebrew].

Lieberman, Saul. *Tosefta Ki-Fshutah: A Comprehensive Commentary on the Tosefta.* Vol. V, *Order Mo'ed, Tractate Rosh Hashanah.* New York: Jewish Theological Seminary in America, 1955-1988 [Hebrew].

Lieberman, Saul. *Tosefta Ki-Fshutah: A Comprehensive Commentary on the Tosefta.* Vol. V, *Order Mo'ed, Tractate Erubin.* New York: Jewish Theological Seminary in America, 1955-1988 [Hebrew].

Lieberman, Saul. *Tosefta Ki-Fshutah: A Comprehensive Commentary on the Tosefta.* Vol. VII, *Order Nashim, Tractate Nezirut.* New York: Jewish Theological Seminary in America, 1955-1988 [Hebrew].

Lieberman, Saul, ed. *The Tosefta: According to Codex Vienna with Variants and a Brief Commentary.* New York and Jerusalem: The Jewish Theological Seminary of America, 1970 [Hebrew].

Linder, Amnon. *The Jews in Roman Imperial Legislation.* Detroit: Wayne State University Press; Jerusalem: Israel Academy of Sciences and Humanities, 1987.

Linder, Amnon. *The Jews in the Legal Sources of the Early Middle Ages.* Detroit: Wayne State University Press; Jerusalem: The Israel Academy of Sciences and Humanities, 1997.

Lotter, Friedrich. "Die Grabinschriften des lateinischen Westens als Zeugnisse jüdischen Lebens im Übergang von der Antike zum Mittelalter (4.-9. Jahrhundert)." In *Jüdische Gemeinden und ihr christlicher Kontext in Kulturraeumlich vergleichender Betrachtung*, edited by Christoph Cluse, Alfred Haverkamp, and Israel J. Yuval, 87-147. Hannover: Verlag Hahnsche Buchhandlung, 2003.

Maimonides. *Responsa.* Vol. 2, edited by Joshua Blau. Jerusalem: Sumptibus Societatis Mekize Nirdamin, 1986 [Hebrew].

Mantel, Hugo D. *Studies in The History of The Sanhedrin ("Mehkarim be-Toldot ha-Sanhedrin").* Tel Aviv: Dvir, 1969 [Hebrew].

Mendels, Doron. *The Rise and Fall of Jewish Nationalism.* 2nd ed. Grand Rapids: Eerdmans, 1997.

Mendels, Doron. *Identity, Religion and Historiography.* Sheffield: Sheffield Academic Press, 1998a.

Mendels, Doron. "Pagan or Jewish? The Presentation of Paul's Mission in the Book of Acts." In *Identity, Religion and Historigoraphy*, 394-419. Sheffield: Sheffield Academic Press, 1998b.

Mendels, Doron. *The Media Revolution of Early Christianity.* Grand Rapids: Eerdmans, 1999.

Mendels, Doron. *Why Did Paul Go West? Jewish Historical Narrative and Thought.* London: Bloomsbury Publishing, 2013.

Merchavia, Chen. *The Church Versus Talmudic and Midrashic Literature [500-1248].* Jerusalem: Bialik Institute, 1970 [Hebrew].

Millar, Fergus. "A Rural Jewish Community in Late Roman Mesopotamia, and the Question of a 'split' Jewish Diaspora." *Journal for the study of Judaism* 42 (2011): 351-374.

Narkis, Bezalel. "Pharaoh is Dead and Living at the Gates of Hell." *Jewish Art* 10 (1984): 6-13.

Neeman, Y. "Tumat Eretz ha-Amim: Hebet Histori." *Sinai* 2 (1997): 56-61 [Hebrew].

Niehoff-Panagiotidis, Johannes. "Review of Nicholas de Lange, *Greek-Jewish Texts from the Cairo Genizah."* *Suedost-Forschungen* 58 (1999): 474-480.

Nitzan, Bilha. *Qumran Prayer and Religious Poetry.* Lieden: Brill, 1994.

Noga-Banai, Galit. *The Trophies of the Martyrs.* Oxford: Oxford University Press, 2008a.

Noga-Banai, Galit. "Between the Menorot: new Lights on a Fourth-Century Jewish Representative Composition." *Viator* 39, no. 2 (2008b): 21-48.

Noy, David. *Jewish Inscriptions of Western Europe.* Vol.1, *Italy (excluding the City of Rome), Spain and Gaul.* Cambridge: Cambridge University Press, 1993.

Noy, David, and Hanswulf Bloedhorn. *Inscriptiones Judaicae Orientis III. Syria and Cyprus.* Tuebingen: Mohr Siebeck, 2004.

Noy, David, Alexander Panayotov, and Hanswulf Bloedhorn. *Inscriptiones Judaicae Orientis I. Eastern Europe.* Tuebingen: Mohr Siebeck, 2004.

Oppenheimer, Aharon. " 'Love of Mordechai or Hatred of Haman'? Purim in the Days of the Second Temple and Afterwards." *Zion* 62 (1997): 408-418 [Hebrew].

Oppenheimer, Aharon. "Rabban Gamliel of Yavneh and his Circuits of Eretz Israel." In *Between Rome and Babylon: Studies in Jewish leadership and society.* Tübingen: Mohr Siebeck, 2005.

Pucci Ben Zeev, Miriam. "The Uprising in the Jewish Diaspora, 116-17." In *The Cambridge History of Judaism* IV, edited by Steven T. Katz, 93-104. Cambridge: Cambridge University Press, 2006.

Rabello, Alfredo Mordechai. "Justinian and the Revision of Jewish Legal Status." In *The Cambridge History of Judaism* IV, edited by Steven T. Katz, 1073-1076. Cambridge: Cambridge University Press, 2006.

Rajak, Tessa. "The Jewish Community and its Boundaries." In *The Jewish Dialogue with Greece and Rome,* 335-354. Leiden: Brill, 2001.

Rappaport, Uriel. "The Jews of Eretz-Israel and the Jews of the Diaspora During the Hellenistic and Hasmonean Periods." *Te'uda* 12 (1996): 1-9 [Hebrew].

Rapoport, Hillel, and Avi Weiss. "In-group Cooperation in a Hostile Environment: An Economic Perspective on Some Aspects of Jewish Life in (Pre-modern) Diaspora." In *Jewish Society and Culture: An Economic Perspective*, edited by Carmel U. Chiswick, Tikva Lecker, and Nava Kahana, 103-128. Bar-Ilan University Press, 2007.

Ravitzky, Aviezer. " 'Way Marks to Zion': The History of an Idea." In *The Land of Israel in Medieval Jewish Thought*, edited by Moshe Hallamish and Aviezer Ravitzky, 1-39. Jerusalem: Yad Izhak Ben-Zvi, 1991 [Hebrew].

Reif, Stefan C. *Judaism and Hebrew Prayer.* Cambridge: Cambridge University Press, 1993.

Rokeah, David. "A New Onomasticon Fragment from Oxyrhynchus and Philo's Etymologies." *Journal of Theological Studies* 19 (1968): 70-82.

Rokeah, David. *Philonis Alexandrini De Providentia-De Decalogo Hypothetica.* Jerusalem: Magnes Press, 1976 [Hebrew].

Rosenfeld, Ben Zion. "The Crisis of the Patriarchate in Eretz Israel in the Fourth Century." *Zion* 53 (1988): 239-257 [Hebrew].

Rosenthal, Abraham. "Torah She'al Peh Ve-Torah Mi-Sinai - Halakhah U-Ma'aseh." In *Mehqerei Talmud: Talmudic Studies Dedicated to the Memory of Professor Eliezer Shimshon Rosenthal.* Vol. 2, edited by Moshe Bar-Asher and David Rosenthal, 448-489. Jerusalem: Magnes Press, 1993 [Hebrew].

Rouwhorst, Gerard. "Jewish liturgical Traditions in early Syriac Christianity." *Vigiliae Christianae* 51 (1997): 36-93.

Roth-Gerson, Lea. "Similarities and Differences in Greek Synagogue Inscriptions of Eretz –Israel and the Diaspora." In *Synagogues in Antiquity, edited by* Arye Kasher, Aharon Oppenheimer, and Uriel Rappaport, 133-146. Jerusalem: Yad Izhak Ben-Zvi, 1987 [Hebrew].

Runia, David T. *Philo in Early Christian Literature, A Survey.* Assen and Minneapolis: Van Gorcum and Fortress Press, 1993.

Rutgers, Leonard V. *The Hidden Heritage of Diaspora Judaism.* 2nd ed. Peters: Leuven, 1998.

Safrai, Shmuel. *Pilgrimage at the Time of the Second Temple.* Tel-Aviv: Am Ha'ssefer Publishing, 1965 [Hebrew].

Safrai, Shmuel. *In Times of Temple and Mishnah: Studies in Jewish History.* Vols. 1-2. Jerusalem: Magnes Press, 1994 [Hebrew].

Safrai, Shmuel. "Contacts between the Leadership of the Land of Israel and the Hellenistic and Eastern Diasporas in the First and Second Centuries." *Te'uda,* 12 (1996): 23-38 [Hebrew].

Safrai, Shmuel, and Ze'ev Safrai. *Haggadah of the Sages.* Jerusalem: Carta, 1998 [Hebrew].

Sanders, E. Parish. *Jewish Law from Jesus to the Mishnah.* London: SCM Press; Philadelphia: Trinity Press International, 1990.

Schreckenberg, Heinz. *Die Christlichen Adversus-Judaeos-Texte und ihr Literarisches und Historisches Umfeld (1.-11. Jh.).* 2nd. ed. Frankfurt am Main: P. Lang, 1990.

Schwartz, Daniel R. *The Second Book of Maccabees.* Jerusalem: Yad Izhak Ben-Zvi, 2004 [Hebrew].

Schwartz, Seth. *Imperialism and Jewish Society: 200 BCE to 640 CE.* Princeton, NJ: Princeton University Press, 2001.

Scribner, Robert. "Germany." In *The Reformation in National Context*, edited by Robert Scribner, R. Porter, and M. Teich, 4-29. Cambridge: Cambridge University Press, 1994.

Shalit, Abraham. *Kadmoniot Ha'yehudim.* Vol. 1. Jerusalem and Tel-Aviv: Bialik Institute, 1967 [Hebrew].

Silberg, Moshe. *Talmudic Law and the Modern State.* Translated by Ben Zion Bokser. New York: Burning Bush Press, 1973.

Simonsohn, Shlomo. "The Hebrew Revival Among Early Medieval European Jews." *American Academy for Jewish Research II,* Salo Baron Jubilee Volume (1974): 831-858.

Simonsohn, Shlomo. *The Jews of Italy: Antiquity.* Leiden: Brill, 2014.

Sterk, Aron C. "*Latino Romaniotes*: The Continuity of Jewish Communities in the Western Diaspora, 400-700 CE." *Melilah, Manchester Journal of Jewish Studies,* 9 (2012): 21-49.

Stern, Menahem. *Greek and Latin Authors on Jews and Judaism.* 2 vols. Jerusalem: Israel Academy of Science and Humanities, 1976-1980.

Stow, Kenneth. *Jewish Dogs: An Image and its Interpreters: Continuity in the Catholic-Jewish Encounter.* Stanford: Stanford University Press, 2006.

Sussmann, Yaakov. "Torah she-Beal Peh Peshutah ke-Mashma." In *Mehqerei Talmud: Talmudic Studies Dedicated to the Memory of Professor Ephraim E. Urbach.* Vol. 3, edited by David Rosenthal and Yaakov Sussmann, 209-305. Jerusalem: Magnes Press, 1993 [Hebrew].

Sznol, Shifra. "Medieval Judeo-Greek Bibliography: Texts and Vocabularies." *Jewish Studies* 39 (1999): 107-132.

Sznol, Shifra. "A Comparative Lexical Study of Greek and Latin Words in Late *Midrashim* and Judeo-Greek Vocabularies from Biblical Translations and Glossaries." *Erytheia* 26 (2005): 87-103.

Sznol, Shifra. "A Mishnaic Hebrew Glossary in Judeo-Greek from Cairo Gniza." *Massorot: Studies in Languages Traditions and Jewish Languages* 8-9 (2006): 225-252 [Hebrew].

Tabory, Joseph. *Jewish Festivals in The Time of the Mishnah and Talmud.* Jerusalem: Magnes Press, 1995 [Hebrew].

Tabory, Joseph. *The Passover Ritual Throughout the Generations.* Tel-Aviv: Hakkibutz Hame'uchad Publishing House, 1996 [Hebrew].

Ta-Shma, Israel M. *Talmudic Commentary in Europe and North Africa.* Vol. 1. Jerusalem: Magnes Press, 1999 [Hebrew].

Ta-Shma, Israel M. "Hebrew-Byzantine Bible Exegesis ca. 1000 from the Cairo Geniza." *Tarbiz* 49, no. 2 (2000): 247-256 [Hebrew].

Toch, Michael. "Mehr Licht: Eine Engegnung zu Friedrich Lotter." *Zeitschrift fuer Geschichte und Kultur der Juden* 11 (2001): 470-474.

Toch, Michael. "The Jews in Europe 500-1050." In *The New Cambridge Medieval History.* Vol. 1, edited by Paul Fouracre, 547-570. Cambridge: Cambridge University Press, 2005.

Tov, Emanuel. *The Text-Critical use of the Septuagint in Biblical Research.* 2nd. ed. Jerusalem: Simor, 1997a.

Tov, Emanuel. *The Textual Criticism of the Bible: An Introduction.* 2nd. ed. Jerusalem: Bialik Institute, 1997b [Hebrew].

Tov, Emanuel. "The Text of the Hebrew/Aramaic and Greek Bible Used in the Ancient Synagogue." In *The Ancient Synagogue from its Origin until 200 C.E.: Papers Presented at an International Conference at Lund University, October 14-17, 2001*, edited by Birger Olsson and Magnus Zetterholm, 237-259. Stockholm: Almqvist & Wiksell, 2003.

Trebilco, Paul R. *Jewish Communities in Asia Minor.* Cambridge: Cambridge University Press, 1991.

Urbach, Ephraim E. *The Sages: Their Concepts and Beliefs.* Jerusalem: Magnes Press, 1978.

Urbach, Ephraim E. *The World of the Sages: Collected Studies.* Jerusalem: Magnes Press, 1998 [Hebrew].

Van der Horst, Pieter W. *Saxa judaica loquuntur, Lessons from Early Jewish Inscriptions.* Leiden: Brill, 2014.

VanderKam, James C. *Introduction to Early Judaism.* Grand Rapids: William B. Eerdmans Publishing Company, 2001.

Vico, Giambattista. *La Scienza Nuova* ("The New Science"). Translated by Thomas Goddard Bergin and Max Harold Fisch. Ithaca, New York: Cornell University Press, 1948.

Wasserstein, Abraham. "Calendaric Implications of a Fourth – Century Jewish Inscription from Sicily." *Scripta Classica Israelica* 11 (1991-1992): 162-165.

Wasserstein, David J. "Langues et frontieres entre Juifs et musulmans en al-Andalus." In *Judios y musulmanes en al-Andalus y el Magreb. Contacos intelectuales*, edited by M. Fierro (Madrid, 2002).

Zeitlin, Solomon. "The Liturgy of the First Night of Passover." *Jewish Quarterly Review* 38 (1948): 431-460.

Zfatman, Sara. *The Jewish Tale in the Middle Ages: Between Ashkenaz and Sepharad.* Jerusalem: Magnes Press, 1993 [Hebrew].

Zipor, Moshe. *The Septuagint Version of the Book of Genesis.* Ramat-Gan: Bar Ilan University Press, 2005 [Hebrew].

Zunz, Leopold. *Ha'drashot Be'Yisrael ve'Hishtalshelutan Ha'historit.* Jerusalem: Bialik Institute, 1954 [Hebrew].

CHAPTER FIVE
# Western Jewry After 70 CE
BERACHYAHU LIFSHITZ[*]

## Introduction

In a stimulating article, my colleagues Arye Edrei and Doron Mendels[1] argue that a language barrier caused a fundamental separation of the Jews of *Eretz Yisrael* (the Land of Israel) who were exiled to the West from both the Jewish communities of *Eretz Yisrael* and the East in general. Whereas the Western Jews spoke Greek, their brethren in the East spoke Hebrew and Aramaic. Consequently, the Jews of the West had no access to the rabbinic *halakhah* that materialized after the destruction of the Temple, especially since this *halakhah* was transmitted orally. In their view, the language barrier prevented the continued unity of the two communities, and that lack of communication effectively sealed the fate of a large segment of Jewry, leading to its severance from the eastern center and its ultimate disappearance. Summing up, the authors enumerate a list of questions still awaiting response in view of their conclusions regarding the decisive importance of the language divide. These include the question of the degree to which the sectarian schism impacted the results that they indicated.

This article responds to the challenge posed by the authors. My claim is that even the partial and fragmented evidence we have indicates a struggle over Jewish identity that persisted into the post-destruction period until towards the end of antiquity. The struggle was not only a response to the challenges posed by the surrounding non-Jewish society, but was also an internal struggle within Judaism and between the Jewish communities. Using their examples, fortified by my own assumption as stated, I will attempt to illuminate this rather obscure period from a different perspective. Due to the lack of concrete, substantial, or clear written evidence we must rely on circumstantial evidence. The preponderance of evidence produces a picture that is more consistent with the position indicated here, and the evidence itself is more plausible in light of our aforementioned assumption. Firstly, a few comments challenging the assumption that language differences were the cause of the split between the diasporas, after which we will examine the facts in view of the well-known dispute over the source of authority for a *pesika* (ruling) and *poskim* (decisors) in the *halakhah*.

## Language

Indeed, "life and death are in the power of the tongue."[2] A language not shared may hinder ongoing communication, but language differences are not an insurmountable barrier where there is a sincere desire to communicate. For example, the Alexandrian Jews spoke Greek, but nonetheless retained close ties with the rabbis of *Eretz Yisrael* and their teachings.[3] Alexandrian Jews directed halakhic questions to the scholars of *Eretz Yisrael*, and occasionally questioned them regarding "matters of wisdom."[4] *Battei din* (rabbinical courts) in Alexandria were relied upon by the sages of *Eretz Yisrael*[5] and the Alexandrians translated the Bible into Greek (Septuagint) for their own needs, as well as other literature that was written in Hebrew in *Eretz Yisrael*. Those who accept the yolk of obligation will read and declaim texts despite not understanding them.[6] Those with the ability will learn the language, which is so singularly important – the language in which their sacred texts are written and orally transmitted. The less talented ones will demand a translation, and if they are many, their wishes will become a public demand from the leaders to attain a proper translation. There were those in the West who not only failed to request a translation of the rabbinic 'Oral Law', but in fact had displayed absolutely no interest in learning the rabbinic doctrine and rejected it altogether, as we will observe below.

On the other hand, even a shared language does not ensure consensus between different communities. The fierce disputes between the Pharisees and the Sadducees were presumably conducted either in Biblical Hebrew or in *Leshon Hachamim* (Mishnaic Hebrew) with which both parties were highly familiar. This was similarly true for the Pharisees' disputes with other sects. The sectarian secession from the Pharisees in general, or the Temple in the case of the Qumran community, was not the result of lingual differences. Even the battles between the Rabbis and the Karaites in different periods and places were conducted in common languages that were familiar to all – Hebrew, Aramaic, or Arabic. Nonetheless, each party categorically rejected the other party's basic positions and beliefs as well as its halakhic-philosophic literature. To a certain extent this was also the case in the dispute between the Geonim of Babylonia and those of *Eretz Yisrael*. Josephus certainly knew both Hebrew and Aramaic by reason of his birth and adulthood in *Eretz Yisrael*, until the period after the revolt. Nonetheless, for the most part, the *halakhah* he describes in his writings was not the rabbinic *halakhah* that crystallized after the destruction but rather the biblical *halakhah*, though he could easily translate the rabbinical traditions into Greek.[7] Thus, though they all spoke the same language, their words and religious worlds were not uniform.

The rival parties did not regard their dispute as an "internal matter" between members of the same camp who despite their differences shared a common starting point, not impaired by their dispute. The dispute concerned the foundations of the system, and those who did not agree with them placed themselves outside the rival's camp. Each party claimed the crown of "the True Judaism," at the exclusion of its rival. The teachings of one were not the teachings of the other. On the contrary, each party banned the holy writings of its rival, referred to it as "external literature" – "apocrypha" – which was prohibited for reading. Reading in the scroll of *Hodayot* (The Thanksgiving Hymns), for example, gives the express feeling of hatred towards the other party.[8] Regarding the sages' position, Prof. Rabin maintained that:

> Pharisee Judaism responded with the banning of an entire series of external writings that were created and read by the mother-sect from which the two groups split off... It is interesting that according to R. Akiva, a person who reads external books has no part in the World to Come, which is precisely the threat enunciated against sinners in matters of faith. This view fortifies the view that the banning of books was part of the battle against heretics... I surmise that the prohibition has its roots in the stylistic similarity of the external books and the writings of the Qumran sect... it was easy to intersperse them with sectarian material. Furthermore, the stylistic similarity created the danger of the members of the sect presenting their books as legitimate external literature.[9]

Both groups only cited the rival group's teachings for polemic purposes and in order to refute both the particulars and the general rules of the other group, not in order to observe and fulfill them as with respect to their own traditions. The separation of the rival communities was the result of this ideological schism.

The same phenomenon also characterized another confrontation that lasted for about a hundred years, three of them soaked in blood according to Talmudic testimony. I refer here to the dispute between *Beth Shammai* (House of Shammai) and *Beth Hillel* (House of Hillel).[10] Both parties claimed that the *halakhah* – all of it – was in accordance with them, until the Heavenly voice came forth with the well-known, yet ambiguous declaration: "Both are the words of the living God, and the *halakhah* is in accordance with the House of Hillel." The result was that the teachings of *Beth Shammai* were also considered part of the *halakhah*, in the general sense, but the accepted practical *halakhah* in all matters was in accordance with *Beth Hillel*.[11] Indeed, in respect of *Beth Hillel* it states that they would teach their own traditions as well as those of *Beth Shammai*.[12] From this affirmative statement we can also infer the reverse, that *Beth Shammai* did not follow this policy and their own teaching had no evidence of *Beth Hillel* because *Beth Shammai* did not recognize its authority, thus regarding it as "external literature." *Beth Hillel* also retracted on a number of occasions in order to rule in accordance with *Beth Shammai*, whereas *Beth Shammai* never did this. Despite this, and perhaps as a result, it was determined that where teachings of *Beth Shammai* contradicted those of *Beth Hillel* they were not considered Mishnah (=*halakhah*)! Some scholars have surmised that the rulings of *Beth Shammai* were actually close to those of the sects,[13] and were it not for the paradoxical compromise of "Both are the words of the Living God," a similar schism would have emerged between *Beth Shammai* and *Beth Hillel*.

To a certain extent, the halakhic division between the Pharisees and the sects lead to physical separation in the form of the sect-members' voluntary exile (Damascus/Judean Desert) and also to a lingual schism, as claimed by Haim Rabin when he addressed the question of "Why were the non-biblical Scrolls written in biblical language?":

> We must ask: What caused the two sects in the same period to develop two so totally different linguistic styles such as the language of the sages (*leshon hachamim*) and the biblical language, in order to express their ideas?...

The halakhic matters in the Scrolls are written in the same language as the non-halakhic matters yet the language is totally different from the halakhic language used by the sages. On the other hand, the earliest dicta of the rabbinic literature are those of aggadah, but their language is nonetheless similar to *leshon hachamim*, which is totally distinct from the language of the Scrolls. We have two groups that used different forms of Hebrew for all of their literary goals.[14]

It would be a distortion to claim that the Mishnaic sages were unable to do what the authors of the Scrolls did... the linguistic differences between the Scrolls and the Talmudic literature cannot be explained against the background of differences in background and education. At all events, we have a number of examples of poetry at the end of the tannaitic period, from which we can see that the sages knew how to write in biblical language when the opportunity arose. The conclusion is that the sages decided to use their own particular language (*leshon hachamim*) by choice and not by necessity.[15]

Whether they intended it or not, the use of pure biblical language in the "publications" of the Qumran sect served the same purpose (of separation – B.L.).[16]

To the extent that the Mishnah was earlier, it bears more indications of biblical language, and where there is a later version of an earlier tradition, the later version will be more rabbinic in its style... this process widened the linguistic gap between the rabbinic doctrine and that of the heretics and indeed this may have been their intention.[17]

Rav Saadia Gaon too claimed that the Karaites not only refused to accept the *halakhah* of the Mishnah and the Gemara, but also its language,[18] and accordingly, they used a different language more akin to biblical language. It is, however, abundantly clear that these differences in language did not prevent communication between the groups in these very same "languages." Ultimately, there were slight variations in the same basic language, and they originated against the background of the desire to be separate in language too. This separation was purely symbolic, but extremely important from the parties' perspective.

The Hellenistic-Roman world was a turbulent one. There was a proliferation of diverse beliefs and opinions among the various nationalities and population groups. They all aspired at the very least to preserve their identity, but also invested tremendous efforts in the dissemination of the features that distinguished them from the surrounding world, both near and far. Jerusalem was a central city in which these kinds of debates were generally conducted in its streets. It was populated by Jews, Greeks, Hellenists, Pharisees, and the members of other sects – Sadducees, Beitusim, Essenes, and Christians – all living side by side.[19] Quite probably among these groups themselves there was a considerable degree of nuances and diversity, and the relations between them were characterized by familiarity and separation, and varying degrees of uniformity and pluralism.[20] Naturally, it cannot be claimed that there was a language barrier between these groups.[21] Disputations with others fulfilled the internal need to convince members of the group of their superiority and the external goal of persuading and subjugating others by way of debate. This need, in addition to communal life per se, lead the members of all the groups (even if not all the members of the groups, without the same degree of knowledge) to familiarize themselves with the languages used by the Jews and the Greeks living in the same general environment.[22] The division as such, and the recognition of the divisions and the borders that created it and which delicately separated one group from another, was not the result of non-communication due to the inability to communicate with one another. Quite the opposite: communication was imperative, as stated, in order to explain the differences in the intellectual "merchandise" of each particular group, both internally and externally. At the same time, neither group taught the teachings of the other, and where possible, imposed reciprocal bans on competing literature. This factor per se, i.e. the need to impose bans and imprecations on each other, indicates that in its absence there would have been no language barrier that prevented the casual perusal of 'external' literature. It is further stressed that the struggle over language might well lead to a schism, but this was only on the condition that language was regarded as a cultural value and as a generator of identity. It is difficult to argue that the Western Jews regarded Greek as their "Holy Tongue." Notwithstanding its importance, being the language in which their everyday life was conducted, both amongst themselves and with their neighbors, this did not oblige them to eschew any connection with or use of Hebrew or Aramaic.

## Multi-factionalism

The totality of sources dealing with Western Jewry gives the impression that in these countries too Judaism was diversified.[23] In other words, it was also split into a variety of sects. Naturally, laymen, both in *Eretz Yisrael* and in the diaspora, were not always fully aware of their "sectarian affiliation," and we may similarly presume that most of them maintained a similar, common system of customs and commandments. On the other hand, the spiritual elites and establishment were well aware of the factors that separated them, and they competed, for influence, both on other Jews and upon the ruling powers. This was the case in *Eretz Yisrael* itself, and it was similarly the case in the various exiles.

There were Jews who were forcibly exiled to the West as a result of the conquest, the rebellion, and as a means of subjugation. There were others who voluntarily uprooted themselves from their homeland and birthplace due to problems of livelihood. Presumably, the members of both of these groups accurately reflected their places of origin at the time of their departure.[24] Their religious characteristics, observance of the commandments, world view, customs, and entire lifestyles were cultural-religious baggage that they had taken to the land of the Edomites, fixed in the form they remembered from their time in the land of their forefathers. Knowledge, common sense, and experience teach us that they clung to these memories and as far as possible meticulously preserved them as a means of establishing and maintaining their unique identity among the other surrounding peoples, and in order to preserve the connection with their remote, beloved homeland. Evidently, the Jewish exile after the destruction of the Temple, much of which was from the Galilee, as well as the Jewish exile immediately after the Great Revolt, was not entirely Phariseeic. This was still before the final Pharisees' victory and the victory of Yavneh and its internalization by most of the dwellers of *Eretz Yisrael* (see below). Prima facie, we may assume the opposite – that many of the exiles were actually identified with other groups that were part of the people, even if only by force of their religious practice and doctrine. The facts indicated by Edrei and Mendels are consistent with this picture because they are interpreted as the identifying characteristics of the different groups.

## Sages in the West

Edrei and Mendels agree that there were rabbis in the West who subscribed to the positions of the rabbis of *Eretz Yisrael*. As mentioned, they probably did not constitute a majority of the Jewish population in these countries, but neither were they a negligible minority. A number of testimonies attest to the existence of a specific group with a clearly defined rabbinic identity. There is the testimony of R. Eliezer b. R. Jose that when he was in Rome he taught a particular *halakhah* concerning menstrual stains which were deemed as being impure, and when relating it to his colleagues they told him "You instructed well" (Tosefta Niddah 7:1). In another context, we learn about a particular *halakaha* concerning ritual baths that "the people of Asia came up to Yavneh for the Three Pilgrim festivals and on the third festival they even purified the hole of a pin. R. Eliezer b. Jose said: I taught this *halakhah* in Rome, and when I came to my friends they told me 'You instructed well'."[25] These laws were thus observed in the practical sense and the testimonies indicate the strictness with which they were observed by residents of "Asia" as well as by those in Rome. It may reasonably be presumed that they had ritual baths even though they have not yet been discovered through archeological digs, and they strictly ensured that they would be built in accordance with the *halakhot* (religious laws) that were codified in Yavneh.[26]

We also know about the journeys of the rabbis to Rome, one of which is related to in the Midrash:

> Rabban Gamliel, R. Joshua, R. Eliezer, and R. Akiba that they went to Rome and taught there: The ways of God are not as those of man, who makes a decree enjoining others to do a thing whilst he does nothing; God not being so. There happened to be a sectarian *(min)* there, who accosted them as they were going out with a taunt: Your words are only falsehood... They replied: Wretch... He replied... They replied... He replied... They replied...[27]

Presumably, this homily was given at an assembly of Jews, among whom there was also "one heretic." The rabbis of that time as a rule tended to intersperse their homilies with halakhic matters.[28] The issue is similarly shown in *Yebbamot* 91a, in the name of Ben Yasyan of a proselyte who said that R. Akiba sat on this bench when he made two statements: "a proselyte may marry the wife of his maternal brother" (*halakhah*), and "And the word of the Lord came unto Jonah…" (*aggadah*), and his statements were preserved (even if in a distorted fashion) for a long time afterwards. Consequently, there are grounds for assuming that those listening also understood R. Akiba's teachings. In this context, it is immaterial if we assume that the homily was in Hebrew – that there were Jews in the West who spoke Hebrew or in Greek – meaning that the Yavneh rabbis knew Greek in order to enable dealings with the representatives of the government, and the Jews, or that they used an interpreter.[29] The above cited source describes an interpretative-theological debate between the Yavneh rabbis and a sectarian. It likewise enables us to assume any of these assumptions, and we therefore have satisfactory and efficient communication between the rabbis and the Western Jews. Concededly, this kind of evidence is not in great supply, and its extent may even be further reduced due to problems concerning the validity and authenticity of the texts, some of which have been viewed of as "*aggadot*" (fables) and no more. However, despite the prevailing skepticism in contemporary research regarding the possibility of inferring historical conclusions from "historical *aggadah*," this approach does not have any blanket justification. The evidence we have contains a kernel of solid truth.

Evidence of a rabbinic community in Rome, which on the face of it accepted the authority of the *Eretz Yisrael* rabbis, is found in the case of Todos, the man of Rome whom the *Tosefta* relates that,

> R. Jose said: Todos of Rome accustomed the people of Rome to take young sheep on Passover eve and make them into offerings. They said to him: He was very near supplying them with sacred meat outside [the Temple], for they called them "pessachim."[30]

The *Jerusalem Talmud* adds the following information:

> The sages sent and said to him: Were you not Todos, would we not put you under a ban? [What does Todos mean? He would send maintenance [support] for the rabbis.] Do you not end up bringing

the public to eat sacrifices (*kodashim*) outside [the holy precinct], "for whoever brings the public to eat sacrifices outside [the holy precincts) should be put under a ban.[31]

And the *Babylonian Talmud* contains additional information, which (as usual) originated in *Eretz Yisrael*:

> The scholars asked: Was Todos the man of Rome a great man or a powerful man? – Come and hear: This too did Todos of Rome teach: What [reason] did Hananiah, Mishael and Azariah give that they delivered themselves for the sanctification of the [Divine] name to the fiery furnace? They argued *a minori* to themselves: if frogs... R. Jose b. Abin said: he cast merchandise into the pockets of scholars. For R. Johanan had said: Whoever casts merchandise into the pockets of scholars will be privileged to sit in the Heavenly Academy.[32]

From all of the above, the following matters at least may be inferred: Todos was a leader, he instructed on halakhic matters in Rome;[33] the rabbis of *Eretz Yisrael* regarded themselves as authorized to excommunicate Todos; and there were those in Rome who would accept that authority and would have complied with such an excommunication (even if in the particular case of Todos they might not have complied). In other words, the relationship between the Roman Jewish community and the rabbis of *Eretz Yisrael* was one of subordination, and the latter regarded themselves as responsible to prevent harm to the diaspora community at large.[34] Todos was familiar with rabbinic-style homilies, as indicated not only by the explicit Talmudic record, but also from the tradition that he authored other homilies which merited the approval of the rabbis. Todos supported rabbinic scholars who were found worthy in the eyes of the *Eretz Yizrael* rabbinic leadership. Concededly, the text does not indicate whether he supported scholars in Rome or in *Eretz Yisrael*. According to the former option, we have evidence of the existence of a class of scholars living in the western diaspora, and presumably they had an established place for study and instruction for others. A notable personage in this category was Matya ben Heresh, who initially lived in *Eretz Yisrael*, but subsequently went to live in Rome and established a *yeshiva* (house of study) there, assuming that there were grounds for thinking that it would be successful and without concern for a language barrier.[35] He asked R. Shimeon b. Yohai a question in aggadah during the latter's visit to Rome (bYom 53a) and in halakhah (bMeil 17a). The principal halakhah was quoted in the matter of saving a life (*pikuah nefesh*) as overriding the Sabbath was cited in his name (mYom 8:6). R. Ishmael, son of R. Yossi, heard from him "three things" (bYom 84a). His *Beth Din* (rabbinical court) in Rome was considered as an eminent court, "a good/important court" to litigate in (bSan 32b), from which we can infer that there were those who needed to resort to this *Beth Din*. From this we may further infer that in the same location there were also other *battei din* that were less recommendable, as a result of which we have a halakhic ruling regarding the *battei din* which should be preferred over those other *battei din*. In the *Tosefta*[36] we read about R. Akiba who was coming from the sea and saw "a ship struggling in the waves and I was saddened at the fate of a disciple of sages (*talmid hachamim*) who was on board. And when I came to Caesarea-Mazaca in Cappadocia I saw him in my session, asking questions regarding *halakhah*." Rabbi Akiba's boat, like the one of the disciple of sages who came to ask him questions in halakhah, sailed from the West to the East. The conclusion is that there were scholars in the West, and they had students who learnt from them and who also came to learn the halakhot of the "rabbinic" R. Akiba. A similar situation prevailed in Caesarea-Mazaca.

R. Gamaliel, R. Eliezer b. Azariah, R. Joshua, and R. Akiba sailed in a ship from Brindisi, which is in south-east Italy (mErub 4:1), and we also know that there were sages in other places in western Europe. All of this supports the conclusion that they were not involved only in money gathering. Money gathering was always done after a scholar had given a public sermon, followed by a request from the listening public to donate generously to the bearers of a message and tradition. The very willingness to donate attests to the feelings of respect and honor that were accorded to them by at least some of the Jews in those places. Naturally, most of the evidence to this effect comes from Rome and not from the smaller places, but still, there are no grounds for rejecting other fragments of knowledge and its implications, all attesting to the existence of communities and individuals who abided by the traditions of Yavneh and the teachings of the rabbis. These included people who went to *Eretz Yisrael* and asked questions about *gittin* (issues dealing with divorce) that were delivered in "the lands of the sea."

In the Jerusalem Talmud (Sanhedrin 7:11, 25d), the following passage appears:

> A story: R. Eliezer, R. Joshua and Rabban Gamliel went up to Rome, they came to a <u>certain place</u> and found children making little piles [of dirt], saying: "The people of the land of Israel make this sort of thing." And they say: "This is heave offering, and that is tithe." The rabbis said: It's likely that there are Jews here. They came to <u>into one place</u> and were received there by a certain person... He said to them, "I have an old father and he has made a decree for himself that he will never go out of that small room until he will see the sages of Israel. They said to him, "Go and tell him, 'Come out here to them, for they are here'."

This paragraph indicates that in their trips to Rome the sages also traveled to other unidentified and remote locations to which Jews had been exiled. We learn that games were used as a means of inculcating children with traditions concerning the commandments connected to the land, which are only obligatory in *Eretz Yisrael*. We may further surmise a fortiori that the same methods also served in inculcating the other universally applicable commandments too. We also learn that these isolated Jews anticipated the arrival of the rabbis, and presumably their anticipations were based on past experience.

We may further conjecture that the letters sent by R. Gamliel and the Elders to the "Greek Diaspora and all of the other Exiles of Israel"[37] may have been written in Aramaic for all of the places, which would imply the addressees' ability to read and understand Aramaic. Alternatively, even if the letters were written to each nation in its own vernacular, it would imply that there was no language barrier to communication between them.

As we are told, R. Simon b. R. Gamliel taught that the Pentateuch could be translated only into Greek, although other rabbis were of the opinion it could be translated into any other foreign language as well. The reason which was supplied by the *Amoraim* for the preference of the Greek language is that it is a beautiful language and a very punctuate one and so the Pentateuch would be translated into it without missing any of its details.[38] It seems that such a ruling must be the result of a perfect knowledge and acquaintance with the Greek language, and others as well, to its nuances. We may suppose that the knowledge of R. Gamliel himself of these languages was not very much different.[39]

However, it is clear either way that there were those to whom these letters were addressed, for whom the letters were meaningful and could be understood, and who were obedient to their orders. This enables us to accept with greater equanimity the fact that *gittin* of Jews came from the distant lands of the sea, and that the rabbis addressed them and their unique problems.

It should also be noted, naturally, that all of these sources are from the tannaitic period, whereas we do not have this kind of information from the amoraic period. Does this mean we can assume that there was some kind of conclusive change in this respect? We will see below that this was not the case.

## Rabbanites and Members of other Sects in the West

As mentioned before, the members of the western diaspora were divided into a multiplicity of groups, just like their brothers in the East. Furthermore, their community was likewise varied, consisting not only of "rabbinic" Jews but also of a large non-rabbinic group. Evidently, as noted, the non-rabbinic groups subscribed to the views of the Sadducees or those ascribed to other extant sects, especially of the sects that were active in *Eretz Yisrael* before the destruction of the Temple, and who remained a part of those groups even after the exile. At the very least one could say that they had these "tendencies." It bears emphasis that their halakhic traditions may have been developed and comprehensive, extending far beyond the limited scripturally based *halakhah*, just as is the case with the Sadducees' *halakhah*. A number of identifying features typify the members of these sects, all of which characterize non-rabbinic positions. Edrei and Mendels cited most of these, but argued that they were the result of the language barrier and used the examples as proof of their theory. We argued above that there are really no language barriers where there is a desire to know, and a need to preserve and observe religious obligations. However, the non-"rabbinic" circles had no interest in translating this literature into Greek or any other language familiar to them. The contents of this literature were certainly known to them, but from their perspective it constituted "external literature" just as the rabbinic circles considered literature in the hands of non-rabbinic circles as "external literature." The Sadducee "people of the west" (i.e. those who were not "rabbinic" according to the teachings of

Yavneh) had Greek pseudepygraphic and apocryphal literature. In contrast to the Alexandrian Jews who translated the accepted literature from *Eretz Yisrael* that was written in Hebrew, viewing it as legitimate, this part of the Western Jewry discontinued the translation of literature originating in Israel because they regarded it as not authorized and thus 'external'. This was an expression of a denial of authority and not of a lingual barrier, and it precluded any attempt to overcome the lingual barriers to the extent that they existed. The result was the creation of separate "Jewish bookshelves" for each of the two communities, which in and of itself widened the gap even further. As is well known, the Sadducees rejected the manner of creation and the binding authority of the Oral Law, as it was created by the Pharisees, and after them the rabbis, or transmitted to them, from generation to generation. On the other hand, it is clear that the Pharisees, and the rabbis in their wake, whose principal feud with the Sadducees pertained to the question of the prohibition of writing the Oral law, were obviously unable to accept any kind of written format of the Oral Law, especially not in a translated format, and not even that of the Mishnah after its compilation.[40]

The victory of the rabbinic position was by no means self-evident, even in *Eretz Yisrael*, and as such there is no reason to suppose that this would have occurred in the western diaspora. In this context, we concur with the words of Tessa Rajak:[41]

> If the Jewries of the Graeco-Roman Diaspora were far removed from the refined debate taking place in Palestine (or Babylon), they need not have accepted the combination of premises from which those debates started and, therefore, would have had as little interest in tolerant rabbinic positions as in hardline ones. In their lives, self-separation for the achievement of purity may not have been an issue in the same terms.

The desire and need to maintain the religious positions that the exiles came with, and the distance from the Jewish center in *Eretz Yisrael*, engendered the crystallization and rigidifying of these positions and the difficulty in refuting or rejecting them. Against this background one can understand the conflict between the two approaches and the steadily growing gap between them.

Naturally, one cannot ignore the fact that life in the Hellenist world, followed by life under Christian propaganda, could have led to a relaxing in the intensity of religious observance, especially as it had developed under the tutelage of the Yavneh Sages. But this is not a sufficient explanation to what was really going on, as we will see below.

## Scriptures, Translation, and the Study of Torah and Halakhah

The dispute over the Greek translation of the Bible provides an example of this. A prevalent assumption in recent scholarship is that "The Translation of the Seventy" – the Septuagint – was the work of Alexandrian Jews intended for local Jews whose language was Greek. The translation is literal and it is almost devoid of interpretations based on rabbinic exegesis. Hints as to the existence of this influence are few and highly tenuous.[42] The rabbis attempted to provide them with a translation that competed with the Septuagint, namely the translation of Akilas:

> The sages attempted to give them (=Jews in the Hellenistic-Roman diaspora) Greek scriptures, which would closely resemble the Hebrew traditional scriptures, as adopted by the "Sages of Yavneh". The reason was that the first translation — of the "Septuagint" — was a far cry from the version accepted in *Eretz Yisrael* at that time (conceivably they may even intended to provide a scriptural text in Greek, in order to counter Christian interpretations, which relied on the Septuagint version.) The extant paragraphs and quotations prove the extent to which they were loyal to the Hebrew scriptures, even at the expense of Greek language and doctrine … to the extent that we can judge based on the numerous testimonies, the Yavneh sages were successful in inculcating the translation of Akilas in all of the diasporas (even though the former translation was not entirely eclipsed).[43]

Indeed, this translation adds elements of *midrash halakhah* and *aggadah* which emerge from Scriptures, and it was praised by the sages for being "the truth of the Torah" that "found expression in Akilas' translation, which was primarily intended to distance the readers (Jews in the diaspora and proselytes) from any affinity to the Septuagint."[44] The translation of Akilas was thus a weapon in the rabbinic battle against their disputants, who adhered to the literal meaning of Scriptures, or more precisely, who deviated from the rabbinic homilies. Hence, the *Tannaim* did not abandon the western communities, but actually attempted to win them over with their doctrine.

Not surprisingly, the question of translation was ultimately addressed by Justinian, who had to decide on the matter:

> When it became clear to us that they (=the Jews) were disputed amongst themselves, we did not permit them to remain in a state of anarchy without any decision. And from the applications (entreaties to the Emperor) submitted to us we learn that there were those who adhered exclusively to Hebrew… and on the other hand there are those who are also prepared to use Greek…. We therefore commanded that for the Jews who so desired, it would be permitted to read the Scriptures in their synagogues in Greek for those who agreed or in their ancestral language (=Italian), or quite simply in any of the other languages… We also order that there will be no freedom of speech for their interpreters, who use Hebrew exclusively in order to distort it so that it accords with their will, exploiting the public's ignorance to hide their malice.
>
> Furthermore, those who read in Greek will use the Septuagint, which is the most accurate of all and is thus preferable to others… but in order to avoid appearing as though we have prohibited the other translations to them, we also give permit them to use Akilas' translation… and in a number of places it differs considerably from the Septuagint.
>
> What they refer to as <u>Mishnah</u> we absolutely forbid, because it is not included in the Holy Scriptures and was not transmitted by the prophets, but is rather an invention of people who generated extensive prattle from a purely human source and it is devoid of any Divine inspiration…
>
> And if any of them attempt to introduce vanities with heretical content, in view of their denial of the Resurrection, or the Final Day of Judgment, or the divinity of the angels, it is our desire that these people be expelled from all places…[45]

This law is relatively late and already incorporates Christian considerations, but it contains elements pertaining to the various foundations of the dispute within the Jewish community. Similarly, it would seem that the dispute was not limited to the time of Justinian, and that the law under discussion was actually a response to an ancient and <u>ongoing</u> dispute, which for various reasons we only know of from external sources and which only came before the Caesar at that time. This confirms our basic thesis: there were a number of active sects between whom there were acrimonious disputes.

One of the disputes concerned the exclusivity of <u>reading</u> in Hebrew, or "quite simply in any of the other languages."[46] The argument is an all embracing one, which could have taken place in all Jewish diasporas, and it indicates that even in places where Hebrew was not the *lingua franca* there were those who demanded that the reading [of Scriptures] be limited to Hebrew. A second dispute concerned the prohibition of <u>exegesis</u> of Scriptures, conducted specifically in Hebrew, and which allegedly exploited the local population's ignorance of the language. The third dispute was over which <u>translation</u> was preferable. The arguments presented and the decision made indicate that the Septuagint was regarded as being more accurate and literal than the translation of Akilas, which differed from the Septuagint in a number of places. As noted, the differences were not just lingual and were primarily expressive of an underlying doctrinal dispute. Nonetheless, the legislator permitted synagogical reading from the Akilas translation, as opposed to exegesis transmitted in Hebrew, which was absolutely interdicted. The difference is, apparently, that with the translation one could not claim it purported to exploit the ignorance of the language and totally mislead, because the translation in its entirety was written in Greek, including its exegetical elements. (Incidentally, the wording of the edict indicates that apart from Akilas there were also other different translations.)[47]

The Mishnah on the other hand, was absolutely proscribed, even for Hebrew speakers. Though, prima facie, the teaching of Mishnah was also forbidden to the speakers of other languages, even if taught in languages other than Hebrew, for the reasons mentioned in the law itself, which negate its <u>actual validity</u>, given its human, non-Divine, source. This was a clearly Sadducean claim[48] that was actually accepted by the Caesar. This kind of dispute is highly appropriate for the West, where the rabbanites had still not prevailed.[49] We are also aware of the Deutorosis, which is usually regarded as the Mishnah, appears in the writings of non-Jews and was attributed to the Jews of all the diasporas.[50] As mentioned above, in Justinian's decision he refers to the reciprocal claims of the <u>Jews</u> regarding this matter. Either way, we learn from this that there were teachers of *mishnayot* (pl. Mishnah, a collection of its units) and *halakhot* within the (western) Jewish communities and those who were interested could learn the *halakhot* of the rabbis. As stated, there were those who refused to do so because it was not a divine halakhah, not because of any language barrier.

This is also the case with the third dispute regarding the "Sadduceean opinions" as they were referred to by the Christians, relating to the denial of the World to Come, the reality of the resurrection of the dead, and the creation of the Angels. These views that had long since been attributed to the Sadducees[51] were still extant in Justinian's time, and he was no doubt aware of them.[52] Justinian's decision was an effective compromise between the competing claims of the two rival movements.

Ultimately, this was a struggle over the control of knowledge, and the authority only secondary. The Emperor wanted to ensure that the Jews would have direct access to the right books and to derive maximum benefit therefrom. Between the lines, we can discern one group's refusal to learn the Mishnah (in the generic sense) of the other group, while on the other hand the authors of the 'Mishnah' were keenly set on instructing and teaching these dissenters. Allegedly, they willfully and intentionally attempted to do this precisely in the language that they did not understand so as to exploit their ignorance in that language.

Thus, direct access to Scriptures was of great importance to the Sadducees of the West, just as it was to their brothers in other countries. They regarded the written Torah as being available and accessible to all who wished to come and learn it, and so they had no need for the Pharisees/rabbinic teachings of the Torah. In this sense, their claims resembled those of the Sadducees in the days of King Yannai.[53] Reading the Torah was not just a ceremonial reading on the Sabbaths and Festivals, but also meant reading for the purpose of deducing commandments directly from the text, a duty that applied and was practiced on the other days of the week too.[54] And so, as mentioned by Edrei and Mendels, the Jews were known precisely as the fulfillers of the Torah of Moses, and not necessarily as the fulfillers of the innovations of the rabbinic teachings and the subsequent Torah of Yavneh.[55]

The method of learning directly from Scriptures written in the Septuagint translation is also evidenced in the *Collatio Legum Mosaicurum et Romanum*. This is an essay that compares the Jewish *halakhah* to Roman law. The laws of the *halakhah* are presented by way of biblical verses, "but it did not make use of the other biblical books. The essay does not contain so much as a single paragraph from the Prophets or the Writings or from halakhic literature such as the Mishnah or any of the other sources, such as the Gospels."[56] Contemporary scholarship attributes this composition to Jewish authorship,[57] and dates its composition to the period before Christianity became the official religion of the Roman empire, in other words before 313 C.E.[58] The author's teaching, which apparently attempted to refute the criticism of the Jews and of their Torah (in this sense he resembled Josephus, whose essay "Against Apion" mentions the proximity of Jewish beliefs and opinions to those of the Romans), differed from the Torah of the Land of Israel.

Indeed, the Roman authorities were not content to learn the Torah of the non-rabbinic members of the West, so they sent commissioners to *Eretz Yisrael* in order to learn directly from the source "what their Torah was."[59]

As mentioned, there were Jews in the West who continued the Sadducee teaching, knowingly and intentionally rejecting the rabbinic form of learning together with its halakhic implications. There was therefore a formidable struggle between two formats of *halakhah*, and our interpretation of what happened in the western diaspora may provide a paradigm for understanding the state of affairs in *Eretz Yisrael*: there too there is a dearth of detailed knowledge of the history of the struggle between these two factions.

To the extent that rabbinical leadership in *Eretz Yisrael* grew stronger, and their teachings proliferated, it became increasingly alienated from those of the Diaspora Jews whose religious beliefs and *halakhot* they rejected as not being a part of its ancestral tradition. We still have no clear knowledge of the process of hegemonization of the rabbinic tradition in *Eretz Yisrael*, therefore we cannot say with certainty whether and to what extent organized non-rabbinic groups continued to operate in *Eretz Yisrael*. Here too, it may reasonably be presumed that there were definitely such groups in the Land of Israel. Initially they were relatively larger but they diminished in time. We may also assume that members of the western diaspora maintained contact with them.

## Payment of Taxes

Our acceptance of these assumptions sheds light on attempts that were finally crowned with success to cancel the obligation to pay taxes to the House of the Patriarch and the central leadership in *Eretz Yisrael*. In this context, Edrei and Mendels claim that the Diaspora Jews were distanced from the center as a result of lingual differences, which lead to a lack of identification with the center and bitterness regarding the tax burden imposed on them. But here too, the fundamental cause was the *halakhah*. The fact is that the Alexandrian Jews participated in fulfilling the commandment of the Half Shekel despite their being speakers of Greek and despite the existence of Honyo's Temple. In the words of Gedaliah Alon:

> Despite the existence of Honyo's Temple, like other Diaspora Jews, the Jews of Egypt too would annually bring the Half Shekel to Jerusalem. Philo waxes eloquently as he describes the ceremonial solemnity with which the Half Shekel was collected, the emissaries chosen and the contribution sent off to Jerusalem, conveying the ardent emotion that accompanied the fulfillment of this national-religious commandment.[60]

When the Temple was destroyed, these funds were given to the Sanhedrin:

> It would seem then, that Rabban Gamliel and his High Court can be credited with establishing a format that lasted for generations and that kept the Jews of the Diaspora involved in maintaining the central institutions of the Jewish people as a whole. It is a reasonable assumption that this format was based on the old half-shekel poll-tax which Jews had been sending to Jerusalem for centuries while the Temple stood, as a means of participating in the maintenance of the Holy city and the Holy sanctuary. After the destruction of the Temple Rabban Gamliel may very well have determined that the revived Sanhedrin ought now be entitled to receive the equivalent of this ancient tax.[61]

This fundraising for support of the sages was reinstated in place of the Half Shekel, and the Sadducees and members of other sects opposed this annual tax. In their view, the Half Shekel was imposed on a person once in his lifetime at the most, and conceivably, the obligation itself was a one-time obligation that had been imposed when the nation was building the sanctuary in the desert.[62] The 'Saduccean' faction in the western diaspora was able to maintain the memory of this opposition to the payment of the Half Shekel and its replacements. It may be assumed that support for the renewed center was not immediately presented as a religious duty, which replaced the Half Shekel of the Temple, but rather as a national duty that came to fortify the national center and its renewal. Consequently, the members of the diaspora were not initially aware of the new religious regime that was being introduced in Israel, and so they were initially prepared to pay this tax to the *Sanhedrin*. However, the motives of the *Sanhedrin* and of the Yavneh teachings gradually became more overt, and to the extent that the call to pay the tax was explained as a replacement for the Half Shekel, the opposition to its applicability and to paying it grew.[63]

## The Sanctification of the Month

This opposition was most definitely an expression of distrust in the new *Beth Din* and its rulings. If this hypothesis is correct, then it can serve as a paradigm to illuminate the subject of the sanctification of the new moon and the determination of the festivals in both of the centers. On this point, Edrei and Mendels pointed out that it is more likely that when the *Eretz Yisrael* lookouts held fire-torches to proclaim the day of the sanctification of the month, they headed exclusively towards the East, in other words, to Babylonia and not to the western countries.[64] This was the permanent practice and there is no evidence of any change in this custom over the years. In other words, there is nothing to indicate the existence of an original custom to light up the West, which was subsequently discontinued. This omission cannot be attributed to ignorance of the Hebrew or Aramaic language. The torch was a consensual sign, with its own independent connotation, and there was no difficulty in understanding its intention. As such, another explanation is required to explain the phenomenon. Firstly, another question must be answered. How did the western Jews observe the festivals? Conceivably, the date of the sanctification of the month became known to them through the emissaries that were sent to the diaspora, because this was the method used for the East too after the Kuthim distorted the calculation by lighting their own torches in order to mislead the other parts of the people.[65] If this was the case, then it is conceivable that the fear of "distortion" in the West was extensive and perhaps even of earlier antiquity due to the divided nature of the Jewish population dwelling there, which included those who disputed the method of calculating the new moons. Accordingly, it was impossible to rely on the accurate conveying of this information, which was entirely dependent on the good will of the lookouts. Furthermore, these sects may have included those for whom sanctification in accordance with viewing and the *Beth Din*'s declaration was totally superfluous, because their calendar was the solar calendar, which was set and by definition calculated in advance.[66] This may also have been a more "regular" and less fundamental dispute that related specifically to the authority of the *Beth Din* in Jerusalem, because this was precisely the dispute that had emerged earlier on between the Jews of *Eretz Yisrael* and Babylon, all of whom spoke the same language, in the period of R. Yehuda Hanasi,[67] as well as during the period of the *Geonim*. It would seem that all of these factors played a part, and that it cannot be reduced only to the issue of the different languages. It is unlikely that the *Eretz Yisrael* sages turned their backs on their brothers in the West and felt no responsibility towards them. The sages would certainly have done all they could to establish their own normative-halakhic hegemony, but on the other hand, they also fought against their opponents, and where there was nothing to be done, they did nothing.

### The Passover Haggadah

As proof of their approach that the absence of a common language caused the divide, Edrei and Mendels cite the absence of a translation of the Passover *Haggadah* into Greek. But it is extremely difficult to explain this absence purely in terms of a lingual barrier. The text of the *Haggadah* is particularly brief, and there was no problem in its transmission and translation, even if the text had not existed in writing and was repeated only orally, which was not the case.[68] It is not just a miracle that there were found in the Cairo Genizah some manuscripts of the *Haggadah* (admittedly, from a later time) written in Hebrew letters but in the Greek language! Where there is a need, a will, and acceptance, a proper solution will usually be found.

Furthermore, there would have been no difficulty in remembering it by heart had someone actually desired to do so. Additionally, the entire purpose of this text was to serve as chapter headings for the oral account, and "He who expounds at length on *yetziat mitzraim* [=exodus from Egypt] is praiseworthy."

In fact, the entire Passover Eve ceremony was structured precisely in the form of a Hellenistic symposium to create a framework for this kind of study, and this framework was obviously also familiar to the western Jews.[69] Only a small part of the *Haggadah's* text was regarded by the rabbis as mandatory, specifically the biblical verses! In fact, also the Karaite *Haggadah* included only biblical verses and presumably was thus submitted to writing.[70] The exodus from Egypt was a story that all could talk about, including the western Jews who had their own traditions written in Greek. According to the Book of Jubilees, "and all of Israel remained eating the flesh of the Passover and drinking wine and praising and blessing and glorifying the Lord, the god of their fathers." Hence, it was only natural that a some kind of ritual framework would crystallize for that praise and glorification. All of this indicates that everyone had some kind of text and that the failure to accept rabbinic *Haggadah* has its roots in the fact that this *Haggadah* was a rabbinic innovation of the post-destruction rabbis, whose authority, intentions, and actions were undesirable in the eyes of a significant portion of the western diaspora. This assumption explains what actually happened.

Two additional considerations buttress this conclusion. First, opposition to the *Haggadah* of the Yavneh Sages was rooted in the fact that it was based on homily, i.e. the exegesis of biblical verses, which in fact is the *Haggadah*.[71] As mentioned, the early text did not include homilies, and consisted exclusively of the biblical verses. The transition to homilies characterizes the Pharisees and accentuated the intentions of the reformers. These intentions were the basic point of controversy with those who were opposed to the doctrines of the Pharisees, and subsequently of Yavneh.[72]

The second consideration was that the sages structured Passover as a festival of the ongoing covenant between God and his people, obliging every person in every generation to regard himself as though he himself had left Egypt. The Book of Jubilees on the other hand, which was widely familiar to all the of western diaspora, endorsed a different conception regarding the festival of *Shavuoth* (Pentecost) as the festival of the renewal of the covenant:

> The festival of *Shavuoth* was regarded as the date of the establishment
> of the first covenant and the renewal of the oath of the covenant in
> the Heavens and Earth… but it deviated from the accepted format,
> which ascribed historical primacy to the Sinai covenant, and the

absolute renewal of this standing, but avoided indicating an exact date for the Sinaitic revelation or connecting it to the *Shavuoth* festival. The Jubilees tradition [on the other hand] regards this covenant as the last in the chain of covenants all of which were contracted in the third month. All of the covenants are connected to weeks and the festival of *Shavuoth* (=oaths).[73]

In the rabbinic tradition, *Shavuoth* was subordinate to Passover and to the date of its determination according to the witnessing of the moon. In Jubilees, on the other hand, *Shavuoth* has a fixed date calculated in accordance with the first day after the Sabbath during Passover, and according to this view Passover is of less importance. There is therefore an inverse relationship between the two positions regarding the connection between Passover and *Shavuoth*. Those who had been accustomed to the Jubilees conception would not replace this perception for the position that became sanctified in post-destruction *Eretz Yisrael*. On the other hand, it may be assumed that the followers of the Yavneh Sages, like those who adopted the teaching of Todus of Rome regarding the burnt lamb, also observed the Passover in accordance with its new format and laws.

## The Beth Midrash

These deep disputes were also expressed in the phenomenon noted by Edrei and Mendels that there were no *yeshivot* and *battei midrash* (institutions for traditional religious study) in the West. As mentioned above it may be presumed that Matya ben Harash established, or attempted to establish a *yeshiva* in Rome, in accordance with the rabbinic custom. On the other hand, the accepted custom in the West was to study the commandments in the synagogue.[74] The distinction is essential because in the synagogue they preserved Temple ritual and sanctified the significance of the number seven and its multiples. This was not the case in the *Beth Midrash* (house of study), which sanctified the freedom of enquiry into all aspects of the *halakhah*. The *halakhah* of the *Beth Midrash* tradition was not transmitted exclusively to the priests who were close to God, but rather was given to the human being as such, and the condition for its study and transmission was human ability. Alternatively, according to another approach to the essence of the Oral Law, it was a tradition that originated at Sinai and was not necessarily given to the priests.[75] For the Sadducees the knowledge of the *halakhah* and its transmission was the legacy of an elite group of individuals, and was not open for general participation. They only taught the ways of performing the commandments. The Pharisees, on the other hand, disseminated the practical knowledge pertaining to the commandments in their homilies, but also taught the Torah and engaged in teaching the principles of ruling on halakhic matters (*pesikat halakhah*) for all those who were interested and able to do so, and also ordained their students to enable them to continue teaching and instructing all Jews.

## Prayer

This fundamental dispute may also explain the possible differences between the prayers of the two sects to the extent that they had divergent understandings of the origin, the purpose, and the meaning of prayer. The claim that the prayer was not originally written down is not persuasive,[76] and would seem to be incorrect and cannot be regarded as a reason for the emergence of the division. What source is there for the view that the prayers were not written? The Pharisees did not consider prayer to be "*halakhah*" but rather an obligation to say certain texts, and as stated, there is no obstacle to its being written down.[77] The various parts of the set prayer include portions from the Bible. What problem was there in putting these in writing? Moreover, the common view of the sages is that all parts of the prayers may be said in any language, certainly in Greek,[78] and the permission to translate assumes an already existing translation. All of the above precludes acceptance of the assumption that the absence of a translation prevented Western Jewry from adapting the prayers in the format established by the sages. In this context, too, the more reasonable assumption is that to the extent that we post-date the formal structuring of the fixed prayers to the post-destruction period, i.e. the Yavneh period, as Edrei and Mendels prove in great detail,[79] the easier it is to regard their rejection by that portion of western Jews as originating in their rejection of the authority, the intentions, and the acts of the rabbis who enacted them.

## Did the Western Jews Disappear?

Did the western diaspora disappear, as claimed by Edrei and Mendels? Are there grounds for assuming that the diaspora in its <u>entirety</u> converted to

Christianity under the influence of Christian indoctrination transmitted in the Greek language, with which they were familiar, without there having been any counter "rabbinic" propaganda? In our view, such an assumption is unfounded. In *Eretz Yisrael* and in Syria Jews converted to Christianity, and Christianity certainly had no monopoly over religious indoctrination. In these countries, Aramaic or Hebrew were spoken languages with which Jews were familiar, and hence even the rabbinic circles could attempt to confront and challenge the Christians in their own language. The Christian missionaries converted souls to their religion on the African continent when the local religious priests who knew the language were present. To think that one may change his well rooted religion, especially members of the elite, just because an apostle is speaking his language is a very unsatisfactory explanation for such an extreme act.

On the other hand, the rabbinic prohibition on the writing of the Oral Law placed them in an inferior position in the confrontation with Christianity, but the source of the inferiority was not the difficulties endemic to language barriers, which in effect did not exist. Rather, it was the fact that they were faced by Christians who had a written text as the principal tool for disseminating their religion.[80] For those accustomed to books, the preference was clear!

We may also raise the claim that Christianity regarded the Western Jewry as partners because of their mutual denial of the rabbinic authority. It was easier for Paul to persuade these Jews to abandon even the commandment of the Bible itself. Since they believed in divine revelation, it was also easier for them to accept the revelation of Jesus instead of the revelation which took place in the Temple, now destroyed. This was not at all the situation in the East where rabbinical authority prevailed, although even there we find Christians and Sadducees as well!

Concededly, there was definitely a phenomenon of conversion among western Jews, and there is no doubt that it was widespread, but it cannot be regarded as something novel. The conversion phenomenon was a recognized one, in all the locations. Christianity liberated Jews from the yoke of the commandments, and by their own claim, freed them from the status of "sinners" inhering by definition in the obligation to fulfill commandments. However, the central kernel of Jewry never disappeared, unless it was expelled from the land. The shaky margins (which occasionally were exceedingly broad) assimilated, and certain distinct groups seceded from the majority but did not assimilate. Just as language was not a real barrier to the performance of the commandments, so too, shared language was not a tool for easy conversion. The wall of religion that enveloped the Jews prevented this as far as possible. It separated them from the surrounding world and united them internally.[81] On the contrary, it may reasonably be presumed that internal rabbinic influence steadily grew and succeeded in bringing increasing numbers of laymen under its wings. These laymen were the people who in their own eyes were never clearly differentiated in a sharp and discernable form as belonging to one or another particular sect. As such, there was "internal assimilation" which originated in the ascendance and subsequent dominance of the rabbinic elite. This is what happened in the Land of Israel and it also happened in the West, during all the periods. The subject of conversion in the East to the religions of Persia and Babylonia, and later on to Islam, is a separate subject.

These western communities constituted the foundation of Italian Jewry and other communities in Europe.[82] Their teachings and their traditions – especially those of Ashkenaz (regions of northern Europe and Germany) – seem to be originated in *Eretz Yisrael*.

Of primary importance was the collection of customs that originated in the halakhic tradition of *Eretz Yisrael*. Needless to say, this collection of customs from *Eretz Yisrael* that we are discussing bears its title by virtue of its true historical origin and not in accordance with the declarations of those who subscribe to it. For the most part, the sources of the custom are not known, but even so we can prove quite clearly, beyond any reasonable doubt, that this indeed was the case.[83]

It is precisely the forgetting of the source that is important here, because it teaches us that it was not the result of rulings (*pesika*) by the book that they abided by, but rather in accordance with the traditions that they preserved from those days of struggle over religious identity, the entire source for which was in *Eretz Yisrael*.[84] The power of the prohibition of the writing of Oral Law and the guarding of the oral tradition transmitted by the spoken and not the written word, led to a situation in which the "Pharisee" members of the West avoided the writing of books, and ineluctably, they were not preserved. Incidentally, we similarly lack books of the Syrian Jews who spoke Aramaic, if there were such. Accordingly, it may be claimed that language was not the controlling factor. The controlling factor was the interest (or lack thereof) in adhering to a particular tradition, rabbinic or otherwise.

On the other hand, it appears that the western Jews did actually have their own books because many of them did not comply with the prohibition on writing the Oral Law. This indeed begs the conclusion that their books were not accepted by the rabbinic elite and were thus regarded as "external books." To the extent that the rabbinic influence grew, so too the books of the western Jews lost their relevance, and ultimately for lack of interest they sunk into oblivion.[85] To this we may add that to the extent that the rabbinic influence grew, so too the ban pronounced on these books and their offshoots, as "external books," became more entrenched.

We also have to bear in mind that western Jews did not write books including new *halakhot*. They were of the opinion that they, and the rabbis as well, were not authorized of doing it! They probably wrote manuals to instruct people on how to act and what to say. This kind of literature does not exist for a long time because of the wear and tear, as we do not find many old prayer books and *Haggadot*.

Nonetheless, the ways of the spirit are inscrutable. We know that part of the literature that originated in Western Jewry was actually preserved by the priests in their monasteries, and were mistakenly ascribed to the Christian.[86] We have also learnt of the connection between the Karaites and the pseudoepigraphic literature and that of the Qumran sects.[87] 'Sadducee portions' (=the Damascus Covenant) in Medieval writings were found in the Cairo Genizah. Suddenly we find ourselves exposed, together with Raabiya of the 14th century, to a unique *ketubba* (Jewish prenuptial agreement) that differs from all of the *kettubot* drafted in the Babylonian format, which indeed was a *ketubba* that originated in *Eretz Yisrael*.[88] There is similarity between the *haftarot* (a series of selections from the books of Prophets publicly read in synagogue) of the Italian custom and those of the Karaites,[89] many of whom had gathered in Turkey and in the areas of Byzantine. Possibly there are additional facts that point in the same direction.

Prof. Israel Ta-Shma directed our attention to the fact that the French sages used sources that originated in Greek-speaking Greece and Southern Italy.[90] For our purposes, particular importance is attached to Prof. Ta-Shma's study of the works of R. Moses the Preacher of Provence, which include pieces based on "external literature."[91] In the footsteps of other researchers,[92] he notes that the external Jewish literature was more extensive than we are used to thinking, some of it being based on the original literature of the Dead Sea Scrolls, which was in possession of the Byzantium Jews. According to Prof. Ta-Shma, that which remained was considerably broader than what was cited in the writings of Rabbi Moses the Preacher. What happened was that various homilies were censored and forgotten anew against the background of internal Christian controversies and in order not to appear as a heretic. However, it may be that the very retention of this "external literature" is salient for our purposes. Once the rabbis triumphed, the external literature was no longer constituted a mortal threat to the accepted canon.[93] This enabled at least some of the books to remain in the hands of the families, for whom it became their official literature, which they used as their accepted canon. The majority, however, continued to view these books as "external literature" and hence did not make extensive use of them thereof.

## Conclusion

The split between the Jewish communities did not occur against the background of divergent *emunot v'de'ot* (abstract beliefs and opinions), which were or could be sufficiently broad so as to accommodate people holding divergent views and belonging to different groups. In the same vein, the divisions between *Beth Shammai* and *Beth Hillel* were not rooted in conflicting halakhic rulings.[94] The argument between them was over the question of authority over halakhic issues, each group claiming "the *halakhah* goes according to us."

The prevalent opinion in research was that the destruction of the Temple lead to the diffusion of the Sadducees and their doctrine, together with all other sectarianism, in so far as the Temple was the focus for their thoughts and their rulings. The new world was therefore a monolithic one.[95] It does not seem reasonable that believers will abandon their belief because of the destruction of their religious center. Surely, there were people who committed suicide and lost their taste for life, as we are informed by the Talmud (bBB 60b), but most of the population moved on with their lives, adjusting themselves to the new reality and reinterpreting it according to their former beliefs. This is exactly what the Qumranic sect did when they left the Temple and turned to the dessert, they continued their spiritual life without the temple, which, for them, it felt as if it was destroyed.

Now, even though ultimately this was the case, we still do not know the exact pace at which things occurred. It may reasonably be presumed that those referred to as Sadducees and the other sects did not 'disappear' immediately. Our comments in this article may indicate that at least in the diaspora, a long way from the Temple, and even after its destruction, the sect did not disperse.[96] In fact it crystallized around its memory, and not necessarily of the actual, functioning Temple.[97] Furthermore, only a very small part of them had actually seen the Temple in its glory, and in fact it lived in a virtual, not real, memory. As such, the effect of the destruction was markedly less among these remote communities, and they were less prone to the influence of the rabbinic doctrines than the sectarians in *Eretz Yisrael*. Their disappearance as differentiated sects was a far more protracted process and no more dramatic than was the descent from the stage of history of the non-Rabbinic sects of *Eretz Yisrael*.[98]

As a matter of fact, we may say that in the days of the Emperor Julianus, in the fourth century, who promised the Jews to rebuild the Temple and already took practical steps towards the fulfillment of his will, Western Jewry was very much alive and vital. Christian sources tell us about the intensive activity that took place everywhere in the Roman Empire where Jews were marching toward Jerusalem, hoping to once again see the Temple which they cherished in their hearts and memory for three centuries.[99] Interestingly enough, we know nothing about the reaction in *Eretz Yisrael* itself. No reaction to the Emperor's letter to the Patriarch regarding this issue was preserved, not even in the Babylonian Talmud, the reduction of which was not yet finished, or in the later homilies.

Still, in the middle of the sixth century, bitter disputes took place between parties. Actually, these disputes were quite violent, and the Emperor Justinian was called to intervene in order to avoid anarchy! This was a religious battle that we read about that was still going on, and not, as Edrei and Mendels try to convince us, take place in the West or otherwise, disregarding the wording and the plain presentation of the issue, as it was always the manner of the Roman Emperor's decrees.

The need to reconstruct the existence of these groups occurred against the background of their omission from rabbinic literature,[100] and from the disappearance and the active silencing of their own literature. Incidentally, non-rabbinic literature in *Eretz Yisrael* did not fare better: has the literature of the 'non-rabbinic' residents of Israel survived? Their views and opinions ultimately survived only very minimally in the secondary literature of liturgical works, in the residuum of local customs and popular beliefs, and in the caves in the Judean desert, where they could not be reached by the rabbis and were preserved there until recently found.

The determinative forces that motivated the people of the period were religion and specifically, the choice of "the correct religion" or the correct nuances thereof. These forces had powerful political and social impacts. For the Jews, the *halakhah*, its commandments, and the right method of instruction were the authentic expression of the Jewish religion, but different streams within Judaism struggled over the birthright in terms of being the true representatives of the Law of Moses. The Oral Law in both of its manifestations was always the central point of contention between disputants. Even though these struggles molded the groups themselves, to a greater or lesser extent, the Oral Law always remained the hallmark of rabbinic Judaism,[101] and those who were defeated were either expelled from the camp or assimilated among the victors.

Somehow, and by still not fully known circumstances, rabbinic influence spread in Western Europe until rabbinic Judaism became the central and largest Jewish movement in the West. Again, the knowledge of Hebrew or Aramaic was not the reason for this phenomenon, but rather the result of it. Eventually, after five hundred years of an ongoing struggle, the rabbinic movement won the battle against the Sadducees and their religious ideas in Western Europe.

It seems the epigraphic, archeological, and documentary evidence at our hands may suggest that what happened is as follows: the Jews were living in the West throughout all the days of Antiquity.[102] Some communities knew more Hebrew than others. Some were affiliated with the rabbinic movement and knowledgeable about rabbinic traditions and teachings, some were not, and some were even hostile to the rabbinic movement and its representatives. Some were influenced by the Eastern Jewry by way of commercial relations and some were not. These parties of the Western Jewry influenced one another, as they were both Jews and spoke the same language, until the rabbinic side, backed up by the Jews in *Eretz Yisrael* and Babylon, won.

The history of Western Jewry tells us about the major failure of the rabbinic movement in the tannaitic and amoraic periods to impose their halakhic system upon all the local Jewish population, despite their many efforts to achieve that goal. It cannot come to us as a surprise to find out that they did not elaborate on this matter. Some information can still be retrieved from the Talmudic material and historical findings, if we just pay attention to what they have to say.

Actually, Edrei, Mendels, and I do agree in almost every relevant fact. We agree that Western Jewry rejected the teachings of the rabbis and that they used the books of "the other side" of rabbis. We also agree that they remained "biblical Jews." In a word, they were acting like the Sadducees did. We differ in the interpretation of these facts. Edrei and Mendels believe that all this is the result of the lack of knowledge of the Hebrew language. I, for one, prefer to call them just Sadducees, as they actually were. Their story is not just a historical accident, as Edrei and Mendels want us to believe, but rather a result of deep religiosity and religious beliefs which should be admired. In those days, not everything was decided by communication, as Edrei and Mendels try to lead us to believe. In fact, it was an emotional religious world, and that is what mattered. Sadducees and Pharisees did not dispute over marginal and procedural matters, as they were administrators, as Edrei and Mendels suggest in order to convince us that when the Temple is already destroyed there is no reason anymore for the dispute and the clerks of the administration just went home. Even a quick glance at the explicit disputes between the Pharisees and the Sadducees in the Mishnah and in the Qumranic writings, and implicitly in these writings as is revealed by recent research, can immediately demonstrate the deep gap between them. In my forthcoming book, I hope to explain this phenomenon in great length. Marginalizing the dispute to administrative issues does not do justice to these spiritual movements (not just "sects"), which were of a tremendous importance to Jewish history and religion.

Yes, the rabbis ultimately won. The world of the Bible ceased to exist, and from that historical moment onwards almost all the Jews were living in the post-biblical world, the world of the rabbis.

I believe that the story which is told by the various sources reflects a richer history of the Jew in this dark and silent age.

* I wish to thank my colleagues who read the article and commented on it: Menahem Blondheim, Doron Mendels, Vered Noam, Amichai Radziner, Daniel Schwartz, and Yaakov Sussman. I would also like to thank the translator, Adv. Michael Prawer z"l, and The Green Foundation for its help.

# *Notes*

1    Arye Edrei and Doron Mendels, "A Split Jewish Diaspora: Its Dramatic Consequences," *Journal for the Study of the Pseudoepigrapha* 16, no. 2 (2007): 91-137; Arye Edrei and Doron Mendels, "A Split Jewish Diaspora: Its Dramatic Consequences II," *Journal for the Study of the Pseudoepigrapha* 17, no. 3 (2008): 163–187. The current article was written and submitted to the editors a very long time ago. Since then, some articles relating to Edrei and Mendels's thesis were published: Fergus Millar, "A Rural Jewish Community in Late Roman Mesopotamia, and the Question of the 'Split' Jewish Diaspora," *Journal for the Study of Judaism* 42 (2011): 351-374; Arye Edrei and Doron Mendels, "A Split Diaspora Again – A Response to Fergus Millar," *Journal for the Study of Pseudepigrapha* 21 (2012): 305-311; Aron C. Sterk, "*Latino Romaniotes:* The Continuity of Jewish Communities in the Western Diaspora, 400-700 CE," *Melilah, Manchester Journal of Jewish Studies* 9 (2012): 21-49; and the last version of Edrei and Mendels's thesis published in this volume. I do not relate here to all of these new writings as I am preparing a longer chapter on this issue in a forthcoming book regarding the dispute between the Pharisees and the Sadducees and their heritage.

2    *Proverbs* 18:21

3    Edrei and Mendels, "A Split Jewish Diaspora…" 112.

4    *Daniel* 1:20

5    See also, Edwin R. Goodenough, *The Jurisprudence of the Jewish Courts in Egypt: Legal Administration by the Jews Under the Early Roman Empire as Described by Philo Judaeus* (New Haven: Yale University Press, 1929).

6    Edrei and Mendels, "A Split Jewish Diaspora…" 119.

7    Edrei and Mendels, "A Split Jewish Diaspora…" 127; See also David Nakman, "The Halakhah in the Writings of Josephus" (PhD diss., Bar-Ilan University, 2004), which surveyed all of the existing material in Josephus's writings and the relevant research literature and drew his own conclusions. On Josephus's disdain for the Pharisees, see ibid, 23. On Josephus's 'religious' affiliation, see ibid, 35 and the following pages. The work in its entirety vacillates on the question of the variety of religious positions and the problems involved in ascribing particular positions to specific groups, in establishing a distinction between the "people" and the various elite classes, and the idea of 'halakhic eclecticism'.

8    *Hodayot,* D II, and in other similar examples in the various writings of the sects. See Yaakov Sussman, "The History of the Halakhah and the Dead Sea Scrolls: Preliminary Observations on Miqsat Ma'ase HaTorah (4QMMT)," *Tarbiz* 59 (1989-1990): 11-76, 21 [Hebrew].

9    Haim Rabin, "The Historical Background of the Hebrew in Qumran," *Linguistic Studies* (1999): 269 [Hebrew].

10   bShab 17a; bEruv 13b.

11   See Berachyahu Lifshitz, "Aggada and Its Role in the Unwritten Law," *Shenaton Ha-Mishpat Ha-Ivri* 22 (2004): 300 and the following pages [Hebrew]. See also Yaakov Sussman, "The History of the Halakhah…" n. 237, stating that the decision to rule in accordance with Beth Hillel was adopted gradually and not always in a definitive manner. There were also those who belonged to Beth Hillel who ruled according to Beth Shammai and vice versa.

12   bEruv 13b.

13  Vered Noam, "Beth Shammai and Sectarian Halakhah," *Jewish Studies* 41 (2002): 45-67 [Hebrew]. See also Yaakov Sussman, "The History of the Halakhah…" text adjacent to n. 117. The dispute therefore concerned the *halakhah*. The Essenes also struggled with the Pharisees over the existence of a different *halakhah*, i.e. the legitimacy of a parallel, alternative perception of the *halakhah,* and finally they separated from them. See ibid., 27-28. And also, ibid., 61 and the following pages, where he points out that the dispute concerned the details of the *halakhah* and was not over the foundations of beliefs and opinions; see Menahem Kister, "Studies in 4QMiqsat Ma'ase HaTorah and Related Texts: Law, Theology, Language, and Calendar," *Tarbiz* 68 (1999): 326 [Hebrew]. Indeed, the dispute over the *halakhah* appears to have been over the manner of deciding the *halakhah,* and by extension, on the particulars that were the product of using different methods of deciding. See my article, Lifshitz, "Aggada and Its Role…" n. 307, and n. 186. The reason for the prohibition on reading the *Book of Ben Sira* was not because it was considered 'Oral Law', and thus not allowed to be written – see Shlomo Naeh, "Karyana de-Igreta: Notes on Talmudic Diplomatics," in *Sha'arei Lashon Vol. II - Rabbinic Hebrew and Aramaic,* eds. A. Maman et al (Jerusalem: The Bialik Institute, 2007), 228 [Hebrew] – but rather because of its contents or because of its claim to be a part of the Holy Scriptures.

14  Rabin, "The Historical Background…" 254.

15  Ibid, 259.

16  Ibid, 269.

17  Ibid, 270. See also William A. Schneidewind, "Qumranic Hebrew as an Antilanguage," *JBL* 118, no. 2 (1999): 235; William A. Schneidewind, "Linguistic Ideology in Qumran Hebrew," in *Diggers at the Well: Proceedings of a Third International Symposium on the Hebrew of the Dead Sea Scrolls and Ben Sira (Studies on the Texts of the Desert of Judah; Vol 36),* eds. T. Mauroca et al. (Leiden; Boston; Koln: Brill, 2000): 245. They were referred to by Magen Broshi and Hanan Eshel, "A Messiah before Jesus Christ," *Tarbiz* 70 (2001): 134, n. 5 [Hebrew] (I was referred to their article by Prof. Daniel Schwartz). They mention the total omission of Greek from the language of the Qumran writings. See also in my article Lifshitz, "Aggada and Its Role…" 153, where I give an additional explanation for the change in language, namely in order to distinguish between the language of the Torah and the language employed in rabbinic *derashot,* because in this sense too, the rabbis were differentiated from the Sadducees and the members of the other sects. See ibid. The same applies to the distinction between the language of the *Amoraim* and that of the *"Stamaim"* – but I cannot expand on this point here.

18  Introduction to his "Book of Seventy Words" [Hebrew]. See Moshe Zucker, "Against Whom Did Se'adya Ga'on Write the Polemical Poem *Essa Meshali*" *Tarbiz* 27 (1958): 73 [Hebrew]. He cites the following paragraph from Rav Saadiah Gaon's "Book of Seventy Words," p. 2, lines 9-11, in *Ignace Goldziher Memorial Volume,* ed. Nehemia Aloni (Jerusalem: Mass, 1958), 14-15: "And I saw Jews who denied the halakhic rulings of the Prophets which are not in writing, and they also deny that part of the nation's language which derives from tradition and is not in the Holy Scriptures." Apparently, his intention is to that part of rabbinic language which differs from biblical language. The claim is that just as one does not accept *halakhah* that is not written, but only transmitted orally, so one should also not accept that part of the language which is not written. Its acceptance would be deemed as an admission of the validity of the tradition, and by extension would also compel acceptance of the traditional *halakhah*. The assumption that rabbinic language is the product of tradition that was transmitted (together?) with the biblical language is particularly interesting. See my article above, Lifshitz, "Aggada and Its Role…" on the entire matter. See also Rina Drori, *Models and Contacts: Arabic Literature and its Impact*

*on Medieval Jewish Culture* (Leiden; Boston; Koln: Brill, 2000). On the extensive and profound familiarity of the Karaites with rabbinic literature, see Ofra Tirosh-Beker, *Ginze Ḥazal ba-sifrut ha-Ḳara'it bi-Yeme ha-Benayim* ("Hidden Rabbinic Literature in Karaite Medieval Literature"), vol. II (Jerusalem: The Bialik Institute, 2012) [Hebrew].

19  At different periods, but also with an overlap, and assuming that these are not just different names for the same sects. Clearly, there was a variety of primary and secondary groups and their precise names and definitions are not important here. See Menahem Kister, "The History of the Essene Sect: Examinations of the Vision of Chayot, Book of Jubilees, and Damascus Scroll," *Tarbitz* 56 (1987): 15-18 [Hebrew].

20  Sussman, "The History of the Halakhah..." 48, n. 165; Ibid., 51, n. 169. Regarding the Jewish-Christians and the plurality of opinions and actions among them, see Burton L. Visotzky, "Prolegomenon to the Study of Jewish Christianities in Rabbinic Literature," *AJSR* 14 (1989): 49. However, see also comments of Charlotte Elisheva Fonrobert, "The Didascalia Apostolorum: A Mishnah for the Disciples of Jesus," *Journal of Early Christian Studies* 9 (2001): 483.

21  Tessa Rajak, *The Jewish Dialogue with Greece-Rome* (Boston-Leiden, 2002), 222; Fergus Millar, "The Jews of the Graeco-Roman Diaspora between Paganism and Christianity, ad 312-438," in *The Jews among Pagans and Christians in the Roman Empire*, eds. Judith Lieu, John A. North, and Tessa Rajak (London and New York: Routledge, 1992), 97, esp. 114 and the following pages; Fergus Millar, "Transformations of Judaism under Graeco-Roman Rule: Response to Seth Schwartz's 'Imperialism and Jewish Society'," *JJS* 57 (2006): 137, 151.

22  Yanai made coins that had Hebrew, Aramaic, and Greek inscriptions. Bar-Kochba also wrote in Greek and some of the bills written in Betar were written in both Hebrew and Greek. Saul Lieberman and Elimelekh E. Halevi proved that the Talmudic rabbis had knowledge of Greek and of the culture of Greece and Rome, and that it influenced them – Saul Lieberman, *Greek in Jewish Palestine* (New York: Jewish Theological Seminary of America, 1942). See also Gedaliah Alon's critique of Lieberman's work, Gedaliah Alon, "The Sociological Approach for the Investigation of the Halakhah," in *Studies in Jewish History in the Times of the Second Temple, the Mishna and the Talmud,* 2 vols. (Tel Aviv: Hakibbutz Hameuchad, 1958) [Hebrew], where he refutes the thesis of Lieberman.

23  Shaye J. D. Cohen, *From the Maccabees to the Mishnah* (Philadelphia: Westminster Press, 1987), 24-26; Lee I. Levine, "Unity and Diversity in Ancient Judaism: The Case of the Diaspora Synagogue," in *The Jews in the Hellenistic-Roman World: Studies in Memory of Menahem Stern,* eds. Isaiah Gafni et al. (Jerusalem: The Zalman Shazar Center for Jewish History, 1996), 379-392 [Hebrew]. In Levine's view, there was pluralism among the different groupings, both in the Land of Israel and in the West, and it found expression in the differences in emphases and customs, but did not embody a fundamental dispute. In our comments below we will present a different understanding of the differences in contents, but the existence of many groups is beyond doubt, although conceivably they are divisible into three (or four) categories, similar to the classification of Josephus into the three (or four) groupings of Jews in his time. See Yoram Erder, *The Karaite Mourners of Zion and the Qumran Scrolls: On the History of an Alternative to Rabbinic Judaism* (Tel-Aviv: Hakibbutz Hameuchad, 2004), 156 [Hebrew], regarding the variety of opinions that existed at that time and their similarities, and the possibility of confusing between them. See also below, n. 92.

24  According to some, "the failure of the Bar-Kochba revolution and the edicts of persecution in its wake lead to waves of refugees... apparently most of them went to Babylonia." Aharon Oppenheimer, "Batei Midrash in Babylonia before the Completion of the Mishnah," in *Yeshivot and Batei Midrash,* ed. Emanuel Etkes (Jerusalem: The Zalman

Shazar Center, 2006), 19 [Hebrew]. While there is no explicit proof of this, it is certainly possible. The character and the tendencies of the Jewish community in Babylonia held greater attraction for the Pharisees, whereas the West tended to attract the Sadducees. See yMa'asS 5:6/56c, and below n. 93.

25  *Tosefta Mikvaot* 4:7.

26  Conceivably, issues of purity did not emerge in the post-destruction, impure exile, as it had emerged in *Eretz Yisrael* prior to the destruction.

27  *Exodus Rabbah,* 30:9. From his question it appears as if the "heretic" was a Christian and not a Sadducee. See bHag 5b, Rashi, s.v. *"mina"* and in *Dikdukei Soferim; Eccles. Rabbah,* 1:24-25 and others. But compare Visotzky, "Prolegomenon to the Study..." regarding the many possibilities of use of this term in rabbinic literature. A *"min"* (= heretic) means 'another' or 'separated' – see Berachyahu Lifshitz, *Law and Action: Terminology of Obligation and Acquisition in Jewish Law* (Jerusalem: The Bialik Institute, 2002), 53 [Hebrew]. The same applies to the interpretation of *'Sadducee'* and *'parush'* – each in the eyes of the other, who determines the difference and the other. See also, Robert Travers Herford, *Christianity in Talmud and Midrash* (London: Williams & Norgate, 1903).

28  See Joseph Heinemann, *Derashot BeTzibbur Betekufat HaTalmud* ("Public Sermons of the Talmud Period") (Jerusalem: Keter, 1974) [Hebrew]. See also in Rashi, bShab 115a s.v. *she'ein korin bahen*: "...on the Shabbat they would preach a sermon to homeowners engaged in their livelihoods on weekdays, and in their *derashot* were interspersed with rulings of ritual law...". And see *Yalkut Or HaAfelah*, cited by Rabbi Menachem Mendel Kasher, ed., *Torah Sheleimah*, 12 vols., *Vayakhel* (Jerusalem: Hotzaat Beit Torah Sheleimah, 1936): "Moshe would gather communities on the Sabbath and preach and teach Israel."

29  See comment of Gedaliah Alon, *History of the Jews in Eretz Yisrael During the Mishnaic and Talmudic Period,* Vol. 1 (Tel-Aviv: Hakibbutz Hameuchad, 1967), 260 n. 25 [Hebrew]. See also *Avot de-Rabbi Nathan,* Ver. A, ch. 16. Rabbi Zaddok and Rabbi Akiba who are mentioned there probably spoke Greek with their listeners. See Joseph Heinemann, "Judaism in the Eyes of the Ancient World," *Zion* 4 (1939): 269, n. 22 [Hebrew].

30  tBets 2:15; Saul Lieberman, ed., *The Tosefta: According to Codex Vienna with Variants and a Brief Commentary* (New York and Jerusalem: The Jewish Theological Seminary of America, 1970), 290-291 [Hebrew].

31  yPes 7:1/34a; yBets 2:7/61c; yMK 3:1/81d.

32  bBer 19a; bPes 53a; bBets 23a; For discussion and bibliography on the subject of Todos, see Haim Licht, "Todus of Rome and the Eating of Holy Sheep on Eve of Passover," *Tura* 4 (1996): 89 [Hebrew]; David Salomon, "Reciprocal Spiritual and Cultural Influences Between Diaspora and Eretz Israel Jewry During the Second Temple Era Until the Revolt Under Trajan" (PhD diss., The Hebrew University of Jerusalem, 1979), 91; Baruch M. Bokser, "Todos and Rabbinic Authority in Rome," in *New Perspectives in Ancient Judaism,* Vol. I, eds. Jacob Neusner et al. (Lanham, MD: University Press of America, 1987), 117-129; Regarding the fear of incurring the wrath of Christians who would see the Pascal sacrifice as a provocation directed at them and the crucifixion of Jesus, who had been likened to a sheep, see Joseph Tabory, *The Passover Ritual Throughout the Generations* (Tel-Aviv: Hakkibutz Hame'uchad Publishing House, 1996), 96 [Hebrew] (I thank Aryeh Edrei for this reference). See also Israel Jacov Yuval, "The Haggadah of Passover and Easter," *Tarbitz* 65 (1996): 26 [Hebrew]. See also, Paul F. Bradshaw and Lawrence A. Hoffman, eds., *Passover and Easter: Origin and History to Modern Times,* vol. 5, Two

*Liturgical Traditions* (Notre Dame: University of Notre Dame Press, 1999). In this context, the word *'mekulas'*, which they had difficulty interpreting, may be understood in the sense of "spreading open" of arms, akin to the explanation given by Saul Lieberman, "Keles Kilusin," in *Studies in Palestinian Talmudic Literature,* ed. David Rosenthal (Jerusalem: Magnes Press, 1991), 433 [Hebrew]. Its description in the sources as a sacrifice in respect of inner entrails is for the purpose of limiting the scope of the prohibition, for in that case it cannot be considered as a "Pessach." Compared to the crucifixion of Haman, which was dated on Pessach Eve, and also carries the same motif, see Elliott Horowitz, *Reckless Rites: Purim and the Legacy of Jewish Violence* (Princeton, NJ: Princeton University Press, 2006); Alfredo Mordechai Rabello, "The First Law of the Emperor Theodosius II," in *Mehkarim B'yahadut: Sefer Hayovel L'david Kotler* ("Studies in Judaica, Jubilee Volume Presented to David Kotlar") (Tel Aviv: Am Hasoffer, 1975), 172-192.

33    Regarding the term *'hinhig'* in the sense of *'hora'* (= instructed in the normative sense), see Berachyahu Lifshitz, " *'Minhag'* and its place on the scale of Norms of the Oral Law," *Shenaton Ha-Mishpat Ha-Ivri* 24 (2006-2007): 123.

34    See Alon, *History of the Jews in Eretz Yisrael During the Mishnaic and Talmudic Period,* 352 (English Version, Vol. 2, p. 566). It is also possible that the practice of eating the paschal sacrifice was preserved by some local inhabitants.

35    The story is based on *Midrash Abchir,* cited in *Yalkut Shimoni, Vayehi,* 161; the story concerning R. Matias b. Harash who sat in the *Beth Midrash* engaged in Torah, does not indicate where the *Beth Midrash* was located.

36    *Yebbamot* 14:5.

37    yMa'asS 5:6/56c.

38    mMieg 8:1; bMeg. 9a; yMeg 9:a, 71a.

39    As we know, Paul was a student of R. Gamliel, and he was a fluent Greek speaker.

40    See in detail in my article, Lifshitz, "Aggada and Its Role...", and recently, the important comments of Paul Mandel, "Scriptural Exegesis and the Pharisees in Josephus," *JJS* 58 (2007): 19. See also the comments of Hieronymus, as cited and translated by Millar, "The Jews of the Graeco-Roman Diaspora..." 151-152, regarding the sages who taught their traditions; see Adiel Schremer, " '[T]he[y] did not Read in the Sealed Book': Qumran Halakhic Revolution and the Emergence of Torah Study in Second Temple Judaism," in *Historical Perspectives: From the Hasmoneans to Bar Kokhba in the Light of the Dead Sea Scrolls,* eds. D. Goodblatt et al. (Leiden-Boston-Kohn: Brill, 2001), 105.

  I will mention the salient points: There is a long-standing dispute regarding the nature of the 'Oral Law'. Was it transmitted to Moshe together with the 'Written Law', after which it was handed down from person to person, or perhaps the sages were given the authority to interpret the 'Written Law', and the 'Oral Law' is the product of that interpretation? According to the first version, there is no possibility of dispute, and it removes and decides all disputes, by virtue of it being the truth. According to the second version, dispute is natural, and hence permitted, and decision is adopted in accordance with the majority opinion, which establishes a "rule of conduct" that does not claim that its result represents "the truth." The history of this dispute is highly intricate and circuitous. One of the descriptions of this duality of positions within the Pharasitic system, appears in the dispute between Hillel the Elder and the Sons of Betheira – tPes 4:13-14, Lieberman ed., *The Tosefta,* 165; Saul Lieberman, *Tosefta Ki-Fshutah: A Comprehensive Commentary on the Tosefta,* Part V, Order Mo'ed, Tractate Pesahim (New York: Jewish Theological

Seminary in America, 1955-1988), 566-567, and its parallels, especially in the version of the Yerushalmi (yPes 6:1/33a) but the point will not be elaborated in the current context. The same applies to the appearance of the heavenly voice that resolved the disputes between the Houses of Hillel and Shammai (see above text adjacent to n. 8 onwards), and another description is the famous story of the 'Oven of Achnai' (bBM 59a). Indeed, this dispute was not totally resolved, and in the colorful language of the Talmudic narrator "they (=the walls) did not fall, in honor of R. Joshua, nor did they resume the upright position, in honor of R. Eliezer; and they are still standing thus inclined." The intellectual pluralism that flows from the second position did not extend to the sectarian views (apart from of *Beth Shammai*) and the right to oppose the majority decision. See Daniel Boyarin, "The Yavneh-Cycle of the Stammaim and the Invention of the Rabbis," in *Creation and Composition: The Contribution of the Bavli Redactors (Stammaim) to the Aggada*, ed. Jeffrey L. Rubenstein (Tubingen: Mohr Siebeck, 2005), 237. See also the article of Devora Steinmetz, "Agada Unbound: Inter-Agadic Characterization of Sages in the Bavli and Implications for Reading Agada," in *Creation and Composition: The Contribution of the Bavli Redactors (Stammaim) to the Aggada*, ed. Jeffrey L. Rubenstein (Tubingen: Mohr Siebeck, 2005), 293. Also see Jeffrey L. Rubenstein, *Talmudic Stories: Narrative Art, Composition, and Culture* (Baltimore: Johns Hopkins University Press, 1999); David Stern, *Midrash and Theory: Ancient Jewish Exegesis and Contemporary Literary Studies* (Evanston, IL: Northwestern University Press, 1996). See also in Daniel Boyarin, "Tale of Two Cities: Yabneh and Nikea," *Continuity and Renewal: Jews and Judaism in Byzantine-Christian Palestine* (Jerusalem: Yad Izhak Ben-Zvi, 2004), 301, which resembles his aforementioned article mentioned in this note. The question  discussed in these articles – and by others mentioned therein, and also by Jeffrey L. Rubenstein, "The Story of the Oven of Achnai: A Literary Analysis," in *Higayon L'Yona: New Aspects in the Study of Midrash, Aggadah and Piyut in Honor of Professor Yona Fraenkel*, eds. Joshua Levinson, Jacob Elbaum, and Galit Hasan-Rokem (Jerusalem: Magnes Press, 2007), 457, n. 1, and the comments of Vered Noam, below in n. 94; see also in my article, Lifshitz, "Aggada and Its Role..." – concerns pluralism in rabbinic *halakhah* after the destruction and the abolishment of the *Sanhedrin*, is connected primarily to the institutional question. It would, however, appear that to the extent that it touches upon the *Babylonian Talmud* it reflects the recognition that the Torah is studied in accordance with the particular understanding of each person, and that there is no "one" provable truth, and certainly not in the hands of Heaven. Every question has an answer, even if tenuous. Every response comes together with its refutation. The halakhic decision therefore becomes a rule of behavior, dependent upon the halakhic authority of each generation and hence the decision to enforce in an unequivocal manner. As a result, 'tolerance' is in fact extremely limited. For a fascinating parallel between the Justinian legal system and Josephus's description of the difference between Sadducees and Pharisees, see Ignazio Castellucci, " Law v. Statute, Ius v. Lex: An Analysis of a Critical Relation in. Roman and Civil Law," *Global Jurist* 8, no. 1 (2008) (Advances), Article 5. Available at https://www.researchgate.net/profile/Ignazio_Castellucci/publication/250147303_Law_v_Statute_Ius_v_Lex_An_Analysis_of_a_Critical_Relation_in_Roman_and_Civil_Law/links/579f9bcd08ae100d38065a0a.pdf?origin=publication_detail

41  Rajak, *The Jewish Dialogue with Greece-Rome,* 340.

42  See Alfredo Mordechai Rabello, "De Collatio Legum Mosaicarum et Romanarum," *Shenaton Ha-Mishpat Ha-Ivri* 1 (1974): 231-262 [Hebrew], comments in n. 61.

43  Alon, *History of the Jews in Eretz Yisrael During the Mishnaic and Talmudic Period,* 352 (English Version, vol. 2, p. 566).

44    Alon, "The Sociological Approach…" 250-251.

45    A Law of Justinian, enacted in 553; Amnon Linder, *The Jews in the Legal Sources of the Early Middle Ages* (Detroit: Wayne State University Press, 1997), 483. Law no. 66. See references and comments by Prof. Linder, *ibid.* See also Jacob Nahum Epstein, *Introduction to the Text of the Mishnah* (Jerusalem: Magnes Press, 1948), 698.

46    Ibid.

47    See Emanuel Tov, "T'nach, Tirgumim" in *Encyclopaedia Biblica,* vol. 8 (Jerusalem: The Bialik Institute, 1982), columns 774-830 [Hebrew]; Avigdor Shinan, *The Biblical Story as Reflected in its Aramaic Translations* (Tel-Aviv: Hakkibutz Hameuchad, 1993) [Hebrew]; Avigdor Shinan, *The Aggada of the Meturgemanim* (Jerusalem: Hotsa'at Makor, 1979) [Hebrew]; Rimon Kasher, "The Beliefs of Synagogue Meturgemanim and Their Audience," in *Continuity and Renewal: Jews and Judaism in Byzantine-Christian Palestine,* ed. Lee I. Levine (Jerusalem: Yad Izhak Ben-Zvi, 2004), 420 [Hebrew]; See also Hanoch Albeck, "External Halakhah in the Eretz Yisrael Translations and in Aggadah," *Jubilee Volume dedicated to B.M. Lewin, ed. Y.L. Fishman* (Jerusalem, 1940), 140 [Hebrew]; Also see recently Daniel Boyarin, "He Who Spoke and the World Came Into Being," in *Higayon L'Yona: New Aspects in the Study of Midrash, Aggadah and Piyut in Honor of Professor Yona Fraenkel,* eds. Joshua Levinson, Jacob Elbaum, and Galit Hasan-Rokem (Jerusalem: Magnes Press, 2007), 155 [Hebrew], on the translations and the reflections of the several kinds of "Jewishness" embedded therein.

48    See my article, Lifshitz, "Aggada and Its Role…"; *Mishnah* indicates here, as in other places, *Torah se'be'al Peh* in general. This should be compared with the famous *midrash* appearing in *Midrash Tanhuma,* Ki-Tisah, 34: "R. Judah b., Shalom said: When the Holy One Blessed Be He said to Moses "Write [for] thyself," Moses requested the *Mishnah* be in writing. And because the Holy One saw that in the future the nations of the world would translate Torah, and read it in Greek, and that they would say "I am Israel, and now the scales are balanced, the Holy One Blessed Be He said to the nations of the world: You say that you are my sons. I do not know, but the one in possession of my secret treasure – he is my son. And what does this refer to *Mishnah*, that was given orally." The Sadducees could easily have replaced the Nations of the World, and all of the elements appearing in the polemics during Justinian's time can easily be replaced by the *Midrash,* as if the *midrash* was an essential component of the Pharisee claim presented to him, and until know the scales are balanced.

49    As mentioned, we are dealing with about the sixth century C.E. and during that period there is already a more solid basis for assuming that the rabbinic trend had prevailed, but nonetheless, the point is still a moot one; see further on. Possibly, the difference between the Akilas translation which was permitted and the *Mishnah,* which was prohibited, was that in the final analysis the translation included less 'Oral Law' than the *Mishnah,* and it presumes to indicate the source of these laws in the version of the scriptural text itself, just as was the case in the sectarian writings.

50    See e.g. Marcel Simon, *Verus Israel: A Study of the Relations between Christians and Jews in the Roman Empire, A.D. 135-425* (London: Littman Library of Jewish Civilization, 1996), and the comments in Fonrobert, "The Didascalia Apostolorum…" Her view is that the term may connote the Torah that was given by God after the sin of the Calf, and that this is the *Mishnah,* which is the same *Mishnah* that was ultimately annulled after the revelation of Jesus. But the Sadducees and the Jews that preceded Justinian made another claim, which was that the *Mishnah* was not of Divine origin being rather of human origin. See also Epstein, *Introduction to the Text of the Mishnah,* and his remarks in his book *Introduction to Tannaitic Literature* (Jerusalem: Magnes Press, 1957), 17.

51 See Flavius Josephus, *Wars of the Jews,* II, 164-166; Flavius Josephus, *Antiquities of the Jews,* XVIII 16-17. See also *Maaseh Shelicin,* 23:6-8. And see *Avot de-Rabbi Nathan,* Ver. A, 8:13b. See in *Maimonides, Commentary on the Mishnah, Avot,* 1:14. The members of the Qumran sect on the other hand believed in the immortality of the soul. Regarding the difference between the different sects, see Albert I. Baumgarten, "Who Were the Sadducees? The Sadducees of Jerusalem and Qumran," in *The Jews in the Hellenistic-Roman World, Studies in Memory of Menachem Stern,* eds. Isaiah Gafni et al. (Jerusalem: The Zalman Shazar Center for Jewish History and The Historical Society of Israel, 1996), 393. See also Erder, *The Karaite Mourners of Zion and the Qumran Scrolls,* 120.

52 On Greek and Latin in the days of the Empire and in the period of its division, see Reuven Yaron, "The Competitive Coexistence of Latin and Greek in the Roman Empire," in *Collatio Iuris Romani: Etudes de'die'es a Hans Ankum a l'occasion de son 65e anniversaire,* vol. 2, ed. Robert Feenstra et al. (Amsterdam: J.C. Gieber, 1995), 657.

53 bKidd 66b.

54 See inscription in the Theodosius tablet, "… he built a synagogue for the reading of the Torah and the study of the commandments (cited in Salomon, "Reciprocal Spiritual and Cultural…" 94); see Mandel, "Scriptural Exegesis and the Pharisees in Josephus," 26-28, who distinguishes between the practice of the sectarians to read the Scriptures and of the Pharisees, who read the law. The question is to which group Theodosius belonged?

55 Edrei and Mendels, "A Split Jewish Diaspora…" 98, 128, and references.

56 Comments of Rabello, "De Collatio Legum…" 232. See also 256, "This essay is remote from the Talmudic spirit that prevailed at that time in *Eretz Yisrael,* and the rabbinic interpretations of the biblical verses that we found when examining the Latin translations of the biblical verses are too rare in the Collatio to justify that assumption (that the Collatio was composed in *Eretz Yisrael*"). See also Alfredo Mordechai Rabello, "Mosaicarum et Romanarum: The Problem of its Secondary Recension or its Use in the Fourth Century," in *For Uriel: Studies in the History of Israel in Antiquity Presented to Professor Uriel Rappaport,* edited by M. Mor, J. Pastor, I. Ronen, and Y. Ashkenazi (Jerusalem: The Zalman Shazar Center, 2005), 385-414 [Hebrew].

57 Rabello, "De Collatio Legum…" 250ff; Baumgarten, "Who Were the Sadducees?" 393; Martin Goodman, "The Roman Identity of Roman Jews", in *The Jews in the Hellenistic-Roman World: Studies in Memory of Menachem Stern,* eds. Isaiah Gafni et al. (Jerusalem: The Zalman Shazar Center for Jewish History and The Historical Society of Israel, 1996), 97. In his view, the work was written by a Jew for Jews, in order to persuade them that they resembled the Romans.

58 Rabello, ibid., 253.

59 See *Sifrei Deut,* 344; yBK 4:3/4b; bBK 38a; the assumption here is that the episode is of historic importance; see Alon, *History of the Jews in Eretz Yisrael During the Mishnaic and Talmudic Period,* 293. Even if there were traces of the rabbinic-*Eretz Yisrael* teachings in Rome, it comes as no surprise that there was a desire to study this Torah from the source in *Eretz Yisrael.*

60 Alon, ibid., 214 (English version, 346). See ibid., 29, regarding the fact that the Jews in Exile were prepared to sacrifice their lives in the fulfillment of this commandment, and battled the edicts issued against its performance.

61  Ibid., 158 (English version, Vol. 1, 251), see also 353 (English version, Vol. 2, 568), "the organic bond between the Diaspora and *Eretz Yisrael* found tangible expression in the regular contributions for the support of the Sages which now replaced the half-shekel which the Jews abroad had used to send to the Temple before the year 70."

62  Jacob Liver, "The Ransom of Half Shekel", in *Yehezkel Kaufmann Jubilee Volume: Studies in Bible and Jewish Religion Dedicated to Yehezkel Kaufmann on the Occasion of His Seventieth Birthday,* ed. Menahem Haran (Jerusalem: Magnes Press, 1960), 54-67; Jacob Liver, "The Half Shekel in the Scrolls of the Judean Desert Sect," *Tarbiz* 31 (1961): 18-22 [Hebrew]; David Flusser, "Mathew XVII, 24-27 and the Dead Sea Sect," *Tarbiz* 31 (1961): 150-156 [Hebrew]; Shmuel Safrai, "Jesus and the Hassidic Movement," in *The Jews in the Hellenistic-Roman World: Studies in Memory of Menachem Stern,* eds. Isaiah Gafni et al. (Jerusalem: The Zalman Shazar Center for Jewish History and The Historical Society of Israel, 1996), 417-420; Vered Noam, *Megillat Ta'anit: Versions, Interpretations, History, with a Critical Edition* (Jerusalem: Yad Ben-Zvi, 2003), 173.

63  See comments of Tessa Rajak, "The Jewish Community and Its Boundries," in *The Jews among Pagans and Christians in the Roman Empire,* eds. Judith Lieu, John A. North, and Tessa Rajak (London and New York, 1992), 14-17, regarding the distinction made by diaspora Jews between the respect that they accorded to the sages, who were regarded as national representatives, and recognition of their laws. From Cicero we learn that even the Jews of Rome sent contributions to the Temple in Jerusalem. Presumably, also the exiles brought by Pompeii to Rome after 63 C.E. and who were thereafter released, gave their contributions after they became established in their new residence, and until the new situation began to become clear, as mentioned.

64  See Lieberman, *Tosefta Ki-Fshutah,* 1028 and the following pages.

65  Ibid. At a later period they could obviously have used the calendar fixed by Hillel.

66  See Rachel Elior, *Temple and Chariot, Priests and Angels, Sanctuary and Heavenly Sanctuaries in Early Jewish Mysticism* (Jerusalem: Magnes Press, 2003), 44, 94, 117, 230, and their following pages. See also Erder, *The Karaite Mourners of Zion and the Qumran,* 118, 124, 152; and *passim* according to the index, under *luach* ("Calendar").

67  yNed 6:13/40a.

68  Apparently, there were no binding halakhot in these matters, and that were all subsumed in the category of *aggadah* and *haggadah*, and given their non-halakhic status, the prohibition on writing halakhot or oral law was not applicable. See my articles referred to above, Lifshitz, "Aggada and Its Role..." and Lifshitz, *Law and Action.* See also below in respect of the prayers.

69  Siegfried Stein, "The Influence of Symposia Literature on the Literary Form of the Pesah Haggadah," *Journal of Jewish Studies* 8 (1957): 13-44; Menahem Blondheim, "Why Is this Book Different from All Other Books? The Orality, the Literacy, and the Printing of the Passover Haggadah" (Paper presented to the Institute of Advanced Studies, The Hebrew University of Jerusalem, 2004). Even according to those who dispute Stein's view, see Baruch M. Bokser, *The Origins of the Seder: The Passover Rite and Early Rabbinic Judaism* (Berkeley: University of California Press, 1984), telling the story of Exodus is natural while the Pascal offering is taking place.

70 See comments of Ernst Daniel Goldschmidt, *The Passover Hagaddah: Its Sources and Its History over the Generations* (Jerusalem: The Bialik Institute, 1960), 18 [Hebrew]: "They certainly fulfilled the commandment in this format in earlier generations and probably reading from the Torah too, without exegesis, and quite possibly every person added his own stories from his own knowledge." See also in the Robert Brodi ed., *Responsa of Rav Natrunai Gaon* (Jerusalem: Ofek Institute, 1994), 258, and the editor's comment in n. 10 to the effect that there was an ancient custom in *Eretz Yisrael* which included citations from the talmudic literature in the *Haggadah,* and which actually match the wording of the *Haggadah* as brought by Rav Natrunai Gaon, which cannot be ascribed to the Karaites. However, the Gaon himself mentioned that this version "does not include any *midrash* at all." They and others preserve this ancient tradition and opposed the *"midrash"* that was appended to the biblical verses for the simple reason that they denied the basic legitimacy and hence authority of *midrash*, as explained below.

71 See my articles, Lifshitz, "Aggada and Its Role..." and Lifshitz, *Law and Action;* see note 67.

72 For a thesis regarding the "political nature" of the *derashot* of the *Haggadah,* see Louis Finkelstein, "The Oldest Midrash," *HTR* 31 (1938): 291-317, and Goldschmidt, *The Passover Hagaddah.*

73 Elior, *Temple and Chariot...*, 144. See further regarding the festival of *Shavuoth* and its meaning for Jubilees (according to index), esp. on pages 220, 235. According to Jubilees (49:2) and the Wisdom of Solomon (18:14-15), the Plague of the Killing of the First Born was carried out by an angel, as distinct from the view of the *Haggadah's* author. See further in Goldschmidt, *The Passover Hagaddah,* 35, on this particular issue. See also Erder, *The Karaite Mourners of Zion and the Qumran,* in the index under *"Hag Shavuoth,"* and also regarding the Sadducean belief in the "corporeality of God." The verses which were the subject of the *derashah* and expounded on in the *Haggadah* appear in Deuteronomy 26:5-9, but the continuation of these verses links *Pessach* to *Shavuoth,* in accordance with the view of the sages. See also in Nahmanides's commentary to Leviticus 23:36. See also Liora Ravid, "Issues in the Book of Jubilees" (PhD diss., Bar Ilan University, 2001).

74 See above, text adjacent to n. 47.

75 Elior, *Temple and Chariot...*, 19, 222.

76 Edrei and Mendels, "A Split Jewish Diaspora..." 125.

77 Edrei and Mendels, ibid., attempt to prove this claim based on the *Tosefta* in *Shabbat,* 13:4 (Lieberman, ed., *The Tosefta,* 157): "As to the scrolls containing blessings, even though they include the Divine Name and many citations from the Torah, one does not rescue them, but they are allowed to burn where they are. Based on this they have stated that those who write blessings are considered as though they burnt the Torah." According to Edrei and Mendels, this text refers to blessings which are part of the prayers, following Rashi's interpretation (bShabb 61b s.v. "the blessings") it refers to "the blessings regulated by the sages such as the nine of *Rosh Hashana* which contains kingship (*malkuyot*), remembrance (*zichronot*) and *shofarot.*" But *Midrash Sechel Tov* (part 2, p. 270 and 291) understood "blessings" as meaning liturgical poems (*piyuttim*). Both of these interpretations are problematic. The wording of the *Bavli* (*Shabbat,* in the same place, 115b) is "the blessings and the amulets..." and the entire passage in tractate *Shabbat* deals specifically with amulets. Rashi, in the same place (s.v. "passages") says: "the many cases which cite verses dealing with healing." However, according to the wording of the *baraita,* the "passages" also relate to the word "blessings" which precedes the word "amulets," and this is certainly of the *Tosefta* in which

the word "amulets" does not appear. It therefore appears that the word "amulets" which the *Babylonian Talmud* adds to the *Tosefta* wording is in effect an interpretation, as indicated by the letter vav which indicates its explanatory status (see Epstein, *Introduction to the Text of the Mishnah,* 1076). This was for the purpose of preventing a mistaken interpretation of "blessings" and indicating that they were essentially amulets for the purposes of receiving blessings and nothing else. In fact, the word "blessings" may have been a euphemism, i.e. the real intention was curses, see Daniel Shperber, *Minhagei Yisrael: Origins and History,* vol. 8 (Jerusalem: Mosssad Harav Kook, 2007), 110, and sources in n. 55. Regarding "letters" see ibid., 108 and n. 49. It bears mention that the language of the prayers and blessings is biblical and not that of *Leshon Hachamim* (the language of the sages). This may also be proof of their antiquity, even though not of the time at which they became religiously fixed, for which there may have been other reasons. This point requires further examination. Shmuel Safrai and Ze'ev Safrai, *Haggadah of the Sages* (Jerusalem: Carta, 1998), 66, who wrote regarding the composition of the *Haggadah of Pessach* that "it is both a format of blessings and prayers and the sages' exegesis. It is a compilation of the scholars of the Oral Law, and was read and transmitted orally, as with the Oral Law in its entirety." They too adduced proof from the *Tosefta* cited above. However, as stated, the claim is not correct with respect to the *Haggadah* of Passover and the *Tosefta* cannot be adduced as proof.

78   The reliance on the conclusions of Hiram Peri (Pflaum), "Prayer in the Vernacular during the Middle Ages," *Tarbiz* 24 (1954/55): 439 [Hebrew], is too far-reaching and imprecise. Prima facie, his conclusions too are too radical. Either way, individual views cannot form a basis for the entire theory.

79   See Ezra Fleischer, "On the Beginnings of Obligatory Jewish Prayer," *Tarbiz* 59 (1990): 397-441 [Hebrew]. But compare critique of Lee I. Levine, *The Ancient Synagogue: The First Thousand Years* (New Haven and London: Yale University Press, 2000), 153 and the following pages.

80   See Harry Y. Gamble, *Books and Readers in the Early Church: A History of Early Christian Texts* (New Haven and London: Yale University Press, 1995), 42 and the following pages.

81   See the highly reasonable comments of John M.G. Barclay, "Diaspora Judaism," in *Religious Diversity in the Graeco-Roman World,* eds. Dan Cohn-Sherbok and John M. Court (Sheffield: *Sheffield* Academic Press, 2001), 47 and the following pages, regarding the possibility that becoming part of the "Hellenistic" world did not preclude the distinguishing characteristics of Judaism. For our purposes, our concern is not so much with the minutiae of the commandments as with the question of authority and its source. We reiterate that the disputes were not between laymen, but rather between the religious elites, irrespective of their sectarian association. In this context see the contribution made by Philip F. Esler, "Palestinian Judaism in the First Century," in *Religious Diversity in the Graeco-Roman World,* eds. Dan Cohn-Sherbok and John M. Court (Sheffield: Sheffield Academic Press, 2001), 21.

82   See Avraham Grossman, "The Immigration of the Kolynumus Family from Italy to Germany – the Beginnings of the Jewish Settlement in Germany in the Middle Ages," *Zion* 40 (1978): 156-185 [Hebrew]; Avraham Grossman, "When Did Palestinian Hegemony Cease in Italy?" in *Mas'et Moshe: Studies in the Culture of Israel and the East Presented to Moshe Gil,* ed. Ezra Fleischer, Mordechai Akiva Friedman, and Joel Kramer (Jerusalem: The Bialik Institute, 1998), 143-157; Reuven Bonfil, "Bein Erez Yisrael le-vein Bavel," *Shalem* 5 (1987): 1-30 [Hebrew]; and see Sara Zfatman, *The Jewish Tale in the Middle Ages: Between Ashkenaz and Sepharad* (Jerusalem: Magnes Press, 1993), Ch. 7 [Hebrew], according to whom

Meshulam Kolynumus may have been the 'fourth prisoner' referred to by Ra'avad in his book of *Kaballah*. See comments of *Baal Ha-Rokeah* regarding the tradition of secret prayers which he had received from R. Kalynumus, who came from Loka, "and it was received one rabbi from another, until Shimeon Ha-Fakuli; and our forefathers, the earlier authorities were very modest and would only transmit it to the modest, righteous of the generation" – Moshe Hershler and Yehudah A. Hershler, *Pirushey Siddur HaTefulah LaRokeach: A Commentary on the Jewish Prayer Book,* vol. 1 (Jerusalem: Machon HaRav Hershler, 1992), 112, and in the commentary to the "Song of the Sea," 228-229. Similar comments were also made by *Rosh* in his responsa, No. 20. s. 20: "I have guarded our tradition, and the *kabbalah* (i.e. tradition) from the sages of Ashkenaz, of blessed memory, who had the Torah bequeathed to them as an inheritance from their forefathers at the period of the destruction." This is proof source for the comments of Yitzhak Baer, *Studies in the History of the Jewish People* (Jerusalem: Israel Historical Society, 1985), 408: "[t]he Alexandrian Jew brought and wrote down what he had heard from the Sages of Israel in his generation, and for a long time the words of the Jewish sages of the Second Temple period were only said in whispers, until they were finally publicized by the scholars of the Kabbalah in the middle ages." In order for this to have happened, there had to have been a tradition of transmission. See Moshe David Cassutto, "Story of Two Tombstones from the Ninth Century in Italy," in *Jews in Italy: Studies Dedicated to the Memory of Umberto Cassuto on the 100th Anniversary of His Birth (Sidrat Sefarim Mi-Yisudo Shel S. Sh. Peri),* ed. Haim Beinart (Jerusalem: Magnes Press, 1988), 1, where he suggests that the communities of southern Italy of that period originated in immigration from *Eretz Yisrael,* and hence the possibility that the literature they brought with them similarly originated in *Eretz Yisrael.* In view of the destitute situation of the Jews and of Judaism in that period in *Eretz Yisrael* during that period and during the periods preceding it, it is difficult to accept that they were the ones who rejuvenated Jewry in southern Italy, unless we assume some kind of joint reunion of communities which generated a general renewal. This is the only way of understanding the well-known adage "The Torah will come forth from Baari and the Word of God from Ottoronto – Rabbenu Tam, *Sefer ha-Yashar,* ed. Ferdinand Rosenthal (Berlin, 1898; repr. Jerusalem, 1975), 90.

83    Israel M. Ta-Shma, *Early Franco-German Ritual and Custom* (Jerusalem: Magnes Press, 1992), 98-100 [Hebrew], and references there. See also ibid regarding additional areas in which *Eretz-Yisrael* influenced Ashkenaz. See Yaakov Sussman, "Manuscripts and Text Traditions of the Mishnah," in *Proceedings of the Seventh World Congress of Jewish Studies: Studies in the Talmud, Halacha and Midrash* (Jerusalem: Magnes Press, 1981), 235, n. 88 [Hebrew], regarding the puzzle surrounding the center of learning in southern Italy, whose Torah traditions were anchored in the traditions and customs of *Eretz Yisrael.* On the influence of the Italian tradition on France, see comments of Simcha Emanuel, *Fragments of the Tablets: Lost Books of the Tosaphists* (Jerusalem: Magnes Press, 2007), 80 [Hebrew].

84    This is not the forum for clarifying the meaning of this 'custom'. See Ta-Shma, *Early Franco-German Ritual and Custom,* and my articles, Lifshitz, " '*Minhag'* and its place…" and Lifshitz, "*Aggada* and Its Role…"

85    See Moshe Amit, "Worlds Which Did Not Meet," in *The Jews in the Hellenistic-Roman World: Studies in Memory of Menachem Stern,* eds. Isaiah Gafni et al. (Jerusalem: The Zalman Shazar Center for Jewish History and The Historical Society of Israel, 1996), 268 and the following pages. In his view, the Jewish Greek literature disappeared because no one was interested in it apart from the Church, and so it was not widely preserved. The Alexandrian Jews abandoned Hellenism.

86    M. D. Herr, "The End of Jewish Hellenistic Literature: When and Why?" in *The Jews in the Hellenistic-Roman World: Studies in Memory of Menachem Stern*, eds. Isaiah Gafni et al. (Jerusalem: The Zalman Shazar Center for Jewish History and The Historical Society of Israel, 1996), 361.

87    Yoram Erder, "When Did the Karaites First Encounter Apocryphic Literature akin to the Dead Sea Scrolls," *Cathedra* 42 (1987): 66 [Hebrew]; Erder, *The Karaite Mourners of Zion and the Qumran*, 428. See also Haggai Ben Shammai, "*Methodological Notes Concerning the Relationship between the Karaites and Ancient Jewish Sects*," *Cathedra 42* (1987): 69; Sussman, "The History of the Halakhah…" 16, 59, and n. 190.

88    R. Eliezer ben Yoel haLevi, *Sefer Ra'avya*, vol. 4, p. 308; Mordechai A. Friedman, *Jewish Marriage in Palestine: A Cairo Geniza Study*. 2 vols. (Tel-Aviv and New York: Tel-Aviv University and The Jewish Theological Seminary of America, 1980), 17.

89    See the comment of Natan Freid, "Alternative *Haftarot* in the Yeini Liturgy and other Early Liturgists," Sinai 31 (1967): 268, n. 7 [Hebrew].

90    Israel M. Ta-Shma, *Studies in Medieval Rabbinic Literature*, vol. 3, *Italy & Byzantium* (Jerusalem: The Bialik Institute, 2005), 177-187 [Hebrew].

91    Israel M. Ta-Shma, "Rabbi Moses the Preacher and the Pseudopigraha," in *Studies in Medieval Rabbinic Literature*, vol. 3, Italy & Byzantium (Jerusalem: The Bialik Institute, 2005), 188-201 [Hebrew]. See in the introduction of R. Hanoch Albeck, ed., *Bereshit Rabbati* (Jerusalem: Mekitzei Nirdamim, 1940), 17 [Hebrew], and in his comments there regarding *Midrash Tadsheh*, which drew from Jubilees and other apocyrpha, such as the writings of Philo. Epstein also took the view that the *Midrash Tadshe* was based on the work of Rabbi Moshe the Preacher. See also in Israel M. Ta-Shma, "Byzantinian Interpretation of Scriptures from the Turn of the Tenth-Eleventh Centuries," in *Studies in Medieval Rabbinic Literature*, vol. 3, *Italy & Byzantium* (Jerusalem: The Bialik Institute, 2005), 241 and the following pages.

92    Michael E. Stone, "The Testament of Naftali," *JJS* 47 (1996): 313-321; Michael E. Stone, "The Geneaology of Bilhah," *DSD* 3 (1996): 20-36; John C. Reeves, "Exploring the Afterlife of Jewish Pseudepigrapha in Medieval Near Eastern Religious Traditions: Some Initial Soundings," *JSJ* 30 (1999): 148-177. See further in material and references brought by Martha Himmelfarb, "R. Moses the Preacher and the Testaments of the Twelve Patriarchs," *AJS Review* 9, no. 1 (1984): 55-78. See n. 5 regarding the literature treating of the influence of the epigrapha on the various *midrashim*, and in n. 7 she claims that the writers did not discuss the question of how these texts were preserved by the writers of these *midrashim*. Himmelfarb states that some of the material was cited by the authors in the name of "our Rabbis of Blessed Memory." In her view, they did this in their ignorance of its source. But perhaps they did it because they did not want to mention the source, of which they were keenly aware?  See also in Himmelfarb's article, Martha Himmelfarb, "Some Echoes of Jubilees in Medieval Hebrew Literature," in *Tracing the Threads: Studies in the Vitality of Jewish Pseudepigrapha*, ed. John C. Reeves (Atlanta: Scholars Press, 1994), 127-136. In that article, she proposes a more complex method to explain the existence of this material in the hands of R. Moshe the Preacher. In fact, the book in which her article appears presents a number of ways of understanding the influence wielded by these writings in different countries and on different religions, and there are a number of different nuances. See also Amos Geula, "Lost Aggadic Works Known only from Ashkenaz: Midrash Abkir, Midrash Esfa and Devarim Zuta," (PhD diss., The Hebrew University of Jerusalem, 2006).

93    Conceivably, the permission that was finally granted for the writing of the Oral Law was also the result of the disappearance of the Sadducees, who demanded the writing down of the law in order to confer its validity (see my article, Lifshitz, "Aggada and Its Role…").

In my comments below I will suggest that there was a distinction between the East and the West with respect to the continued, parallel existence of the two sects. In fact, the "book" (=*Talmud*) arrived in Ashkenaz at a later period than in Babylonia and North Africa, and there was a greater and more longstanding reliance on Oral Law traditions. This may indicate the effect of the parallel existence of two diasporas. For a similar format for honing Jewish identity against the background of the "other," see Seth Schwartz, "Interactions between Jews and Christians at the end of Antiquity," in *Continuity and Renewal: Jews and Judaism in Byzantine-Christian Palestine,* ed. Lee I. Levine (Jerusalem: Yad Izhak Ben-Zvi, 2004), 343-354 [Hebrew]; Joshua Levinson, "Mother and Nation, Literary Identities in Changing Reality," in *Continuity and Renewal: Jews and Judaism in Byzantine-Christian Palestine,* ed. Lee I. Levine (Jerusalem: Yad Izhak Ben-Zvi, 2004), 465-485 [Hebrew].

94 mYeb 1:4 and above, in text adjacent to n. 8 onwards. See also comments of Baumgarten, "Who Were the Sadducees?"; See also in articles of Noam, "Beth Shammai and the Sectarian Halakhah," 45-67; Vered Noam, "Between Polemic and Dispute: Why Was Rabbi Eliezer Excommunicated?" *Masechet* 5 (2006): 125-144 [Hebrew]; Vered Noam, "Traces of Sectarian Halakha in the Rabbinic World", in *Rabbinic Perspectives: Rabbinic Literature and the Dead Sea Scrolls, Proceedings of the Eighth International Symposium of the Orion Center,* eds. Steven D. Fraade et al. (Leiden: Brill, 2006), 67-85.

95 See Sussman, "The History of the Halakhah..." nn. 235, 238, and literature cited there. (He also mentions those who dealt with identifying the traces of Sadduccean *halakhah.*) This is no longer the prevalent view. See Lee I. Levine, "Between Rome and Byzantine in Jewish History: Records, Reality and Periodicization," in *Continuity and Renewal: Jews and Judaism in Byzantine-Christian Palestine,* ed. Lee I. Levine (Jerusalem: Yad Izhak Ben-Zvi, 2004), 7-48. See also Martin Goodman, "Sadducees and Essenes after 70 C.E.," in *Judaism in the Roman World: Collected Essays* (Leiden: Brill, 2007) 153-162. Emphasis should be placed on his assertion that despite the paucity of sources indicating the continued religious and social differentiation between the other sects and the rabbis, they cannot be ignored. The dearth of sources may be attributable to the sages' intentional disregard of their rivals (my thanks to Daniel Schwartz for this reference). The material and the explanation presented here complement the sources recording the dispute. An additional relevant factor in this context is the renewed assent of the Priestly class. See Oded Irshai, "The Priesthood in Jewish Society of Late Antiquity," in *Continuity and Renewal: Jews and Judaism in Byzantine-Christian Palestine,* ed. Lee I. Levine (Jerusalem: Yad Izhak Ben-Zvi, 2004), 67-106 [Hebrew], and see article of David Amit, "Priests and the Memory of the Temple in the Synagogues of Southern Judea," in *Continuity and Renewal: Jews and Judaism in Byzantine-Christian Palestine,* ed. Lee I. Levine (Jerusalem: Yad Izhak Ben-Zvi, 2004), 143-155 [Hebrew], and on the other hand, the article of Zeev Weis, in same collection, Zeev Weis, "Biblical Stories in Early Jewish Art: Jewish-Christian Polemic or Intracommunal Dialogue," in *Continuity and Renewal: Jews and Judaism in Byzantine-Christian Palestine,* ed. Lee I. Levine (Jerusalem: Yad Izhak Ben-Zvi, 2004), 245-269 [Hebrew]; Dalia Trifon, "The Jewish Priests from the Destruction of the Second Temple to the Rise of Christianity," (PhD diss., Tel-Aviv University, 1985) [Hebrew]. Presumably, their traditions are not only evidenced by their political practices, and their status also influenced their spiritual life. It bears mention that these influences are also discernible in secondary literature, liturgy, and the *heichalot* literature, see Levine, "Between Rome and Byzantine in Jewish History..." p. 32.

96 See Sussmann, "The History of the Halakhah..." 60, and n. 191, regarding the research on the Sadducees done indirectly. Their history in the western exile also provides similar indirect evidence. Apparently, there were "Sadducees" in Babylonia too in the times of Rabba: see bMacc 22b, where he mentions the distinction between honoring the Scroll of the Torah and failing to accord respect to a rabbi, which is essentially the distinction between the belief in

the Written law and the non-belief in the Oral Law that is predicated of the debates during the tannaitic period. This formulation is similar to that stated by the members of the sects, as interpreted by Kister, "Studies in 4QMiqsat Ma'ase HaTorah and Related Texts..." 331! See also bErub 21b, where Rabba emphasizes the extra severity attaching to the Words of Scribes over the words of the (Written) Torah. bSan 100a (members of the family of Benyamin, the doctor, who scorned the rulings of the sages); bHull 84a (dispute with Jacob the heretic [*min*]). See at length in comments of Yaakov Elman, "Acculturation to Elite Persian Norms and Modes of Thought in the Babylonian Jewish Community of Late Antiquity," in *Netiot le-David: Jubilee Volume for David Weiss Halivni* (Jerusalem: Orhot, 2004), 31 [Hebrew]. On the disputations with Christians in Babylonia, see Richard Kalmin, "Christians and Heretics in Rabbinic Literature of Late Antiquity," *Harvard Theological Review* 87 (1994): 158. See bSan 43a; bPess 48b; and see also Moshe Halbertal and Shlomo Naeh, "Fountains of Redemption: Exegetical Contradiction and the Repentance of the Heretics," in *Higayon L'Yona: New Aspects in the Study of Midrash, Aggadah and Piyut in Honor of Professor Yona Fraenkel*, eds. Joshua Levinson, Jacob Elbaum, and Galit Hasan-Rokem (Jerusalem: Magnes Press, 2007), 179-198 [Hebrew].

See Maimonides, *Mishneh Torah, Hilchot Avadim*, 6:7, on the status of Sadducees in this time, and see also in *Hilchot Avodat Yom HaKippurim* 1:7: "In the days of the Second Temple heresy sprouted in Israel and the Sadducees – may they fast perish – who did not believe in the Oral Law..." It emerges from this ("may they fast perish") that according to Maimonides, the Sadducees or Sadduceanism still existed in his own time. See also in his comments in *Hilchot Mamerim* 3:3, where he distinguishes between Sadducees and Karaites in a matter pertaining to practical *halakhah* at that time, from which we learn that they were distinct sects. On this matter see the observations of Isadore Twersky, *Introduction to the Mishneh Torah of Maimonides*, trans. M. B. Lerner (Jerusalem: Magnes Press, 1991), 66, n. 159. See also in the *Zohar* 3, 156a-b: "there is no bread – this refers to the Oral Law; and there is no water – this refers to the Written Law, and this is moldy bread, for in their eyes the words of Oral Law were defective." Even during the period of the author of the Zohar there were those for whom the Oral Law carried no weight. See also Moisés Orfali Levi, *In the Struggle Over the Status of the Torah: The Numerology of Rabbi Imanuel Aboab* (Jerusalem: Yad Izhak Ben-Zvi, 1997), in the introduction [Hebrew]; Yosef Kaplan, *From New Christians to New Jews* (Jerusalem: The Zalman Shazar Center, 2003) [Hebrew].

The choice of using either of the two conceptions of Oral Law existing simultaneously in the world of Judaism, and the choice to emphasize either of the conceptions, depends on the historical context and changing needs. See above, n. 40.

97   See also in Isaiah Gafni, "Punishment, Blessing, or Universal Mission? Jewish Dispersion in the Second Temple and Talmudic Period," in *The Jews in the Hellenistic-Roman World: Studies in Memory of Menahem Stern*, edited by Isaiah Gafni, Aharon Oppenheimer, and Daniel R. Schwartz (Jerusalem: The Zalman Shazar Center for Jewish History, 1996), 299-250 [Hebrew]; Isaiah Gafni, "The Status of Eretz-Yisrael in Jewish Consciousness Following the Bar-Kochba Revolt," in *Studies in Jewish History During the Mishnah and Talmud*, ed. Isaiah Gafni (Jerusalem: The Zalman Shazar Center, 1994), 178 [Hebrew]. See also in the representation of the Temple in the post-destruction artwork, by Bianca Kohnel, "Jewish Art in the Pagan-Christian Context: Questions of Identity," in *Continuity and Renewal: Jews and Judaism in Byzantine-Christian Palestine*, ed. Lee I. Levine (Jerusalem: Yad Izhak Ben-Zvi, 2004), 49-65 [Hebrew].

98   Seth Schwartz, *Imperialism and Jewish Society: 200 B.C.E. to 640 C.E.* (Princeton, NJ: Princeton University Press, 2001). Even if we totally reject the approach of Schwartz (and see critique of Millar, "Transformations of Judaism under Graeco-Roman Rule...") it would seem that the influence of the rabbis was not total and all embracing. Indeed, from

the perspective of the heretics, all of the Jews belonged to the same category, and hence Schremer's thesis is of limited validity, see Adiel Schremer, "Seclusion and Exclusion: The Rhetoric of Separation in Qumran and Tannaitic Literature," in *Rabbinic Perspectives: Literature and the Dead Sea Scrolls, Proceedings of the Eighth International Symposium of the Orion Center*, eds. Steven D. Fraade et al. (Leiden: Brill, 2006), 127, 139.

In this context, it is interesting to note that there is a "black hole" between the closing of the *Talmud* in the sixth century and the beginning of the Geonic period in the eighth century, and in a wondrous manner it was precisely during that obscure period that the *Babylonian Talmud* was edited by the *stamaim*. This "hole" exists also in Europe, but the light of the Ashkenzai communities – Italy, France, and Provence, issued precisely from that blackness. Contemporary research is still groping in the darkness in its attempt to understand how this happened. We are similarly in the dark regarding the history of Babylonian Jewry from after the destruction of the First Temple and until the beginning of the Amoraic period. Despite this, great scholars of Torah came up from Babylonia, such as Hillel and R. Nathan, with their own Torah during the tannaitic period. We also know of the Torah in Babylonia based on our knowledge of sages such as R. Shila, the father of Shmuel, Karna, and others. It may reasonably be presumed that they learned from somebody, but that the nation did not preserve the names of their teachers. In this case too, no literature seems to have been preserved, but it would nonetheless seem that Babylon was home to a defined form of Judaism. Otherwise it would not have suddenly "come back to life." It was under a cloud of secrecy and ignorance in all of these diasporas and on every occasion, whether it be the Pharisee Judaism or the Rabbinic Judaism, according to the time and place. We cannot elaborate in this current context.

99 See Yohanan Levy, *Worlds Meet: Studies on the Status of Judaism in the Greek-Roman World* (Jerusalem: The Bialik Institute, 1960), 227 [Hebrew]; Michael Avi-Yonah, *In the Days of Rome and Byzantium* (Jerusalem: The Bialik Institute, 1970), 168 [Hebrew].

100 See Menahem Kister, "Observations on Aspects of Exegesis, Tradition and Theology in Midrash, Pseudoepigrapha, and Other Jewish Writings," in *Tracing the Threads: Studies in the Vitality of Jewish Pseudepigrapha,* ed. John C. Reeves (Atlanta: Scholars Press, 1994), 1, nn. 22, 23.

101 A thesis warranting examination in this context is that Babylonian Jewry at the early stages, and certainly the major part thereof (even though there were also Sadducees there – see M. D. Herr, "The End of Jewish Hellenistic Literature..."), accepted the concept and the authority of the 'Oral Law' already in the times of Hillel, who came to *Eretz Yisrael* from Babylonia and was already equipped with traditions regarding methods of exegesis of Scriptures (see above n. 35). As such the rabbis felt more comfortable conducting a dialogue with them than they did in their battles with the other sects that were in *Eretz Yisrael* and in the western diaspora.

102 See Sterk, "Latino Romaniotes..."

# Bibliography

Albeck, Hanoch. "External Halakhah in the Eretz Yisrael Translations and in Aggadah," *Jubilee Volume dedicated to B.M. Lewin*, edited by Y.L. Fishman, 93-104. Jerusalem, 1940 [Hebrew].

Albeck, Hanoch, ed. *Bereshit Rabbati.* Jerusalem: Mekitzei Nirdamim, 1940 [Hebrew].

Alon, Gedaliah. "The Sociological Approach for the Investigation of the Halakhah." In *Studies in Jewish History in the Times of the Second Temple, the Mishna and the Talmud.* 2 vols. Tel Aviv: Hakibbutz Hameuchad, 1958 [Hebrew].

Alon, Gedaliah. *History of the Jews in Eretz Yisrael During the Mishnaic and Talmudic Period.* Vol. 1. Tel-Aviv: Hakibbutz Hameuchad, 1967 [Hebrew].

Aloni, Nehemia, ed. *Ignace Goldziher Memorial Volume.* Edited by Ignaz Goldziher and Samuel Löwinger. Budapest: Globus Nyomdai Müintézet; Jerusalem: Mass, 1948-1958.

Amit, David. "Priests and the Memory of the Temple in the Synagogues of Southern Judea." In *Continuity and Renewal: Jews and Judaism in Byzantine-Christian Palestine*, edited by Lee I. Levine, 143-155. Jerusalem, Yad Izhak Ben-Zvi, 2004 [Hebrew].

Amit, Moshe. "Worlds Which Did Not Meet." In *The Jews in the Hellenistic-Roman World: Studies in Memory of Menahem Stern*, edited by Isaiah Gafni, Aharon Oppenheimer, and Daniel R. Schwartz, 260-267. Jerusalem: The Zalman Shazar Center for Jewish History, 1996 [Hebrew].

Avi-Yonah, Michael. *In the Days of Rome and Byzantium.* Jerusalem: The Bialik Institute, 1970 [Hebrew].

Baer, Yitzhak. *Studies in the History of the Jewish People.* Jerusalem: Israel Historical Society, 1985.

Barclay, John M.G. "Diaspora Judaism." In *Religious Diversity in the Graeco-Roman World*, edited by Dan Cohn-Sherbok and John M. Court. Sheffield: *Sheffield* Academic Press, 2001.

Baumgarten, Albert I. "Who Were the Sadducees? The Sadducees of Jerusalem and Qumran." In *The Jews in the Hellenistic-Roman World: Studies in Memory of Menahem Stern*, edited by Isaiah Gafni, Aharon Oppenheimer, and Daniel R. Schwartz, 393-412. Jerusalem: The Zalman Shazar Center for Jewish History, 1996 [Hebrew].

Ben Shammai, Haggai. "Methodological Notes Concerning the Relationship between the Karaites and Ancient Jewish Sects." *Cathedra* 42 (1987): 69–84 [Hebrew].

Blondheim, Menahem. "Why Is this Book Different from All Other Books? The Orality, the Literacy, and the Printing of the Passover Haggadah." Paper presented to the Institute of Advanced Studies, The Hebrew University of Jerusalem, 2004.

Bokser, Baruch M. *The Origins of the Seder: The Passover Rite and Early Rabbinic Judaism.* Berkeley: University of California Press, 1984.

Bokser, Baruch M. "Todos and Rabbinic Authority in Rome." In *New Perspectives in Ancient Judaism*, Vol. I, edited by Jacob Neusner, Peder Borgen, Ernest S. Frerichs, and Richard Horsley, 117-129. Lanham, MD: University Press of America, 1987.

Bonfil, Reuven. "Bein Erez Yisrael le-vein Bavel." *Shalem* 5 (1987): 1-30 [Hebrew].

Boyarin, Daniel. "Tale of Two Cities: Yabneh and Nikea." In *Continuity and Renewal: Jews and Judaism in Byzantine-Christian Palestine*, edited by Lee I. Levine, 301-332. Jerusalem: Yad Izhak Ben-Zvi, 2004 [Hebrew].

Boyarin, Daniel. "The Yavneh-Cycle of the Stammaim and the Invention of the Rabbis." In *Creation and Composition: The Contribution of the Bavli Redactors (Stammaim) to the Aggada*, edited by Jeffrey L. Rubinstein, 237-289. Tubingen: Mohr Siebeck, 2005.

Boyarin, Daniel. "He Who Spoke and the World Came into Being." In *Higayon L'Yona: New Aspects in the Study of Midrash, Aggadah and Piyut in Honor of Professor Yona Fraenkel*, edited by Joshua Levinson, Jacob Elbaum, and Galit Hasan-Rokem. 151-164. Jerusalem: Magnes Press, 2007 [Hebrew].

Bradshaw, Paul F., and Lawrence A. Hoffman, eds. *Passover and Easter: Origin and History to Modern Times*. Vol. 5, *Two Liturgical Traditions*. Notre Dame: University of Notre Dame Press, 1999.

Brodi, Robert, ed. *Responsa of Rav Natrunai Gaon*. Jerusalem: Ofek Institute, 1994.

Broshi, Magen, and Hanan Eshel. "A Messiah before Jesus Christ." *Tarbiz* 70 (2001): 133-138 [Hebrew].

Cassuto, Moshe David. "Story of Two Tombstones from the Ninth Century in Italy." In *Jews in Italy: Studies Dedicated to the Memory of Umberto Cassuto on the 100th Anniversary of His Birth (Sidrat Sefarim Mi-Yisudo Shel S. Sh. Peri)*, edited by Haim Beinart. Jerusalem: Magnes Press, 1988.

Castellucci, Ignazio. "Law v. Statute, Ius v. Lex: An Analysis of a Critical Relation in. Roman and Civil Law." *Global Jurist* 8, no. 1 (2008) (Advances), Article 5. Available at: https://www.researchgate.net/profile/Ignazio_Castellucci/publication/250147303_Law_v_Statute_Ius_v_Lex_An_Analysis_of_a_Critical_Relation_in_Roman_and_Civil_Law/links/579f9bcd08ae100d38065a0a.pdf?origin=publication_detail

Cohen, Shaye J. D. *From the Maccabees to the Mishnah*. Philadelphia: Westminster Press, 1987.

Drori, Rina. *Models and Contacts: Arabic Literature and its Impact on Medieval Jewish Culture*. Leiden-Boston-Koln: Brill, 2000.

Edrei, Arye, and Doron Mendels. "A Split Jewish Diaspora: Its Dramatic Consequences." *Journal for the Study of the Pseudoepigrapha* 16, no. 2 (2007): 91-137.

Edrei, Arye, and Doron Mendels. "A Split Jewish Diaspora: Its Dramatic Consequences II." *Journal for the Study of the Pseudoepigrapha* 17, no. 3 (2008): 163–187.

Edrei, Arye, and Doron Mendels. "A Split Diaspora Again – A Response to Fergus Millar." *Journal for the Study of Pseudepigrapha* 21, no. 3 (2012): 305-311.

Elior, Rachel. *Temple and Chariot, Priests and Angels, Sanctuary and Heavenly Sanctuaries in Early Jewish Mysticism*. Jerusalem: Magnes Press, 2003.

Elman, Yaakov. "Acculturation to Elite Persian Norms and Modes of Thought in the Babylonian Jewish Community of Late Antiquity." In *Netiot le-David: Jubilee Volume for David Weiss Halivni*, 21-42. Jerusalem: Orhot, 2004 [Hebrew].

Emanuel, Simcha. *Fragments of the Tablets: Lost Books of the Tosaphists*. Jerusalem: Magnes Press, 2007 [Hebrew].

Epstein, Jacob Nahum. *Introduction to the Text of the Mishnah*. Jerusalem: Magnes Press, 1948.

Epstein, Jacob Nahum. *Introduction to Tannaitic Literature*. Jerusalem: Magnes Press, 1957.

Erder, Yoram. "When Did the Karaites First Encounter Apocryphic Literature akin to the Dead Sea Scrolls." *Cathedra* 42 (1987): 53-68 [Hebrew].

Erder, Yoram. *The Karaite Mourners of Zion and the Qumran Scrolls: On the History of an Alternative to Rabbinic Judaism.* Tel-Aviv: Hakibbutz Hameuchad, 2004 [Hebrew].

Esler, Philip F. "Palestinian Judaism in the First Century." In *Religious Diversity in the Graeco-Roman World,* edited by Dan Cohn-Sherbok and John M. Court, 21-46. Sheffield: *Sheffield Academic Press,* 2001.

Finkelstein, Louis. "The Oldest Midrash." *HTR* 31 (1938): 291-317.

Fleischer, Ezra. "On the Beginnings of Obligatory Jewish Prayer." Tarbiz 59 (1990): 397-441 [Hebrew].

Flusser, David. "Mathew XVII, 24-27 and the Dead Sea Sect." Tarbiz 31 (1961): 150-156 [Hebrew].

Fonrobert, Charlotte Elisheva. "The Didascalia Apostolorum: A Mishnah for the Disciples of Jesus." *Journal of Early Christian Studies* 9 (2001): 483-509.

Freid, Natan. "Alternative *Haftarot* in the Yeini Liturgy and other Early Liturgists." *Sinai* 31 (1967): 267 [Hebrew].

Friedman, Mordechai A. *Jewish Marriage in Palestine: A Cairo Geniza Study.* 2 vols. Tel-Aviv and New York: Tel-Aviv University and The Jewish Theological Seminary of America, 1980.

Gafni, Isaiah. "The Status of Eretz-Yisrael in Jewish Consciousness Following the Bar-Kochba Revolt." In *Studies in Jewish History During the Mishnah and Talmud,* edited by Isaiah Gafni. Jerusalem: The Zalman Shazar Center, 1994 [Hebrew].

Gafni, Isaiah. "Punishment, Blessing, or Universal Mission? Jewish Dispersion in the Second Temple and Talmudic Period." In *The Jews in the Hellenistic-Roman World: Studies in Memory of Menahem Stern,* edited by Isaiah Gafni, Aharon Oppenheimer, and Daniel R. Schwartz, 229-250. Jerusalem: The Zalman Shazar Center for Jewish History, 1996 [Hebrew].

Gamble, Harry Y. *Books and Readers in the Early Church: A History of Early Christian Texts.* New Haven and London: Yale University Press, 1995.

Geula, Amos. "Lost Aggadic Works Known only from Ashkenaz: Midrash Abkir, Midrash Esfa and Devarim Zuta." PhD diss., The Hebrew University of Jerusalem, 2006.

Goldschmidt, Ernst Daniel. *The Passover Hagaddah: Its Sources and Its History over the Generations.* Jerusalem: The Bialik Institute, 1960 [Hebrew].

Goodenough, Edwin R. *The Jurisprudence of the Jewish Courts in Egypt: Legal Administration by the Jews Under the Early Roman Empire as Described by Philo Judaeus.* New Haven: Yale University Press, 1929.

Goodman, Martin. "The Roman Identity of Roman Jews." In *The Jews in the Hellenistic-Roman World, Studies in Memory of Menachem Stern,* edited by Isaiah Gafni, Aharon Oppenheimer, and Daniel R. Schwartz, 85-99. Jerusalem: The Zalman Shazar Center for Jewish History, 1996 [Hebrew].

Goodman, Martin. "Sadducees and Essenes after 70 C.E." In *Judaism in the Roman World: Collected Essays,* 153-162. Leiden: Brill, 2007.

Grossman, Avraham. "The Immigration of the Kolynumus Family from Italy to Germany – the Beginnings of the Jewish Settlement in Germany in the Middle Ages," *Zion* 40 (1978): 156-185 [Hebrew].

Grossman, Avraham. "When Did Palestinian Hegemony Cease in Italy?" In *Mas'et Moshe: Studies in the Culture of Israel and the East Presented to Moshe Gil*, edited by Ezra Fleischer, Mordechai Akiva Friedman, and Joel Kramer, 143-157. Jerusalem: The Bialik Institute, 1998.

Halbertal, Moshe, and Shlomo Naeh. "Fountains of Redemption: Exegetical Contradiction and the Repentance of the Heretics." In *Higayon L'Yona: New Aspects in the Study of Midrash, Aggadah and Piyut in Honor of Professor Yona Fraenkel*, edited by Joshua Levinson, Jacob Elbaum, and Galit Hasan-Rokem, 179-198. Jerusalem: Magnes Press, 2007 [Hebrew].

Heinemann, Joseph. "Judaism in the Eyes of the Ancient World." *Zion* 4 (1939): 269-293 [Hebrew].

Heinemann, Joseph. *Derashot BeTzibbur Betekufat Hatalmud* ("Public Sermons of the *Talmud Period*"). Jerusalem: Keter, 1974 [Hebrew].

Herford, Robert Travers. *Christianity in Talmud and Midrash*. London: Williams & Norgate, 1903.

Herr, M. D. "The End of Jewish Hellenistic Literature: When and Why?" In *The Jews in the Hellenistic-Roman World: Studies in Memory of Menahem Stern*, edited by Isaiah Gafni, Aharon Oppenheimer, and Daniel R. Schwartz, 361-379. Jerusalem: The Zalman Shazar Center for Jewish History, 1996 [Hebrew].

Hershler, Moshe, and Yehudah A. Hershler. *Pirushey Siddur HaTefulah LaRokeach: A Commentary on the Jewish Prayer Book*, Vol. 1. Jerusalem: Machon HaRav Hershler, 1992.

Himmelfarb, Martha. "R. Moses the Preacher and the Testaments of the Twelve Patriarchs." *Association for Jewish Studies Review* 9, no. 1 (1984): 55-78.

Himmelfarb, Martha. "Some Echoes of Jubilees in Medieval Hebrew Literature." In *Tracing the Threads: Studies in the Vitality of Jewish Pseudepigrapha*, edited by John C. Reeves, 127-136. Atlanta: Scholars Press, 1994.

Horowitz, Elliott. *Reckless Rites: Purim and the Legacy of Jewish Violence*. Princeton, NJ: Princeton University Press, 2006.

Josephus, Flavius. *Wars of the Jews* II.

Josephus, Flavius. *Antiquities of the Jews*.

Kalmin, Richard. "Christians and Heretics in Rabbinic Literature of Late Antiquity." *Harvard Theological Review* 87 (1994): 155-169.

Kaplan, Yosef. *From New Christians to New Jews*. Jerusalem: Zalman Shazar Center, 2003 [Hebrew].

Kasher, Menachem Mendel, ed. *Torah Sheleimah*. 12 vols. *Vayakhel*. Jerusalem: Hotzaat Beit Torah Sheleimah, 1936.

Kasher, Rimon. "The Beliefs of Synagogue *Meturgemanim* and Their Audience." In *Continuity and Renewal: Jews and Judaism in Byzantine-Christian Palestine*, edited by Lee I. Levine, 420-442. Jerusalem: Yad Izhak Ben-Zvi, 2004 [Hebrew].

Kister, Menahem. "The History of the Essene Sect: Examinations of the Vision of Chayot, Book of Jubilees, and Damascus Scroll." *Tarbitz* 56 (1987): 15-18 [Hebrew].

Kister, Menahem. "Observations on Aspects of Exegesis, Tradition and Theology in Midrash, Pseudoepigrapha, and Other Jewish Writings." In *Tracing the Threads: Studies in the Vitality of Jewish Pseudepigrapha*, edited by John C. Reeves, 1-34. Atlanta: Scholars Press, 1994.

Kister, Menahem. "Studies in 4QMiqsat Ma'ase HaTorah and Related Texts: Law, Theology, Language, and Calendar." *Tarbiz* 68 (1999): 317-371 [Hebrew].

Kohnel, Bianca. "Jewish Art in the Pagan-Christian Context: Questions of Identity." In *Continuity and Renewal: Jews and Judaism in Byzantine-Christian Palestine*, edited by Lee I. Levine, 49-65. Jerusalem, Yad Izhak Ben-Zvi, 2004 [Hebrew].

Levine, Lee I. "Unity and Diversity in Ancient Judaism: The Case of the Diaspora Synagogue." In *The Jews in the Hellenistic-Roman World: Studies in Memory of Menahem Stern*, edited by Isaiah Gafni, Aharon Oppenheimer, and Daniel R. Schwartz, 379-392. Jerusalem: The Zalman Shazar Center for Jewish History, 1996 [Hebrew].

Levine, Lee I. *The Ancient Synagogue: The First Thousand Years*. New Haven and London: Yale University Press, 2000.

Levine, Lee I. "Between Rome and Byzantine in Jewish History: Records, Reality and Periodicization." In *Continuity and Renewal: Jews and Judaism in Byzantine-Christian Palestine*, ed. Lee I. Levine, 7-48. Jerusalem: Yad Izhak Ben-Zvi, 2004 [Hebrew].

Levinson, *Joshua*. "Mother and Nation, Literary Identities in Changing Reality." In *Continuity and Renewal: Jews and Judaism in Byzantine-Christian Palestine*, edited by Lee I. Levine, 465-485. Jerusalem, Yad Izhak Ben-Zvi, 2004 [Hebrew].

Levy, Yohanan. *Worlds Meet: Studies on the Status of Judaism in the Greek-Roman World*. Jerusalem: The Bialik Institute, 1960 [Hebrew].

Licht, Haim. "Todus of Rome and the Eating of Holy Sheep on Eve of Passover." *Tura* 4 (1996): 89-106 [Hebrew].

Lieberman, Saul. *Greek in Jewish Palestine*. New York: Jewish Theological Seminary of America, 1942.

Lieberman, Saul, ed. *The Tosefta: According to Codex Vienna with Variants and a Brief Commentary*. New York and Jerusalem: The Jewish Theological Seminary of America, 1970 [Hebrew].

Lieberman, Saul. *Tosefta Ki-Fshutah: A Comprehensive Commentary on the Tosefta*. Vol. V, *Order Mo'ed, Tractate Pesahim*. New York: Jewish Theological Seminary in America, 1955-1988 [Hebrew].

Lieberman, Saul. "Keles Kilusin." In *Studies in Palestinian Talmudic Literature*, edited by David Rosenthal. Jerusalem: Magnes Press, 1991 [Hebrew].

Lifshitz, Berachyahu. *Law and Action: Terminology of Obligation and Acquisition in Jewish Law*. Jerusalem: The Bialik Institute, 2002.

Lifshitz, Berachyahu. "Aggada and Its Role in the Unwritten Law." *Shenaton Ha-Mishpat Ha-Ivri* 22 (2004): 233-328 [Hebrew].

Lifshitz, Berachyahu. " '*Minhag*' and its place on the scale of Norms of the Oral Law." *Shenaton Ha-Mishpat Ha-Ivri* 24 (2006-2007): 123-255 [Hebrew].

Linder, Amnon. *The Jews in the Legal Sources of the Early Middle Ages*. Detroit: Wayne State University Press, 1997.

Liver, Jacob. "The Ransom of Half Shekel." In *Yehezkel Kaufmann Jubilee Volume: Studies in Bible and Jewish Religion Dedicated to Yehezkel Kaufmann on the Occasion of His Seventieth Birthday*, edited by Menahem Haran, 54-67. Jerusalem: Magnes Press, 1960 [Hebrew].

Liver, Jacob. "The Half Shekel in the Scrolls of the Judean Desert Sect." *Tarbiz* 31 (1961): 18-22 [Hebrew].

Maimonides. *Commentary on the Mishnah,*

Maimonides. *Mishneh Torah,*

Mandel, Paul. "Scriptural Exegesis and the Pharisees in Josephus." *Journal of Jewish Studies* 58 (2007): 19-32.

Millar, Fergus. "The Jews of the Graeco-Roman Diaspora between Paganism and Christianity, ad 312-438." In *The Jews among Pagans and Christians in the Roman Empire*, edited by Judith Lieu, John A. North, and Tessa Rajak, 97-123. London and New York: Routledge, 1992.

Millar, Fergus. "Transformations of Judaism under Graeco-Roman Rule: Response to Seth Schwartz's 'Imperialism and Jewish Society'." *Journal of Jewish Studies* 57 (2006): 137-158.

Millar, Fergus. "A Rural Jewish Community in Late Roman Mesopotamia, and the Question of the 'Split' Jewish Diaspora." *Journal for the Study of Judaism* 42 (2011): 351-374.

Naeh, Shlomo. "Karyana de-Igreta: Notes on Talmudic Diplomatics." In *Sha'arei Lashon Vol. II - Rabbinic Hebrew and Aramaic*, edited by A. Maman, S.E. Fassberg, and Y. Breuer (Jerusalem: The Bialik Institute, 2007), 228-255 [Hebrew].

Nakman, David. "The Halakhah in the Writings of Josephus," PhD diss., Bar-Ilan University, 2004.

Noam, Vered. "Beth Shammai and Sectarian Halakhah." *Jewish Studies* 41 (2002): 45-67 [Hebrew].

Noam, Vered. *Megillat Ta'anit: Versions, Interpretations, History, with a Critical Edition.* Jerusalem: Yad Ben-Zvi, 2003.

Noam, Vered. "Between Polemic and Dispute: Why Was Rabbi Eliezer Excommunicated?" *Masechet* 5 (2006): 125-144 [Hebrew].

Noam, Vered. "Traces of Sectarian Halakha in the Rabbinic World." In *Rabbinic Perspectives: Rabbinic Literature and the Dead Sea Scrolls, Proceedings of the Eighth International Symposium of the Orion Center*, edited by Steven D. Fraade, Aharon Shemesh, and Ruth A. Clements, 67-85. Leiden: Brill, 2006.

Oppenheimer, Aharon. "Batei Midrash in Babylonia before the Completion of the Mishnah." In *Yeshivot and Batei Midrash,* edited by Emanuel Etkes, 19-29. Jerusalem: The Zalman Shazar Center, 2006 [Hebrew].

Orfali Levi, Moisés. *In the Struggle Over the Status of the Torah: The Numerology of Rabbi Imanuel Aboab.* Jerusalem: Yad Izhak Ben-Zvi, 1997 [Hebrew].

Peri (Pflaum), Hiram. "Prayer in the Vernacular during the Middle Ages." Tarbiz 24 (1954/55): 428-430 [Hebrew].

R. Eliezer ben Yoel haLevi, *Sefer Ra'avya,* Vol 4.

Rabbenu Tam. *Sefer ha-Yashar*, edited by Ferdinand Rosenthal. Berlin, 1898; repr. Jerusalem, 1975.

Rabello, Alfredo Mordechai. "De Collatio Legum Mosaicarum et Romanarum." *Shenaton Ha-Mishpat Ha-Ivri* 1 (1974): 231-262 [Hebrew].

Rabello, Alfredo Mordechai. "The First Law of the Emperor Theodosius II." In *Mehkarim B'yahadut: Sefer Hayovel L'david Kotler* ("Studies in Judaica, Jubilee Volume Presented to David Kotlar"), 172-192. Tel Aviv: Am Hasoffer, 1975.

Rabello, Alfredo Mordechai. "Mosaicarum et Romanarum: TheProblem of its Secondary Recension or its Use in the Fourth Century." In *For Uriel: Studies in the History of Israel in Antiquity Presented to Professor Uriel Rappaport*, edited by Menahem Mor, Jack Pastor, Israel Ronen, and Yakov Ashkenazi, 385-414. Jerusalem: The Zalman Shazar Center, 2005 [Hebrew].

Rabin, Haim. "The Historical Background of the Hebrew in Qumran." *Linguistic Studies* (1999): [Hebrew].

Rajak, Tessa. "The Jewish Community and Its Boundries" In *The Jews among Pagans and Christians in the Roman Empire*, edited by Judith Lieu, John A. North, and Tessa Rajak, 9-28. London and New York, 1992.

Rajak, Tessa. *The Jewish Dialogue with Greece-Rome.* Boston-Leiden: Brill, 2002.

Ravid, Liora. "Issues in the Book of Jubilees." PhD diss., Bar Ilan University, 2001.

Reeves, John C. "Exploring the Afterlife of Jewish Pseudepigrapha in Medieval Near Eastern Religious Traditions: Some Initial Soundings." *JSJ* 30 (1999): 148-177.

Rubenstein, Jeffrey L. *Talmudic Stories: Narrative Art, Composition, and Culture.* Baltimore: Johns Hopkins University Press, 1999.

Rubenstein, Jeffrey L. "The Story of the Oven of Achnai: A Literary Analysis." In *Higayon L'Yona: New Aspects in the Study of Midrash, Aggadah and Piyut in Honor of Professor Yona Fraenkel*, edited by Joshua Levinson, Jacob Elbaum, and Galit Hasan-Rokem, 457-480. Jerusalem: Magnes Press, 2007.

Safrai, Shmuel. "Jesus and the Hassidic Movement." In *The Jews in the Hellenistic-Roman World: Studies in Memory of Menachem Stern*, edited by Isaiah Gafni, Aharon Oppenheimer, and Daniel R. Schwartz, 417-420. Jerusalem: The Zalman Shazar Center for Jewish History, 1996 [Hebrew].

Safrai, Shmuel, and Ze'ev Safrai. *Haggadah of the Sages.* Jerusalem: Carta, 1998 [Hebrew].

Salomon, David. "Reciprocal Spiritual and Cultural Influences Between Diaspora and Eretz Israel Jewry During the Second Temple Era Until the Revolt Under Trajan." PhD diss., The Hebrew University of Jerusalem, 1979.

Schneidewind, William A. "Qumranic Hebrew as an Antilanguage." *JBL* 118, no. 2 (1999): 235-252.

Schneidewind, William A. "Linguistic Ideology in Qumran Hebrew." In *Diggers at the Well: Proceedings of a Third International Symposium on the Hebrew of the Dead Sea Scrolls and Ben Sira (Studies on the Texts of the Desert of Judah; Vol 36)*, edited by Takamitsu Mauroca and John F. Elwolde, 245-255. Leiden-Boston-Koln: Brill, 2000.

Schremer, Adiel. " '[T]he[y] did not Read in the Sealed Book': Qumran Halakhic Revolution and the Emergence of Torah Study in Second Temple Judaism." In *Historical Perspectives: From the Hasmoneans to Bar Kokhba in the Light of the Dead Sea Scrolls*, edited by David Goodblatt, Avital Pinnick, and Daniel R. Schwartz, 105-126. Leiden-Boston-Kohn: Brill, 2001.

Schremer, Adiel. "Seclusion and Exclusion: The Rhetoric of Separation in Qumran and Tannaitic Literature." In *Rabbinic Perspectives: Literature and the Dead Sea Scrolls, Proceedings of the Eighth International Symposium of the Orion Center*, edited by Steven D. Fraade, Aharon Shemesh, and Ruth A. Clements, 127-145. Leiden: Brill, 2006.

Schwartz, Seth. *Imperialism and Jewish Society: 200 B.C.E. to 640 C.E.* Princeton, NJ: Princeton University Press, 2001.

Schwartz, Seth. "Interactions between Jews and Christians at the end of Antiquity." In *Continuity and Renewal: Jews and Judaism in Byzantine-Christian Palestine*, edited by Lee I. Levine, 343-354. Jerusalem, Yad Izhak Ben-Zvi, 2004 [Hebrew].

Shinan, Avigdor. *The Aggada of the Meturgemanim.* Jerusalem: Hotsa'at Makor, 1979 [Hebrew].

Shinan, Avigdor. *The Biblical Story as Reflected in its Aramaic Translations.* Tel-Aviv: Hakkibutz Hameuchad, 1993 [Hebrew].

Shperber, Daniel. *Minhagei Yisrael: Origins and History*, Vol. 8. Jerusalem: Mosssad Harav Kook, 2007.

Simon, Marcel. *Verus Israel: A Study of the Relations between Christians and Jews in the Roman Empire, A.D. 135-425.* London: Littman Library of Jewish Civilization, 1996.

Stein, Siegfried "The Influence of Symposia Literature on the Literary Form of the Pesah Haggadah." *Journal of Jewish Studies* 8 (1957): 13-44.

Steinmetz, Devora. "Agada Unbound: Inter-Agadic Characterization of Sages in the Bavli and Implications for Reading Agada." In *Creation and Composition: The Contribution of the Bavli Redactors (Stammaim) to the Aggada*, edited by Jeffrey L. Rubinstein, 293-338. Tubingen: Mohr Siebeck, 2005.

Sterk, Aron C. "*Latino Romaniotes*: The Continuity of Jewish Communities in the Western Diaspora, 400-700 CE." *Melilah, Manchester Journal of Jewish Studies* 9 (2012): 21-49.

Stern, David. *Midrash and Theory: Ancient Jewish Exegesis and Contemporary Literary Studies.* Evanston, IL: Northwestern University Press, 1996.

Stone, Michael E. "The Testament of Naftali." *Journal of Jewish Studies* 47 (1996): 313-321.

Stone, Michael E. "The Geneaology of Bilhah." *DSD* 3 (1996): 20-36.

Sussman, Yaakov. "Manuscripts and Text Traditions of the Mishnah." In *Proceedings of the Seventh World Congress of Jewish Studies: Studies in the Talmud, Halacha and Midrash*, 215–250. Jerusalem: Magnes Press, 1981 [Hebrew].

Sussman, Yaakov. "The History of the Halakhah and the Dead Sea Scrolls: Preliminary Observations on Miqsat Ma'ase HaTorah (4QMMT)." *Tarbiz* 59 (1989-1990): 11-76 [Hebrew].

Ta-Shma, Israel M. *Early Franco-German Ritual and Custom.* Jerusalem: Magnes Press, 1992 [Hebrew].

Ta-Shma, Israel M. *Studies in Medieval Rabbinic Literature*, vol. 3, *Italy & Byzantium.* Jerusalem: The Bialik Institute, 2005 [Hebrew].

Tabory, Joseph. *The Passover Ritual Throughout the Generations.* Tel-Aviv: Hakkibutz Hame'uchad Publishing House, 1996 [Hebrew].

Tirosh-Beker, Ofra. *Ginze Ḥazal ba-sifrut ha-Ḳara'it bi-Yeme ha-Benayim* ("Hidden Rabbinic Literature in Karaite Medieval Literature"). Vol. II. Jerusalem: The Bialik Institute, 2012 [Hebrew].

Tov, Emanuel. "T'nach, Tirgumim." In *Encyclopaedia Biblica*, vol. 8, columns 774-830. Jerusalem: The Bialik Institute, 1982 [Hebrew].

Trifon, Dalia. "The Jewish Priests from the Destruction of the Second Temple to the Rise of Christianity." PhD diss., Tel-Aviv University, 1985 [Hebrew].

Twersky, Isadore. *Introduction to the Mishneh Torah of Maimonides*. Translated by M. B. Lerner. Jerusalem: Magnes Press, 1991.

Visotzky, Burton L. "Prolegomenon to the Study of Jewish Christianities in Rabbinic Literature." *AJS Review* 14 (1989): 47-70.

Weis, Zeev. "Biblical Stories in Early Jewish Art: Jewish-Christian Polemic or Intracommunal Dialogue." In *Continuity and Renewal: Jews and Judaism in Byzantine-Christian Palestine*, edited by Lee I. Levine, 245-269. Jerusalem, Yad Izhak Ben-Zvi, 2004 [Hebrew].

Yaron, Reuven. "The Competitive Coexistence of Latin and Greek in the Roman Empire." In *Collatio Iuris Romani: Etudes de'die'es a Hans Ankum a l'occasion de son 65e anniversaire*, Vol. 2, edited by Robert Feenstra, A. S. Hartkamp, J. E. Spruit, P. J. Sijpesteijn, and L. C. Winkel, 657-664. Amsterdam: J.C. Gieber, 1995.

Yuval, Israel Jacov. "The Haggadah of Passover and Easter." *Tarbitz* 65 (1996): 5-29 [Hebrew].

Zfatman, Sara. *The Jewish Tale in the Middle Ages: Between Ashkenaz and Sepharad*. Jerusalem: Magnes Press, 1993 [Hebrew].

Zucker, Moshe. "Against Whom Did Se'adya Ga'on Write the Polemical Poem *Essa Meshali*." *Tarbiz* 27 (1958): 61-82 [Hebrew].

CHAPTER SIX

# Communications and the Cultural Origins of Ashkenazic Jewry*

HAYM SOLOVEITCHIK

The contention of this article is that the scholarship of communication of the past several decades undermines a major tacit assumption of the regnant theory of cultural origins of the Ashkenazic community. First, however, we should define some terms.

The term "Ashkenazic Jewry" in the Middle Ages refers to the Jews of northern Europe, as opposed to those of southern France — Languedoc and Provence — and the Iberian Peninsula. The Ashkenazic community was comprised of the Jewish communities of the German Empire (with the possible exception of parts of northern Italy), northern France (roughly north of the Loire) and England. Culturally, they have a common point of origin, eastern part of lower Lotharingia (what Jews then called "Lotir") and the Rhineland, more specifically, the middle and upper Rhine from Köln to Worms.[1] In the course of the late Middle Ages the expulsion from England and France and the recurrent persecutions of Jews in the Empire led to their resettlement in eastern Europe. Thus, the religious culture of the Jews of central and eastern Europe until the Holocaust is correctly termed "Ashkenazic."

There are two Talmuds, the Babylonian and the Palestinian; the former was concluded in the sixth or seventh century, the latter in the fourth. The Oral Law, which governs Jewish religious practice to this day, was first set down in writing by R. Yehudah ha-Nasi in the second century in a work called the Mishnah. This work was expounded and developed by the scholars of Palestine and Babylonia in the subsequent centuries and summed up in their respective Talmuds. The Palestinian Talmud is almost purely Palestinian, that is to say, it reflects the thought of Palestinian scholars exclusively. The larger and more complex Babylonian Talmud contains material from both cultures. Palestinians figure prominently in this composite work. By the ninth or tenth century the Babylonian Talmud had generally achieved dominance in the Jewish Diaspora, though places were still to be found outside of Palestine that followed Palestinian prescriptions.

୶

Nineteenth-century Jewish scholars who founded the academic study of Judaism (*Wissenschaft des Judentums*) discovered that the Ashkenazic rite had strong Palestinian influences, and the past half century has witnessed a vigorous reassertion of this viewpoint. It has been claimed that the underlying religious culture of Early Ashkenaz was Palestinian, and that only later, some say only as late as the mid-eleventh century, does the Babylonian Talmud achieve the dominance in the religious life of Ashkenaz with which we commonly associate it. Whether one dates the Babylonian supercession in this culture to the mid-eleventh century or advances it the late tenth century, the Palestinian origins of the Ashkenazic culture is agreed upon by all; indeed, it may currently be called a scholarly commonplace.[2]

I have long had my doubts about scholarly truism on methodological grounds and, more recently, on empirical ones.

Let us begin with methodology. Assume that there are roughly some 200 laws regulating the observance of numerous laws of Passover, i.e. the elimination of leavened bread, the preparation of *matsah* and the observance of the *seder*. Suppose two or three are discovered to reflect Palestinian law, what this would mean is that, at most, some 2% of the Ashkenazic practices of Passover have Palestinian roots. However, no religious culture is a monolith, and a two or three percent mixture of the religious practices of other cultures is only natural. For example, in the lighting of Hanukkah candelabra, a field with far fewer laws than that of Passover, the Jews of Eastern Europe follow the ruling of the Sephardic scholar, Maimonides, and Sephardic Jews follow that of the famed, medieval Franco-German glossators, known as the Tosafists![3] Other examples of such crossovers could easily be provided. All this is common knowledge; yet no one would contend that the east European religious culture has Sephardic roots. For it is understood that to speak of influence one must have critical mass, a sufficient number of examples that one cannot suspect the results of being a product of happenstance.

Critical mass, however, is precisely what has been lacking in the numerous articles published on the Palestinian origins of Ashkenaz. Most articles take an instance or two from a specific area, be it Sabbath, Passover or priestly tithes, show that they are of Palestinian origin and then draw broad inferences. There are several areas where there does, indeed, seem to be critical mass. The laws of mourning for the destruction of the Second Temple during the three weeks preceding *Tish'ah be-Av* is unquestionably of Palestinian origin (something medieval scholars already noted[4]); liturgy would seem to be another such instance. Nineteenth-century scholars pointed out to some dozen or two instances where the Ashkenazic liturgy has formulas drawn from the Palestinian rite. However, many years ago the distinguished editor of liturgical texts, Daniel Goldschmidt, pointed out to me that this inference was valid in the nineteenth century before the Genizah[5] was discovered and its texts published. Now that we know that the differences in liturgy between the Palestinian and Babylonian rites runs into the many hundreds and even thousands, the significance of a score of Palestinian formulas in the Ashkenazic rite dwindles dramatically.[6] Dwindle though it may, nevertheless, there is critical mass for some claim of influence. Fifteen to twenty instances cannot be the product of chance. In most of the other instances adduced for the Palestinian influence, the sparse evidence rarely rises above claims of the random.

The only approach that will yield substantive results is the "area study." That is to say, to take an entire field of Jewish law, Sabbath or Passover for example, study *all* of its laws in all their complexity, and then assess whether there are sufficient correlations with distinctive Palestinian dicta to justify a claim of influence. I recently published just such a study of the laws of *yein nesekh*, the ban on all wine that a Gentile has made or even so much as touched, and discovered two things: First, that prior to Rashi (Troyes, Champagne, d. 1105), Ashkenazic scholars had a very imperfect knowledge of the tractate of the Babylonian Talmud, *'Avodah Zarah*, that governed the laws of *yein nesekh*. This should have made pre-Crusade Ashkenaz fertile soil for Palestinian influence and, even more importantly, for its continuance down to the closing decades of the eleventh century. Yet, and this was the second finding, the practices recorded in the pre-Rashi literature, reflect entirely the prescriptions of the Babylonian Talmud. Indeed, several of the pre-Crusade rulings stand in stark opposition to the directives found in the Palestinian one.[7]

Let us broaden the scope of our discussion and introduce the results of recent studies in the Ashkenazic manuscript traditions of the Baylonian

Talmud. This may seem somewhat esoteric, but its relevance will soon be apparent. The work of the last quarter of a century has recently been well summarized by Vered Noam:

> [E. S.] Rosenthal noted that there are two manuscript traditions [of the Talmud]: An eastern one [best] reflected in the writings of R. {H.} anan'el [of Kairuoan], and another widespread version, which he called the "vulgata," which is reflected not only in the writings of Rashi and the Franco-German Tosafists, but also in Spanish manuscripts and even in very old eastern manuscripts and Genizah fragments. This would indicate that the split in the traditions occurred already in the East, and that the Ashkenazic tradition is an eastern one. Friedman found that the text of the Ashkenazic manuscripts of the tractate *Bava Metsi'a* reflects the same text as found in the writings of the Babylonian Ge'onim. Siegel's researches revealed that there are striking similarities between the Ashkenazic version of the tractate *Megillah* and fragments from the Genizah. A striking similarity was found to exist between the superb Sephardic manuscript of the tractate *Megillah* (located in Göttingen) and the Franco-German textual traditions. Sabato found two clear textual traditions in the tractate *Sanhedrin*: an eastern one reflected in the Yemenite manuscripts and in the works of Rabbi Isaac of Fez (Alfasi); the other reflected in the Ashkenazic tradition which is mirrored, surprisingly, in the version used by Rabbenu {H.}anan'el [of Kairuoan] and that of R. Meir Abulafiah [Ramah] of Toledo. He further surmised that the split took place quite early and in the east and that this eastern version got somehow to Ashkenaz. This tradition has readings as good as [the Yemenite one] and at times even superior [to it]. The general picture that emerges from all these "partial" studies [i.e., of individual tractates] are confirmed by a broad study of the orthography of [the majority of] extant Talmudic manuscripts. Friedman's morphological study showed that many of the so-called "Palestinian" spellings are, in fact, Babylonian ones, and that to a large extent this orthography is found in late Ashkenazic manuscripts. These manuscripts preserve many of the distinctive Babylonian spellings, as do the [highly regarded] Yemenite manuscripts.[8]

The upshot of all this is that the Babylonian material that reached Yemen, Kairouan (near Tunis, in the Maghreb), and Spain, equally arrived in Ashkenaz, or that Ashkenaz received their traditions from these locales. A third possibility is that Ashkenaz received some of its manuscripts independently from the East, others via the mediation of Yemen, Kairouan and Spain. One might argue that Ashkenazic manuscripts are late — the earliest is from 1177[9] and most others are far later. What relevance can these manuscript findings have for pre-Crusade Ashkenaz? Let us turn to the emendations of Rashi. In the same article, Noam has shown that in the tractate *Sukkah*, seventy-one percent of his emendations are confirmed by eastern or Spanish manuscript traditions. This is an extraordinarily high figure. Shai Secunda's research shows that in the tractate *'Avodah Zarah* there is a forty-three percent congruence of Rashi's emendations with manuscripts which, to use Friedman's typology, are either Mediterranean or of Spanish provenance.[10] (Unfortunately we have no Yemenite manuscripts on *'Avodah Zarah*.) One might argue that a congruence of forty-three percent could equally be random; chance would have it that at least close to fifty percent of all good emendations would be corroborated by some manuscript or another. Reply can be made that first, there are only three and not a dozen manuscripts of this tractate. Second, Friedman has shown that one of the two manuscripts, Jewish Theological Seminary 15, is a composite. The first half (up to f. 43) is of the "Mediterranean" type (in Friedman's orthographical typology), the second half (f.s 43-76) of the Spanish one.[11] In the first half of this manuscript, the congruence of its readings with Rashi's emendations is forty-seven percent, in the latter half — only thirty-three percent. The degree of congruence of Rashi's emendations changes noticeably with the change of the textual tradition to which it is being compared. Apparently, Rashi was working off a manuscript that had more in common with the Mediterranean type than with the Sephardic one, and that differed very considerably from the one that came to be called "Ashkenazic." Nor is the tractate *'Avodah Zarah* unique. Thirty-one percent of Rashi's emendations in the tractate *Sanhedrin* correspond to the Yemenite tradition. Thirteen percent are found only in the Yemenite textual tradition.[12]

Truth to tell we need not resort to Rashi's emendations. Friedman has shown that in the eighth chapter of the tractate *Bava Metsi'a*, Rashi's *incipits* reflect a "Mediterranean" text, rather than what came to be known as the "Ashkenazic" version of the tractate.[13] Rashi didn't import these manuscripts. They were apparently in circulation at the time and he took care to obtain them. No doubt Rashi was a brilliant commentator and, quite possibly, he was equally talented in emendation; nevertheless, a seventy-one percent congruence in *Sukkah* is too high for intuition alone, and the marked change in degree of correlations with alternative textual traditions to which the emendations are being compared, as happens in *'Avodah Zarah* is, again, too salient to be happenstance. It seems clear that alongside intuition, Rashi also employed a broad spectrum of manuscripts of different provenances and traditions, all of which came from places far removed from the city of Troyes, where he lived, and from the Rhineland academies of Mainz and Worms where he had studied.

Can we push yet further back in time? I believe that we plausibly can. R. Geshom of Mainz, more commonly known as Rabbenu Gershom Ma'or ha-Golah (Light of the Exile) (d. 1028) issued a ban on anyone who emended the text of the Talmud.[14] Let us remember that he wrote at the dawn of Ashkenazic culture, in a period before any commentary on the Talmud had been composed. The ban issues from a time prior to the commentaries of the school of Mainz (that go currently under the name of R. Gershom), prior to the famed commentaries of Rashi and those of R. {H.}anan'el of Kairouan and R. Yosef Ibn Megas. Who was so confident of his understanding of the abrupt and gnomic text of the Talmud that he would regularly presume to emend it? Who was so confident of his control of western Aramaic that he *could* emend the Talmudic text? To give a contemporary example: what Talmudist of today could regularly emend the text of the *Bereshit Rabah* — a text written in the dialect of third and fourth century Galilean Aramaic? The Babylonian Aramaic of the Talmud was as new and as alien to them as the Galilean Aramaic of the *midrashim* is to us today. No doubt there were then, as now, bold souls who rushed in where angels fear to tread, but was the phenomenon so frequent that it demanded a communal ban? Is it not more plausible that if emendation was rampant or in danger of becoming rampant, these emendations were being made on the basis of extant manuscripts? Let us assume for a moment (we shall soon see why such an assumption is plausible) that many different textual traditions were circulating in Ashkenaz in the late tenth and early eleventh century. Whenever a group of Jews gathered to study the Talmud, each held in his hand a different manuscript, quite possibly a manuscript of a different tradition. When the group encountered a difficulty in the Talmud, nothing was more natural than to check the differing texts of the various members and to emend the other manuscripts according to the reading that they felt was best.

The pressing need for emendation unquestionably existed at the time. What is meant by such Ashkenazic medieval terms as "the book [i.e., version of the Talmud] of Rabbenu Gershom Ma'or ha-Golah" or "the book of R. Yits{h.}ak ben Yehudah [of eleventh century Mainz]"?[15] Not that they personally copied the book; this would have invested that text with no authority; but rather that its readings had received their imprimatur. It had been edited by them and contained the version that they had judged best — either by their choice of manuscript reading or by their emendation. The need for an authoritative text was felt by all; the danger was that it would be attempted by the unqualified. It seems reasonable that the purpose of R. Gershom's ban was both to preserve for qualified scholars the wide range of versions that were circulating and to preclude their corruption at the hands of the ignorant.

Why should we assume that different manuscript traditions were at that time circulating in Ashkenaz generally, and in Mainz, the city of Rabbenu Gershom, in particular? The economic role of Mainz at that time leads to this assumption. A Jewish traveler from Spain, Ibrâhim b. Yaq`ub, who traveled about northern Europe during R. Gershom's youth (ca. 965), reported thus of Mainz: "This is a great city... she dwells in the land of the Franks on a river called 'Rin' ... One sees there dirhams that were minted in Samarkind with the name of the Master of the Mint and the date of 301-302 [i.e., 913-914]... It is astonishing that a person can find in Mainz, that is to say at the far ends of the West, perfumes and spices that originate at the far ends of the East, as pepper, ginger, clove, Indian nard, "custus" and galingale. These plants are brought from India where they grow in abundance."[16] Ibrâhim b. Ya`qub need not have been surprised. Mainz was the final station of two of the three overland trade routes to the Near and Far East. One road led from the Black Sea through Kiev, Przemýsl, Krakow, Prague, Regensburg and thence to Mainz. The other followed the Danube to Esztergöm (Hungary), Raffelstettin (on the eastern border of the German Empire), Regensburg, and ended equally at Mainz.[17] Jewish merchants were active in these trails. Jews were equally active in the lucrative trade of luxury goods that arrived in Mainz from the

East via the port of Venice and the Alpine passes; so much so that the Venetian authorities sought to have them expelled from Mainz.[18] These trade routes led to Mainz because it was situated opposite Ingelheim, the seat of the major palace of the German emperors. In the tenth and eleventh century Germany there were no wealthy, independent urban centers. All large, nodal points of settlement belonged either to a bishop, an abbey or to the Emperor. Wealth was concentrated in the hands of the masters of these centers, and they alone had the buying power to attract large-scale luxury trade.[19] The Rhineland was the richest area in Germany of the time and constituted one of the economic pillars of the Empire. No one was richer than the Emperor, nor could there be any greater consumer of luxuries that the main Imperial palace.

In the mid-ninth century Jewish merchants, the Radhanites, traveled to India and China. Upon their return from the East, some of them made for Constantinople to sell their treasures to the "Romans" (the Byzantines); others headed towards "the residence of the king of the Franks to dispose of their wares."[20] Many scholars believe that the trade with the East was predominantly in Jewish hands, others deny this.[21] All, however, are agreed that the Jews were lively participants in this commerce.

At this time, we hear also of "hordes" (*cohortes*) of merchants that traveled from Germany to Saragossa, Spain, and not surprisingly they stopped at Mainz.[22] We also know that in 876 Charles the Bald sent ten pounds of silver for the reconstruction of the church in Barcelona by means of his Jewish emissary, Judas. It would appear that cultivating the Spanish periphery of the Empire was equally the policy of Louis the Pious, two generations before, when he took under his protection Abraham the Jew from Saragossa. Historians have assumed that the release from the numerous tolls that he accorded Abraham was not simply an act of benevolence, but rather part of a policy to encourage trade with Muslim Spain or to insure for the Imperial palace a steady supply of goods from Islamic countries, similar to requirement made of merchants with Imperial protection "to appear in our palace in mid-May once every year or two."[23] Rather than detailing each and every contact that the Rhineland had with Spain, Italy, Kairouan, Egypt, Palestine, Constantinople, and Baghdad, I believe that the map drawn by McCormack entitled "Trade and Communications, 700-900" will vividly illustrate to what extent the Rhineland was linked with the wider world of the time.[24]

Spices and condiments from the East arrived in Mainz in abundance; so too did material objects of religious significance. The Christian world attached great importance to relics, palpable remains of their sacred past, as the hem of the robe of Jesus or of one of the Apostles, a chip of the rock on which Mary had sat, a staff that a saint or martyr had held, and the like. These fragments of wood, cloth and stone radiated potent sanctity and were held in awe and reverence by their believers; they added great prestige, even power, to those fortunate enough to possess them. Churches and monasteries vied for their possession and were willing to pay steeply for their acquisition. Christians imported them frequently from Mediterranean countries and took care to authenticate these imports. Some of these authenticating labels or tags have survived. Around 800 Charlemagne sent his famous delegation to Haroun al Rashid in Baghdad, which included Isaac the Jew, who served possibly as the guide, possibly as the interpreter. About this time, the aristocratic nunnery in Chelles, not far from Paris, received a relic whose authenticating tag stated that it came from an area "[between] the rivers of the Tigris and the Euphrates."[25] Is it implausible that Isaac the Jew or his attendants sought equally to obtain in Baghdad or Sura or from other Jewish centers "[between] the Tigris and the Euphrates," religious objects dear to them? Jews were not interested in a patch from the cloak of Elijah or in pieces of Moses' rod, but they were starved for knowledge: for some *midrashim* that would flesh out the sparse Biblical narratives and tell of the country from which they came and something of the world in which they would dwell after their death, for books that would tell them something about their God, who was so different from the God of their neighbors  (as did the *Shiur Komah*  — the book of the mystical dimensions of the Godhead), of His palaces and attendants and His infinite glory (as did the books of the *Heikhalot*) and, perhaps above all, of His law, to whose upholding they were committed and which set them so apart from their Gentile neighbors.[26] Let us never forget that both Christianity and Judaism were Eastern religions, and the Jews of Ashkenaz and their Gentile neighbors lived in the far end of the West. Both eagerly sought out the sources of their religion in the East and endeavored to bring home some of their tangible remains. Man does not live by bread alone. Religion is a need and need creates demand, and the avenues of trade and communication will supply that need, for people will pay well for what they deeply wish, be it material or spiritual consignments.

Moreover, in these centuries the Oral Law was being first committed to writing. In the famed Babylonian academies of Sura and Pumpedita no texts were employed, but rather were recited by *tanna'im* or *garsanim*, carefully selected individuals who had meticulously committed large sections of the Talmud to memory.[27] Some texts did circulate in the Diaspora, but they were few and very far between. One can also reasonably assume that some written guides to religious conduct did circulate then in Ashkenaz, but they were unofficial and non-binding, more in the nature of cribs than of codes. The tiny clusters of Jews in Ashkenaz lived their life by mimetic transmission, by observing and reproducing the way of life of parents and teachers. What could have been more important, indeed epoch-making, for these meager settlements, than to have received for the first time in their history some authoritative guide to the observance of Sabbath or of Passover from the legendary academies of Sura and Pumpedita, not to speak of a text of a tractate the Talmud or some parts of the famed Geonic codes, as the *Halakhot Pesukot* or the *Halakhot Gedolot*? To possess such an authoritative work was truly a blessing. It also bestowed on its possessor considerable prestige and not inconsiderable religious authority.

Many routes led from West to East, not the least of which was the slave route. The Radhanites, Jews who may have originated in the environs of Baghdad, were active, possibly even played a controlling role in this trade.[28] Around 745, a bubonic plague swept through the lands of Islam. It is estimated that Islam lost about 25-35% of its population in the seven years of this scourge. There was a desperate need for labor, and the door opened wide to slave trade. Christian Europe, in turn, saw this as an opportunity to reverse its negative trade balance with Islam. Christians were forbidden to enslave their co-religionists; however, to the east, in Slavic lands, pagans lived, and war parties set out to enslave and sell them to the Muslims. So ubiquitous was this trade that the word for "slave" in English, French, German and Italian is derived from "Slav."[29] Medieval Jews, in turn, called Moravia (which was then pagan) "the land of Canaan" after the Biblical verse: "Accursed be Canaan. He shall be his brother's meanest slave."[30]

The current scholarly consensus is that the Jews were the major slave traders in the early Middle Ages.[31] The Christian world would not allow Muslim infidels to traverse and trade freely in its territory. The Christians in

Moslem countries were also a tolerated minority. However, they were bitterly divided into sects, and it is doubtful if one sect would lend sufficient help, if any, to Christian traders of another sectarian persuasion. The Jews, however, were a tolerated minority — and a reasonably "monolithic" one — both in the Islamic and Christian worlds. The Jewish Diaspora provided them with an international network of contacts, communities that would welcome, house, and advise them during their stay. These co-religionists could further serve as intermediaries between them and the different populations through which they moved. A merchant who traveled internationally also passed through many different legal systems. If he sought to do some business in these locales, he had to master their legal intricacies. The ability to have local, knowledgeable co-religionists serve as intermediaries between the merchant and the general population lightened that burden considerably. Again a map of McCormick will serve to illustrate the multiple routes of the slave trade.[32]

Recently historians, most notably Michael Toch, have begun to challenge vigorously both the scope of the Ashkenazic Jewish involvement in international trade in general, and in the slave trade in particular.[33] However, all agree that Ashkenazic Jews were predominantly traders and more importantly, were purveyors to the Imperial and ecclesiastical courts. They appear thus in Latin sources from the sixth century chronicle of Gregory of Tours down to documents from the end of the tenth century from Vienne (*negotia monachorum*).[34] A similar picture emerges from the Hebrew sources of Ashkenaz, from the *responsa* literature that first appears in the tenth and the early eleventh centuries. Jews are there frequently portrayed as selling to the courts of bishops, local rulers and even to the Queen of Hungary.[35] We further find there the institution of *ma'arufya*, a widely employed communal ordinance that forbade a Jew from competing with a co-religionist who until then had been the exclusive purveyor to Gentile or his factotum. As Toch has written: "The customers of these [Jewish] merchants [governed by the *ma'arufya* ban] came exclusively from the Christian elite, both secular and ecclesiastical."[36]

Imagine a Gentile merchant who is bringing luxury items from the East to sell local rulers in the German Empire. He knows that among the buyers are Jewish purveyors to the court and naturally, he would like to get on their good side. He also knows that for some reason they are eager to receive any written material, even the smallest work, from Babylonia or Palestine. Would he not take care to bring some of this material with him as presents or to sell them at a high price when reached the Ashkenaz? Wouldn't Jewish purveyors order on their own such books or scrolls? Would they abstain from making contact with the historic, vital centers of their religion? Would they forgo such an opportunity for enlightenment, for taking instruction from the ancient and far-famed seats of learning in Babylonia?

The links with the East were not simply commercial ones. Numerous pilgrims and envoys also made their way to Constantinople and Jerusalem during this period. Charlemagne kept an eye on the Franks in Jerusalem, and a survey that he instituted showed that close to one quarter of the priest and monks in Jerusalem were of Latin (i.e., west European) origin. Between the years 700 and 900, no less than 239 emissaries and pilgrims made their way to sacred places in the East, primarily to Constantinople (the city richest in *reliquia*) and to Jerusalem. Sixty-two percent came from Italy and twenty-six percent from the Carolingian Empire.[37] Would not a Jewish pilgrim or merchant have made some effort to reach the famed, almost sacred academies of Sura and Pumpedita, in whose halls the Talmud had been composed and bring home some scrolls or codices? Nor need these travelers to have gone so far afield as Babylonia. There was no lack of wish settlements in Jerusalem, Ramlah, Tiberias and Damascus that followed the Babylonian teachings. Damascus even served as an "entrepot" for donations from the Mahgreb to the Babylonian *yeshivot*.[38] Travelers for Ashkenaz could have acquired Babylonian works with equal ease in Fustāt (Old Cairo) and in the Maghreb. Finally, one should note that, most probably, Jewish merchants who visited the fair at St. Denis, outside of Paris, sent a query in Jewish law in the middle of the ninth century to the head of one of the Babylonian academies, R. Natrona'i Ga'on of Pumbedita.[39]

The map of the slave trade shows many roads leading to Baghdad and the map of communication and trade shows many lines converging on Aachen, the capital of the Carolingian Empire, and on the Rhineland, a major pillar of the Ottonian Empire. Is it at all surprising that a superb Spanish manuscript of the tractate *Megillah* has many characteristic readings with Ashkenazic manuscripts or that there are striking similarities between readings in Ashkenazic manuscripts and those found in the Cairo Genizah? Is it any wonder that the Ashkenazic manuscripts of the tractate *Sanhedrin* reflect scribal traditions of the Maghreb (R. {H.}anan'el) and of Spain (R. Me'ir Abulafiah), or that Rashi's textual emendations to that tractate reflect a text in part similar to that found in Yemen? With spices came books and even perhaps, as Noam has surmised,[40] commentarial traditions. Yemen and Ashkenaz, seemingly the antipodes of the Jewish world, were linked in this period by ongoing commercial contacts.

Early Ashkenaz was not located in some remote and isolated region in the far ends of the known earth of the time, whose only link to other Jewish centers was via some Alpine paths that led to Italy and from there somehow to Palestine. The Rhineland, in which the Imperial palace of Ingelheim was located, and nearby Aachen, the Carolingian capitol, were the very heartland of the Carolingian and Salian Empire, what Otto of Friesing in the twelfth century called "maxima vis regni," "the major strength of the kingdom," more colloquially, "the backbone of Imperial power."[41] The unparalleled purchasing power of the estates and palaces of the Emperor, local bishops and rulers attracted goods from four ends of the earth — China, India, Babylonia, Palestine, Spain and the Maghreb. The port of Venice further linked them with Egypt and Yemen. Ashkenaz and "Lotir" may well have been the richest zone of Europe and from the point of view of demand and consumption, the economic center of Latin Christendom. Not surprisingly they served as a magnet for all the treasures of the East, including those of the spirit.

In brief, there is no more reason to assume a Palestinian base for the culture of Ashkenaz than a Babylonian one. Ashkenaz had equal access to the treasures of both of these Near Eastern Jewish cultures. From the polemical letter against the Jews that Agobard of Lyon wrote to Emperor Louis the Pius in Aachen in the third decade of the ninth century we know that in the area of *kashrut*, Carolingian Jews followed the Babylonian prescriptions when they conflicted with those of Palestine.[42] We also know that in the area of *yein nesekh*, the ban of wine that had been touched by a Gentile, the rulings of Early Ashkenaz were in keeping with those of Babylonia rather than those of Palestine.[43]

I should emphasize that this in no way precludes Palestinian influences in other spheres of religious life. We have seen that such influence exists to a small degree in prayer, and it may equally exist to a far greater extent in other areas. It certainly does not forestall influences in the interstices of the halakhah, as in the pre-Av mourning for the destruction of the Second Temple, about which the Babylonian Talmud says nothing. Such influences, however, must be proven rather than assumed. For the tacit assumptions of some century and a half are no longer valid.

In retrospect, these assumptions seem only natural. Like all scholars, the nineteenth-century erudites of *Wissenschft des Judentums* were only too eager to demonstrate the novel results of their discipline, to show how their findings would dispel common misconceptions. It was axiomatic in that century, as in previous centuries, that Ashkenazic Jewry had lived by the lights of the Talmud, which meant of course the Babylonian Talmud which had guided Jews for a millennium. Nothing was then more natural when *Wissenschaft* uncovered the Palestinian origin of a score or so of liturgical formulas, or that here and there a custom made sense only in light of Palestinian data, to proclaim that the origins of Ashkenaz were not what they had seemed, that the religious cradle of north European Jewry had all the while been located in Palestinian Talmud. Partially from unconscious Zionist motivation, partially because the Pirenne thesis had portrayed Christian Europe as being wholly cut off from the Muslim world, twentieth-century scholars have viewed Ashkenaz as tenuously connected to the East. The advances in the study of liturgical poetry (*piyyut*) had further demonstrated that Ashkenazic liturgical poetry had been patterned after Italian models, and Italian models were unquestionably developments of the Palestinian ones.[44] *Piyyut* originated in Palestine; indeed, it had scarcely existed in Babylonia. So it was assumed that Ashkenazic religious practices equally had its roots in the same soil. This then linked up with a "founding story" that told of the translation of R. Kalonymous from Lucca to Mainz, and with it the establishment of Ashkenazic culture. That the story claimed only that the esoteric messages encoded in text of the prayers were an Italian tradition was overlooked.[45] The roots of Ashkenaz lay in Italy; Italy had, in the Byzantine period, ongoing contacts with Palestine; ergo, Ashkenazic culture was rooted in Palestine. Thus, the common notion of the cultural origins of the Ashkenazic community was born and maintained for well over a century and a half.

Liturgy was more than simply a component of this viewpoint. The enormous progress made over the past four decades in the field of liturgical poetry, fueled primarily by the Herculean labors of the late Ezra Fleischer, has endowed that poetry with significance greater than it deserved. Not that the significance of *piyyut* in the Ashkenazic culture was exaggerated; its importance was indeed great. However, its evolution cannot serve as the bellweather of Ashkenazic culture generally. Developments in liturgical poetry are one thing, developments in Jewish law another, and those in religious praxis may yet be different from both. Each area demands investigation on its own terms and in light of the differing possibilities of influence. In liturgical poetry, Ashkenaz could be influenced only by Italy and Palestine, for there was no other competing model; not so for other religious spheres. In liturgy itself, as distinct from liturgical poetry, we have seen that the influence of Babylonia far outstripped that of Palestine. Indeed, there is no reason even to assume that the Ashkenazic liturgy is cut from one cloth. Certainly, its textual tradition of the Talmud points to variegated and multicultural origins. If any place in Europe had broad cultural exposure, free access to the cultural artifacts of both Palestine and Babylonia, and those of Fustāt, Yemen and the Maghreb too, it was the Rhineland and "Lotir," the heartland and great emporium of the Carolingian and Ottonian Empires.

ᥦ

As a coda, I would note that a recent revolutionary essay of Mendels and Edrai undermines another unarticulated assumption of the Palestinian origins of Ashkenaz.[46] It was reasonably assumed that most (though not all) settlers in northern Europe came from the south, from the Mediterranean littoral with its ancient Jewish settlements. Coming from the former Roman Empire, the Jews brought with them naturally the Palestinian religious way of life, the practices reflected and formulated in the Palestinian Talmud. The practices of the Jews in the East mirrored, more or less, the Babylonian Talmud, and so it was only natural to assume that the practices of the Jews in the West mirrored those of the Palestinian Talmud. However, if Mendels and Edrei are correct, as I believe them to be, the Jews from the Empire, west of Anatolia, brought with them nothing other than a vague Biblical Judaism. Ashkenazic culture, rabbinic to the core, must then be seen not as a continuation and transformation of Jewish religious identity of the later Roman Empire, but as a break with an indistinct and tenuous past and a fresh and sharply etched beginning. A new religious civilization emerged in "Lotir" and the adjacent Rhineland about whose origins and nature we at present know very little.

## *Notes*

\* This essay is an abridged version of Chapter 9 of my *Ha-Yayin bi-Yemei ha-Beinayim: Yein Nesekh – Perek be-Toledot ha-Halakhah be-Ashkenaz* (Jerusalem: Zalman Shazar Center, 2008). This English translation was first published in Collected Essays, Volume II by Haym Soloveitchik, published by the Littman Library of Jewish Civilization (Oxford and Portland, Oregon 2014). I wish to thank Michael Toch for reading and commenting on this essay.

1    For a rough map of "Jewish Lotir," see Max Weinreich, History of the Yiddish Language (Chicago: YIVO Institute for Jewish Research, 1980), 1.

2    Avraham Grossman, "Zikatah shel Yahadut Ashkenaz ha-Kedumah el Erets Yisra'el," *Shalem* 3 (1981): 57-92; Israel M. Ta-Shma, *Minhag Ashkenaz ha-Kadmon* (Jerusalem: Magnes, 1992), 98-103 and passim; Reuven Bonfil, "Bein Erets Yisra'el le-Bavel: Kavim le-{H.}eker Toledot ha-Tarbut shel ha-Yehudim be-Italyah ha-Dromit u-ve-Eropa ha-Notsrit bi-Yemei ha-Beinayim-ha-Mukdamim," *Shalem* 5 (1987): 1-30, especially 13-19; Reuven Bonfil, " 'Eduto shel Agobard mi-Lyon 'al 'Olamam ha-Ru{h.}ani shel Yehudei 'Iro ba-Me'ah ha-Teshi'it," in *Me{h.}karim be-Kabbalah, be-Filosofyah u-ve-Sifrut ha-Musar, Muggashim le-Yesha'ayahu Tishby bi-Mel'ot Lo Shive'im ve-{H.}amesh Shanim,* eds. Yosef Dan et al (Jerusalem: Magnes, 1986), 327-348, especially 339-347. An abridged, English version of this article is available in Yoseph Dan, ed., *Binah: Studies in Jewish History, Culture, and Thought, III, Jewish Intellectual History in the Middle Ages* (Westport, CT: Praeger Publishers, 1994), 1-17; Ivan Marcus, "The Dynamics of Jewish Renaissance and Renewal in the Twelfth Century," in *Jews and Christians in Twelfth Century Europe* (Notre Dame: University of Notre Dame Press, 2001), 36-39. See also Yaakov Sussman, "Kitvei-Yad u-Mesorot Nusa{h.} shel ha-Mishnah," in *Divrei ha-Kongres ha-'Olami ha-Shevi'i le-Mada'ei ha-Yahadut* (August 7-14, 1977): *Me{h.}karim be-Talmud, Halakhah ve-Midrash* (Jerusalem: Magnes, 1981), 236, n. 89.

3    *Tosafot, Shabbat* 21c, s.v. *u-mehadderin; Mishneh Torah, {H.}anukkah* 4: 1; *Shul{h.}an 'Arukh, Ora{h.} {H.}ayyim* 671:2.

4    *Tosafot Rashba 'al Pesa{h.}im* 40b, *s.v. aval; Tosafot Ri Sirleon 'al Berakhot* 18a, s.v. *dalyeh; Or Zaru'a,* II (Zhitomir, 1862) #421 and parallel passages cited in the first two works.

5    The vast assortment of torn and discarded texts from the tenth through the twelfth century that was discovered in the attic of a synagogue in Old Cairo (Fustāt) in the late nineteenth century.

6   Goldschmidt's point was later strikingly illustrated by Ezra Fleischer, *Tefilah u-Minhagei Tefilah Erets Yisra'eliyim bi-Tekufat ha-Genizah* (Jerusalem: Magnes, 1988).

7   Soloveitchick, *Ha-Yayin bi-Yemei ha-Beinayim*, 321-327.

8   Vered Noam, "Mesorot Nusa{h.} Kedumot be-Haggahot Rashi ba-Talmud," *Sidra* 17 (2001-2002): 110-111.

9   David Rosenthal, "Mavo," in *Talmud Bavli: Ketav-Yad Firentseh, 'im Mavo me'et D. Rosenthal* (Jerusalem, 1972), 1.

10  Shai Secunda's paper, written for a seminar of mine, contains both an analysis of the variants and emendation together with a transcription of all the manuscripts readings (including those of the Genizah fragments) of the Talmudic passages emended by Rashi, both as found in the printed version of his Commentary and in Ms. Parma de Rossi 1292 (Richler 727). Deciding which version an author had in front of him often hinges on fine nuances. One may disagree with one point or another of Secunda's analysis, but the overall picture that he draws is, to my thinking at least, beyond question. As both the paper and the transcriptions variants have been placed online, the reader may draw his own conclusions: Shai Secunda. "Rashi's Emendations of the Text of Avodah Zarah," *Avodah Zarah Yein Nesekh,* last modified August 9, 2007, http://azyn.blogspot.co.il/.

11  Shamma Friedman, "Masekhet 'Avodah Zarah', Ketav Yad New York, Ketav Yad she-Hu'atak bi-Shenei Shelavim," *Leshonenu* 56 (1992): 371-374.

12  Mordechai Sabato, *Ketav Yad Teimani le-Masekhet Sanhedrin (Bavli) u-Mekomo be-Masoret ha-Nusa{h.}* (Jerusalem: Yad Izhak Ben-Zvi, 1998), 231-278, especially the table on p. 258.

13  S. Y. Friedman, *Talmud 'Arukh, Perek ha-Sokher et ha-Umanim – ha-Nusakh 'im Mavo Kelaly* (Jerusalem, 1997), 48, 57-69.

14  Rabbenu Tam, "Introduction," in *Sefer ha-Yashar: {H.}elek {H.}iddushim,* ed. Simon Solomon Schlesinger (Jerusalem: Kirjath Sefer, 1959), 9.

15  Rabbenu Gershom: sources in Avigdor Aptowitzer, *Mav'o le-Sefer ha-Ravyah* (Jerusalem: Mekitze Nirdamim, 1938), 332, n. 10; R. Yits{h.}ak ben Yehudah: sources in Avraham Grossman, *{H.}akhmei Ashkenaz ha-Rishonim: Koroteihem, Darkam be-Hanhagat ha-Tsibbur, Yetsiratam ha-Ru{h.}anit me-Reshit Yishuvam ve-'ad li-Gezerot Tatnu (1096),* 3rd ed. (Jerusalem: Magnes, 2001), 316-317. See also Avraham Grossman, *{H.}akhmei Tsarfat ha-Rishonim: Koroteihem, Darkam be-Hanhagat ha-Tsibbur, Yetsiratam ha-Ru{h.}anit,* 3rd ed. (Jerusalem: Magnes, 2001), 113, for "the book of R. Yits{h.}ak ben Mena{h.}em."

16  André Miquel, "L'Europe occidentale dans la relation arabe d'Ibrâhim b. Yaq'ub (Xe s.)," *Annales: ESC* 21 (1966): 1059-1060.

17  Aleksander Gieysztor, "Les Juifs et leurs activités économiques en Europe orientale," in *Gli Ebrei Nell'alto Medioevo,* vol. I. *Settimane di Studio del Centro Italiano di Studi Sull'alto Medioevo* 26 (Spoleto, 1980), 506-511; Tadeusz Lewicki, "Les commerçants juifs dans l'Orient islamique non méditerranéen au IXe-XIe siècle," in *Gli Ebrei Nell'alto Medioevo,* vol. I. Settimane di Studio del Centro Italiano di Studi Sull'alto Medioevo 26 (Spoleto, 1980), 375-401; W. G. Haussig, "Praxis und Verbreitung des jüdischen Handels in Südrussland," in *Untersuchungen zu Handel und Verkehr der vor- und frühgeschichtlichen Zeit in Mittel- und Nordeuropa / Teil 6: Organisationsformen der Kaufmannsvereinigungen in der Spätantike und im frühen Mittelalter,* eds. Herbert Jankuhn, W. Kimmig, and E. Ebel. *Abhandlungen-Akademie der Wissenschaft in Göttingen Philologisch Historische Klasse* 183 (Göttingen, 1989), 27, 31-32.

18    Michael McCormick, *Origins of the European Economy: Communications and Commerce 700-900* (Cambridge: Cambridge University Press, 2001), 796, 970; Georg Caro, *Sozial- und Wirtschaftsgeschichte der Juden* 2. Aufl. (Frankfurt/Main, 1924), I, 193. A letter from both the Doge and Archbishop of Venice requested that the Jews be either banned from handling items with crosses, as they desecrated them, or be expelled from the city. Caro pointed out that numerous Ottonian coins had embossed crosses, such an injunction then would have effectively excluded Jews from commerce. The commercial implications of the request would also explain why the Doge of Venice joined the Archbishop of Venice in what was ostensibly a purely religious matter.

19    Timothy Reuter, *Germany in the Early Middle Ages: 800-1056* (London/New York: Longman, 1991), 233; Alfred Haverkamp, "Die 'frühbürgerliche' Welt im hohen und späten Mittelalter: Landesgeschichte und Geschichte der städtischen Gesellschaft," *Historische Zeitschrift* 221 (1975): 571-602.

20    Robert Sabatino Lopez and Irving Woodworth Raymond, trans., *Medieval Trade in the Mediterranean World: Illustrative Documents* (New York: Columbia University Press, 1955), 32. For a German translation from the original Arabic account (rather than an English translation of a French translation as is the case of Lopez and Raymond's text), see the references in McCormick, Origins of the European Economy, 689, n. 72. A Hebrew translation from the original can be had in Moshe Gil, *Be-Malkhut Yishma'el bi-Tekufat ha-Ge'onim,* I (Tel Aviv: Tel Aviv University, 1997), 614, and see pp. 611-635 for a comprehensive discussion of the Radhanite narrative.

21    See above n. 17 and see the rich bibliography in Michael Toch, "Jews and Commerce: Modern Fancies and Medieval Realities," in Il *ruolo economico delle minoranze in Europa. Secc. XIII-XVIII (Atti dela XXXI Settimana di Studi, Istituto Francesco Datini, Prato),* ed. S. Cavaciocchi (Firenze, 2000), 43-58. See also the cautious formulation of J. P. Devroey and C. Brouwer, "La participation des Juifs au commerce dans le monde franc (VIe-Xe siècles)," in *Voyages et voyageurs à Byzance et en Occident du VIe au XIe siècle,* eds. A. Dierkins and J. M. Sansterre avec la collaboration de J.L. Kupper. Bibliothèque de la Faculté de Philosophie et Lettres de l'Université de Liège, 278 (Genève, 2000), 339-374.

22    McCormick, *Origins of the European Economy,* 674-677.

23    Fritz Rörig, "Magdeburgs Entstehung und die ältere Handelsgeschichte," in *Wirtschaftskräfte im Mittelalter. Abhandlungen zur Stadt- und Hansegeschichte,* hrsg. von P. Kaegbein, 2. Aufl. (Wien/Köln/Graz/Böhlau, 1971), 607-610; Bernhard Blumenkranz, *Juifs et Chretiens dans le monde occidentale:* 430-1096. Ecole des Hautes Etudes – Sorbonne, Etudes juives 2 (Paris, 1960), 17-18.

24    McCormick, *Origins of the European Economy,* 676. Our interest lies with the rich network of communication that McCormick has traced, not with any specific thesis of his, as for example, that it was the growing trade in the Mediterranean rather than the upsurge of commerce in the North that proved instrumental in the economic revival of the West. See, for example, the issue of *Early European History* 12 (2003) devoted to a discussion of McCormick's book.

25    McCormick, *Origins of the European Economy,* 313, 283-318.

26    See Agobard Lugdunensis, "De judaicis superstitionibus," *Opera Omnia,* ed. L. van Acker, *Corpus Christianorum, Continuatio Medievalis* 52 (Turnhout: Brepols, 1981), 199-221, 205-206. On the Jewish sources to which Agobard refers and which were then circulating in the Carolingian Empire, see the references in Bernhard Blumenkranz, *Les auteurs chrétiens latins du Moyen Age sur les Juifs et le Judaïsme* (Paris, 1963), 165, n. 62. On the

date of the missive, see most recently Christof Geisel, *Die Juden im Frankenreich: Von den Merowingern bis zum Tode Ludwigs des Frommen* (Frankfurt/Main, 1998), 575-581.

27   See Yaakov Sussman, "Torah she-Be-'al Peh Peshutah ke-Mashma'ah: Ko{h.}o shel Kutso shel Yod," *Me{h.}kerei Talmud* 3 (2005): 209-384; Nachman Danzig, "Mi-Talmud 'al Peh le-Talmud bi-Khetav: 'Al Derekh Mesirat ha-Talmud ha-Bavli ve-Limudo bi-Yemei ha-Beinayim," *Sefer ha-Shanah shel Universitat Bar-Ilan: Mada'ei ha-Yahadut u-Mada'ei ha-Rua{h.}* 30-31 (2006): 49-112.

28   Moshe Gil, "The Radhanite Merchants and the Land of Radhan," *Journal of the Economic and Social History of the Orient* 17 (1974): 299-328. See, however, Jacobi's critique, cited by McCormick, *Origins of the European Economy,* 688, n. 71.

29   The fullest and most recent discussion of the slave trade with Islam is that of McCormick, *Origins of the European Economy,* 733-776; on the bubonic plague, ibid., 504-505, 753 and 113, n. 124.

30   *Genesis* 8: 25-26. The translation is that of the *Jerusalem Bible* (London, 1966).

31   See the literature cited by Toch, "Jews and Commerce..." 43-58.

32   McCormick, *Origins of the European Economy,* 762.

33   See Toch, "Jews and Commerce..." 43-58, to which add Michael Toch, "Wirtschaft und Verfolgung: die Bedeutung der Ökonomie für die Kreuzzugspogrome des 11. und 12. Jahrhunderts. Mit einem Anhang zum Sklavenhadel der Juden," in *Juden und Christen zur Zeit der Kreuzzüge, ed. Alfred Haverkamp* (Sigmaringen: Jan Thorbecke Verlag, 1999), 253-285. A fuller discussion of the issue of slavery is available in his Hebrew article, Michael Toch, "Yehudei Eropa bi-Yemei ha-Beinayim ha-Mukdamim: So{h.}arei 'Avadim?" *Zion* 64 (1999): 39-64. See also his general survey, Michael Toch, "The Jews in Europe: 500-1050," in *The New Cambridge Medieval History,* I (Cambridge: Cambridge University Press, 2005), 555-561.

34   Julius Aronius, *Regesten zur Geschichte der Juden im fränkischen und deutschen Reiche bis zum Jahre 1273* (New York: Hildesheim, 1970), 122, 129, 132, 133, 134; Blumenkrantz, *Juifs et Chretiens,* 15-19; Devroey and Brouwer, "La participation des Juifs au commerce..." 361-363; Toch, "Jews and Commerce..." 43-58, and previous note.

35   On *ma`arufya,* see Shlomo Eidelberg, "Ma`arufia in Rabbenu Gershom's Responsa," *Historia Judaica* 15 (1953): 59-67.

36   Michael Toch, "Pe'ilutam ha-Kalkalit shel Yehudei Germaniah ba-Me'ot ha-'Asirit 'ad ha-Sheteim-'Esreh: Bein Historiografyah le-Historyah," in *Yehudim mul ha-Tselav: Gezerot Tatnu ba-Historiografyah u-va-Historyah,* eds. Yom Tov Assis et al (Jerusalem: Magnes, 2000), 43-44.

37   McCormick, *Origins of the European Economy,* 129-173, especially 153-158.

38   Gil, *Be-Malkhut Yishma'el bi-Tekufat ha-G'eonim,* 153, 149-205.

39   Robert Brody, ed., *Teshuvot R. Natronai be-Rabbi Hil'ai Ga'on* (Jerusalem: Mekhon Ofek, 1994), 243, and see McCormick, *Origins of the European Economy*, 650-651 and n. 44. For the meaning of "Farangia" in this *responsum,* see Gil, *Be-Malkhut Yishma'el bi-Tekufat ha-G'eonim,* 625, n. 349. (There remains an outside chance that the letter concerned the market in Ephesus in Asia Minor and not that of St. Denis.)

40   Vered Noam, "Mesorot Nusa{h.} Kedumot..." 117-134.

41   Otto von Freising, *Ottonis et Rahewini Gesta Friderici I. imperatoris,* eds. Georg Waitz and Bernhard von Simson (Hannover/Leipzig: Impensis Biblipolli Hahniani, 1912), 28.

42    Agobard Lugdunensis, "De insolentia judaeorum," *Opera Omnia,* ed. L. van Acker, *Corpus Christianorum, Continuatio Medievalis* 52 (Turnhout: Brepols, 1981), 193. Agobard's letter certainly is informative of the conduct of the Jews in Lyon. To my thinking, it is equally revelatory of the Jews in Lotharingia, the seat of the Empire. I cannot believe that Agobard, who saw himself as being the object of persecution by influential Jews of the court, would not have taken care to see that these Jewish practices were equally observed in and around Aachen, even more broadly, in Lotharingia generally. Otherwise, the court Jews could prove him a liar, by simply asking the Emperor to ascertain in local Jewish settlements if Agobard's descriptions were accurate. See "Agobard of Lyons and the Babylonian Orientation of Early Ashkenaz." On the date of Agobard's missives, see most recently Geisel, *Die Juden im Frankenreich,* 575-581.

43    Soloveitchick, *Ha-Yayin bi-Yemei ha-Beinayim,* 321-326.

44    Ezra Fleischer, *Shirat ha-Kodesh ha-'Ivrit bi-Yemei ha-Beinayim* (Jerusalem: Magnes, 1975), 79-276, 425-484.

45    Text in Yosef Dan, *Torat ha-Sod shel {H.}asidei Ashkenaz* (Jerusalem: The Bialik Institute, 1968), 14-20. Discussion in Grossman, *{H.}akhmei Ashkenaz,* 29-44; Joseph Schatzmiller, "Politics and the Myth of Origins," in *Les Juifs au regard de l'histoire. Mélange en l'honneur de Bernhard Blumenkrantz,* ed. Gilbert Dahan (Paris: Picard, 1985), 52-54, 61.

46    Arye Edrei and Doron Mendels, "A Split Jewish Diaspora: Its Dramatic Consequences," *Journal for the Study of the Pseudoepigrapha* 16, no. 2 (2007): 91-137.

## Bibliography

Aptowitzer, Avigdor. *Mav'o le-Sefer ha-Ravyah.* Jerusalem: Mekitze Nirdamim, 1938.

Aronius, Julius. *Regesten zur Geschichte der Juden im fränkischen und deutschen Reiche bis zum Jahre 1273.* New York: Hildesheim, 1970.

Blumenkranz, Bernhard. *Juifs et Chretiens dans le monde occidentale: 430-1096.* Ecole des Hautes Etudes – Sorbonne, Etudes juives 2. Paris, 1960.

Blumenkranz, Bernhard. *Les auteurs chrétiens latins du Moyen Age sur les Juifs et le Judaïsme.* Paris, 1963.

Bonfil, Reuven. " 'Eduto shel Agobard mi-Lyon 'al 'Olamam ha-Ru{h.}ani shel Yehudei 'Iro ba-Me'ah ha-Teshi'it." In *Me{h.}karim be-Kabbalah, be-Filosofyah u-ve-Sifrut ha-Musar, Muggashim le-Yesha'ayahu Tishby bi-Mel'ot Lo Shive'im ve-{H.}amesh Shanim,* edited by Yosef Dan and Yosef Hacker, 327-348. Jerusalem: Magnes, 1986.

Bonfil, Reuven. "Bein Erets Yisra'el le-Bavel: Kavim le-{H.}eker Toledot ha-Tarbut shel ha-Yehudim be-Italyah ha-Dromit u-ve-Eropa ha-Notsrit bi-Yemei ha-Beinayim ha-Mukdamim." *Shalem* 5 (1987): 1-30.

Brody, Robert, ed. *Teshuvot R. Natronai be-Rabbi Hil'ai Ga'on.* Jerusalem: Mekhon Ofek, 1994.

Caro, Georg. *Sozial- und Wirtschaftsgeschichte der Juden.* 2. Aufl. Frankfurt/Main, 1924.

Dan, Yosef. *Torat ha-Sod shel {H.}asidei Ashkenaz.* Jerusalem: The Bialik Institute, 1968.

Dan, Yoseph, ed. *Binah: Studies in Jewish History, Culture, and Thought,* III, *Jewish Intellectual History in the Middle Ages.* Westport, CT: Praeger Publishers, 1994.

Danzig, Nachman. "Mi-Talmud 'al Peh le-Talmud bi-Khetav: 'Al Derekh Mesirat ha-Talmud ha-Bavli ve-Limudo bi-Yemei ha-Beinayim." *Sefer ha-Shanah shel Universitat Bar-Ilan: Mada'ei ha-Yahadut u-Mada'ei ha-Rua{h.}* 30-31 (2006): 49-112.

Devroey, J. P., and C. Brouwer. "La participation des Juifs au commerce dans le monde franc (VIe-Xe siècles)." In *Voyages et voyageurs à Byzance et en Occident du VIe au XIe siècle*, edited by A. Dierkins and J. M. Sansterre, avec la collaboration de J.L. Kupper. Bibliothèque de la Faculté de Philosophie et Lettres de l'Université de Liège, 278. Genève, 2000.

*Early European History* 12 (2003).

Edrei, Arye, and Doron Mendels. "A Split Jewish Diaspora: Its Dramatic Consequences." *Journal for the Study of the Pseudoepigrapha* 16, no. 2 (2007): 91-137.

Eidelberg, Shlomo. "Ma`arufia in Rabbenu Gershom's Responsa." *Historia Judaica* 15 (1953): 59-67.

Fleischer, Ezra. *Shirat ha-Kodesh ha-'Ivrit bi-Yemei ha-Beinayim*. Jerusalem: Magnes, 1975.

Fleischer, Ezra. *Tefilah u-Minhagei Tefilah Erets Yisra'eliyim bi-Tekufat ha-Genizah*. Jerusalem: Magnes, 1988.

Friedman, Shamma. "Masekhet 'Avodah Zarah, Ketav Yad New York, Ketav Yad she-Hu'atak bi-Shenei Shelavim." *Leshonenu* 56 (1992): 371-374.

Friedman, S. Y. *Talmud 'Arukh, Perek ha-Sokher et ha-Umanim – ha-Nusakh 'im Mavo Kelaly*. Jerusalem, 1997.

Geisel, Christof. *Die Juden im Frankenreich: Von den Merowingern bis zum Tode Ludwigs des Frommen*. Frankfurt/Main, 1998.

Gieysztor, Aleksander. "Les Juifs et leurs activités économiques en Europe orientale." In *Gli Ebrei Nell'alto Medioevo*. Vol. I. *Settimane di Studio del Centro Italiano di Studi Sull'alto Medioevo 26*, 480-528. Spoleto, 1980.

Gil, Moshe. *Be-Malkhut Yishma'el bi-Tekufat ha-Ge'onim*, I. Tel Aviv: Tel Aviv University, 1997.

Gil, Moshe. "The Radhanite Merchants and the Land of Radhan." *Journal of the Economic and Social History of the Orient* 17 (1974): 299-328.

Grossman, Avraham. "Zikatah shel Yahadut Ashkenaz ha-Kedumah el Erets Yisra'el." *Shalem* 3 (1981): 57-92.

Grossman, Avraham. *{H.}akhmei Ashkenaz ha-Rishonim: Koroteihem, Darkam be-Hanhagat ha-Tsibbur, Yetsiratam ha-Ru{h.}anit me-Reshit Yishuvam ve-'ad li-Gezerot Tatnu (1096)*. 3rd ed. Jerusalem: Magnes, 2001.

Grossman, Avraham. *{H.}akhmei Tsarfat ha-Rishonim: Koroteihem, Darkam be-Hanhagat ha-Tsibbur, Yetsiratam ha-Ru{h.}anit*. 3rd ed. Jerusalem: Magnes, 2001.

Haussig, W. G. "Praxis und Verbreitung des jüdischen Handels in Südrussland." In *Untersuchungen zu Handel und Verkehr der vor- und frühgeschichtlichen Zeit in Mittel- und Nordeuropa / Teil 6: Organisationsformen der Kaufmannsvereinigungen in der Spätantike und im frühen Mittelalter*, edited by Herbert Jankuhn, W. Kimmig, and E. Ebel. *Abhandlungen-Akademie der Wissenschaft in Göttingen Philologisch Historische Klasse 183*. Göttingen, 1989.

Haverkamp, Alfred. "Die 'frühbürgerliche' Welt im hohen und späten Mittelalter: Landesgeschichte und Geschichte der städtischen Gesellschaft." *Historische Zeitschrift* 221 (1975): 571-602.

*Jerusalem Bible*. London, 1966.

Lewicki, Tadeusz. "Les commerçants juifs dans l'Orient islamique non méditerranéen au IXe-XIe siècle." In *Gli Ebrei Nell'alto Medioevo*. Vol. I. *Settimane di Studio del Centro Italiano di Studi Sull'alto Medioevo 26*, 375-401. Spoleto, 1980.

Lopez, Robert Sabatino, and Irving Woodworth Raymond, trans. *Medieval Trade in the Mediterranean World: Illustrative Documents*. New York: Columbia University Press, 1955.

Lugdunensis, Agobard. "De judaicis superstitionibus." *Opera Omnia*, edited by L. van Acker, *Corpus Christianorum, Continuatio Medievalis* 52. Turnhout: Brepols, 1981.

Lugdunensis, Agobard. "De insolentia judaeorum," *Opera Omnia*, edited by L. van Acker, *Corpus Christianorum, Continuatio Medievalis 52*, 189-195. Turnhout: Brepols, 1981.

Marcus, Ivan. "The Dynamics of Jewish Renaissance and Renewal in the Twelfth Century." In *Jews and Christians in Twelfth Century Europe*, 36-39. Notre Dame: University of Notre Dame Press, 2001.

McCormick, Michael. *Origins of the European Economy: Communications and Commerce 700-900*. Cambridge: Cambridge University Press, 2001.

Miquel, André. "L'Europe occidentale dans la relation arabe d'Ibrâhim b. Yaq'ub (Xe s.)." *Annales: ESC* 21 (1966): 1048-1064.

Noam, Vered. "Mesorot Nusa{h.} Kedumot be-Haggahot Rashi ba-Talmud." *Sidra* 17 (2001-2002): 110-111.

Rabbenu Tam. "Introduction." In *Sefer ha-Yashar: {H.}elek {H.}iddushim*, edited by Simon Solomon Schlesinger. Jerusalem: Kirjath Sefer, 1959.

Reuter, Timothy. *Germany in the Early Middle Ages: 800-1056*. London/New York: Longman, 1991.

Rörig, Fritz. "Magdburgs Entstehung und die ältere Handelsgeschichte." In *Wirtschaftskräfte im Mittelalter. Abhandlungen zur Stadt- und Hansegeschichte*, hrsg. von P. Kaegbein, 2. Aufl. Wien/Köln/Graz/Böhlau, 1971.

Rosenthal, David. "Mavo." In *Talmud Bavli: Ketav-Yad Firentseh, 'im Mavo me'et D. Rosenthal*. Jerusalem, 1972.

Sabato, Mordechai. *Ketav Yad Teimani le-Masekhet Sanhedrin (Bavli) u-Mekomo be-Masoret ha-Nusa{h.}*. Jerusalem: Yad Izhak Ben-Zvi, 1998.

Schatzmiller, Joseph. "Politics and the Myth of Origins." In *Les Juifs au regard de l'histoire. Mélange en l'honneur de Bernhard Blumenkrantz*, edited by Gilbert Dahan. Paris: Picard, 1985.

Soloveitchik, Haym. *Ha-Yayin bi-Yemei ha-Beinayim: Yein Nesekh – Perek be-Toledot ha-Halakhah be-Ashkenaz*. Jerusalem: Zalman Shazar Center, 2008.

Secunda, Shai. "Rashi's Emendations of the Text of Avodah Zarah." *Avodah Zarah Yein Nesekh*. Last modified August 9, 2007. http://azyn.blogspot.co.il/.

Sussman, Yaakov. "Kitvei-Yad u-Mesorot Nusa{h.} shel ha-Mishnah." In *Divrei ha-Kongres ha-'Olami ha-Shevi'i le-Mada'ei ha-Yahadut (August 7-14, 1977): Me{h.}karim be-Talmud, Halakhah ve-Midrash*. Jerusalem: Magnes, 1981.

Sussman, Yaakov. "Torah she-Be-'al Peh Peshutah ke-Mashma'ah: Ko{h.}o shel Kutso shel Yod." *Me{h.}kerei Talmud* 3 (2005): 209-384.

Ta-Shma, Israel M. Minhag Ashkenaz ha-Kadmon. Jerusalem: Magnes, 1992.

Toch, Michael. "Wirtschaft und Verfolgung: die Bedeutung der Ökonomie für die Kreuzzugspogrome des 11. und 12. Jahrhunderts. Mit einem Anhang zum Sklavenhadel der Juden." In *Juden und Christen zur Zeit der Kreuzzüge*, edited by Alfred Haverkamp, 253-285. Sigmaringen: Jan Thorbecke Verlag, 1999.

Toch, Michael. "Yehudei Eropa bi-Yemei ha-Beinayim ha-Mukdamim: So{h.}arei 'Avadim?" *Zion* 64 (1999): 39-64.

Toch, Michael. "Jews and Commerce: Modern Fancies and Medieval Realities." In *Il ruolo economico delle minoranze in Europa. Secc. XIII-XVIII (Atti dela XXXI Settimana di Studi, Istituto Francesco Datini, Prato)*, edited by S. Cavaciocchi, 43-58. Firenze, 2000.

Toch, Michael. "Pe'ilutam ha-Kalkalit shel Yehudei Germaniah ba-Me'ot ha-'Asirit 'ad ha-Sheteim-'Esreh: Bein Historiografyah le-Historyah." In *Yehudim mul ha-Tselav: Gezerot Tatnu ba-Historiografyah u-va-Historyah*, edited by Yom Tov Assis, Jeremy Cohen, Ora Limor, Aharon Keidar, and Michael Toch, 43-44. Jerusalem: Magnes, 2000.

Toch, Michael. "The Jews in Europe: 500-1050." In *The New Cambridge Medieval History*, I, 547-570. Cambridge: Cambridge University Press, 2005.

Von Freising, Otto. *Ottonis et Rahewini Gesta Friderici I. imperatoris*, edited by Georg Waitz and Bernhard von Simson. Hannover/Leipzig: Impensis Biblipolli Hahniani, 1912.

Weinreich, Max. *History of the Yiddish Language*. Chicago: YIVO Institute for Jewish Research, 1980.

CHAPTER SEVEN

# The Ordinances Attributed to Rabbi Gershom of Mainz as Regulations of Diasporic Communications

### A Proposition

MENAHEM BLONDHEIM

## I.

A series of medieval ordinances (*takanot*), attributed to Rabbi Gershom son of Judah of Mainz (ca. 960-1028),[1] has proved of enduring importance. These ordinances came to be considered legally binding by Jews of Northwestern Europe, and the best known among them – a ban on polygamy, and its "twin ordinance" a ban on divorcing a woman against her will – became fundamental to Jewish personal status law, and hence to Israeli law.[2] These medieval ordinances thus resonate in courts of law in contemporary Israel a full millennium after their enactment.

Given their relevance, and with the increased awareness of gender issues in the study of Jewish law and Jewish history, these bans have been receiving considerable attention from legal scholars and social historians.[3] Yet this lively interest has tended to focus on the two gender-related bans, in isolation from the rest of the ordinances attributed in subsequent generations to Rabbi Gershom. This chapter redirects attention from the specific bans to the group of ordinances as a whole, and it adds communications history to social and legal history as a relevant context for understanding them. Further, it proposes a common substantive denominator to most of the ordinances identified with Rabbi Gershom, who became known (quite significantly, *vide infra*), as the "Light of the Exile."

Over the ages, scholars have grappled with a variety of aspects of the *takanot*, one major issue being the correctness of their attribution to the venerable Rabbi Gershom. In addition, versions of the *takanot* in the various sources which have survived are inconsistent: they provide conflicting enumerations of the *takanot*, and present glaring differences in phrasing.[4] Finally, doubt pervades our current understanding of the process through which the *takanot* were enacted and adopted by Franco-German communities. The literature on these textual and historical issues is, in the words of an embattled contemporary scholar, "infinite."[5]

Nevertheless, from the Middle Ages to modernity, a core of specific *takanot* was consistently and persistently attributed to Rabbi Gershom by authoritative sources. While many scholars accept their authenticity, very little effort has been devoted to making sense of them as a whole—to find how they cohere. Historians have traditionally seen the *takanot* as the foremost legal expression of the dramatic medieval departure in Jewish social and religious organization: the emergence of the community (*kehillah*) as an autonomous entity and its becoming the fundamental political unit of diasporic Judaism.[6] Thus, the leading authority on Ashkenazi religious leadership in the middle ages, Avraham Grossman, has suggested that the *takanot*, taken together, addressed "the ways of organization of the communities (*kehillot*) and the nature of the relationship between them and the individual."[7] Simha Goldin, in a subsequent study of the social implications of the *takanot*, similarly highlighted their role in community building and internal organization, focusing on their tendency to buttress solidarity and maintain social control within the local communities.[8]

This paradigm works well for a few of the *takanot*, but most of them—the ban on polygamy and non-consensual divorce are prominent examples—do not fit this rationale of framing communal law and regulating public-private relations. This chapter proposes an alternative rationale for the *takanot* as a whole, and it takes its clue from a pioneering study, published three generations ago by Louis Finkelstein, that highlighted the institutional enactment of the ordinances. One and all were special, Finkelstein argued, in that they were apparently legislated for, and adopted by, many communities outside of Mainz, in the Northwestern European diaspora. He found it remarkable that Rabbi Gershom, a scholar from 'a little town in Germany', could generate and launch, possibly even mastermind and engineer, what became a pan-European consensus.[9]

Indeed, it is precisely this supposed supra-local authority of the *takanot*, pointed out and celebrated by Finkelstein, that is relevant to a major substantive thrust of the corpus, surprisingly overlooked in the "infinite" and erudite extant scholarship. We propose that the *takanot* were widely accepted by numerous local communities precisely because they addressed legal issues that were not confined within the boundaries and jurisdictions of these communities. A major substantive theme in the cluster of *takanot*, we submit, is the regulation of the interface of the local community and that which is external to it. In other words, they pertain to the interaction of Jews from different communities in Northwestern Europe (and even beyond it, as we shall see). In this view, a considerable share of the *takanot* attributed to Rabbi Gershom are primarily ordinances regulating communications—broadly construed to include travel, letter, text, and rumor—between, and to an extent within, the Jewish communities of Western Europe.[10] This suggestion is based on a review of the 16 *takanot* Grossman has identified as contemporary with Rabbi Gershom's age, and two other *takanot* that appear to have a strong claim to authenticity.[11]

Of this group, four *takanot* relate directly to travel between communities, and at least two others appear to have been occasioned by the consequences of such travel. This group includes the obligation of Jews from the hinterland sojourning in larger communities for the Day of Atonement to deposit their candles in the host community's place of prayer. Another *takana* dictates that pledges made in synagogue by a visitor are to be donated to the community where they were pledged, not to the visitor's home community. Similarly, a third *takana* establishes that travelers in the Purim season must give their obligatory Purim donations to the poor of the localities along their route, not of the community in which the traveler resides. A fourth *takana*, of considerable significance to legal procedure, also responds to the contingency of inter-communal travel. It establishes the local court as the proper jurisdiction for conducting suits brought by local community members against visitors, in apparent contradiction of traditional Talmudic legal procedure.

Travel between Jewish communities thus launched four of the lesser-celebrated *takanot*. Recent scholarship, however, has pointed to inter-diasporic communications as the circumstance giving rise to the two most famous ones. Polygamy was apparently exceedingly rare, if practiced at all, within Ashkenazi communities of the 11th century. Why then would Rabbi Gershom or subsequent leaders go to the trouble, and daring, of legislating to ban it? The answer, according to Grossman, lay far beyond the Rhineland, in the Jewish communities of Muslim Spain and North Africa, where polygamy was condoned by both Jews and gentiles.[12] While Rhineland Jewish males did not usually cohabit with more than one wife, when they engaged in long distance trade-related travel to, and extended sojourns in, Muslim lands, some married men wedded local woman, to have sex and create a home away from home.[13] But as trade routes and fortunes changed, the practice created problems of *aginut* that vexed the Jewish communities in Muslim lands, and threatened the smooth intercourse between them and sojourners from Christian Europe. The solution was to ban polygamy and also a potential loophole: *seriatim*, divorce without consent.[14] Hence the two most famous ordinances of Rabbi Gershom.

That the personal-status ordinances were understood at their time, or not long after their issuance, as an element of the inter-communal regulation of marriage is supported by the stipulations which developed for their relaxation in particular cases. When unusual circumstances recommended parallel marriage (such as a first wife's insanity or conversion), only the consent of 100 Jews (or rabbis) from at least three "countries" or "states" could effect a relaxation of the ban.[15] The necessity to generate what amounted to an international consensus for overruling the ordinance would suggest that its raison d'etre concerned the regulation of marriage practices across Jewish communities. At the same time, it reflected a pan-European, or even global, vision of rabbinical authority, and more concretely the feasibility of communicating with numerous rabbis over long distance.

Beyond face-to-face communications between individuals from different places, the *takanot* also address mediated communications. Legal issues concerning the flow of information, as distinct from individual travel, are represented, most conspicuously, in legislating the inviolability of mails. The *takana* forbidding the reading of letters by anyone but the sender or addressee had the power to enhance the exchange of letters between Jews of different communities by guaranteeing confidentiality and hence the efficacy of communication by written messages. At the same time, the legislation of the ordinance would appear to indicate that communication by written messages between Jewish communities was widespread. In fact, it has recently been argued that the *takanot* themselves were diffused among the communities of Ashkenaz and Northern France and adopted by them through their conveyance from one community to the next in writing, rather than in conference or synod.[16]

The *takanot* also address less tangible flows of information. Most notably, they take issue with the spread of information and rumors from place to place. Two *takanot* stand out in this respect: the obligation to provide information about lost or stolen property, and the ban on disclosing information about past apostasy of individuals (later understood to include family members as well). Legal cases emerging under these two *takanot* demonstrate that at issue was information at a distance: individuals who had lost merchandise along trade routes attempted to enforce the disclosure of information about it from members of congregations located along the route by applying the *takana*. Similarly, cases invoking the ban on disclosing information about apostasy indicate that at issue was family reputation, particularly in cases of marriage between families in different communities. The latter ban was thus intended to curtail the flow of damaging gossip between communities, just as the former worked to encourage the spreading of useful information from place to place.

Three *takanot* focus on the handling and preservation of texts. The thrust of these ordinances is to promote not only the diffusion of a uniform heritage in space, but also its preservation through time. One of them, forbidding the "proofing" of traditional texts (*hagaha*) was apparently intended to prevent the corruption of the classical texts and the compromising of their authenticity. Irresponsible editing could introduce local variance to traditions of learning and observance in Jewish space, as well as disrupt the chain of transmitting the canon over time.[17]

A further *takana*[18] forbidding the cutting of margins of pages, even for the purpose of their secondary use, apparently reflected the same rationale: by eliminating the margins, readers' comments and corrections would have to be made in the text itself, potentially corrupting it, and ultimately causing a multiplicity of local traditions. Further afield, a *takana* of a distinct commercial–law nature forbids retaining books, received for safekeeping, as collateral against any outstanding claims on their owner. Here too, the rationale appears to have been the negative effect of such a practice on the diffusion of knowledge. Indeed, an exception to the *takana* (considered by some authorities to constitute a separate one) was made in the case of teachers holding texts for safekeeping, and using them for teaching while in their possession. In such cases, allowing the teacher to keep the books in his possession as collateral is seen to serve the cause of disseminating knowledge. It was therefore permitted.

Finally, the *takanot* also appear to address problems relating to potential or actual migration to and from established communities. One of the *takanot* forbids the renting of a real estate property occupied by another Jew, or one that a Jew had occupied within the preceding year. The *takana* was apparently intended to prevent landowners (usually gentiles) from leveraging demand for their properties to raise rents and evict tenants who could not afford the higher rates. It is quite plausible that the circumstance for legislating this *takana* was increased demand for urban property due to migratory pressures, at a time when the Jewish communities of the Rhineland were in the process of growth. On the other hand, the *takana* forbidding the owner of a property which serves as the communal synagogue from preventing an enemy from attending prayers on his property could serve to check forced migration out of the community: after all, preventing a Jew from public prayer was tantamount to forcing him out of the community and joining another.[19]

According to the foregoing, most of the ordinances attributed to Rabbi Gershom could be construed as legislation addressing inter-communal issues and shaping inter-diasporic communications. In this analysis, all but three of 18 *takanot* here considered to be part of the corpus could have communicative rationales—some more obvious than others. In contrast, the prevailing understanding of the thrust of the *takanot* as the solidifying of intra-communal arrangements and regulating the relations between the community and its individual members can explain, at best, 8 of the 18 *takanot* comprising the corpus.[20]

## II

A few general considerations would tend to buttress the foregoing proposition's power to explain and to be explained. To begin with the former: should the organizing principle of the *takanot* attributed to Rabbi Gershom indeed be the regulation of communications, that principle may be productively seized on in an attempt to better interpret or re-interpret specific *takanot*. A case in point would be the second *takana* in the compilations considered by Finkelstein to be our best sources for the corpus. It is one of the few *takanot* that does not appear to square with the foregoing proposition.

This *takana* regulates the right of plaintiffs to interrupt synagogue services in a plea to have their case come to court. While prima facie a purely intra-communal procedure, addressing, in Finkelstein's view, freedom of speech, it is listed immediately after the opening *takana* upholding the local court as the proper jurisdiction for the prosecution of visitors. A plausible explanation for the proximity of these first two *takanot* is that the second complements the first: it spells out the visitor's procedural privileges in bringing a suit against local community members, complementing the first *takana*'s legislation of the local court's jurisdiction in suits brought against visitors. Indeed, there are both examples and explicit statements demonstrating that the *takana* was invoked in cases of stopping prayers by visitors to the community. In fact, in one of our best sources, the issues of suing visitors and interrupting prayer to sue a local community member appear as two clauses linked by an "and" (--*vav ha-xibur*). More speculative is to assume that the next ban (no. 3 in the lists preferred by Finkelstein), which forbids the owner of a house of prayer to prevent an adversary from praying there, relates to the case of a visitor to town who intends to interrupt prayer and petition the community for legal redress against the owner. Nevertheless, the subsequent *takana* (no. 4), once again relates to the case of a petition to the community, most probably by a visitor.

Be that as it may, the second *takana* just discussed concerning the interruption of prayer, which has heretofore been understood as an element of communal public law, can plausibly be re-understood as a precursor of "international" private law, thus falling in line with the other, supra-local *takanot*. Future students may find ways to creatively re-interpret the remaining few ordinances that have traditionally been understood as regulating merely intra-communal affairs, so that they too fit the inter-communal mold.

In pursuing such a course, scholars would not be straying far from what is known to have been the prevailing legislative trend and social process of Northwestern Jewry of the 11th and 12th centuries. By the time of Rabbi Gershom, historians tell us, Ashkenazi Jewry was well on its course of lodging religious authority in communal institutions, rather than looking to religious authority lodged in distant institutions, dynasties, and individuals. By the 11th century *cherem Beit Din*, *cherem hayishuv*, and other institutions which established the authority of the local community were well established, as were institutions regulating the relations of the individual and his community, such as interrupting prayers. Synods of communal leaders or other arrangements for reaching a pan-communal consensus on the legitimacy of the community wielding power over its own affairs, and regulating the duties and rights of community-members, were no longer necessary. Nor would the great prestige of Rabbi Gershom of Mainz be necessary to legitimize these firmly established practices.

Synods or other processes for engineering inter-communal consensus, and the prestige of Rabbi Gershom, were, however, necessary for launching a new departure and engineering a further project. This project was extending the authority of the community beyond its own boundaries, or rather, arranging the diaspora as a lateral coalition of communities, in place of the previous vision of the diaspora as a hierarchical field subject to the supremacy of a distant authority. Through such a project, the legal sphere outside of the local communities was to be adjusted, filling, as it were, the legal void between them. As proposed above, this is precisely what most of the ordinances attributed to Rabbi Gershom dealt with. In the process, a few intra-communal issues may have also been addressed.

The realities of social life pointed to this departure as both necessary and proper. In the first place, the assumption of internal authority by the *kehillot* reflected the gradual demise of authority exercised from the Near-Eastern centers of Jewish leadership. Not only were the Exilarchs, the *Yeshivot*, and their *Geonim* in a process of decline, but thoroughgoing change in patterns of Jewish demographics, commerce, and communication made the potential exercise of authority from afar unrealistic. As more and more Jews moved into the Northern European regions, patterns of travel and trade were shifting from the long-haul to the inter-regional and the intra-regional loop. Commercial and civic interaction was rapidly increasing between the emerging cities of Northwestern Europe, with many more Jews, as well as gentiles, moving in competition along the thickening web of routes and destinations in Christian Western Europe. As the intensity of mid-range travel and communication was increasing, traffic on the long-distance trade routes to the Near and Far East, to North Africa, and even to Muslim Spain, was in decline.[21] The increasing activity and interaction between Jews of Northwestern Europe challenged the internal workings of the *kehillot* and highlighted the realm of contact between them—the spheres of communication, interaction, and interdependence.[22]

It was to this challenge of vastly increased social and business communication between Northwestern European Jews that communal leaders of the 11th and 12th centuries found it necessary to respond. They did so by framing a layer of ordinances regulating the consequences of increased travel, migration, and communication between their communities. This was the core of the cluster of *takanot* that emerged in the 11th century.

Responding to these circumstances, the *takanot*, over time, were compiled into a single list. Precisely what was compiled, and precisely when, therefore represents an interesting, but only secondary, matter of historical detail. Nor is the problem of the attribution of any, some, many, or all of the inter-communal *takanot* to Rabbi Gershom a very significant one. The new departure of establishing a body of law regulating inter-communal affairs required a modicum of legitimacy. The splendid reputation of Rabbi Gershom as scholar and leader could provide that legitimacy.

Indeed, Rabbi Gershom's real or imagined personal authority could be construed as a bridge between the universal authority of the *tana'im* and *amora'im*, later exilarchs, *rashey yeshiva* and *geonim*, whose authority supposedly covered ecumenical Jewish space, and the new era of the communal self-rule. In such a construction, Rabbi Gershom, who rose to prominence after the communities had seized authority over their own affairs, could launch a second step. It was up to him to exercise his potential authority over Jewish space not controlled by the *kehillot*, and he could do it by way of conferring that potential authority to a coalition of the *kehillot*. Hence the persistent attribution of the cluster of inter-communal *takanot* to Rabbi Gershom.

And in fact, to a greater or lesser extent Rabbi Gershom appears to have been among the initiators of this novel legislative thrust, or identified with it from early on. His role as the authority that legitimized the extension of the communal authority over great expanses was subsequently highlighted and celebrated. Like the Sun [*hama'or hagadol*][23], which shines over the entire ecumene, the project attributed to him was extending the light of Jewish law beyond the confines of the community and over the entire Jewish space. As "legislator for the entire diaspora," if not for the internal affairs of its communal enclaves, Rabbi Gershom was styled "the light of the exile."

# Notes

1   This dating, proposed in Avraham Grossman, *The Early Sages of Ashkenaz: their Lives, Leadership and Works, 900-1096* (Jerusalem: Magnes Press, 2001), 109-111, is widely accepted.

2   An exhaustive summary of the impact of these ordinances in subsequent halakhic discourse and ruling is provided in Meyer Berlin and Shlomo Josef Zevin, eds., "Cherem d'Rabenu Gershom," in *Talmudic Encyclopedia,* vol. XVII (Jerusalem: Talmudic Encyclopedia Press, 1947-2015), 378-454.

3   Works that focus on these *takanot* include: Ze'ev Falk, *Marriage and Divorce: Ordinances in Laws of the Family in German and French Jewry* (Jerusalem: Hebrew University Faculty of Law, 1961), 14-31; Avraham Grossman, "The Historical Background to the Ordinances on Family Affairs Attributed to Rabbenu Gershom Me'or ha-Gola ('The Light of the Exile')," in *Jewish History: Essays in Honour of Chimen Abramsky,* eds. Ada Rapoport-Albert and Steven J. Zipperstein (London: Peter Halban, 1988), 3-23; Avraham N. Z. Roth, "On the History of Monogamy Among the Jews," in *Jewish Studies in Memory of Yehiel Michal Guttman,* ed. Samuel Loewinger (Budapest: 1946), 114-136; Elimelech Westreich, *Traditions in the Legal Status of the Wife in Jewish Law: A Journey Among Traditions* (Jerusalem: Magnes Press, 2002), 62-96; Shlomo Zalman Havlin, "The Ordinances of Rabbi Gershom the Light of the Exile in Family Affairs in Spain and Provance," *Shnaton ha-Mishpat ha-Ivri* 2 (1975): 200-258 [Hebrew]; Mordeccai Akiva Friedman, *Polygamy Among the Jews: New Sources from the Cairo Geniza* (Jerusalem: The Bialik Institute, 1986), 19-25, 268; Peretz Tishbi, "Was the *Takana* not to Marry Two Wives Issued by Rabbi Gershom?" *Tarbitz* 34 (1965): 49-55 [Hebrew].

4   See Finkelstein's discussion of the 17 sources he used: Louis Finkelstein, *Jewish Self-Government in the Middle Ages* (New York: Philipp Feldheim, Inc., 1964), 111-118. For a comprehensive list of references and versions of the *takanot* from before 1492, see Meyer Berlin and Shlomo Josef Zevin, eds., "Appendix," in *Talmudic Encyclopedia,* vol. XVII (Jerusalem: Talmudic Encyclopedia Press, 1947-2015), 757-572.

5   Simha Goldin, *Uniqueness and Togetherness: The Enigma of the Survival of the Jews in the Middle Ages* (Tel Aviv: Hakibbutz Hameuchad, 1997), 75.

6   The literature on the *takanot* as an element of Jewish communal organization is vast. See, e.g., Haim Hillel Ben-Sasson, *On Jewish History in the Middle Ages* (Tel Aviv: Am Oved, 1977), 84-121; Haim Hillel Ben-Sasson, ed., *A History of the Jewish People* (Cambridge: Harvard University Press, 1976), 421-38; Finkelstein, *Jewish Self-Government in the Middle Ages,* 1-19; Mordechai Breuer, *The Rabbinate in Ashkenaz During the Middle Ages* (Jerusalem: The Zalman Shazar Center, 1976), 9-16.

7   "... their purpose was to establish arrangements and leaderships in many areas of life, especially the ways in which the communities were organized and the nature of the relationships between them and the individual." Grossman, *The Early Sages of Ashkenaz,* 132.

8   Goldin, *Uniqueness and Togetherness,* 74-80.

9   Finkelstein, *Jewish Self-Government in the Middle Ages,* 20-22.

10  This aspect of Medieval Jewish life has recently been receiving some of the attention it deserves. See Menahem Blondheim, "Channels, Means, Boundaries: Communications in Germany and France in the 10th-12th Centuries According to the Responsa Literature" (The Hebrew University of Jerusalem), an extensive unpublished paper available from this author upon request. Sophia Menache, "Communication in the Jewish Diaspora: A Survey," in *Communication in the Jewish Diaspora: The Pre-Modern World,* ed. Sophia Menache (Leiden: Brill, 1996), 15-57, provides an excellent introduction; and other

articles in that volume provide more detailed analysis. Among them, Avraham Grossman, "Communication among Jewish Centers during the Tenth to the Twelfth Centuries," in *Communication in the Jewish Diaspora: The Pre-Modern World, ed. Sophia Menache* (Leiden: Brill, 1996), 107-125, is of particular importance to the problems addressed in the text. A valuable early study which provides considerable detail on communication related aspects of Medieval Jewish life is Irving A. Agus, *Urban Civilization in Pre-Crusade Europe,* 2 vols. (New York: Yeshiva Universiy Press, 1965).

11 These *takanot,* the first of which Grossman too appears to accept as authentic (*The Early Sages of Ashkenaz,* 136, n. 112, p. 144), forbid the editing of books and cutting their margins. Ben Zion Dinur, *Israel in Exile,* vol. 1, *Book 3* (Tel Aviv: Dvir, 1961), 273 [Hebrew]; Shlomo Eidelberg, "Gershom the Legislator, Author of Responsa, and Poet," *Sinai* 36 (1956): 60.

12 Grossman, "Ordinances on Family Affairs."

13 Roth, "On the History of Monogamy," 124, cites, with disapproval, a parallel, but opposite, solution: the *takana* was supposed to regulate bigamy by traders from Muslim countries sojourning in Ashkenaz. A charming literary rendering of such a scenario is provided in Abraham B. Yehoshua, *Massa el Tom ha-Elef* (Tel Aviv: Hakibbutz Hameuchad, 1997) [Hebrew].

14 Westreich, *Traditions in the Legal Status of the Wife in Jewish Law,* 69-70, is critical of Grossman's suggestion due to the lack of contemporary supporting sources. This reservation is strange: Westreich appears to accept the attribution of the bigamy *takana* to Rabbi Gershom, although no sources for the enactment of the *takana* survived. He thus expects that sources for the rationale of the *takana* should survive when the *takana* itself didn't.

15 Grossman, *The Early Sages of Ashkenaz.*

16 Goldin, *Uniqueness and Togetherness,* 77-80.

17 Yaakov Shmuel Spiegel, *Chapters in the History of the Jewish Book: Scholars and their Annotations* (Ramat Gan: Bar Ilan University Press, 1996), 101-115. Compare to Aryeh Grabois, "The Use of Letters as a Communication Media," in *Communication in the Jewish Diaspora: The Pre-Modern World, ed. Sophia Menache* (Leiden: Brill, 1996), 102.

18 Included by Dinur, *Israel in Exile,* 1:273, in the list of R. Gershom's ordinances on the authority of *Tshuvot Maharam,* 113/a.

19 Grossman convincingly demonstrates that until the late 11th century Mainz and other Rhineland communities could not sustain more than a single synagogue: Grossman, *The Early Sages of Ashkenaz,* 146, n. 141.

20 Numbers 2, 3, 5, 7, 11, and at a stretch also 1, 4, 15 in Grossman's list (*The Early Sages of Ashkenaz,* 134-35). The two *takanot* we added, the ban on altering texts and cutting their margins, do not fit the category.

21 For the erstwhile long-haul see Grossman, Communication Among Jewish Centers, 107-126.

22 Kenneth R. Stow, *Alienated Minority: The Jews of Medieval Latin Europe* (Jerusalem: The Zalman Shazar Center, 1997), 208-210; Ben Sasson, *On Jewish History,* pp. 61-66; Mark R. Cohen, *Under Crescent and Cross: The Jews in the Middle Ages* (Lod: Zmora Bitan, 2001), 188-192.

23 Sidur Rashi, p. 106.

# Bibliography

Agus, Irving A. *Urban Civilization in Pre-Crusade Europe*. 2 vols. New York: Yeshiva Universiy Press, 1965.

Ben-Sasson, Haim Hillel, ed. *A History of the Jewish People*. Cambridge: Harvard University Press, 1976.

Ben-Sasson, Haim Hillel. *On Jewish History in the Middle Ages*. Tel Aviv: Am Oved, 1977.

Berlin, Meyer, and Shlomo Josef Zevin, eds. "Cherem d'Rabenu Gershom." In *Talmudic Encyclopedia*, Vol. XVII, 378-454. Jerusalem: Talmudic Encyclopedia Press, 1947-2015.

Berlin, Meyer, and Shlomo Josef Zevin, eds. "Appendix." In *Talmudic Encyclopedia*, Vol. XVII, 757-572. Jerusalem: Talmudic Encyclopedia Press, 1947-2015.

Blondheim, Menahem. "Channels, Means, Boundaries: Communications in Germany and France in the 10th-12th Centuries According to the Responsa Literature." Unpublished paper, available from the author upon request.

Breuer, Mordechai. *The Rabbinate in Ashkenaz During the Middle Ages*. Jerusalem: The Zalman Shazar Center, 1976.

Cohen, Mark R. *Under Crescent and Cross: The Jews in the Middle Ages*. Lod: Zmora Bitan, 2001.

Dinur, Ben Zion. *Israel in Exile*. Vol. 1, Book 3. Tel Aviv: Dvir, 1961 [Hebrew].

Eidelberg, Shlomo. "Gershom the Legislator, Author of Responsa, and Poet." *Sinai* 36 (1956): 60.

Falk, Ze'ev. *Marriage and Divorce: Ordinances in Laws of the Family in German and French Jewry*. Jerusalem: Hebrew University Faculty of Law, 1961.

Finkelstein, Louis. *Jewish Self-Government in the Middle Ages*. New York: Philipp Feldheim, Inc., 1964.

Friedman, Mordeccai Akiva. *Polygamy Among the Jews: New Sources from the Cairo Geniza*. Jerusalem: The Bialik Institute, 1986.

Goldin, Simha. *Uniqueness and Togetherness: The Enigma of the Survival of the Jews in the Middle Ages*. Tel Aviv: Hakibbutz Hameuchad, 1997.

Grabois, Aryeh. "The Use of Letters as a Communication Media." In *Communication in the Jewish Diaspora: The Pre-Modern World*, edited by Sophia Menache. Leiden: Brill, 1996.

Grossman, Avraham. "The Historical Background to the Ordinances on Family Affairs Attributed to Rabbenu Gershom Me'or ha-Gola ('The Light of the Exile')." In *Jewish History: Essays in Honour of Chimen Abramsky*, edited by Ada Rapoport-Albert and Steven J. Zipperstein, 3-23. London: Peter Halban, 1988.

Grossman, Avraham. "Communication among Jewish Centers during the Tenth to the Twelfth Centuries." In *Communication in the Jewish Diaspora: The Pre-Modern World*, edited by Sophia Menache, 107-125. Leiden: Brill, 1996.

Grossman, Avraham. *The Early Sages of Ashkenaz: their Lives, Leadership and Works (900-1096)*. Jerusalem: Magnes Press, 2001.

Havlin, Shlomo Zalman. "The Ordinances of Rabbi Gershom the Light of the Exile in Family Affairs in Spain and Provance.," *Shnaton ha-Mishpat ha-Ivri* 2 (1975): 200-258 [Hebrew].

Menache, Sophia. "Communication in the Jewish Diaspora: A Survey." In *Communication in the Jewish Diaspora: The Pre-Modern World*, edited by Sophia Menache, 15-57. Leiden: Brill, 1996.

Roth, Avraham N. Z. "On the History of Monogamy Among the Jews." In *Jewish Studies in Memory of Yehiel Michal Guttman*, edited by Samuel Loewinger, 114-136. Budapest, 1946.

Spiegel, Yaakov Shmuel. *Chapters in the History of the Jewish Book: Scholars and their Annotations*. Ramat Gan: Bar Ilan University Press, 1996.

Stow, Kenneth R. *Alienated Minority: The Jews of Medieval Latin Europe*. Jerusalem: The Zalman Shazar Center, 1997.

Tishbi, Peretz. "Was the *Takana* not to Marry Two Wives Issued by Rabbi Gershom?" *Tarbitz* 34 (1965): 49-55 [Hebrew].

Westreich, Elimelech. *Traditions in the Legal Status of the Wife in Jewish Law: A Journey Among Traditions*. Jerusalem: Magnes Press, 2002.

Yehoshua, Abraham B. *Massa el Tom ha-Elef*. Tel Aviv: Hakibbutz Hameuchad, 1997 [Hebrew].

CHAPTER EIGHT

# Putting the World on Paper in Hebrew

## Early Journalism and the Modernization
## of Socio–Political Discourse

OREN SOFFER

The second half of the nineteenth century saw the establishment of several Hebrew journals in Eastern Europe which provided a platform for a lively political discourse reflecting varied ideological approaches. These Hebrew journals were part of an extensive network of Jewish journals, published not only in Hebrew but in Yiddish and other European languages.[1] In the multilingual context of Jewish communities, Hebrew was not an obvious choice for a journal. It was merely an embedded language within the framework of the other two languages of daily communication—Yiddish and the state vernacular.[2] Of course, Hebrew was never a "dead language." Jewish collective existence was based on Hebrew texts. Children studied Hebrew to some extent, and it continually functioned as a written language.[3] But in the first half of the nineteenth century, Hebrew was far from suitable for journalistic discourse, as it lacked an active basic vocabulary for many spheres of modern life.[4] It existed separately from the discussion about everyday and political matters.[5]

The centrality of Hebrew in the Zionist revolution could lead one to assume that this emerging journalistic use of Hebrew was related to early nationalist considerations. But this is not necessarily the case. At least some of the main figures who took part in this journalistic enterprise saw the use of Hebrew as an intermediary stage. In their vision, Hebrew had two functions: first, it allowed Jews to leave behind Yiddish, which was seen as a corrupted German dialect, a "language without grammar"[6]; and second, it allowed Jews to bypass the use of their resident country's language, which most readers were unfamiliar with. It was thought that by using Hebrew, which most Jews knew to some extent through religious rituals, it would be possible to present new and modern spheres of life to the public, such as popular science and technological innovations or international affairs. These, usually discussed in the state vernacular, were not previously accessible to Jewish readers.[7] This Hebrew discourse was seen as a sort of "training period" to accustom readers to discussing these themes. It was expected that Jews would eventually be able to deal with these matters in the state language.[8]

As in other discursive domains of the body of *Haskalah* (Jewish enlightenment movement) literature, the use of Hebrew within the journalistic framework needed to be adapted to modern reality and experience. But as I will argue in this paper, because of journalism's immediate connection to the "real world," it was not only the language that had to be modernized. Hebrew *discourse*—the way this language was used to frame utterances and arguments relating to social, political, cultural issues[9]—had to go through a major shift. In other words, the discursive characteristics of traditional Jewish communities had to be transformed to fit the modern socio-political discourse of journalism.

Nineteenth-century Hebrew discourse was "thrown" into a new and modern "discursive reality." After the Western scientific revolution, the perception of discourse was founded on the assumption that texts can and should literally reflect objective facts as they are observed in the "real world." The reference for "truth"—for these "real facts"—was seen to be outside the text, and the text aimed to represent these facts in an accurate way. The influence of this extratextual perception emerged not only in scientific discourse but also in other domains of life, such as politics and journalism. This modern discursive model was radically different from both the traditional/religious perception of discourse in general and the Jewish perception in particular. This latter perception was based upon a model of inquiry that was both intertextual—focused on the relationship *between* different components in the textual mosaic—and intratextual—focused on attempts to plumb the God-given meanings hidden *inside* the text. The adaptation of Hebrew discourse to modern life therefore incorporated a changing perception of the relationship between text and reality. In other words, whereas the traditional perception (in which the Hebrew text is a holy language with hidden layers) saw the literal text merely as a starting point, the modernization of Hebrew (adopting the Western extratextual perception) focused on this literal level and aimed to describe "reality as it is."

My hypothesis is therefore that the journalistic discourse of the second half of the nineteenth century and the beginning of the twentieth reveals the transition towards the modern, extratextual perception of discourse. *HaTzfira*,[10] a long-running journal first published in Warsaw in 1862, provides an ideal case study for this modernization process. In its early years, this journal was characterized by a popular scientific ethos (scientific themes were dominant in other Hebrew journals at the time as well), and this ethos went on to influence the journal's method of political argumentation (and later its Zionist orientation). But it is important to note that *HaTzfira* had no monopoly on the socio-political trends which it reflected and shaped. Furthermore, these trends were not hegemonic: they did not constitute the sole road towards modernizing Hebrew discourse.

I will first outline the changes in the perception of discourse in Western Europe following the scientific revolution. My second step will be to compare this modern perception of discourse with the traditional Jewish perception of discourse. I will show that these two models were distinct in how they saw the role of discourse and the connection between text and reality. These differences will allow us to better understand how Hebrew discourse changed in the process of modernization, and will hopefully lead to a better understanding of the social role of journalism at the time.

## *The Scientific Revolution and the Extratextual Perception of Discourse*

The scientific revolution was directly related to a social change in the perception of the discourse and methods of public investigation: the inter/intratextual method of the pre-scientific forms of investigation were transformed. In the Middle Ages, texts were perceived to be the source of divine knowledge: the truth was hidden within them. This created an atmosphere that invited the breaking down of texts, correspondence with other texts, and the use of allegorical methodology.[11] But the scientific revolution established that truth existed in—and could be revealed through observation of—the extratextual "real world," creating an atmosphere in which texts aimed to mirror reality: to "put the world on paper."[12] As Olson argues, the changes that occurred between the Middle Ages and the Renaissance were a matter of "moving away from reading between the lines to reading what was on the lines—giving increased importance to the information explicitly represented in the text."[13] Expressions were to be taken literally, neither more nor less than what was said.[14] The role of language in the way truths were reached was reconsidered: "Language does have a place, but it must be well disciplined, obedient and modest, almost unnoticeable; the reader has to try hard to catch even a glimpse of it."[15] This is therefore an apparently transparent language that does not conceal a thing.

Within this view, an issue of concern is the preciseness of the language. To this point, Thomas Hobbes describes words as the "wise men's counters," and notes that "a man that seeketh precise *truth* had need to remember what every name he uses stand for, and to place it accordingly, or else he will find himself entangled in words; as a bird in lime twigs, the more he struggles the more belimed."[16] In a similar spirit, Leibniz thought that every single element or "first idea" should have one signifier to represent this idea alone.[17] Complicated ideas should be composed of combinations of such simple signifiers. Leibniz believed that the adoption of this kind of language would lead to a certainty of conclusion, as in the field of mathematics.[18]

The idea that facts are perceived by the senses and reliably reported through textual means influenced how scientific experiments were conducted and reported. The need to "show" inventions—to prove that they worked and were founded upon general scientific laws—led to public experiments, such as Robert Boyle's demonstration of his vacuum pump.[19] Boyle's results were written in detail to make readers feel they had participated in the experiment: like "virtual witnesses."[20] The increased importance of the visual dimension in proving what was "true" was also linked to the new print technology. The printed text itself was seen as a fixed and visual testament. A belief in the closure of the printed text—in its being "a datum, separate from any utterer or hearer or reader"[21]—was integral to the belief in a transparent language: in the text's ability to reflect facts exactly and reliably. The modern extratextual model is intimately linked to the concept that all readers receive the same fixed message from the reporter-transmitter. Print technology also enabled mass production of pictures for the first time, contributing to the development of visual communication, which was seen to be part of the attempt to give words accurate meanings.[22] Being able reproduce the same picture of a specific event increases its reliability: the perceived objectivity of these pictures gives them the authority to reflect reality. Furthermore, through pictures, which were more and more widespread, it was possible to give a wider circle of people a visual idea of things they had no direct access to.

Evidence of this new conception of text as a tool to present objective reality was to be found not only in the discourse of natural sciences: it had much broader social effects. In the nineteenth century, scientific methods were adopted by the social sphere. Scientific quantitative methods diffused into academic social studies, influencing the discussion and presentation of political content.[23] Politics was seen as a realm of observable powers and forces; and the idea that language could and should present "reality" led to the attempt to reveal "objective social facts" in politics.[24] In this spirit, American journalists believed they should describe only what they saw and leave the conclusions to others.[25] Journalists were "naive empiricists", believing that facts were aspects of the world itself.[26] By the 1890s, the American press had separated editorial writing from news, the latter dominating.[27] This objective ethic was a defining mark of journalism as a profession,[28] and "information" became a key word for journalists.

As already mentioned, this modern perception of text and discourse differs from a religious perception, in which the text, much more than a tool for transferring objective knowledge, is seen to have intrinsic importance. According to the religious model, one must read between the lines of the holy texts to uncover concealed truths. The traditional Jewish perception of Hebrew religious texts in Eastern Europe provides an illustrative and radical case of inter/intratextual perception.

## The Intertextual and Intratextual Talmudic Perception

The discursive patterns in Eastern European communities were heavily influenced by the study of the Babylonian Talmud. According to Jacob Neusner, Jewish society was a textual community: its members all read the same texts, and communication among them was guided by the thinking patterns imprinted by these texts, mainly the Babylonian Talmud.[29] This dominance of the Talmud in the Jewish world led scholars to analyze its unique characteristics.

The Talmud is by its nature an intertextual project—a text whose task is to deeply investigate another text: the Mishna. This task is explicitly expressed through the term *Talmud*, which means interpretation, explanation, or hypothesis.[30] As Louis Jacobs argues, Talmudic study is academic in character—its main role is to better understand the Mishna.[31] David Kraemer notes that one of the exceptional traits of Talmudic discourse is that it often refrains from reaching any obvious conclusion.[32] Attention is given to the arguments in support of each view: one view is not chosen over the rest. The Babylonian Talmud opens up possibilities, but usually does not allow for the practical implementation of any clear law decided upon in the discussion.[33] The position of the Talmud is rather to acknowledge the impossibility of reaching a clear verdict concerning absolute truth, and hence to provide alternative positions reflecting different aspects of a general truth.[34] The very contrast in the arguments, interpretations, and rulings is itself considered a religious commandment (*mitzvah*).

In contrast to the modern extratextual perception, the Talmudic texts and methods of study endeavored to unveil truths hidden within the text. The Talmudic proof for an argument was *textual* verification. This inter/intratextual mode of study (*derash*) was seen as superior to literal reading (*pshat*). Talmudic textual study is characterized also by a continuous movement from one argument to the next—the same dialectic moves through each point in an endless flow of dialogue.[35] The readers of the Talmud, because of its oral nature, did not feel that it was a sealed book; they were called upon to take part in its writing through discussion and innovative commentary. In addition, since the Talmud dealt with rabbinic discussion in Babylon—in a time and place far from its readers—this discussion seemed fragmented, requiring the readers themselves to complete ideas and sentences.[36]

Talmudic learning patterns in Jewish communities of Eastern Europe are an extreme illustration of inter/intratextual methodology. In the sixteenth and seventeenth centuries, these characteristics were embodied in the scholarly *pilpulic* method of study adopted by the Polish yeshivas. The original sense of the Hebrew word "*pilpul*" (casuistic) was "turning something this way and that," and it was adopted to describe the dialectical activity of studying Jewish lore.[37] Discussion had to be defined within the limits of the Talmudic issue, and thus it was totally localized. Within such a strict method of study, all the intellectual energies of the student were directed at the Talmudic issue alone. This increased the tendency to concentrate on every small textual detail, and it put excessive stress on nuances of stronger and weaker tone, early and late mention, exact wording, and the progress of the Talmudic negotiations.[38] Using a philological method, this type of study analyses every issue to its basic components and assigns equal value to each of these components. Since the methodology of the Talmud is deliberately harmonizing, the *pilpulic* method of study aimed to prove the coherence within the Talmudic system—and it did this by uncovering the concealed "true" meaning of the text.[39]

A few restrictions should be noted here. First, the dichotomy of the Talmudic perception and the extratextual perception might not hold when referring to the relationship between the Talmudic text and reality *at the time the Talmud was composed.* In fact, the Talmud contains many terms and questions that relate to nature—animals, plants, and so on. But, as Harshav argues, these terms appeared in different contexts, and over time they lost their representative character since the reality they were describing was not part of the life of the Talmudic readers.[40] We should also note that rabbinic literature was composed of different trends or genres. The Responsa literature, for example, included *halakhic* (religious) rulings by the rabbinic elite in response to concrete questions sent to them by the public.[41] A focus on actual time and place can also be seen in the *drush* literature, which included a written version of the oral homilies.[42] In addition, attempts were made over the generations to integrate scientific principles into the rabbinic Talmudic literature.[43] However, in these cases, the methodology remained within the same tradition of exegetical, inter/intratextual study; and the integration between scientific knowledge and traditional methods does not necessarily prove the adoption of a modern way of thinking, as scientific knowledge had many times been absorbed into traditional homiletic way of thought.[44]

In conclusion, the traditional Jewish model, influenced by Talmudic-*pilpulic* methods of study, differed radically from the modern discursive methods which developed after the scientific revolution. The latter saw the text as a reliable mirror for facts in the real world and consequently emphasized the text's literal layer and its precision. The traditional Hebrew discursive model of the Eastern European communities, on the other hand, emphasized the need to reveal the hidden layers of the text and examined its interrelations with other texts. The modern text was seen as complete and fixed, therefore creating a passive reading atmosphere in which the reader was held captive by the author. The Talmudic discursive atmosphere, due to its oral nature, created an atmosphere that invited active commentary and contribution to the text by its readers. With these differences in mind, I will analyze the implications of the move from traditional methods of textual study to modern extratextual methods, as evidenced on the pages of *HaTzfira*.

## The Telegraph: From the Inter/Intratextual to the Extratextual Perception

Booki Ben Yogli's[45] tale in *The Jubilee Book of HaTzfira* sheds light on the implication of the discursive transition from inter/intratextual to extratextual methods.[46] In the tale, the mystery of the telegraph becomes the focus of a heated debate among the students of a *Beit Midrash* (house of study) for a whole year. Rabbi Avigdor, the teacher, whom the boy Booki Ben Yogli describes as a great scholar—so versed in the book *The Binding of Isaac* by Rabbi Isaac Arma that he almost knew it by heart[47]—did not believe such a thing as a telegraph existed, saying that it went against nature. Rabbi Avigdor even used the verse "The fool shall believe anything" to refer to his students who believed the phenomenon existed. But a distinguished merchant—described as one who "forced himself" on the students and was not the type to deceive people— told the students that he himself sent a telegram to Warsaw and received the "right" response immediately afterwards, which could not possibly have been counterfeit. The students accepted this testimony as reliable proof of the existence of the telegraph, and even Rabbi Avigdor came to assent to it.

Two worlds of knowledge are expressed in this discussion about the telegraph. The first world, that of Rabbi Avigdor, is inter/intratextual: Booki Ben Yogli describes him as "a great scholar," but his scholarship is in the rabbinic literature. In Rabbi Avigdor's model of inquiry, based on the rabbinic inter/intratextual facts, the telegraph went against nature. But the distinguished merchant—the practical figure who deals with everyday matters and therefore does not belong to the student band—brings another sort of knowledge into the picture. This is extratextual knowledge, which is supposedly based on observation and experience. Significantly, the "empirical" knowledge of the merchant defeats the inter/intratextual rabbinical knowledge of Rabbi Avigdor.

But even if it had been proven that there was indeed such a "wondrous" instrument as the telegraph, the way it worked remained a mystery. Booki Ben Yogli describes his personal quest to understand the mechanism behind it, a quest that reveals the influence of inter/intratextual patterns of inquiry on his mode of reasoning and choice of sources. The Talmud and other Jewish works of inquiry (*HaKhazary*, *Hovat HaLevavot*) serve as his starting point: "I read much and understood but little… Only this I learned, that the world is made up of four elements: fire, water, air and earth, and four basic qualities: cold and hot, dry and moist. I have tried to combine these elements and qualities and reveal through them, by my best *pilpul* argumentation skills, the secret of the telegraph—but in vain."[48] Jewish Enlightenment literature also did not provide answers about the telegraph; this literature used slogans to expound its form of redemption: the victory of light over dark. But in these works, according to Booki Ben Yogli, proper scientific knowledge was nowhere to be found.[49]

Booki Ben Yogli the boy had much wider access to sources of knowledge than had the general Jewish public. But still, to him the telegraph was a query with no answer. It should be noted that around the time that the telegraph was invented, even those with technical knowledge found its operation difficult to understand. As Menahem Blondheim[50] argues, unlike technological innovations related to quick motion in space (such as steam ships or rail trains) whose movements were observable and consecutive, the transmission of a message from place to place without any visible motion was difficult for people to comprehend. The lack of visibility of the telegraph's operation made its reliability hard to perceive and accept.[51]

It is against this background that Booki Ben Yogli describes his first encounter with *HaTzfira* as a veritable revelation. Haim Zelig Slonimsky, the editor of *HaTzfira*, responded to the public's yearning to understand innovations such as the telegraph, and indeed detailed explanations about its operation appeared in the first three issues. As Booki Ben Yogli testifies, "I unfold the first issue before me and lo—great God above—in big shiny letters at the top of the very first article the word 'Telegraph' is glowing before me! Could it be that very same telegraph that intrigued me so this past year? I found myself reading Slonimsky's article, swallowing every word as someone taken by a great frenzy, till from excess of joy and elation of spirit my soul had all but departed."[52] Thus the journal provided a gateway to whole new (extratextual) world, totally unfamiliar to *Beit Midrash* students like Booki Ben Yogli, who said of the first issues of *HaTzfira*: "I saw before me a new world, a world filled with miracles and wonders, but not such miracles that are shrouded in mist, rather ones that are shining as bright as the heavens. I thought that day that I had grown wings behind both my shoulders, such as the wings of a stork, and there I was rising upwards, sailing through the air, in short—I was as one who is losing his wits."[53]

Articles on the telegraph were accompanied in *HaTzfira* by sketches intended to aid the readers in comprehending this new technological domain. Slonimsky refers in several places to the contribution of these sketches as part of the spirit of European visual culture (as exemplified in the scholarship of Johann H. Pestalozzi or Amos Comenius). These images were intended to give the readers a visual conception of the subject discussed, but they were also part of the adjustment of Hebrew to the surrounding modern world.[54] The detailed explanation of telegraph operation systems or the discussion of synthesis and decomposition of water molecules required the invention of new words. This was part of the renewal of the connection between the Hebrew language and reality.

Pictures—sketches of technical instruments such as telegraph parts—gave meaning to words that were renovated, unfamiliar, or imported from other languages. These sketches (like other printed pictures, such as the beaver,[55] rocks,[56] and landscape pictures) were accompanied by meticulous verbal description,[57] imbuing the article with reliability and ensuring that the readers felt they were dealing with "real objective things." At the same time, they reshaped the perception of social truths within Jewish society, by giving priority to what was perceived as extratextual empirical verification. Slonimsky regarded this focus on nature as an alternative to the over-sophistication of the Jewish public's thinking and knowledge: "And how great is the benefit of such nature stories among our people! The reader will take much pleasure from looking at genuine wonders, without burdening himself with excess inquiries."[58] It also should be noted that the use of visual images may have helped counter the skepticism (as can be seen in Rabbi Avigdor's attitude) and superstition about natural phenomena that was common at the time.

We see another example in *HaTzfira* of the attempt to "put the world on paper": the repeated use of maps. While the art of drawing maps is ancient—the use of cartography is evident as early as 2000 BCE—the perception of maps changed following the scientific revolution and the development of printing techniques.[59] Modern maps intended to reflect nature "as it is." Maps were seen as autonomous texts, free from the influences of authorial subjectivity. Reading maps was likened to reading the book of nature, reflecting a realistic scientific orientation toward the world. As Richard Helgerson argues, "Maps were the undeniable makers and markers of modernity, the signs, as well as the tools, of a distinctly new age."[60]

In *HaTzfira* in 1877, maps were translated into Hebrew.[61] These translated maps are of marked symbolic importance. They reflect an attempt to present the world in a modern, visually accurate way through the use of Hebrew. With these translated maps we clearly see a change in the perception of language within the Jewish community. These translated maps, like other visual descriptions, reveal a yearning to harness Hebrew to the natural world and everyday life.

These pictures, maps, and sketches also reflect the introduction of new visual communication patterns into Jewish communities. Because most Jewish readers did not comprehend their state's vernacular language, and because maps were part of the literature published in this language, they would not have been familiar with the maps' markings. By calling the series of twisted lines within a map the "Black Sea" (in Hebrew, *yam ha-shakhor*) and by marking cities with graphic points on a map, the journal exposed readers to a new world of symbols, allowing them to adjust gradually to map reading.

## The Yearning for Modern Extratextual Political Discourse

As Lederhendler argues, the Jewish press reflected the beginnings of autonomous Jewish politics.[62] But Hebrew journals were not only structurally important: that is to say, their significance was not simply in their role as a political channel. They also reflected and contributed to a change in Jewish political thought: its adaptation to modern life.

The yearning for a "scientific" discussion of political issues in *HaTzfira* was an expression of the modernization of Hebrew political discourse. The aim was to rely on extratextual proof. In this spirit Slonimsky argued, "We don't wish to give our readers small talk and *pilpulim* [*pilpul* in plural] about nothing, but clear reports and news from the practical world."[63] When Nahum Sokolov joined the editorial board of *HaTzfira* in the early 1880s, these trends strengthened and became much more sophisticated in his discussions of political issues. For Sokolov—influenced by Warsaw positivism[64]—identifying political discussion in *HaTzfira* with science became a sort of virtue. Even in 1910, when *HaTzfira* no longer had a scientific agenda, scientific discourse was still considered a model for political discourse:

> When *HaTzfira* was first formed, it was dedicated to science. Those days have partly passed and have partly not yet arrived. The period within which it was justified [to publish] a scientific journal that mainly translated articles about natural sciences passed, and the day when we can establish a Hebrew newspaper for general sciences has not yet come. But one thing we want to continue as a tradition is the scientific method. A newspaper should be a newspaper in each and every line, but the method of the observation and the way conclusions are drawn from life experiences, we wish to borrow from science. In light and vulgar journalism, there is a race after exaggerations, wanderings, embellishments, meaningless and unreal terrifying words, flowery speeches, and outlandish colors. In the sciences, there is no such race, as they are not meant to . . . blind the eyes, but to illuminate the eyes.[65]

According to this perception, the newspaper is scientific in the "yearning of the editorial board and the authors towards truth and exactness, to move away from the exaggeration that confuses the mind."[66]

An illustrative example of the attempt to examine political issues according to scientific methods relates to the immigration of Jews to the land of Israel. It should be clarified that the question of the settlement of the land was part of an ongoing debate at this time. As Kressel argues, the attitude of *HaTzfira* on this issue was lukewarm.[67] This was in contrast to other journals, such as *HaMaggid*,[68] which supported settlement, and *HaMelitz*,[69] which adopted an attitude similar to that of *HaMaggid* after the pogroms ("*Sufot Banegev*") of 1881 (27). Although *HaTzfira* does not espouse a complete and consistent opposition to settlement, the argument repeatedly appears to draw away from the national enthusiasm—based on the imagination—which prevents sober scientific judgment and pragmatic analysis of the issue. This reserved attitude of *HaTzfira* was at the center of its controversy with *HaMelitz*, which reflected the attitude of *Hovevei Tzion* (the lovers of Zion) movement. Of course, *HaTzfira*'s so-called scientific intentions could be seen as a rhetorical strategy to legitimize, and thus recruit support for, its ideological stance towards the settlement. However, it still reflects the shift to modern lines of argumentation—dealing with the matter using seemingly extratextual facts.

In this spirit, *HaTzfira* declared its aim to inquire, clarify, and examine the issue of settling the land of Israel in the light of the sciences.[70] In order to fulfill this "scientific" political task, *HaTzfira*'s board established a new series: "On the Land and its Fruit." The first article lays out the scientific purpose of the series, and sets up observation and inquiry in opposition to (according to *HaTzfira*) common phraseologies and claims:

Since the movement of settlement in the Land of Israel began to pave its way among our brothers, the Children of Israel, and to recruit heroes to its force, we have said again and again that the imaginations of the authors and their philosophizing is not useful or helpful but disgraces and shames; because the matter of the settlement in the Land of Israel is a political plan … not through empty idioms or useless discussion will we reach the target, but through study and inquiry, through effort and scientific examination. And the author who aspires to help his people in resolving the query of the settlement of the holy land has the duty to refine, explain, and clarify: to weigh up the wisdom, consider all the geographers' studies, and look into the matter to the extent of his intelligence whether by observing it with his eyes or with his mind. To this opinion we have been devoted since then and until today, and to the same extent that our soul despises the flowery phrases of the imaginative men who repeat again and again what is already known—harping phrases of nonsense that most educated readers are fed up with—so we wholeheartedly admire and respect the study and inquiry that scholars gather about the characteristics of the holy land—the condition of its land and its weather and its residents. And as most of these studies and inquiries were yet to be gathered within the framework of our literature and are scattered and divided among different books and languages, we have therefore decided to gather like the sheaf to the granary the discussions of reliable scholars, and to divide them into different chapters, and we hope that these purified, clear, and deeply sifted discussions, enlightened by the torch of inquiry, will help much more to carry out the settlement of the land of Israel than all those articles written with great enthusiasm and little inquiry. [71]

Before *HaTzfira* turned to discuss the extratextual, objective facts about the land of Israel, such as its weather and demography, it clarified the reliability of the sources and the methodology which would guarantee avoiding biased analysis. The article discussed the four geographers upon whose studies the series would be based, stressing their professionalism and reputations.

The conclusion drawn from analysis of the scientific observations in the political-geographical sphere was that the settlement of the land of Israel is problematic and unrealistic:

> It is amazing and peculiar that the supporters of the settlement of the land of Israel among us are demanding without knowing what they demand for, wishing without knowing what they wish for. It is a repeated thing for them to say that the salvation of Israel will come from the colony in the land of Judea, and they don't pay attention to the whole land of Judea; or more precisely, to the fact that the size of all the western land of Israel is no bigger than that of the Vhaline district, and that this land is settled by Christians and Moslems in their different companies and divisions, Arab city residents, and Bedouins, and peasants, and Christian residents and foreigners—and how many Colonialists would we finally be able to insert through the eye of this needle? . . . Where, therefore, is there space in the western land of Israel for one hundred thousand people? Or maybe you believe in miracles, that the land of Israel will expand and enlarge; is it not that you believe in salvation only through the natural way and not by miracles, and if your hope is in the natural way, why won't you pay attention to nature—that a small place cannot hold the many, if we will not trust and believe that in our great force we will remove the Ottomans and the Arabs and the different sectors of Christians from the eastern land of Israel. [72]

It is interesting to see in this series of articles an early awareness of the existence of Arab residents in the land of Israel and the acknowledgement of this presence as an obstacle to Jewish settlement plans. But this issue aside, although the scientific issue here was related to rhetorical consideration—scientific, logical, and reasonable discourse versus unauthorized, imaginative, and nationalist discourse—a modern political discussion which claimed to be relying on facts and observations—on nature and geography—was clearly framed by Hebrew political discourse. As in the early days of *HaTzfira* when popular science was dominant, the journal took an abstract topic (that of the land of Israel) along with the spiritual, religious, and nationalist meanings accompanying it, and made it a concrete issue—part of the real world. Sokolov made data which was previously only available in a foreign language accessible to his readers, emphasizing the empirical natural world—that of the land of Israel. Spiritual or unseen forces were thus replaced by public facts and observations, a shift that reflects the modern perception of political discourse.[73]

This trend of scientizing political discourse gained momentum and became much more sophisticated with the introduction of statistics. This yearning for statistics as the definitive (extratextual) information in the public sphere diffused from Western discourse in general, as well as from Jewish scholarly discourse (see Hart, 2000; Efron, 1994; Penslar, 2001).[74] The yearning to base political discourse on the "real world" progressed into a yearning for the politics of numbers, as statistics are perceived as having an ultimate ability to capture the objective political condition, which is seen as the basis for any pragmatic political discussion.

Basing political arguments on statistics was encouraged through confrontation with anti-Semites, who backed their claims with statistics that allegedly proved, for example, the laziness of Jews. *HaTzfira* saw its role as the "overseer of the nation"—that is, as a medium linking and coordinating the various Jewish communities and thus obligated to serve as its spokesman[75]—and answered the anti-Semites with statistics of its own. Sokolov called upon readers to count and send reports on the numbers of merchants and other occupations of Jews in their communities: "Our brothers in the world of commerce, industry, and workers of the land have the obligation to gather handfuls of trustworthy information regarding their numbers, occupations, and the benefits of their skills so that our defenders will possess the correct and true statistics with which to oppose the falsehoods and distortions in the hands of our enemy."[76] More and more "statistics" appeared in the special new column ("What Does Israel Do?"). Thus, for example, the following "statistical" article arrived from Kamin:

> In order that our city, though it is but a small town, not be considered useless, it excels in statistical matters; thus I was roused to bring exact statistics to the portal of *HaTzfira* to show our enemies and our ostracizers that it is a lie to attribute Jews with eating the bread of the lazy and that even in a small town like ours, many more eat from the sweat of their brow than the bread of the lazy.
>
> The number of our brother Children of Israel residing in our town is 200 families. One post office proprietor, 1 forest lumberjack, 29 shopkeepers, 7 sellers of eggs, 1 oil presser, 1 maker of raisin wine, 3 bakers, 4 builders of wooden houses, 7 traveling salesmen in the villages, 2 roofers, 2 workers with coal and sledges, 1 assistant, 4 tinsmiths, 5 wood craftsmen, 13 tailors, 10 assistants, 9 shoe makers and belt makers, 5 assistants, 2 hat makers, 1 assistant, 1 book binder, 1 candle maker, 4 glass cutters, 2 yeast salesmen, 3 hotels, 3 oven builders, 2 assistants, 3 sellers of grappa [*ya"sh*], 13 butchers, 2 cloth dyers, 2 barbers, 9 tutors, 1 teacher of writing and language, 4 sellers of hides, 1 water drawer, 1 bath attendant, 2 brick makers, 5 bull traders, 2 sellers of rags, 1 soda water maker by machine, 2 assistants, 3 wool combers by machine, 2 assistants, 1 *sofer stam* [scribe of holy writings], 1 Rabbi, 1 cantor, 1 keeper of the synagogue [*shamash*], 3 slaughterers, 1 house of study [*beit midrash*], 2 Hasidic houses, 3 Sha"s Societies [*sha"s* – the six orders of the *Mishna*], 3 *Misnayot* Societies, 1 Psalms Society, 1 Jewish Burial Society [*Hevra Kadisha*]. From the above account all can easily see that almost all the sons of our town are employed, and some as craftsmen.[77]

Incoming "statistics" referred not only to economics, but also to the social life and public institutions of the Jewish community.[78] Thus, for instance, "statistical" reports arrived regarding the number of seminaries, tutors, Sha"s societies, charitable societies, Talmud Torah societies, hospitality, and so on.[79] The call for "statistical material" clearly made a great impression on the readers as evidenced through the number of letters that included "counts" sent to *HaTzfira* and through the positive introductory sentences of the articles. The letters revealed that readers saw themselves as taking part in the war against anti-Semitism by being connected to the statistical project.[80]

The editor of *HaTzfira* was probably surprised by the great responsiveness of the readers. These "counts" were claimed as an expression of the new period of pragmatism in Jewish political discourse. The discourse of the past was concerned with disputes, questions of religion, imagination, and phraseology, and referred to the romantic period that was now over.[81] In contrast, the collection of statistical information was described as reflecting a new era, discussing in Hebrew the real-life economic and secular issues that the essence of the nation depended on. The journal's enthusiasm for the mere possibility of merging political discourse with real life was evident: "A sign of truth is among us and among the community, because there are readers who read the articles in order to do something, because there is actually a connection and relationship between literature and life."[82] Another article claimed that in general Jews tended to use dialectic argumentation to expose the hidden meanings of the text (in *drash* fashion). It argued that the seeds of change in the character of Jewish thought—its adjustment to the pragmatic world— would be found in statistics (even if the process is slow).[83]

The statistical leanings both reveal and contribute to changes in authoritative sources (and the perception of these sources) in political debate. This was an authority that relied on "reality," on observed facts that would testify to evidence and that were seen to be neither arbitrary nor subjective.[84] It reflects aspirations toward the establishment of a society based upon *knowledge* and not upon *belief.* Knowledge was understood to represent objectivity: it is seen to teach us about actual phenomena, not merely about those in possession of the knowledge. Belief, on the other hand, is subjective, saying something about its holder.[85] Politics based on numbers—on precise statistics—was perceived and described through the metaphor of being conducted in the full light "of the noon-day sun."[86] This was the antithesis of the politics of darkness— conducted, for example, by bureaucrats and policemen. The hopes for changing politics were based upon the transparency that numbers seemingly offered: on their very ability to allow one to "see" the data which reflects the extratextual reality "as it is" thus providing conclusive proof. This stood in contrast to anti-Semitism's "closing its eyes" to the reality before it.[87]

## Concluding Remarks: The Triumph of the Pilpul?

As we have seen, in its earlier stage *HaTzfira* was dominated by the popular sciences. This scientific discourse appears to reflect the beginnings of the modernization of Hebrew discourse. *HaTzfira*'s content at that stage tried to "pull" the readers to the natural world, to the truths of extratextual reality—of empirical matters—as the text presented them. But in the same way that Western socio-political patterns were influenced by the scientific revolution (observing and reporting social phenomena as physical facts), the political discourse developed in *HaTzfira* saw the scientific ethos as appropriate for modern, rational political argumentation.

This yearning for the scientization of socio-political discourse was reflected in the general tendency to challenge rabbinic discourse, which was part of the agenda of the *Haskalah*. This challenge was already evident in the eighteenth century in the work of the early *maskilim* in Berlin. By revising the school curriculum, these *maskilim* stressed the method of plain meaning (*peshat*) and Hebrew grammar, and criticized the Talmudic *pilpul* method.[88] We should also note that the connection between Hebrew journalism and popular sciences did not begin with the appearance of *HaTzfira* or with the Eastern European journals in general, but can be found in *HaMasef*, the journal established by Moses Mendelssohn's students in 1783 in Germany.[89] The modernization of Hebrew discourse can also be seen as the roots of the discursive processes of the *Yishuv* pre-state era, which aimed to emphasize the pragmatic use of Hebrew. As Penslar argues, the shift towards pragmatic discourse was part of a national existential change: "Scientific discourse—spare, practical, and universal— was music to the ears of Zionist ideologues hostile to rabbinic declamation and the shrill cry of the hawker."[90] Learning programs from those days articulated the yearning for visualizing texts—an attempt to present punctilious visual descriptions in order to help students in the process of learning.[91] This desire for visualization developed over time into a national need to observe the "homeland" (*moledet*) as part of reconnecting Jews to the natural world, to the soil of the land of Israel. These discursive trends can also be related to the Israeli *dugri* speech culture. According to Tamar Katriel, the *dugri* "antistyle" mode, which stressed plain talk and simple discursive patterns, was part of the general Zionist tendency to repudiate all aspects of rabbinic-Diaspora culture, including the *pilpul* style, and to adapt modern cultural trends.[92]

But this allegedly linear progress of the modernization of Hebrew discourse should be evaluated with much caution. In fact, evidence from *HaTzfira* proves that a fundamental discussion took place in Jewish society about the possibility of a rabbinic influence on general social discourse, and especially with regard to Zionism. Discussion of the influences of the rabbinic *pilpul* on politics appeared again and again: political and later Zionist debates in Eastern Europe were described as complex, tending toward circuitous argumentation, negation, and opposition in "the opposite holds true" style:

> Indeed especially we see the curvature within our people. Speak into someone's ear clear matters, right and reliable, matters that are easy to understand and true to the linguistic form of the learned, in a language of the steadfast, and he answers you: what is the meaning of that? The obvious meaning? Ho, on the contrary! It is just the opposite! Because he is accustomed to intrigue and to go round about and to seek ruses and to confine and to hook and to dance upon a rope in his gloomy affairs and his odd condition. Speak to him strange things and miracles, marvelous news—and then he will thank you; add to that enigmatic Talmudic legends and verses that are hard to understand, and to them add many queries, and all the crowd will so wonder about the wisdom that is so concealed that it cannot be understood. They will expectantly anticipate the speaker, who speaks wonders, and expect that with his witty and sharp reasoning he will explain enormous wonders and will turn the complex into plain and will continue to dig and to strive and to ascend, and then all the listeners will be content and pleased.[93]

It was argued that, like the endless dialectic discourse of the Talmud, Zionist discussion had become endless too: a discourse with no ability to translate the political debate into practical decisions. In the manner of *pilpul* in the Talmud texts, every word, article, or speech in the political sphere became the basis for analogy and deep textual study. This mode of argumentation, it was claimed, took up endless time and energy. Because the debate did not end even after a vote was set and decisions were accepted, one could never act upon them. A national movement that aims to act in the practical world cannot allow itself to keep overturning its decisions. Over time, the attitude towards the influences of the rabbinic methods, and especially towards the influence of the *pilpul*, became more decisive and explicit. Sokolov described it as the illness of the exile period and demanded that the public stop dealing with political and Zionist content in the style and structure of the rabbinic (inter/intratextual) methods:

> There is to be no discussion about things that were never born. There is to be no analogy from the clear to the unclear. There will be no permission [*ein reshot*] to analogize. There is no permission to be [characterized by] over-*pilpul*.[94]

It is true that mere reference to the influence of the rabbinic discursive methods does not necessarily mean that such influence was expressed in the textual "reality." But we should take into account that the spokesmen or writers who took part in shaping Zionist discourse in Eastern Europe had absorbed rabbinic discursive patterns and were accustomed to seeing them as the "right way" of reaching the truth. As discursive perceptions are absorbed into a society's culture, their replacement requires a lengthy processes of adaptation. It is therefore not realistic to expect that traditional discursive patterns, shaped during the exile generations, would be left behind all at once.[95] The existence of such influences of Talmudic studies on early Hebrew political discourse, and its possible clash with modern discourse, therefore deserves further in-depth study.

## Notes

1    Israel Bartal, " 'Herald and Informer to a Jewish Man': Jewish Journalism as a Channel to Innovation," *Katedra* 71 (1994): 160 [Hebrew].

2    Benjamin Harshav, *Language in Time of Revolution* (Los Angeles: University of California Press, 1993), 119.

3    Ibid., 116-117.

4    Ibid., 119.

5    Gezel Kressel, *The History of the Hebrew Press in Erez-Israel* (Jerusalem: The Zionist Library, 1964), 10 [Hebrew].

6    Haim Rabin, *Principles of the Hebrew Language* (Jerusalem: Jewish World Federation, 1977), 47-48 [Hebrew].

7    Shalom Jacob Abramovitz, *Fountain of Judgement* (Zitamir: A. S. Shadaw Press, 1867), 24-25 [Hebrew].

8    Ibid., 26-27.

9    Adam Jaworski and Nikolas Coupland, "Introduction: Perspectives on Discourse Analysis," in *The Discourse Reader,* eds. A. Jaworski and N. Coupland (London and New York: Routledge, 1999), 1-44.

10   The journal *HaTzfira* was founded in 1862 by Haim Zelig Slonimsky, who served as its editor and publisher. Publication ceased after six months; it was re-established twelve years later. Until 1886 it appeared as a weekly and thereafter as a daily. Publication was halted several times over the years, and from 1906 onward it did not appear regularly. From a popular, scientifically-oriented journal it became a politically-oriented one, maintaining an emphasis on issues related to the future of the Jewish people. The change is linked, among other things, to Nahum Sokolov's entry onto *HaTzfira*'s editorial board. Another change in the journal's content came with the adoption of Zionist ideological concepts. This trend, beginning at the time of the first Zionist Congress (1897), was a characteristic of the paper until it finally faded away at the beginning of the 1930s. For more detail of the periods in which the paper stopped appearing, as well as references to changes in its format, see Menuha Gilboa, *Lexicon of Hebrew Periodicals in the Eighteenth and Nineteenth Centuries* (Tel Aviv: The Rosenberg School of Jewish Studies, 1992) [Hebrew].

11   Richard Harland, *Literary Theory from Plato to Barthes* (New York: St. Martin's Press, 1999), 25; Oren Soffer, "The Textual Pendulum," *Communication Theory* 15, no. 3 (2005): 268.

12   David R. Olson, *The World on Paper* (Cambridge: Cambridge University Press, 1994), 195.

13   Ibid., 143.

14   Ibid., 196.

15   Ilse Nina Bulhof, *The Language of Science* (Netherlands: E.J. Brill, 1992), 3.

16   Thomas Hobbes, *Leviathan: With selected variants from the Latin edition of 1668,* edited by Edwin Curley (Cambridge: Hackett Publishing Company, 1994), 19.

17   James Knowlson, *Universal language schemes in England and France 1600-1800* (Toronto: University of Toronto Press, 1975), 108.

18   Ibid., 109.

19   Steven Shapin and Simon Schaffer, *Leviathan and the Air-Pump: Hobbes, Boyle and the Experimental Life* (Princeton: Princeton University Press, 1985).

20   Olson, *The World on Paper,* 173-176.

21   Walter J. Ong, "Writing Is a Technology That Restructures Thought," in *The Linguistics of Literacy,* eds. P. Downing, S. D. Lima, and M. Noonan (Amsterdam: John Benjamins Company, 1992), 308.

22   William M. Ivins, *Prints and Visual Communication* (Cambridge: Harvard University Press, 1953), 159.

23   M. C. McGee, "Against Transcendentalism: Prologue to Functional Theory of Communication Praxis," in *Form, Genre, and the Study of Political Discourse,* eds. H. W. Simons and A. A. Aghazarian (Columbia: University of South Carolina, 1986), 115.

24   Yaron Ezrahi, *The Descent of Icarus* (Cambridge: Harvard University Press, 1990), 170.

25   Michael Schudson, *Origins of the Ideal of Objectivity in the Professions: Studies in the History of American Journalism and American Law, 1830-1940* (New York and London: Garland Publishing, 1990), 162.

26   Michael Schudson, *Discovering the News: A Social History of American Newspapers* (New York: Basic Books, 1978), 6.

27    David T. Z. Mindich, *Just the Facts: How "Objectivity" Came to Define American Journalism* (New York and London: New York University Press, 1998), 114.

28    Ibid., 115.

29    Jacob Neusner, *The Making of the Mind of Judaism* (Atlanta Georgia: Scholars Press, 1987).

30    Chanoch Albeck, *Introduction to the Talmud, Babli and Yerushalmi* (Tel Aviv: Dvir, 1987), 3 [Hebrew].

31    Louis Jacobs, *Structure and Form in the Babylonian Talmud* (Cambridge: Cambridge University Press, 1991).

32    David C. Kraemer, *The Mind of the Talmud* (New York: Oxford University Press, 1990).

33    Ibid., 6-7.

34    Ibid., 139.

35    Neusner, *The Making of the Mind of Judaism,* 147.

36    Adin Steinsaltz, *Talmud for Everyone* (Jerusalem: Eidannim, 1977), 195 [Hebrew].

37    Dov Rapel, *The Dispute over Disputations (pilpul)* (Tel-Aviv: Dvir, 1979), 11 [Hebrew].

38    Haim Zalman Dimitrovsky, "On Ways of Pilpul," in *The Jubilee Book in Honour of Shalom Baron* (Jerusalem: The American Academy of Jewish Studies, 1975), 117 [Hebrew].

39    David Assaf, *Poland: Chapters in The History of the Eastern European Jews and Their Culture (Units 5-6)* (Tel-Aviv: The Open University, 1990), 62 [Hebrew].

40    Benjamin Harshav, *Language in Time of Revolution* (Los Angeles: University of California Press, 1993), 83.

41    See Solomon B. Freehof, *The Responsa Literature* (Philadelphia: The Jewish Publication Society of America, 1959).

42    Hava Tornyanski, "The Homily (Drasha) and the Written-Homily as a Mediator Between the Canon Culture and the Wide-Public," in *Popular Culture: Collections of Researches, ed. B. Z. Kedar* (Jerusalem: Shazar Center for the History of Israel, 1996) [Hebrew].

43    See Tal Kogman, "The Creation of Images of Knowledge in Texts for Children and Young Adults Published during the Haskalah Period" (Ph.D. diss., Tel Aviv University, 2000) [Hebrew].

44    See Jacob Katz, *Out of the Ghetto* (Cambridge: Harvard University Press, 1973), 36.

45    Booki Ben Yogli is the penname of Judah Loeb Kazenelson (1847-1917): historian, author of Hebrew literature, and physician.

46    Booki Ben Yogli, "Fleeting Memories from the Days of the First HaTzfira," in *The Jubilee Book of HaTzfira* (Warsaw: HaTzfira Press, 1912).

47    Ibid., 70-71.

48    Ibid., 72.

49    Ibid., 73.

50    Menahem Blondheim, *News Over the Wires: The Telegraph and the Public Information in America* (Cambridge and London: Harvard University Press, 1994).

51    Ibid., 30-46.

52    Booki Ben Yogli, "Fleeting Memories from…" 73.

53   Ibid., 75.

54   See Oren Soffer, *There Is No Place for Pilpul: HaTzfira Journal and the Modernization of Sociopolitical Discourse* (Jerusalem: Mosad Bialik and the Center for the Study of Polish Jewry and Their Culture, 2007); Oren Soffer, "The Case of the Hebrew Press: From the Traditional Model of Discourse to the Modern Model," *Written Communication: An International Quarterly Research, Theory and Applications* 21, no. 2 (2004b): 141-170.

55   "The Beaver," *HaTzfira* 13 (5th of Iyar, 1862) [Hebrew].

56   "Meteors," *HaTzfira* 7 (18th of 2nd Adar, 1862) [Hebrew].

57   Soffer, "The Case of the Hebrew Press..."

58   Haim Zelig Slonimsky, "Letter from Rabbi Ch. Z. Slonimsky to Abramovich, July 1864," in *The History of Marbei Haskala B'Israel Company in the Land of Russia,* Part 2 (St. Petersburg: Moshe Ha'Levi Rosenthal, 1890), 41.

59   L. Jakels, *The Art of Map-Maker in Essex 1566-1860* (Chelmsford: Essex County Council, 1947), vii.

60   Richard Helgerson, "The Folly of Maps and Modernity," in *Literature, Mapping, and the Politics of Space in Early Modern Britain,* eds. A. Gordon and B. Klein (Cambridge: Cambridge University Press, 2001), 241.

61   "Chronicles," *HaTzfira* 20 (18th of Sivan, 1877) [Hebrew]; "Chronicles," *HaTzfira* 32 (13th of Elul, 1877) [Hebrew].

62   Eli Lederhendler, *The Road to Modern Jewish Politics* (New York & Oxford: Oxford University Press, 1989), 133.

63   "To Our Authors," *HaTzfira* 23 (8th of Tevet, 1875) [Hebrew].

64   See Shoshana Stiftel, "Nohom Sokolov: From Judaic-Polish Positivism to the Zionist Movement" (PhD diss., University of Tel Aviv, 1994) [Hebrew]; Stanislaus A. Blejwas, *Realism in Polish Politics: Warsaw Positivism and National Survival in Nineteenth Century Poland* (New Haven: Yale Concilium on International and Area Studies, 1984).

65   *HaTzfira* (11th of Tishrei, 1910) [Hebrew]. The expanded spacing between the letters appears in the source for the purpose of emphasis.

66   Ibid.

67   Gezel Kressel, "Nahum Sokolov, His Way and Activities," in *N. Sokolov, Scouts for the House of Israel,* ed. G. Kressel (Jerusalem: Zionist Library, 1961) [Hebrew].

68   The journal *HaMaggid* was founded by Eliezer Lipmann Silbermann in a small town (Lyck) on the border between Prussia and Russia. Silbermann emphasized the moderate tone of his journal, rejected suggestions for religious reforms, and avoided adopting radical *maskilic* attitudes. *HaMaggid* had readers in many countries but most resided in the Russian Empire. In 1858 David Gordon became Silbermann's assistant and in time functioned, in effect, as the journal's editor. *HaMaggid* emphasized the importance of the use of Hebrew and described this language as the common denominator binding the Children of Israel. *HaMaggid* saw itself as obliged to provide its readers with information about current political events, but also gave space to articles that dealt with popular science, medical issues, Jewish history, and so on. In 1880 the ownership of the journal passed to David Gordon. The journal continued to appear after Gordon's death in 1886 under variations of the journal's original name and under different editors until it finally faded away in 1903 (see: Gilboa, *Lexicon of Hebrew Periodicals*, 117-135; Kressel, *The History of the Hebrew Press,* 14-15; Yosef Salmon, "David Gordon and Ha-maggid: Changing Attitudes toward

Jewish Nationalism 1860-1882," *Modern Judaism* 17, no. 2 (1997): 109-124; Ya'akov Shavit, "Window on the World," *Qesher* 4 (1988): 3-10 [Hebrew]).

69 The journal *HaMelitz* was founded in 1860 in Odessa by Alexander Ha-Levi Ziderboime. It was the first weekly journal in Tsarist Russia. According to Gilboa, *Lexicon of Hebrew Periodicals,* in its first years *HaMelitz* emphasized the historical aspects of Jewish life. From its second year onwards, the journal published political articles as well as articles dealing with popular science and the economy. The journal became a major stage for internal Jewish social and political debates, in which many young and radical writers published their articles. In 1866 *HaMelitz* began to appear daily. Ziderboime died in 1893, and Leon Rabinovitz became the new editor of the journal. The journal disappeared in 1904 (ibid., 137-157).

70 "Scouts for the House of Israel," *HaTzfira* 29 (4th of Av, 1883) [Hebrew].

71 "On the Land and its Fruits," *HaTzfira* 42 (24th of Heshvan, 1885) [Hebrew].

72 "On the Land and its Fruits," *HaTzfira* 2 (4th of Shvat, 1885) [Hebrew].

73 Yaron Ezrahi, "The Cultural Dimension of the Concept of Modern Democratic Power," *Zmanim* 6 (1994): 4-16 [Hebrew].

74 John M. Efron, *Defenders of the Race* (New Haven and London: Yale University Press, 1994); Derek J. Penslar, *Shylock's Children* (Los Angeles and London: University of California Press, 2001).

75 Oren Soffer, "'Paper Territory': Early Hebrew Journalism and Its Political Roles," *Journalism History* 30, no. 1 (2004c): 31-39.

76 "What Does Israel Do?" *HaTzfira* 151 (26th of Tamuz, 1887) [Hebrew].

77 Ya'akov Tzukkerman, *HaTzfira* 252 (12th of Kislev, 1887) [Hebrew].

78 See Oren Soffer, "Anti-Semitism, Statistics, and the Scientization of Hebrew Political Discourse: The Case Study of HaTzfira," *Jewish Social Studies: History, Culture and Society* 10, no. 2 (2004a): 55-79.

79 "What Does Israel Do?" *HaTzfira* 217 (1st of Heshvan, 1887) [Hebrew].

80 "What Does Israel Do?" *HaTzfira* 191 (15th of Elul, 1887) [Hebrew].

81 Seek Our Paths and Investigate!" *HaTzfira* 215 (28th of Tishre, 1887) [Hebrew].

82 Ibid.

83 Yitzchak Shlomo Fox, "The Counting of the Sons of Israel," *HaTzfira* 90 (23rd of Iyar, 1888) [Hebrew].

84 Yaron Ezrahi, *The Descent of Icarus* (Cambridge: Harvard University Press, 1990), 62.

85 Bruno Latour, *Science in Action* (Cambridge: Harvard University Press, 1987), 182.

86 "Scouts for the House of Israel," *HaTzfira* 16 (20th of Iyar, 1885) [Hebrew].

87 Soffer, "Anti-Semitism, Statistics, and the Scientization of Hebrew Political Discourse..." 55-79.

88 David Sorkin, *The Berlin Haskalah and German Religious Thought* (London & Portland: Vallentine Mitchell, 2000), 42-45.

89 Z. Zeimerion, "The Cultivation of Hebrew within HaMeasef," in *Dr. Baroch Ben-Yhoda Book,* ed. Ben-Zion Luria (Tel Aviv: The Society of Bible Research, 1981), 438 [Hebrew].

90 Derek J. Penslar, *Zionism and Technocracy* (Bloomington and Indianapolis: Indiana University Press, 1991), 154.

91   Joseph Ozrakovski, Mordechai Krishevski, and Ychiel Ychieli, *Observation Lessons and the Knowledge of the Homeland* (Jaffa: Kohelet, 1912) [Hebrew].

92   Tamar Katriel, *Talking Straight: Dugri Speech in Israeli Sabra Culture* (Cambridge: Cambridge University Press, 1986), 17-18.

93   Katravitch, "Zion Erstwhile Times and Future," *HaTzfira* 50 (2nd of Nisan, 1899) [Hebrew].

94   "Basis of the Revival," *HaTzfira* 268 (17th of Kislev, 1905) [Hebrew]. The expanded spacing between the letters appears in the source for the purpose of emphasis.

95   See Oren Soffer, "Zionist Discourse and the Rabbinic Genre," *Jewish Culture and History* 7, no. 3 (2004d): 53-76.

# Bibliography

Abramovitz, Shalom Jacob. *Fountain of Judgement*. Zitamir: A. S. Shadaw Press, 1867 [Hebrew].

Albeck, Chanoch. *Introduction to the Talmud, Babli and Yerushalmi*. Tel Aviv: Dvir, 1987 [Hebrew].

Assaf, David. *Poland: Chapters in The History of the Eastern European Jews and Their Culture (Units 5-6)*. Tel-Aviv: The Open University, 1990 [Hebrew].

Bartal, Israel. " 'Herald and Informer to a Jewish Man': Jewish Journalism as a Channel to Innovation." *Katedra* 71 (1994): 154-164 [Hebrew].

Blejwas, Stanislaus A. *Realism in Polish Politics: Warsaw Positivism and National Survival in Nineteenth Century Poland*. New Haven: Yale Concilium on International and Area Studies, 1984.

Blondheim, Menahem. *News Over the Wires: The Telegraph and the Public Information in America*. Cambridge and London: Harvard University Press, 1994.

Booki Ben Yogli. "Fleeting Memories from the Days of the First HaTzfira." In *The Jubilee Book of HaTzfira*, 70-71. Warsaw: HaTzfira Press, 1912.

Bulhof, Ilse Nina. *The Language of Science*. Netherlands: E.J. Brill, 1992.

Dimitrovsky, Haim Zalman. "On Ways of Pilpul." In *The Jubilee Book in Honour of Shalom Baron*. Jerusalem: The American Academy of Jewish Studies, 1975 [Hebrew].

Efron, John M. *Defenders of the Race*. New Haven and London: Yale University Press, 1994.

Ezrahi, Yaron. *The Descent of Icarus*. Cambridge: Harvard University Press, 1990.

Ezrahi, Yaron. "The Cultural Dimension of the Concept of Modern Democratic Power." *Zmanim* 6 (1994): 4-16 [Hebrew].

Freehof, Solomon B. *The Responsa Literature*. Philadelphia: The Jewish Publication Society of America, 1959.

Gilboa, Menuha. *Lexicon of Hebrew Periodicals in the Eighteenth and Nineteenth Centuries*. Tel Aviv: The Rosenberg School of Jewish Studies, 1992 [Hebrew].

Harland, Richard. *Literary Theory from Plato to Barthes*. New York: St. Martin's Press, 1999.

Harshav, Benjamin. *Language in Time of Revolution*. Los Angeles: University of California Press, 1993.

Helgerson, Richard. "The Folly of Maps and Modernity." In *Literature, Mapping, and the Politics of Space in Early Modern Britain*, edited by Andrew Gordon and Bernhard Klein, 241-262. Cambridge: Cambridge University Press, 2001.

Hobbes, Thomas. *Leviathan: With selected variants from the Latin edition of 1668*, edited by Edwin Curley. Cambridge: Hackett Publishing Company, 1994.

Ivins, William M. *Prints and Visual Communication*. Cambridge: Harvard University Press, 1953.

Jacobs, Louis. *Structure and Form in the Babylonian Talmud*. Cambridge: Cambridge University Press, 1991.

Jakels, L. *The Art of Map-Maker in Essex 1566-1860*. Chelmsford: Essex County Council, 1947.

Jaworski, Adam, and Nikolas Coupland. "Introduction: Perspectives on Discourse Analysis." In *The Discourse Reader*, edited by Adam Jaworski and Nikolas Coupland, 1-44. London and New York: Routledge, 1999.

Katriel, Tamar. *Talking Straight: Dugri Speech in Israeli Sabra Culture*. Cambridge: Cambridge University Press, 1986.

Katz, Jacob. *Out of the Ghetto*. Cambridge: Harvard University Press, 1973.

Knowlson, James. *Universal language schemes in England and France 1600-1800*. Toronto: University of Toronto Press, 1975.

Kogman, Tal. "The Creation of Images of Knowledge in Texts for Children and Young Adults Published during the Haskalah Period." Ph.D. diss., Tel Aviv University, 2000 [Hebrew].

Kraemer, David C. *The Mind of the Talmud*. New York: Oxford University Press, 1990.

Kressel, Gezel. *The History of the Hebrew Press in Erez-Israel*. Jerusalem: The Zionist Library, 1964 [Hebrew].

Kressel, Gezel. "Nahum Sokolov, His Way and Activities." In *N. Sokolov, Scouts for the House of Israel*, edited by Gezel Kressel. Jerusalem: Zionist Library, 1961 [Hebrew].

Latour, Bruno. *Science in Action*. Cambridge: Harvard University Press, 1987.

Lederhendler, Eli. *The Road to Modern Jewish Politics*. New York & Oxford: Oxford University Press, 1989.

McGee, M. C. "Against Transcendentalism: Prologue to Functional Theory of Communication Praxis." In *Form, Genre, and the Study of Political Discourse*, edited by Herbert W. Simons and Aram A. Aghazarian, 108-158. Columbia: University of South Carolina, 1986.

Mindich, David T. Z. *Just the Facts: How "Objectivity" Came to Define American Journalism*. New York and London: New York University Press, 1998.

Neusner, Jacob. *The Making of the Mind of Judaism*. Atlanta Georgia: Scholars Press, 1987.

Olson, David R. *The World on Paper*. Cambridge: Cambridge University Press, 1994.

Ong, Walter J. "Writing Is a Technology That Restructures Thought." In *The Linguistics of Literacy*, edited by Pamela Downing, Susan D. Lima, and Michael Noonan, 293-319. Amsterdam: John Benjamins Company, 1992.

Ozrakovski, Joseph, Mordechai Krishevski, and Ychiel Ychieli. *Observation Lessons and the Knowledge of the Homeland*. Jaffa: Kohelet, 1912 [Hebrew].

Penslar, Derek J. *Zionism and Technocracy*. Bloomington and Indianapolis: Indiana University Press, 1991.

Penslar, Derek J. *Shylock's Children*. Los Angeles and London: University of California Press, 2001.

Rabin, Haim. *Principles of the Hebrew Language*. Jerusalem: Jewish World Federation, 1977 [Hebrew].

Rapel, Dov. *The Dispute over Disputations (pilpul)*. Tel-Aviv: Dvir, 1979 [Hebrew].

Salmon, Yosef. "David Gordon and *Ha-maggid:* Changing Attitudes toward Jewish Nationalism 1860-1882." *Modern Judaism* 17, no. 2 (1997): 109-124.

Schudson, Michael. *Discovering the News: A Social History of American Newspapers*. New York: Basic Books, 1978.

Schudson, Michael. *Origins of the Ideal of Objectivity in the Professions: Studies in the History of American Journalism and American Law, 1830-1940*. New York and London: Garland Publishing, 1990.

Shapin, Steven, and Simon Schaffer. *Leviathan and the Air-Pump: Hobbes, Boyle and the Experimental Life*. Princeton: Princeton University Press, 1985.

Shavit, Ya'akov. "Window on the World." *Qesher* 4 (1988): 3-10 [Hebrew].

Slonimsky, Haim Zelig. "Letter from Rabbi Ch. Z. Slonimsky to Abramovich, July 1864." In *The History of Marbei Haskala B'Israel Company in the Land of Russia*, Part 2. St. Petersburg: Moshe Ha'Levi Rosenthal, 1890 [Hebrew].

Soffer, Oren. "Anti-Semitism, Statistics, and the Scientization of Hebrew Political Discourse: The Case Study of *HaTzfira*." *Jewish Social Studies: History, Culture and Society* 10, no. 2 (2004a): 55-79.

Soffer, Oren. "The Case of the Hebrew Press: From the Traditional Model of Discourse to the Modern Model." *Written Communication: An International Quarterly Research, Theory and Applications* 21, no. 2 (2004b): 141-170.

Soffer, Oren. " 'Paper Territory': Early Hebrew Journalism and Its Political Roles." *Journalism History* 30, no. 1 (2004c): 31-39.

Soffer, Oren. "Zionist Discourse and the Rabbinic Genre." *Jewish Culture and History* 7, no. 3 (2004d): 53-76.

Soffer, Oren. "The Textual Pendulum." *Communication Theory* 15, no. 3 (2005): 266-291.

Soffer, Oren. *There Is No Place for Pilpul:* HaTzfira *Journal and the Modernization of Sociopolitical Discourse*. Jerusalem: Mosad Bialik and the Center for the Study of Polish Jewry and Their Culture, 2007.

Sorkin, David. *The Berlin Haskalah and German Religious Thought*. London & Portland: Vallentine Mitchell, 2000.

Steinsaltz, Adin. *Talmud for Everyone*. Jerusalem: Eidannim, 1977 [Hebrew].

Stiftel, Shoshana. "Nohom Sokolw: From Judaic-Polish Positivism to the Zionist Movement." PhD diss., University of Tel Aviv, 1994 [Hebrew].

Tornyanski, Hava. "The Homily (*Drasha*) and the Written-Homily as a Mediator Between the Canon Culture and the Wide-Public." In *Popular Culture: Collections of Researches*, edited by B. Z. Kedar. Jerusalem: Shazar Center for the History of Israel, 1996 [Hebrew].

Zeimerion, Z. "The Cultivation of Hebrew within *HaMeasef*." In *Dr. Baroch Ben-Yhoda Book*, edited by Ben-Zion Luria. Tel Aviv: The Society of Bible Research, 1981 [Hebrew].

CHAPTER NINE

# "With our Pens and Words Alone We Conquered Public Opinion"

## Herzl's Campaigns of Persuasion and His Travels Through Communication Genres[1]

### TAMAR LIEBES

## *Introduction*

In the broader context of the question discussed in this book regarding the role of the media in *the survival of the Jewish people in the diaspora*, I examine the central role of the media campaign designed to ensure the continued existence of the Jewish people by rather *putting an end to the diaspora*. While, as we perceive from the chapters of this book, communication between Jewish communities in Europe (for the purpose of commerce, familial ties, and halakhic matters) indicates relatively stable conditions, the purpose of Benjamin Ze'ev Herzl's campaign of persuasion for establishing the Zionist movement was to warn the Jewish diaspora of the impending disaster originating from the new kind of anti-Semitism gaining momentum after the emancipation. Herzl's idea was to unite the traditional and assimilating Jews as one around a revolutionary movement designed to relocate the diaspora communities from their places of residence to a land in which they can establish their own state. From the two options of the end of the Jews (assimilation) and the end of the diaspora, the latter was chosen. In this perspective, Herzl's media campaign, discussed below, was not intended towards *conserving the existing*, but rather *to affect change*.

My objective in this chapter is to examine the two aspects of Herzl's groundbreaking activity. Firstly, I will examine how Herzl's intuitions concerning the interactions between media, public, and leadership can be mapped and interpreted while using contemporary terms from media studies. Secondly, I will examine how Herzl's understanding of the power of journalistic, dramatic, and literary genres to influence the public, his talents on the stage and behind the scenes, as a main actor and the impresario of the Zionist movement is manifested. I will do this by analyzing a series of media campaigns Herzl adapted for the specific target audience he marked in each stage of his thought development. Herzl was a prominent charismatic orator, abundantly imaginative event producer, as the creative author of newspaper articles, stage plays, work plans for philanthropists, popular literature for the general Jewish public, and as a historical documenter (Herzl made sure that the collection of scrawled notes – notes his doting father turned into a diary – were published in book form after his death). In this context, I would like to examine the process and underlying dilemmas of choosing the medium and genre in each and every stage of Herzl's efforts to solve the Jewish problem, as an indication of Herzl's perception of the target audience and the specific appropriate persuasion campaign for that audience.

## Herzl and the Media

Herzl was a sworn devotee of using the latest technological inventions of his time, not just those used for improving the communication between people. He admired the technological achievement of the Suez Canal more than the beauty of the Acropolis, because the canal is the manifestation of the great abilities of human will.[2] Also in his novel, *The Old New Land* (German: *Altneuland*), which outlined the vision of the Zionist state, technologies and their usage were awarded a place of honor.

Herzl made good use of the printed word in order to distribute his ideas. Through it he reached out in a rather sophisticated way to a variety of audiences – from the religious Jews in the ghetto to the secular Jews that had abandoned it and moved out to live in other places. Herzl established is leadership not only on the grounds of his impressive visage, charismatic personality that charmed his surroundings (many of the ghetto Jews saw him as a reflection of Sabbatai Zevi,[3] who was perceived as the Messiah and alternatively the false Messiah during his time period), and the enchanting rhetoric of his speeches, but also on a wide range of genres in print. Throughout his long and hindered journey to establish the Zionist movement and propelling it forward, Herzl published in print a play, manifesto (position paper), novel, and opinion pieces in various newspapers. Herzl made a living working for the liberal and influential Vienna newspaper *Neue Freie Presse*, and among other things was a reporter in France during the Dreyfus trial. He was the editor of the feuilleton section of the newspaper and an esteemed and respected literary critic. Later, in the midst of his Zionist activity, he founded his own magazine (also in German), *Die Welt*, which offered a printed stage for managing the Zionist discourse in the public sphere. Despite his brilliant writing career, Herzl did not overlook the benefits of other persuasion techniques, such as conferences, ceremonies, and public speeches. Avineri claims that due to his unique communication skills, Herzl was the right person in the right time and place for dealing with his generation's task – finding a national solution for the Jews in light of rising anti-Semitism. Indeed, his leadership was based first and foremost on his being media savvy: not only in the context of an intimate conversation or a public impassioned speech in congress hall, but in a much broader sense. Herzl's skills as a journalist and his capabilities of analyzing European politics led him to the firm conclusion that the option supposedly given to the Jews in central and western Europe to integrate in the society around them, in practice turned into a kind of "new ghetto" (like the name of the play he wrote about the bitter fate of educated young people who had just left the ghetto, *The New Ghetto*). In his opinion, the dangers of this ghetto were greater than the life in the old ghetto, where Jewish life was run within the framework of clear rules and was relatively stable. Another political-media insight of Herzl's reflected that he was the first of the Zionist leaders who understood the power of impact on the non-Jewish public opinion as a strong tool in modern politics, especially for the Jews, who had no other political force. He realized that public relations and media exposure are vital for political success, even if they create a representation of a greater strength than that which exists in reality – and perhaps due to this.[4]

It is important to note that despite his skills and great understanding of the ways of propaganda, Herzl did not comprehend what many others did – the importance of a national language as a device for national unity. He himself, as someone fluent in a number of languages (Hebrew not being one of them), assumed the national model did not require a common language for all residents. Herzl never inclined to implement the use of the print medium for the dissemination of the national language, as was done in many other places.[5] Furthermore, he publicly stated that he intended to continue speaking German until his dying day, and wrote that the same principle should apply to all Jews: "Everyone retains his own language. I am a German-speaking Jew from Hungary and can never be anything but a German. At present I am not recognized as a German. But that will come once we are over there. And so let everyone keep his acquired nationality and speak the language which has become the beloved homeland of his thoughts. Switzerland offers visible proof that a federated state of different nationalities can exist."[6] Herzl, who's reference group was the German aristocracy, preferred the national model of Switzerland – a federation of cantons, each with its own language, with all the cultural implications that involved.

## The importance of changing the public's opinion in Herzl's Zionist project

Throughout his entire public career, Herzl was aware of the media's central role in leveraging his ideas and influencing public opinion about the Jewish question. In a letter that he wrote to his friend Max Nordau on December 13th, 1897, Herzl made an interim assessment of the success of the Zionist project: "The way the matter stands today, after winning public opinion for our 'crazy idea', something that we accomplished with our mere pens and words, we only need the *simulacre* [semblance] of this syndicate of guarantors to make the subscription a tremendous success, this letting Zionism grow into a real power."[7] Beyond being aware that the movement's success was a result of eloquent oral and written articulation, Herzl believed that the general public needed to be convinced there was a large financial power supporting the movement. In his opinion, it was important that the leaders of the western countries and even the clients themselves (the Jewish communities) believe these wealthy men backed Herzl, more than their actual support. The belief that there existed a financial force behind the movement is what would ultimately realize this power.

Turning to public opinion in order to realize the vision was particularly daring, one can say revolutionary. Herzl bridged the gap between two central groups that dealt with a solution to the Jewish problem. On the one hand, the utopists who described Judaism as a nation and fantasized about the connection with the Land of Israel (such as Moses Hess, Leon Pinsker, Judah Alcalay, and Zvi Hirsch Kalischer) but never thought to ask whether and how the Zionist idea will be realized. One the other hand, the Jewish philanthropists, the wealthy men engaged in real and immediate solutions through the resettlement of places far from Europe, but insisted that things will be done discreetly while keeping a low profile. Herzl's was singular in the combining of utopian ideology and practical solutions, the two poles that until then remained isolated from one another. In any case, his claim to solve the Jewish problem by means of "political Zionism" and not through a philanthropic company demanded publicity, transparency, and the convincing of Jewish public opinion to follow him, as well as the non-Jewish public opinion to support the idea. Herzl understood, therefore, that as a public relations person he must speak to four different target audiences and find the appropriate strategies for each of them. Among the non-Jews, Herzl directed his words to the liberals and anti-Semites, who were expected to support the idea of political Zionism, each group for its own motives. Among the Jews, Herzl turned both to those who left the ghetto a generation or more ago that have become educated and integrated into the surrounding society, and to those who remain in it. This attempt was particularly complex, since the Jews themselves were far from being a united community, and the need to enlist the two completely separate groups to the Zionist movement was a challenge no less than that of enlisting the non-Jewish public opinion to support the solution. In order to convert the Jews into Zionists – that is, to make them believe in the radical solution of a voluntary transfer – a change of consciousness was required. Herzl needed to bring everyone – those who eft the ghetto and those who remained in it – to see themselves as part of the Zionist nation.

In his attempt to enlist the ghetto Jews, Herzl thought in terms of appealing to the imagination, emotion, and a sense of belonging. In a letter that he sent a German statesman in 1902, he explained that "only the fantastic excites people." When he suggested setting up a permanent Congress Office in Basel, Herzl wrote "the public knows only headlines and slogans. It's stupid, but that is how it is." He then added, "With nations one must speak in a childish language: a house, a flag, a song are the symbols of communication."[8] In a distressed letter that he sent to the Baron Hirsch, Herzl described the necessary measures for the realizing of the Zionist vision, and emphasized the centrality of propaganda, the use of symbols, and appealing to emotions:

> "Money, money, and more money; means of transportation; the provisioning of great multitudes (which does not mean just food and drink, as in the simple days of Moses); the maintenance of manly discipline; the organization of departments; emigration treaties with the heads of some states, transit treaties with others, formal guarantees

from all of them; the construction of new, splendid dwelling places. Beforehand, tremendous propaganda, the popularization of the idea through newspapers, books, pamphlets, talks by travelling lecturers, pictures, songs. Everything directed from one center with the sureness of purpose and with vision. but I would have had to tell you eventually what flag I will unfurl and how. and then you would have asked mockingly: A flag, what is that? A stick with a rag on it? – No, sir, a flag is more than that. With a flag one can lead men wherever one wants to, even into the Promised Land. For a flag men will live and die; it is indeed the only thing for which they are ready to die in masses, if one trains them for it; believe me, the policy of an entire people – particularly when it is scattered all over the earth – can be carried out only with imponderables that float in thin air. Do you know what went into the making of the German Empire? Dreams, songs, fantasies, and black-red-and-gold ribbons – and in short order. Bismarck merely shook the tree which the visionaries had planted. What! You do not understand the imponderable? And what is religion? Consider, if you will, what the Jews have endures for the sake of this vision over a period of two thousand years. Yes, vision alone grip the souls of men. And anyone who has no use for them may be an excellent, worthy, sober-minded person, even a philanthropist on a large scale; but he will not be a leader of men, and no trace of him will remain."[9]

Herzl's words about the influential capabilities of symbolic institutions, monumental buildings, a flag and anthem ("song") – may indeed be reminiscent of fascist and communist regimes. However, presumably the importance he attached to unifying symbols and mass ceremonies derived from the attempt to create national unity between communities that did not see eye to eye on substantive issues to the new national culture. As mentioned, Herzl even aspired to preserve the unique language of each community. Either way, Herzl envisioned another purpose for these symbols – he did not intend for them to be used as tools in the hands of cynical leaders who want to enslave through the minds and bodies of their citizens, or that they play a manipulative and dangerous role leading to the destruction of society and state. Herzl viewed the general public very differently, in his mind appealing to the emotion and fantasy of the masses was intended to persuade them to voluntarily join the movement and society that were based on cooperation, liberal spirit, cosmopolitanism, and multiculturalism. The "firm foundation" of these popular fantasies were based on the "educated proletariat": engineers, architects, technologists, chemists, lawyers, doctors that like him left the ghetto over the past generation.

Another example of Herzl's distrust of the people's ability for rational thinking can be seen in his expressed reservations regarding the uncontrolled exposure characteristic of democracy. "The publicity brings about the loss of that respect which is necessary for government. All the world finds out that the men who govern us are merely human beings too – and in so many cases laughable, narrow persons."[10] Literary expression of this sentiment can be found in the pages of his novel, *Altneuland,* there lies insight into the *phonograph's* proper use, of which the manner of operation is intended for maintaining leadership through controlled exposure and spurring admiration towards the leader. Several people can receive the message simultaneously through this device – and yet, the speaker's authority is maintained due to his distance from the audience. Further along in the novel, Herzl tells the story of a Seder in the utopian society built in Palestine. During the evening, the participants wish to become acquainted with Joseph Levy, the Director General of the Ministry of Industry in the Jewish state, shown as a doer in the nascent Zionist movement. "I thought," said the host, "that you would be interested in meeting this all-round man. You shall hear him speak after dinner, since I cannot otherwise show him to you except in a photograph."[11] This is not a telephone, he stresses, but an invention that will allow "not only yourselves, but posterity, will listen to this speech." And here he presents the new phonograph machine. Indeed, Herzl as the author adds, the phonograph has been around for two decades, but the new device is more sophisticated than the existing: the lecture can be paused, discussed, and then continued to be listened to.

Herzl describes the participants sitting closely around phonograph that is placed on a small table. The phonograph is activated and Joe Levy's "strong masculine voice" emanates from it, detailing to the astonished listeners a rich depiction of the economic and commercial activity designed to provide a strong footing for the Zionist enterprise. Joe Levy was created in the form of a man that admires these technologies, which are meant to cater towards effective management, requesting his subordinates to receive updates at any time by telegraph, since reporting by letter seemed too slow to him. Herzl therefore portrays a dynamic, busy, and preoccupied leader, who moves around from place to place and from country to country, and utilizes the phonograph to remotely control his audience's agenda.

The authoritative voice is used as a means for control. The absence of an image, however, prevents supervision concurrently in the opposite direction, the public's supervision of the speaker. Indeed, over-exposure to the media has become a major issue in the 21st century, where the television camera creates visibility and removes the leader's protective walls. This situation is different than the era in which a leader had at his disposal a system of means for representation, which enabled him to control his public appearance and meticulously upheld his "face," the desired public image that he wished to adopt. Many researchers, such as John Thompson in his book, *The Media and Modernity*,[12] discuss the effects of the "era of visibility" on the status of political leaders. On the one hand, politicians have the opportunities of creating quasi-intimacy by talking directly to viewers at home. On the other hand, however, the cameras reveal their weaknesses, defects, moments of embarrassment and loss of control, which are documented in the media and can be devastating for them. Nonetheless, it is needless to mention the benefits of overexposure for leaders in democracies, as it allows voters to get to know a little more closely those nominated to lead them. Yet Herzl, concerned about these vulnerabilities, does not envision a technology that will allow the masses to see the leader in his true form. He settled in portraying the leader's character through painting, sculpture, engraving, and print, in a manner that serves his image and does not threaten the interests of the leader who is supposed to be exalted.

We wonder why Joe Levy was not presented as someone who speaks on the phone with his audiences. Presumably, there are two reasons: The first, the phonograph, which transmits a one-way communication, serves Herzl's perception that the message should go through in its entirety from the leader's heightened position. While with a telephone conversation, which is bidirectional, the message is jointly built during the interaction between the conversationalists. Secondly, the voice recorded on the phonograph instrument is perpetuated, while the things being said in a telephone conversation (as it was known at the time of writing *Altneuland*) fade.

The description of the use of the phonograph bears testimony to the tremendous importance Herzl attributed to documentation. This concept is reflected in the meticulous manner in which he documented all of his actions and thoughts. The story of Herzl's meeting with Emperor Wilhelm should be mentioned in this context. At an event that took place during his singular journey to Israel in 1898, Herzl met with German Emperor Wilhelm II at Mikveh Israel. The star of the event, as it turned out later, was the camera that recorded it. Herzl held great hope in his ability to recruit the Emperor in favor of the Zionist enterprise. Previous talks gave him the impression that the Emperor will meet with him and treat him with respect, but Herzl was very disappointed with the Emperor's position on the matter. However, there was a moment in that meeting where the opportunity arose to correct the public opinion's impression. Max Bodenheimer, Herzl's friend, took out his camera and documented the Emperor conversing with Herzl. None of the people present understood at that moment the great importance of that photograph. We do not know what was said at that chance meeting – the words faded and were not documented, but the photograph indicates that the leader of world Jewry at that time gained the sympathetic ear of the German Kaiser, one of the influential leaders in those days.

## Founding the Zionist movement as leaps between media campaigns

Herzl's first attempt to raise the question of the Jews on the public's agenda was the idea of an "initiative" he conceived and dreamed produce. It was in 1891, four years before he resolved that Zionism is the only solution to the Jewish problem following the Dreyfus trial. Herzl envisioned a festive parade of the Jewish children of Vienna that would conclude with an impressive public Christian conversion ceremony, to be conducted by the Pope, and held at St. Stephen's Cathedral. Herzl, in his naivety, was certain that the head of the Christian Church would be happy to lend a hand to his plan:

> The conversion was to take place in broad daylight, Sundays at noon, in Saint Stephen's Cathedral, with festive processions and amidst the pealing of bells. Not in shame, as individuals have converted up to now, but with proud gestures. And because the Jewish leaders

would remain Jews, escorting the people only to the threshold of the church and themselves staying outside, the whole performance was to be elevated by a touch of great candor.[13]

The plan description included such details as the march route of Herzl and his colleagues on the main street of Vienna and the curious masses standing on the sides. The participants would be baptized at the ceremony for all to see. Herzl saw himself as the producer of the initiative, and the rest of the participants as actors-extras – both the participants marching to the church and the audience watching from the sidewalk – who were supposed to function according to their place in the script. He imagined along the route dozens of reporters from local and foreign media, who came to cover the unusual media event. This media coverage was supposed to be the engine that would kick-start a public and extensive process of religious conversion. The general consensus among the participants, spectators on the sidewalks, and those exposed to it after the fact via the newspapers, would neutralize the sense of shame and guilt that characterized those who already converted earlier, in secret.

From Herzl's point of view, therefore, this was a symbolic, ritual extravaganza genre, which carries the meaning of a religious, social, and cultural transformation: the participants/actors in the show were the authentic representatives of the Jews. This is a historical moment for the Jewish people, a sort of seminal event on the main road towards the honorable end of the thousands-year-old religion of Judaism. In Austin's terms, the ceremony is a performative act, in which the words spoken in a specific context and by the right people serve as an action and generate change.[14] In this case, it is the power of the baptism act and ritual words spoken by a supreme religious authority that enable an ancient people abandon their identity, which was a burden to them, and provide them with a new identity.

Herzl's immediate target audience in this ceremony are assimilated Jews but also Christians from birth to witness the seriousness of the Jews' intentions. Herzl assigned himself roles throughout the whole process. Before the ceremony, he will negotiate with the church leaders and persuade them to support the process. During the ceremony, he will be the standing producer behind the scenes of the show. He is also the leader accompanying the procession, but does not convert to Christianity in order to show that he is not supposed to benefit from this constitutive act of Jewish conversion. Like Moses on Mount Nevo, Herzl will observe the new world from his perch on its boarder, not entering it. Although the television did not exist yet in those days, we ca refer to the similarity of the public production as imagined by Herzl and the motifs that precede their time – as a "media event" decades before the emergence of the "media events" genre of the radio, and later of television. Elihu Katz and Daniel Dayan defined this genre for the first time as a direct transmission of historical moments, pre-planned with the cooperation of the leadership, the public, and the media.[15] We can identify similarities between the baptism event Herzl conceived and an initiative conducted in a similar spirit decades later: the dramatic visit of Egyptian President, Anwar Sadat, which revolutionized Israeli public opinion. These two transformative and radical events establish new relationships between two groups that are in a state of hostility. Until that visit, Egypt was perceived among the Israeli public as belligerent and dangerous, and following the visit it was accepted as a possible peace process partner.

In the imaginary event before us, the leaders are Herzl on the one hand, and the heads of the Catholic church on the other. Print media, the mass media of the time, according to Herzl's vision, should rally around the event and report extensively on it in order to bring in an audience to watch it. The viewers on the sidewalks, along with the newspaper readers, should feel the historical significance, which would give a constitutive revolutionary meaning to the event. This is not a live and direct media coverage, as is customary these days, and there is no television picture to present the event from various angles; however, even without them, the event Herzl planned meets the criteria of a public, planned, ceremonial performance that receives massive publicity in advance and brings a crowd out into the streets to watch it. This is, therefore, a sort of model that illustrates in miniature the new relationships created between the two groups that were in a state of hostilities until now. This is one of the most radical reality-changing event, after which the participants and those exposed to it will be ready to revolutionize their lives.

The event is described in poetic terms in Herzl's personal diary, but this grandiose idea was destined to be archived before it was even publicized and developed. David Vital, one of his biographers, studied Herzl's merits and shortcomings as a propagandist striving to realize the objectives of a plan that was never carried out:

> The impudence of this simplistic plan, the belief in the power of this rational, transparent idea to influence the minds of people, the tendency for theatrical, luxurious gestures, the attention to the smallest details of direction, and on the other hand, the amazing ignorance and numbness towards the subjects of his plan, the Jews themselves, whose relationship with the Catholic church – its nature of enduring suffering and humiliation – does not need to be expanded on.[16]

Thus, despite the original idea and meticulous planning, the first phase of Herzl's political thought is characterized by his ignorance of the field, the radical unfamiliarity and communication disconnect between him and most of the potential audience – the traditional Jewish communities. It seems that Herzl initially thought about the solution in terms of his own disillusionment and the other assimilated-educated people like him who were disappointed by the promise of emancipation and the realization that this process will not only not solve the Jewish problem, but in fact has become the source of new anti-Semitism. Instead of allowing Jews to be part of society by creating the opportunity for them to integrate into the general society, the emancipation created a "new ghetto" with a glass ceiling for the educated Jews who left the ghetto.

Herzl was aware of – and at times even partner to – the negative stereotype attributed Jewish businessmen as swindlers, yet he searched for a way to create an immediate and drastic impact to urge Christian leaders to curb anti-Semitism. As someone who exclusively listened to the (critical) voices of his cosmopolitan surroundings, Herzl viewed the anti-Semitism problem only as an image problem, and the solution he fancied was creating a switch in the non-Jewish public opinion concerning the image of Jews. While his goal to improve the image of the Jews in the eyes of society, Herzl treated the Jews themselves as objects, pawns in a game, or as his "subordinates" that were expected do their job when called upon.

In practice, however, the entire Jewish community was infinitely diverse and completely different from the assimilated Jewish community of Vienna that Herzl was familiar with. Vienna was home to the descendants of Jewish immigrants who abandoned the ghettos of Eastern Europe and were exposed to secular education and Western culture, but left behind were hundreds of thousands of Jews who still lived in ghettos in Poland and Russia. Their religious faith remained strong, they felt no need to change it, and some were even angry at those who abandoned their Jewish environment and tradition and changed their way of life. Moreover, Herzl never knew the Jewish communities in Islamic countries. This disconnect is evident down the road, after Herzl outlined the vision of the Jewish state, not realizing that the only territorial solution acceptable to the Jewish Diaspora incorporated the Land of Israel. As Herzl and his friend Max Nordau admitted, the driving force of their actions wasn't the return to the Land of Israel, but rather "anti-Semitism, and nothing else, made us Jews." And indeed, in 1904, Herzl attacked the Zionist idea and argued that "if the Jews truly returned to their home they would discover the very next day that there is no longer any interaction between them, for centuries they were rooted in the new homelands and are different from one another."

For Herzl, becoming attached to the Jews in a pre-emancipation status, such as the communities in Austrian Galicia, let alone the poverty and primitiveness of Eastern Jews, the *Ostjuden*, that "were almost impossible to speak to" and "whose exterior was sickening" – was not an option. His return to Judaism was on the condition that "there will be a compromise on their part, too, on the basis of a radical change," both social and political, of the Jewish reality.[17] Only at a later stage, when he discovers that obliterating Judaism in order to save the Jews is not acceptable for most Jews, he changes his attitude and begins to listen to his people. It is quite ironic that the leader of the Zionist movement did not know the objects of his plan, and indeed later on Herzl equated himself with Moses who grew up as an Egyptian in Pharaoh's palace.

Not only was the idea of the public conversion of Vienna's Jews to Christianity at St. Stephen's Cathedral never put into action, but it was never publicized. It was only mentioned in Herzl's diaries that were published after his death (as aforementioned, his father wrote the diaries based on Herzl's scribbled notes). Only after the diaries were published in print in 1927 – over two decades after his death – the public was informed about this earlier thinking of Herzl's. Later, in 1944, Stefan Zweig highlighted these lines from Herzl's diaries in his autobiography, "The World of Yesterday" (German: *Die Welt von Gestern*). As described below, Herzl turned to entirely different solutions that preserved the Jewish identity. Nevertheless, we can already view this project as part of the communication principles on which the next stages of his later and more developed plan are based on: belief in the potential of public-status showcase events that would give dignity and class status to the Jews who take part in it, and spark the imagination of the community members and outsiders viewing it. Indeed, like the unripe public conversion idea, so were the steps towards the territorial solution –culminating in the Zionist Congress initiative – to be performed in public and through publicized maneuvers, not in secret.

Since Herzl's initial goal was to solve the Jewish problem, namely, to fight anti-Semitism (rather than preserving Jewish religion and culture), from his perspective he urgently needed to create an immediate impact and drastically hurry up the Christian leaders in curbing the anti-Semites. One of the turning points in the transition from the idea of eliminating Judaism (in order to put an end to anti-Semitism) to the idea of establishing a Jewish state was Herzl's conversation with Moriz Benedikt, one of his two newspaper publishers. Herzl turned to him in order to get the newspaper's support for the new initiative he was planning: appealing to the Pope. The "deal" he tests out on Benedikt reveals Herzl's knowledge of the behind the scenes world of negotiation between the press and powerful players.

Herzl thought that as the *Neue Freie Presse*'s representative he could offer the Pope, behind closed doors, a diplomatic peace agreement (between liberals and anti-Semites), for the services of the leading liberal newspaper. This type of deal between a newspaper and a government would have perhaps motivated the Pope to do something, to publish a clarification or imply a positive hint on this issue. To Herzl's great disappointment, Benedikt rejected the idea of approaching the Pope, and slammed the brakes on the bold public relations idea. However, Herzl notes that Benedikt contributed to his advancing another step in thinking about the Jewish problem. Benedikt explained to Herzl that it is not in his power, and that he must not, block Judaism: "For a hundred generations your line has preserved itself within the fold of Judaism. Now you are proposing to set yourself up as the terminal point in this process. This you cannot do and have no right to do." This speech, Herzl writes, "struck me as being true."[18] Herzl's failure taught him, among other things, the importance of recognizing the "distribution of innovations" mechanism and the importance that a new product's success relies on the compatibility between the new idea and the community's existing values.[19]

It should be noted that even after reaching the conclusion that the solution is a voluntary transfer, as we shall see later, Herzl continued to attribute great importance to improving the image of Jews in the eyes of the European public. This objective was more important than even the wealthy Jews' support of the Zionist movement. This is apparent from Herzl's decision to publish the manifesto, *The Jewish State* (written ahead of his meeting with Rothschild), despite his fear that its publication will cause an unrepairable disconnect with the philanthropists he had worked so hard to recruit to participate in the Zionist project. As he deliberates the publication of the plan in his diary, Herzl writes:

> Yet the publication will be of indirect benefit to the Jews.— Many of my thoughts, such as those about dueling, suicide, support of inventors, a stock exchange monopoly, traveling complaint commissions, are good for all nations. Therefore people may treat the Jews more gently because these suggestions were born of their sufferings and their spirit.[20]

## *The New Ghetto*

Following his deliberations, not only did Herzl change his perception of the nature of the solution to the Jewish problem, but he also changed the persuasion strategies that will lead him to this goal. Thus, he repeatedly utilized his writing talent and increasingly exploited the distribution and preservation capabilities of the printing technology. In 1894 Herzl wrote a play titled *The New Ghetto* (*Das Neue Ghetto*) intended for the population of assimilated Jews, his contemporaries. He wanted the play to reflect the structural difficulty of his people to integrate into Vienna's cosmopolitan society. This is the last text he wrote to promote the Jews' integration in Western society, and the adoption of its values. Herzl realized only later that the Jews of the ghetto, in the limited living conditions imposed on them, were not capable to adopt these lifestyles.

The idea for the play came to Herzl after a conversation with the sculptor Samuel Frederick Beer in Paris, while he was sculpting his bust. Following this conversation, Herzl concluded that "it does a Jew no good to become an artist and free himself from the taint of money. The curse still clings. We cannot get out of the Ghetto." The issue "still glowed in[him]," and after crossing a few streets the outline for the play *The New Ghetto* was "already finished in [his] mind," and was published in print under a pseudo name.[21]

The play's protagonist is Jacob Samuel, an assimilated Jew, a lawyer, and an idealist, who refuses to recognize the social restrictions imposed on him by his religion. He is not afraid to openly spend time with his wife's Jewish friends, although his fellow Christian friends are afraid of losing their social status because of this and shun him. At the center of the story is the hero's effort in helping the workers in a coal mine struggle to secure their rights. This action ignites a conflict between him and the owner of the mine, an anti-Semitic count, and eventually they duel each other and our hero meets his end. In the last moments of his life, Samuel gains insight into something he tried suppressing his whole life: Jews like himself were not given real emancipation, and even if they would live outside of the ghetto, they would have no choice but to live in a kind of ghetto.

The views presented in the play were revolutionary, but its dramatics quality was controversial. Due to its contents, it was treated as a hot potato that no one wants to hold it in their hand. Europe's top theater directors at the end of the 19th century were afraid to deal with sensitive, controversial social genres. In that sense, they are similar to today's television producers, who prefer equal entertainment for all that does not stimulate thinking and does not upset the target audience. The emancipation of European Jews was considered too sensitive to bring to the stage, and when a Prague theater finally agreed to put on the play, a new difficulty arose. The city's Jewish community leaders did not want to spark a public debate on the issue raised in the play, they feared it would negatively affect the relations between Jews and Christians. They realized, apparently, that the theater and the press covering its plays have the power to bring issues to the public's agenda.

Thus, the play The New Ghetto did not make it onto the stages in 1894, but thanks to its perpetuation in print (as opposed to Herzl's thoughts about the conversion to Christianity plan) it could be pulled out of the drawer and look at again four years later, in 1898, and again until today. During this period (after the First Zionist Congress in Basel), Herzl was confident in himself and in his persuasion abilities, and therefore decided to stop hiding behind a pseudonym and to openly stand behind the play he wrote. Indeed, this time, the play showed in theaters in Vienna and other cities, followed by a public debate regarding the solution of the Jewish question.

## The campaign to recruit the wealthy Jewry

Following the Dreyfus trial (1895), Herzl came to the unequivocal conclusion that the emancipation has failed, and therefore – the only solution to the Jewish problem is a voluntary transfer. While often subjected to mood swings of despair and hope, and having a clear sense that his and Jewish diaspora's time is running out, Herzl simultaneously and alternately ran a variety of advocacy campaigns using an abundance of media. Through trial and error, Herzl tried out different political and communication strategies for different audiences in order to see which of them has a chance to succeed. Herzl explained the rationale for each and every one of them in his diaries, from which we learn the tactics of persuasion he has taken in order to achieve his objectives, the choice of media and genre for distribution as an indication of the type of solution he offered and how he viewed his role in this fabric of media.

First, in order to achieve this goal, Herzl believed that there was no point in appealing to the general public, but rather that he must convince people of wealth, who can finance the emigration of Jews. Although he believed in the importance of public action, Herzl actually preferred to act secretly during the early stages. Indeed, Herzl initially turned to the wealthy and powerful in order to create a lobby to support the resettlement of Jews away from Europe. The first place that had been discussed was a territory in Argentina. Herzl tried to convince the barons Hirsch and Rothschild, who were already involved in helping Jewish settlers, that international recognition of the Jews as a nation would give them back their dignity – even in a territory that is a temporary shelter. Herzl soon found himself faced with a difficult dilemma: on the one hand, the wealthy persons he contacted demanded secrecy, and on the other hand, he himself felt how important and necessary the publicity was. This feeling intensified when he realized that the negotiations with the wealthy was not producing results.

## The Jewish state

When Herzl finally realized that he could not proceed with the assistance of philanthropists, it occurred to him that he must leverage the power of the Jewish community through public actions. Had intended to speak about the situation of the Jews to the Baron Rothschild, but following his new insight he put down his words in writing to reach wider target audiences. These words were written in his book, *The Jewish State*, which has the attributes of a manifesto and presents Herzl's political vision. It is a dull document that deals with legal aspects and operational guidelines for the establishment of a Jewish national state, and it builds the proposed state's society, economy, culture, and courts. For several weeks in 1896, Herzl poured over reworking the document in the attempt to approach the widest audience possible. He hoped that the book will appeal to reason rather than to emotion, and in order to give it sanction, he reiterated and underscored his academic degree as a Doctor of Law. At first, he couldn't find a publisher who was willing to publish the booklet, but in the end, he found someone who agreed to do it despite his doubts about the commercial success. The short, resonating, marketable name *The Jewish State* was born on a whim, at the moment the contract is signed.[22]

At the end of the process, the booklet was published by 79 independent publications and in 18 languages.[23] It was the first time that Herzl's political ideas appeared in the public sphere. Its rapid distribution made the short booklet topic of conversation across Europe. Some of the readers were outraged about the book's contents and Herzl's newspaper employers believed that the document's apparent enormous distribution would only increase anti-Semitism. According to them, the booklet's main claim that it is impossible to assimilate the Jews as equal citizens in the European national communities provides ammunition for anti-Semites who consider Jews to be outsiders. One of the newspaper publishers went so far as to try and bribe Herzl to destroy all of the copies.

But print has a power of its own and it wasn't within those gatekeepers' power to block the accessibility of the text. Indeed, Herzl's plan to reach as many people as possible worked out well. Although some newspapers in Austria, including his own newspaper, intentionally ignored the book, three thousand copies of *The Jewish State* were distributed across Europe. Many heard of the booklet's contents by word of mouth or through its media coverage. Its audience was therefore much broader and diverse than those who read it from start to finish. As Ernst Pawel writes, by the end of that year Herzl was already a familiar figure across Europe – from the "Pale of Settlement" in Russia to slums of England.[24]

## Altneuland

Herzl was not content with the policy document he prepared and circulated. He understood that an essay of a technical nature such as *The Jewish State*, which is a sort of "User's Guide," is not enough in order to recruit the Jewish Diaspora to his vision. Already at the beginning of his advocacy campaign of distributing the Zionist idea Herzl pondered on what he should invest his time and effort: Would it be better to write a scholarly essay or a fiction novel? Indeed, it is interesting to see that the outlines for the utopian novel *Altneuland* were written prior to the essay *The Jewish State*, but the novel was published only a few years after it. It seems that whenever Herzl gave up on the political venture's chance of success in the short term, he returned to the drafts of his novel *Altneuland*, which was supposed to excite the readers and persuade them to support his ideas. And just like his *The New Ghetto* play initiative, Herzl got the idea to write a novel following a conversation with a friend, this time with the French author Alphonse Daudet. In that conversation, Herzl recounts that he intends to write a book "for and about the Jews"; "[Daudet] asked: A novel? – no, I said, preferably a man's book! – Whereupon he said: [The message of] A novel reaches farther. Think of *Uncle Tom's Cabin*."[25] Indeed, Herzl was convinced that a novel could have an emotional impact, as had happened with the American bestseller that softened the hearts of those tens of millions of readers that delved into reading about the black slave family's series of adventures.

*Altneuland* was published in 1902. A few weeks before the book appeared in print, Herzl wrote a letter to the Lord Rothschild where he documented their dispute about the nature of the desired solution of the Jewish question. Rothschild believed that settlements in which only Jews lived will eventually become ghettos and therefore will treat its inhabitants with disrespect.[26] Herzl, however, had other ideas. In his opinion, *Altneuland* was not merely a story, but a systematic doctrine for taking action disguised as a work of fiction. At a basic level, it was a melodramatic story. The hero, Dr. Friedrich Lowenberg, woos Ernestine Loeffier, who does not accede to his courting. In order to disconnect from her, he joins a hedonist Prussian nobleman who married a girl whose looks resemble those of Ernestine. Out of this passion-fraught affair, which could have been a great source of material for a current day soap opera, Herzl's national utopia was conceived. The two friends sail around the world, and for some unclear reason they dock on the shores of the Land of Israel. They discover blooming views, thriving cities, non-polluting industries, and above all – a collective community, whose members, all of them Jews, solve their problems through the spirit of volunteering and reciprocity. Zionism brought the Jews of the world home and allowed them to create a perfect society in which they realize their wonderful talents.

The Jews changed beyond recognition and became similar to the Gentiles, except for a few people, including Ernestine, who rejected the hero earlier and from an object of desire turned into an aging matron. According to Pawel, this work coherently illustrates Herzl's political worldview.[27] Pawel claims that the novel, *Altneuland*, is an anarchist utopia where equality and comradeship between men supersede the state's suppression mechanisms. In other words, although born into the romance novel genre (also known to us today as a "Soap Opera"), *Altneuland* proved itself as having a greater historical significance than the genre for which it was written. Herzl enlisted a melodramatic, accessible, and enticing story in order to widely spread an ideological message he considered to be of great importance to his readers.

*Altneuland*, which unlike its dull predecessor is quite titillating, inspired many people, including the founders of Tel Aviv. Akiva Aryeh Weiss, one of the founders, describes his book, *New Society* (Hebrew: *Hevrah Hadasha*), the impact of Herzl's novel on him: "The words '*Alt-Neu-Land*' strongly impacted me, both openly and secretly. They seemed to demand of me actions on any foothold. It seemed to me as if I received an order from above: 'Speak little, and do much'. To revive the spirit of Herzl after his death, devote myself to continuing his work, to aim towards the goals he set and to build in this spirit, in the Land of Israel, the '*Alt-Neu-Land*' in Tel Aviv."[28]

Another area in which Herzl tried to act is the journalism field. At first, he tried to solicit the two Jewish editors of the newspaper he worked at, *Neue Freie Presse*, to adopt the Zionist project. When they refused, for obvious reasons, Herzl established his own newspaper, *Die Welt* (in the Spring of 1897), in preparation for the First Zionist Congress, designed to be a representative institution and meeting place for representatives of the different communities. The idea of territory in itself, wrote Herzl, would lead to national identity even before it is reached, if at all.

## The Zionist Congress

As Herzl continued developing his ideas, it became clearer to him that he needed to reach a wider Jewish audience and present them with his vision of a Jewish state. Over time, it seemed that Herzl's public and interpersonal influence was immense. One of the two *Neue Freie Presse* editors was excited by the American press' fascination with Herzl's character, and called him "the Pied Piper, who captivated the whole world."[29]

Just then, when his popularity soared, Herzl began to realize that he set himself too big of a challenge for one person to handle. He realized that he would have to join ranks with other people to serve him as partners from the starting point. It was a difficult compromise on his part, since Herzl was an individualist by nature and relied primarily on himself. This change in his mindset is apparent in the large-scale Congress initiative, which was to bring together for the first time representatives of communities from eastern and central Europe to discuss the Zionist agenda. Herzl's first references to this venture appeared in his diaries in January 1897, just seven months before the mission was completed. Herzl dedicated five feverish months to organizing the Congress and integrated his capabilities as a theater person and orator towards his efforts. He had to know every detail and do almost everything alone, even sending out the invitation letters. Pawel wrote: "With the same loving attention to detail that he had once used to describe the mass conversion ceremony of the Jews to Christianity, he set himself to direct the first meeting of the first Jewish parliamentary body in modern history."[30]

According to Herzl's plan, the Congress convention was supposed to be "a spectacular demonstration of national solidarity that would ignite the imagination of Jews throughout the world and legitimize their political representatives."[31] Within a week all of the invitations were sent out from Herzl's home office, which Pawel called "the advertising blitzkrieg command center."[32] While still in the planning stage, Herzl began envisioning how the event will look and what the participants will wear: he planned that they will come to the opening session in full evening dress. After the Congress, Herzl wrote in his diary: "This worked out splendidly. Formal dress makes most people stiff. This stiffness immediately gave rise to a sedate tone – one they might not have had in light-colored summer suits or travel clothes – and I did not fail to heighten this tone to the point of solemnity."[33]

Herzl was not content with only these public actions, and delved into the thick of things in the political sphere. He had to struggle with the different factions of the Zionist movement, but found out that the larger dispute between the various factions the greater the publicity of the Congress, which raised it to the level of a seminal, impactful, and dramatic event. Indeed, as Pawel wrote: "As the campaign against the Congress went into high gear from within and out, so was the issue publicized beyond anything Herzl could have hoped for."[34] Just like more people heard about the booklet *The Jewish State* than those who read it, the discussion around the Congress employed more people than those who took part in it. This falls in line with canonical media researchers Paul Lazarsfeld and Robert Merton's claim in their important paper, which was published fifty years later, about the effect of "status conferral."[35] According to them, the publicity of a message grants it status and importance, whether agreed upon or not. This approach is also consistent with Elizabeth Eisenstein's argument about the role of the print technology in the Protestant revolution.[36] Eisenstein describes Martin Luther's astonishment when he saw his intellectual theses reaching the thresholds of different communities that he never thought of in the first place. Indeed, in the end, the Jewish Congress participants arrives from over 16 countries across Europe, but also from Algeria and the United States.[37]

Herzl's impressive capabilities as a propagandist and a member of the press were also reflected in his design of the space where the conference was held. Herzl came to Basel a few days before the opening of the Congress, and in this short period he had revolutionized the design. He abandoned the pitiable beer cellar originally allotted for the Congress, and instead he chose an elegant and impressive hall to conduct the conference in and hung up on the building a festive, large-scale blue and white flag, in accordance with his vision of the future Jewish state flag.

As abovementioned, Herzl also gave his opinion in regards to the dress code. He sported coattails and a white tie, but his partner, Max Nordau, appeared in a simple outfit and refused to change it. Herzl himself testified that he considered the attire as one of the status symbols through which he could provide prestige to the occasion and the movement: "I drew [Nordau] aside and begged him to do it as a favor to me. I told him: today the presidium of the Zionist Congress is nothing at all, we still have to establish everything. People should get used to seeing the Congress as a most exalted and solemn thing. He allowed himself to be persuaded, and in return I hugged him gratefully. A quarter of an hour later he returned in formal dress."[38] Herzl's talents as a theater person were also enlisted for the task of producing the event: "Finally a huge hit for the frustrated playwright of unimportant farces. He staged a spectacle that not only excited people, but also included them in the game, and in doing so hit the mark in a manner instinctive to alchemy of mass manipulation, and managed to convert fantasy into power."[39] Thus, it can be said that from Herzl's perspective a variety of measures were implemented in order to achieve the goal, including the theatrical features of the event, the impressive building with the big flag specially hung as decoration, and the organizers' fancy attire. "This work of art successfully turned a random group of intellectual, idealistic, and opportunistic Jews into a representative body imbued with a sense of their historic role."[40]

In a sense, the First Zionist Congress was an act of creation of a mass movement through organizing a public, respectable event that gained massive media coverage. The Congress, Avineri writes, is the establishment of a mass movement, which proves Herzl's loyalty to democratic institutionalization, after his preferred solution of recruiting wealthy Jews had failed. This is despite the fact that Herzl was far from the populist enthusiasm, in France and Vienna, which he viewed as a danger to the values of freedom and democracy.

Indeed, when comparing the founding of the Congress to the baptism idea, we come full circle in that the Congress actually brings to fruition many of Herzl's initial thoughts. Initially, Herzl utilized theatrical thinking and planned a seminal, public event that will lead to a mass conversion to Christianity of the Jews of Europe, and in doing so will solve (in his opinion in those days) the problem of anti-Semitism. Less than a decade later, his political thinking was completely different, but his perception of change-generating ceremonies remained the same as it was. This time, unlike the previous attempt, he brought his thoughts from imagination to realization. Herzl already new how to distribute and preserve them using the media at his disposal. In the planning of the two events, creating a respectable image for the participating Jews is perceived as an essential element, however, there is one crucial difference: Herzl, who ignored the masses of Jews in the beginning, now provides them with sovereignty.

In an early formulation of Benedict Anderson's[41] concept of the "imagined community," Herzl wrote in his diary: "Territory is only the material basis; the State, even when it possesses territory, is always something abstract." And future generations are left with his greatest, echoing remark, "At Basel I founded the Jewish State":

> Were I to sum up the Basel Congress in a word - which I shall guard against pronouncing publicly - it would be this: At Basel I founded the Jewish State. If I said this out loud today, I would be answered by universal laughter. Perhaps in five years, and certainly in fifty, everyone will know it.[42]

This slogan is imbedded in the Jewish collective memory as a basis for the creation of a nation in the Land of Israel. This statement, which today sounds to us common and perhaps banal, was innovative and surprising at the time, and Herzl's communication skills helped him engrave it into the Jewish consciousness in an unforgettable manner.

## Epilogue: Herzl as the scribe, Herzl as the Messiah

Herzl's personal diaries, which he began to write when he was captivated by the "Jewish issue," is his initiation novel (*Bildungsroman*), throughout which he evolved from a journalist into a political leader.[43] Herzl himself attached great importance to the diaries documenting the considerations that led to his changing actions. He considered the diaries his spiritual heritage, and in his will he asked that they be published soon after his death in order to preserve the historical record of the movement and his own role in its development. Herzl's letters are also an important source for understanding the strategies he chose in the various stages of his work. For instance, in an "agitated" letter to a Prague director, Herzl intimately revealed the emotional upheaval he experienced in order to convince the director to immediately bring to the stage his play, *The New Ghetto*. In his diary, Herzl explains to us how he believes the persuasion strategy in this letter should work, and that the tactical need of the intimate exposure to the Prague director stems from the need to motivate him.

The diaries expose the turmoil created by the author's mental strength. Herzl's diaries reveal that he constantly jumped between two options for the realization of Zionism: the long-term utopian vision that will penetrate the hearts of his readers and become a driving force for the political movement after a generation or two; and the immediate establishment of a political movement, which will realize the vision in the short-term. The diary pages reveal the vital role of the various media, and how Herzl saw himself as a super-producer in charge of all of the stages.

In terms of solving the Jewish problem concept, the diaries divulge two successive stages, radically different from each other. The first stage is based on the idea that the problem can be solved without leaving Europe (but also without saving the Jewish people, only their safety). In this early stage, Herzl is toying with the radical idea of conversion, and then compromising on assimilation, which means 'appropriate behavior' that is free of the characteristics of the ghetto Jews. In the second stage, having recognized that the solution of assimilation is hopeless, Herzl does a complete turnaround that brings to a radical makeover of his political approach: if Jews are not allowed to integrate then they have no choice but to completely disconnect and create a new Jewish society, which will be run according to the principles of Enlightenment, at a location far from Europe.

At this stage, the exclusivity of the Zionist solution is being recognized. In terms of the nature of the solution Herzl offers – building a society according to the principles of modernity and liberalism – the difference between the two phases is purely technical in regard to the geographical space where the solution will be implemented. However, if Herzl was familiar with his audience he would know that the geographic change will massively expand his target audience, who would enthusiastically accept the solution, but for the wrong reasons (in his mind). Indeed, the immigration to the Land of Israel, and perhaps even his personality as a modern Messiah who will make this happen, are what motivated the masses, rather than the idea of building a modern society. Over time and as he became better acquainted with the Eastern Jews, Herzl learns how to communicate with the Jewish masses and adapts the Zionist project to the new target audience. Indeed, some of the projects Herzl depicted in detail in his journals, such as the baptism Vienna's

Jews or the description of a ceremony held aboard the first pioneers ship, "the Jewish Mayflower," upon its arrival on the shores of the Jewish State – were not put into action. But the most important project of all was produced with great success and became the defining moment of the Zionist movement until the present day: The World Zionist Congress.

By way of conclusion, we consolidated into a table the series of initiatives that Herzl conceived, carried, and sometimes only imagined, on the road to achieving the goal of establishing a Jewish state in the Land Israel. In this manner, Herzl's ability to analyze his audiences and adapt to each one the genre, medium, and unique initiative that will advance the realization of his vision is made clear. This table can teach us about the short-term actions aimed at achieving an immediate and powerful impact, as well as long-term actions whose effect, he believes, will take place after his death.

## Table 1. Herzl's initiatives according to characteristics

| INITIATIVE | GENRE/ MEDIUM | RANGE | TARGET AUDIENCE | THE MEANS FOR TRANSFORMING THE JEWISH PEOPLE | THE ACTORS | HERZL'S ROLE |
|---|---|---|---|---|---|---|
| A procession to the church | Ceremony/ media event: mass street show | Short | Assimilated Jews | Through an external event | The Jewish masses | Producer/ publicist community leader |
| The New Ghetto | Theater play | Short | Christian Jews | Through internal conviction | Professional actors | Playwright/ publicist |
| The Jewish State | Manifesto/ article (essay) | Short | Philanthropists/ educated Jewish public | Immigration to Israel following rational persuasion | Philanthropists and politicians | Journalist/ leader |
| Altneuland | Novel/ textbook | Long | Jews | Immigration to Israel through emotional persuasion | Fictional characters | Author/ leader |
| The First Zionist Congress | The "Congress" as a media event | Short | Jews and Christians | Through an external event | The representatives | Leader/ messiah |
| Herzl's diaries | Personal diary | Long (for next generation) | For himself in the present and for the Jews in their country in the future | The diary was published after the establishment of the state | Herzl | Reflection |

This table of initiatives would not be complete without drawing attention once more to Herzl the man. Beyond the adoption of communication strategies and various media channels, Herzl found that he was carrying an additional channel for all the audiences he came in contact with: his noble personality, which sparked feelings of admiration, awe, and an almost religious reverence in the people he met. The Turkish Sultan viewed Herzl as an "ancient Hebrew," as having "royal stature," and Franz Rosenzweig (and Martin Buber in turn) saw him as a "Messiah." Herzl himself was aware of this image through which he could create a direct, courageous, and deep connection with traditional Jews, and he took advantage of this in order to deepen his emotional bond with them.

Evidence of his awareness of the connection between his image as a leader and the idea of a Messiah can be found in his diary, where among other plans Herzl intended to write a book about Moses "from Pharaoh's court." He also does not out rightly reject the similarity between himself and Sabbatai Zvi: "I am not a Theologian and so I do not know," writes Herzl, and adds in another place: "The difference between myself and Sabbatai Zvi (the way I imagined him), apart from the difference in the technical means inherent in the times, is that Sabbatai made himself great so as to be the equal of the great of the earth, I, however, find the great small, as small as myself."[44] Anita Shapira also makes a connection between the messianic movements and the Zionist movement, which "reflected the mindset that served as the messianic movements' psychological infrastructure in various policies."[45] According to Shapira, one needs to only lightly scratch the layer of empiricism on the Zionist leader to discover a vibrating messianic belief that bursts out in times of crisis, or in moments of what Talmon refers to as "revolutionary breaching." [46]

Perhaps in the Eastern Jews' acceptance of Herzl, in those moments of crisis, the historical connection between the messianic longings and the political movement is revealed. And in the words of David Ben-Gurion:

> Perhaps Pinsker and Herzl often held the messianic vision in their hearts, but in the hearts of the masses in Israel – if I remember them as a child – time and time. When I was ten years old, I heard talk about a Messiah that appeared in Vienna and his name was Herzl.

# Notes

1   This chapter was redacted by the book's editors from the drafts left by the author. We dedicate this edited work to Tamar, an esteemed researcher and cherished teacher, who encouraged her students to inquire, be curious, and deepen their knowledge. Tamar's published works encompass many research areas in the media field, including the study of the interface between communication and the Bible and the role of the media in the Zionist project – topics which were close to her heart.

2   Shlomo Avineri, *Herzl* (Jerusalem: Zalman Shazar Center, 2007).

3   Sabbatai Zevi founded a messianic movement that was named after him (Sabbatean) in the 17th century, and caused a profound upheaval in the Jewish world.

4   Avineri, *Herzl,* 105-106.

5   See Benedict Anderson, *Imagined Communities: Reflections on the Origin and Spread of Nationalism* (London: Verso, 1991).

6   Theodor Herzl, *The Complete Diaries of Theodor Herzl, vols. I-V,* ed. Raphael Patai, trans. Harry Zohn (New York: Herzl Press and Thomas Yoseloff, 1960), 171.

7   Ibid., 607.

8   Ibid., 645.

9   Ibid., 27-28.

10  Ibid., 124.

11  Theodor Herzl, *Old New Land (AltNeuLand),* trans. D. S. Blondheim (Berlin: Hofenberg, 1902), 117-118.

12  John B. Thompson, *The Media and Modernity: A Social Theory of the Media* (Stanford, CA: Stanford University Press, 1995).

13  Herzl, *The Complete Diaries of Theodor Herzl,* 7.

14  John L. Austin, *How to Do Things with Words* (Oxford, UK: Oxford University Press, 1962).

15  Daniel Dayan and Elihu Katz, *Media Events: The Live Broadcasting of History* (Cambridge, MA: Harvard University Press, 1992).

16  David Vital, *The Zionist Revolution. Vol. I: The Beginnings of the Movement,* trans. B. Moran (Tel Aviv: Am Oved, 1978), 184.

17  Ibid., 181.

18  Herzl, *The Complete Diaries of Theodor Herzl,* 8.

19  Everett M. Rogers, *Diffusion of Innovations,* 1st ed. (New York: Free Press of Glencoe, 1962); Elihu Katz, "The Two-Step Flow of Communication: An Up-To-Date Report on an Hypothesis," *The Public Opinion Quarterly* 21, no. 1 (1957): 61-78.

20  Herzl, *The Complete Diaries of Theodor Herzl,* 80.

21  Ibid., 11.

22  Ernst Pawel, *The Labyrinth of Exile: A Life of Theodor Herzl,* trans. Bruria Ben-Baruch (Tel Aviv: Zmora, 1997), 195.

23  H. Avrahami and A. Bein, "The editions of the 'Jewish State' by Theodor Herzl," in *Zionism: Studies in the History of the Zionist Movement and of the Jews in Palestine,* ed. Daniel Carpi (Tel Aviv: Hakibbutz Hameuchad, 1970), 464-474.

24  Pawel, *The Labyrinth of Exile.*

25  Herzl, *The Complete Diaries of Theodor Herzl,* 12.

26  Pawel, *The Labyrinth of Exile,* 338

27  Ibid., 340.

28  Akiva Aryeh Weiss, *Hevrah Hadasha – Hashalom* (Tel Aviv: Dfus Herzliyah, 1938), 35; In the first translation into Hebrew of *Altneuland,* edited in 1902 by Nahum Sokolov, the novel was called in the biblical phrase "Tel Aviv." The founders of the first all-*Jewish* city chose to name it something that will directly connect it to Herzl's vision.

29  Avineri, *Herzl,* 135.

30  Pawel, *The Labyrinth of Exile,* 234.

31  Ibid.

32  Ibid., 235.

33  Herzl, *The Complete Diaries of Theodor Herzl,* 581.

34  Pawel, *The Labyrinth of Exile,* 236.

35  Paul F. Lazarsfeld and Robert K. Merton, "Mass Communication, Popular Taste, and Organized Social Action," in *The Communication of Ideas,* ed. L. Bryson (New York: Harper, 1948).

36  Elizabeth L. Eisenstein, *The Printing Press as an Agent of Change: Communications and Cultural Transformations in Early Modern Europe,* Vols. I-II (Cambridge, UK: Cambridge University Press, 1979).

37  According to Pawel (*The Labyrinth of Exile,* 243), between 199-256 people from twenty different countries attended the Congress.

38   Herzl, *The Complete Diaries of Theodor Herzl,* 581.

39  Pawel, *The Labyrinth of Exile,* 242.

40  Ibid.

41  Anderson, *Imagined Communities.*

42  Herzl, *The Complete Diaries of Theodor Herzl,* 581.

43  Avineri, *Herzl.*

44  Herzl, *The Complete Diaries of Theodor Herzl,* 960.

45  Anita Shapira, "The Religious Motifs of the Labor Movement," in *Zionism and Religion,* eds. S. Almog et al. (Hanover, NH: Brandeis University Press, 1998), 251-272.

46  Jacob Leib Talmon, The Riddle of the Present and the Cunning of History: Studies in *Jewish History from a Universal Perspective* (Jerusalem: Bialik Institute, 2000).

## Bibliography

Anderson, Benedict. *Imagined Communities: Reflections on the Origin and Spread of Nationalism.* London: Verso, 1991.

Austin, John L. *How to Do Things with Words.* Oxford, UK: Oxford University Press, 1962.

Avineri, Shlomo. *Herzl.* Jerusalem: Zalman Shazar Center, 2007.

Avrahami, Hila, and Alex Bein. "The editions of the 'Jewish State' by Theodor Herzl." In *Zionism: Studies in the History of the Zionist Movement and of the Jews in Palestine*, edited by Daniel Carpi, 464-474. Tel Aviv: Hakibbutz Hameuchad, 1970.

Eisenstein, Elizabeth L. *The Printing Press as an Agent of Change: Communications and Cultural Transformations in Early Modern Europe*. Volumes I-II. Cambridge, UK: Cambridge University Press, 1979.

Herzl, Theodor. *Old New Land (AltNeuLand)*, translated by D. S. Blondheim. Berlin: Hofenberg, 1902.

Herzl, Theodore. *The Complete Diaries of Theodor Herzl*. Volumes I-V, edited by Raphael Patai, translated by Harry Zohn. New York: Herzl Press and Thomas Yoseloff, 1960.

Katz, Elihu. "The Two-Step Flow of Communication: An Up-To-Date Report on an Hypothesis." *The Public Opinion Quarterly* 21, no. 1 (1957): 61-78.

Katz, Elihu, and Daniel Dayan. *Media Events: The Live Broadcasting of History*. Cambridge, MA: Harvard University Press, 1992.

Lazarsfeld, Paul F., and Robert K. Merton. "Mass Communication, Popular Taste, and Organized Social Action." In *The Communication of Ideas*, edited by L. Bryson. New York: Harper, 1948.

Pawel, Ernst. *The Labyrinth of Exile: A Life of Theodor Herzl*, translated Bruria Ben-Baruch. Tel Aviv: Zmora, 1997.

Rogers, Everett M. *Diffusion of Innovations*. 1st edition. New York: Free Press of Glencoe, 1962.

Shapira, Anita. "The Religious Motifs of the Labor Movement." In *Zionism and Religion*, edited by S. Almog, J. Reinharz, and A. Shapira, 251-272. Hanover, NH: Brandeis University Press, 1998.

Talmon, Jacob Leib. *The Riddle of the Present and the Cunning of History: Studies in Jewish History from a Universal Perspective*. Jerusalem: Bialik Institute, 2000.

Thompson, John B. *The Media and Modernity: A Social Theory of the Media*. Stanford, CA: Stanford University Press, 1995.

Vital, David. *The Zionist Revolution. Vol. I: The Beginnings of the Movement*, translated by B. Moran. Tel Aviv: Am Oved, 1978.

Weiss, Akiva Aryeh. *Hevrah Hadasha – Hashalom*. Tel Aviv: Dfus Herzliyah, 1938.

CHAPTER TEN

# Responsa Between Two Worlds
## America, Eastern Europe, & the Connection
## Between Distance and Authority
## at the Turn of the 19th Century
### ZEF SEGAL AND MENAHEM BLONDHEIM

Responsa literature is a traditional rabbinical genre, dating back to the ninth century. Responsa are written replies to questions submitted in writing to a rabbinic authority. In general, each reply repeats the question, analyzes the issue, and then provides a resolution. Although usually dealing with everyday practical matters connected with the application of Jewish law, responsa have in fact been written on virtually every aspect of Jewish life and thought. Such texts became the standard mode of circulating rabbinic legal decisions, especially throughout the Diaspora. The responsa literature thus offers a rich source for reconstructing the history of rabbinic law as well as for illuminating the details of day to day life in Jewish communities. Furthermore, the flow of questions and answers reveals communication networks and rabbinical hierarchies; the latter is reflected through the inherent asymmetry between the questioned and the questioner.

The present study focuses on the communicational aspects of responsa literature, with respect to America and American Jewry in particular. References to America in European responsa literature appear as early as the seventeenth and eighteenth centuries, as described by Eisenstein and Freehof, but these were rarities.[1] Acknowledgement of America in this genre only became frequent during the late nineteenth century, and especially towards the turn of the century. This corresponds with the large Jewish migration to North America at that time, and serves as evidence of transborder communication between individuals and communities in the "new world" and those in the "old world". This kind of contact was particularly significant with regards to the orthodox community in America, since rabbinical authority was largely based on communication networks. However, these connections have never been mapped in order to identify which networks actually existed, and why some existed while others did not. As this paper will demonstrate, a spatial analysis of these connections provides counter-intuitive findings regarding the intra-orthodox division between Hasidim and Mitnagdim and their relationship to their American counterparts.

## Responsa literature as a source of communication networks

Responsa literature, which has existed for well over a thousand years, consists of queries, submitted by individuals and communities from all over the world, to the outstanding Jewish authorities in each generation, and the decisions given by those authorities in accordance with the Talmudic system of Jewish law.[2] Almost all the queries and answers deal with the application of Talmudic precepts to actual questions concerning the various problems of community life as well as of private behavior. The portrayal of real-life problems spanning a multitude of private and public arenas had made this genre very useful for historians almost since the inception of modern Jewish historiography. Besides being an invaluable source of evidence for historical Jewish life through the problems it depicts, it also manifests patterns of inter-communal relationships between Jewish Diasporas.[3] By focusing on the correspondence as the main object of analysis, and not necessarily on the content of the correspondence, social networks within rabbinical life can be revealed. In addition, the asymmetrical nature of the "questions and answers" format depicts rabbinical hierarchies within those social networks.

As a result, late nineteenth and early twentieth century responsa literature might better clarify our understanding of the inter-communal exchange between the European orthodox community and the emerging American community of migrants. The main question followed in this research is that of location: which European communities corresponded with America and which did not? An answer to such a question reflects on many other facets of the lives of orthodox communities in the new world, such as the role of the local rabbi, American Jews' ties with their original communities, and the emergence of an autonomous American rabbinate.

The evidence at hand only surveys one side of the communication network, which is the European reply to a query regarding America. Unfortunately, publishers of printed responsa were chiefly concerned with the preservation of the Halachic decisions, and omitted everything else which they regarded as superfluous. As a result, the queries are in most cases either abridged or not extant. In addition, in many cases the names of the correspondents, their places of residence, and their dates of composition are not mentioned. Consequently, it is often very difficult to fix the place and the time of an event or custom we find in the responsa.[4] Because of this, our chief points of information regarding an existent network are the responding rabbi, the date of publication, and the mentioning of America in the correspondence.

## Methodology

Fortunately, much of the responsa literature printed over the ages has remained extant, and is now available in digital form. Huge digital databases such as *Otzar Hahochma, Hebrew Books*, and the *Bar Ilan Responsa Project* enable a digital analysis of 594 responsa publications appearing between 1890 and 1930.[5] On the down side, and as noted, responsa do not necessarily document the time, place, and identity of the asker or even the text of the query: each responsum usually repeats the gist of the question(s), analyzes the legal issue and then provides a resolution, that commonly is not dated either. Therefore, in this study, when the date of the query is not provided, we used the publication date of the responsum as the basis for dating. We found in a sample of queries that appeared with dates that an average of eight years separated the actual communication from its publication of the query in a responsa book. We therefore subtracted this average interval of eight years from the publication dates upon charting responsa exchanges relevant to America over time.

The database was narrowed down to all queries that mention the toponym "America". However, since there are a few different Hebrew and Yiddish transcriptions of the word, we searched all the standard variations: "אמריקה"; "אמעריקע"; "אמריקא"; etc. Once we omitted all the references to America that were not connected to the query or the response, our new American-oriented database was complete.[6] This included queries that came from American laymen, queries from American rabbis, and queries that discussed America-related matters between European rabbis. The latter form did not imply directly that American-European communication existed, but it did reflect this indirectly due to the implicit involvement with the affairs of American Jewry.

The cartographic visualization was created by placing all the locations of authors who mentioned America in their responsa as nodes on the map of Europe, using Arcmap software. Discrete mapping is very unreliable as an analytical tool, since separate points confuse the observer and make it much harder to distinguish between masses of points; by using the ArcMap point-density function, the discrete mapping was transformed into a continuous map of American references in Europe. Point density calculates the density of points in each neighborhood, by summing up the number of points that fall within the neighborhood and dividing by the area of the neighborhood. The outcomes, Maps 1 and 2, reflect the degree of connection between European regions and American Jewry. To be more exact, these maps locate orthodox communities with intensive ties to Jews in America.

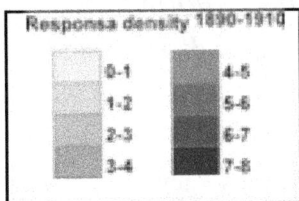

*Map 1- Responsa density 1890-1910*

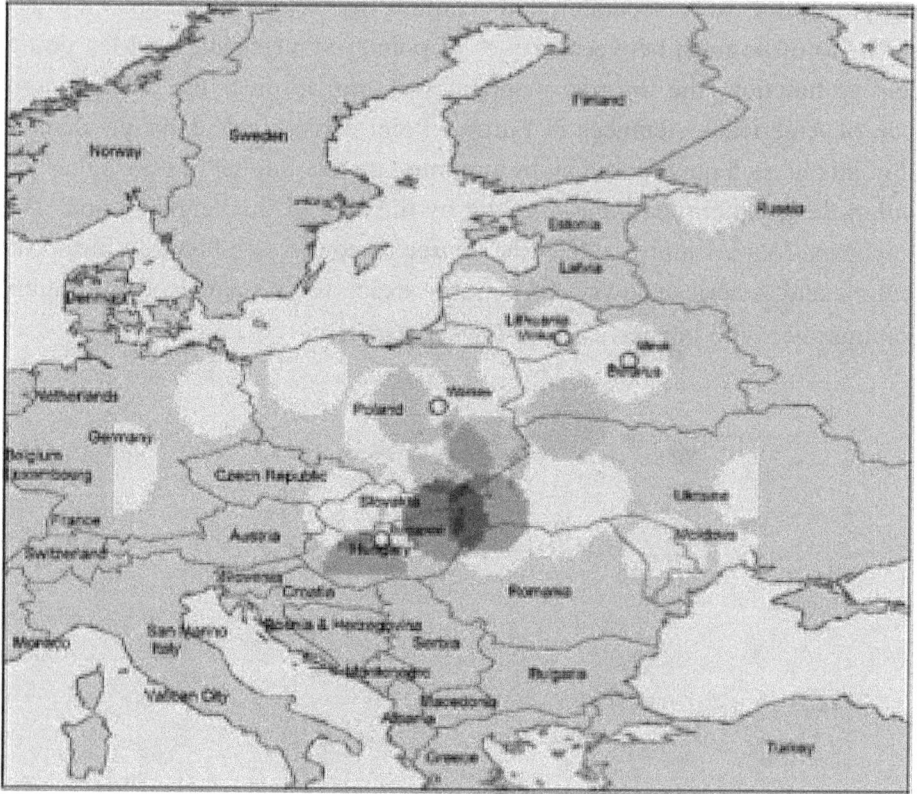

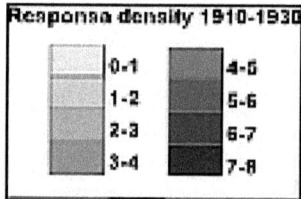

*Map 2- Responsa density 1910-1930*

## Initial observations and hypotheses

The ordered manner of lighter and darker colored regions in the map suggests that the distribution of corresponding rabbis was not uniform across Europe, and that some territorial logic hides behind the locations of the central areas. Moreover, a comparison of Maps 1 and 2 demonstrates a temporal change in the locations of communications with America. Until 1910, the gravitational center of these locations was the adjacent territories of east Poland, west

Ukraine and a part of east Hungary. In the following decades, the map portrays a south-eastwards shift towards Hungary and Ukraine.

The problem is that these maps reflect only the existence of such territorial clustering, but do not provide explanations for it. The intuitive hypotheses, which we will subsequently cancel out, would include three obvious variables: the first would be the spatial distribution of the Jewish emigration to America; one would expect American Jews to correspond with the centers whence they originated. As least as significant would be the demographic distribution of European Jewry; that is, one would expect more correspondence with the more highly populated Jewish centers. Finally, since we are tracing a specific genre of correspondence, halachic responsa, the findings may reflect the spatial distribution of responsa literature publications and nothing more. However, as we shall briefly show, none of these bear any correlation to the maps above.

The most obvious of these hypotheses would be the first, namely, the local origins of emigration. Obviously, the larger the emigration is from a certain territory, the more questions from America a rabbi in that territory should receive. This corresponds to the idea that immigrants are mediators who connect their community of origin to their new communities, thus forming transnational communities.[7] From this perspective, emigration to America forged transnational congregations: Landsmanschaftn representing the transnational extensions of the original communities in the new world.

While the number of Jews who immigrated to America is relatively well known and accounted for, the geographical origins of these immigrants has been a complex topic, especially with regard to immigrants from Russia. A seminal study was Simon Kuznetz's "Immigration of Russian Jews to the United States: Background and Structure", which identified the distribution of immigrants based on social statistics of remaining Jewish communities in Russia.[8] Shaul Stampfer complemented Kuznetz's sources by analyzing Jewish Landsmanschaften in the United States.[9] In more recent studies, Gur Alroey, Joel Perlmann, and Yannay Spitzer each reconstructed the places of origin of Jewish immigrants using distinct but large samples of Russian immigrant documents.[10] While the sources and perspectives of each research differed tremendously, the spatial conclusions were rather similar: east-European Jewish immigration in the years 1880-1930 had an over-representation of Lithuanian

Jews and an under-representation of south-eastern Russian Jewry. These results stand in sharp contrast to our Maps 1 and 2, in which communication is focused on south-eastern regions. Indeed Perlmann's cartographic depiction of the origins of Jewish immigration to the United States can almost be described as a mirror image to our maps. This appears to demonstrate that Lithuanian rabbis rarely refer to America in their responsa publications, while Ukrainian and Hungarian rabbis refer extensively to America. Nevertheless, we shouldn't overemphasize the contrast, since Poland was both a center of Jewish emigration and a center of American references. As it appears, the premise of a correlation, whether positive or negative, between rates of immigration and the extent of responses with America does not hold.

As noted, another possible demographic characteristic that might have affected the distribution of American references is the general distribution of the Jewish population in Europe. But here too, statistical data from the years 1900-1939 display a lack of correlation between the two.[11] For example, Hungarian Jews accounted for 10% of European Jewry in 1900, and 5% in 1939, and yet constituted 26% of all American responsa. On the other hand, Poland, with approximately 36% of total European Jewry in 1939, accounted a mere 24% of American responsa during the years 1890-1930. Furthermore, Richard H. Rowland's regional analysis of Jewish demographics in the Pale, which included cartographic depiction, shows no resemblance to Maps 1 or 2.[12] Thus, Jewish demographics cannot explain the spatial distribution of transnational communication.

This leaves us with the third preliminary hypothesis: rather than being related to demographic attributes, it was related to the geography behind the publishing of responsa literature as a genre, and not to communication with America at all. This would mean that the concentration of references to America in responsa published in a certain community should match its weight in responsa publishing in general. However, over-representations and under-representations are the norm, which disproves this suggestion. Between the years 1890 and 1910, Ukraine and Hungary accounted for 29% and 14% respectively of the responsa regarding America, compared to 14% and 8% of total responsa literature in those two decades.[13] On the other hand, Romania and Lithuania accounted for a mere 5% and 9% of American responsa respectively, compared to 12% of total literature. Similar results can be found in the later responsa between the years 1910 and 1930, with an even greater discrepancy. Hungary accounted for 31% of American responsa compared to 4% of total European responsa. In contrast, Lithuania accounted for 3% of American responsa yet published 15% of total European responsa.

Clearly, the spatial distribution of transnational communication in responsa literature must be attributed to more subtle characteristics of orthodox communities. One such potential factor emerges from recent advances in the study of the historical geography of Jewish Eastern Europe: the social and institutional divide between the Hasidic and non-Hasidic communities (Mitnagdim) and in particular their socio-geographical structure.

## The Hasidic movement

European Orthodox Judaism has been divided into two major factions since the mid-eighteenth century: the Hasidic movement founded by Rabbi Israel ben Eliezer, known as "Ha-Ba'al Shem Tov", and the non-Hasidic communities, or Mitnagdim.[14] The Hasidic movement started as a small alternative group surrounding Ha-Ba'al Shem Tov, which opposed the contemporary way of Jewish worship, specifically the emphasis on Jewish legalism (Halacha).[15] The astonishing success of the Hasidic movement transformed what was initially a theological conflict into geographical separation with relatively delimitated boundaries. By the early nineteenth century, notes Simon Dubnow, "Hasidism had conquered almost all the communities of the Ukraine and eastern Galicia, most of the communities of central Poland, and a considerable number of communities in Romania and Hungary".[16] A recent paper by Marcin Wodzinski and Uriel Gellman analyzed the geography of Hasidic distribution on a historical timeline and illustrated the delimitation of the Hasidic movement and the development of its territorial expansion.[17]

Strikingly, their results and especially their cartographic outcomes are almost identical to the maps in this article. This finding is quite unexpected since responsa literature is supposed to reflect a more scholarly orientation highlighting the legal aspects of Judaism, which opposes the basic tenets of Hasidism. However, this surprising result is also strengthened by the biographies of the various authors in our corpus. Of the 80 European references to America between the years 1890 and 1910, 45 authors were Hasidic, 16 were Mitnagdim and 19 are unknown.[18] Similarly, of the 131 European references between the years 1910 and 1930, 87 were Hasidic, 33 were Mitnagdim, and 11 are unknown.

The correlation between references to America and Hasidic communities offers a historical reasoning for the differences between Map 1 and Map 2. In Map 1, Hasidic centers such as west Ukraine and East Poland are very dominant, while Lithuania, the center of the Mitnagdim, is almost negligible. The south-eastern shift in Map 2 correlates temporally and spatially with the interwar period migration of Hasidic courts away from Soviet territories, especially to Hungary.[19]

The circumstantial evidence suggests a strong connection between Hasidism and rabbinical responses regarding America, but why should this be so? Two characteristics of the European Hasidic movement could explain the reasons for this correlation: the spatial-institutional structure of a Hasidic court, and the unique experiences of Hasidic immigrants to the United States.

## Spatial-institutional structure of the Hasidic movement

The Hasidic movement was initiated in the mid-eighteenth century as an alternative to traditional rabbinical Judaism. It sought to replace the customary scholarly faith with charismatic leadership and ecstatic devotion to God. The movement ceased to exist as a unified form of pietistic religious ideology once it expanded. It evolved into separate groups of followers (Hasidim) of a specific tsadik (righteous man, usually referred to as the rebbe), each with its own theological directives.[20] This was perhaps the main innovation of the Hasidic movement: the creation of a figurehead role, filled by one who was not necessarily known for his intellectual abilities but rather for his spiritual devotion and approach to life.[21]

Since the success of a specific rebbe depended on his personal charisma, accessibility to his followers was a critical feature of Hasidic courts.[22] Therefore, the expansion of Hasidism across Europe was largely a result of new courts founded by disciples of traditional Hasidic rebbes. This form of expansion, which Adam Teller describes as an imitation of the monastery system in Poland, resulted in a widespread network of independent Hasidic centers.[23] In time, the location of a rebbe's court became a brand name defining both the followers and the heirs to the throne.[24] In a way, this form of branding minimized the tension between different branches of the same Hasidic court, but provided a stronger symbolic hold of a Hasidic court on peripheral communities.

The new network, established during the eighteenth century, was only effective as long as the different rebbes were distant from each other. However, this was rarely the case, since rebbes were looking to expand their dominion.[25] This was initially done by sending emissaries representing the rebbe to peripheral Jewish communities.[26] The new communities would attach themselves to the Hasidic court by accepting the spiritual leadership of the rebbe. This was only possible since a separation was maintained between the rebbe as a moral role-model and the rabbi, or rav, as the daily halachic leader. The rabbi was the educated expert, well-read in the letters of Jewish law, while the rebbe was an expert in the way of life suitable for his Hasidim.[27]

As a result, peripheral Hasidic communities were paradoxically both territorially bounded and separated from neighboring Jewish communities, and distant from their own rebbe.[28] This was overcome by three important modes of communication between the rebbe and his disciples: pilgrimage, official visits from the court, and written communication. Although the journey to the Hasidic court was considered a high point in the life of a Hasid, this was very seldom undertaken, due to the major financial burden of such a voyage.[29] Another form of communication was the deployment of emissaries or, on a smaller scale, visits of the rebbe himself. Teller describes the similarity between these visits and the visits made by Polish noblemen through their estates.[30] However, visits were only a partial solution, since transportation was slow and costly. Therefore, written correspondence between individual followers and the rebbe were essential as a means of sending out personal requests and questions.[31]

## Hasidic immigration to America

Consequently, the Hasidic court structure, usually described as a tight knit centralized system, had plenty of room for peripheral outposts, connected to the core through various modes of correspondence. This was indeed the case with the Hasidic immigration to America. However, this immigration has largely been overlooked by immigration research.[32] Moreover, the customary claim was that Hasidim only started immigrating after the Second World War. One of the main supporting arguments was the nature of the Hasidic court and the unwillingness of followers to distance themselves from their rebbe, who did not immigrate to America.[33] Some even claim that Hasidic rebbes objected to the migration of their followers to such extent as to not just prevent American immigration, but to even prevent Hasidic communities from forming in Western Europe.[34] These rebbes saw America as a land of ungodliness (Trefa), where "even the stones are impure".[35] However, others claim that Hasidic rebbes were largely inattentive to the concept of immigration.[36] According to them, America was actually considered an "unknown land" and was therefore not regarded at all.[37] This is supported by references to America in European responsa between 1890 and 1930, since objections to America are rarely discussed. In fact, only two European rabbis during this period outspokenly criticized America in their responsa, and both appeared in the late 1920s, decades after the big Jewish migration.[38] Furthermore, both of them, Mordechai Dov Eidelberg of Mykolaiv and Reuven David Burstein of Kamenitz, were Lithuanian – and not Hasidic rabbis. We can conclude that their pronounced objections to godless Jewish lives in America were the exception and not the norm, and cannot be attributed to Hasidic disapproval of immigration.

While the no-immigration argument is largely dependent on the false premise that Hasidim had to reside in close proximity to their rebbe, evidence proves the existence of Hasidim and Hasidic communities in America from the 1880s. Steven Lapidus describes, for example, the personal tales of isolated Hasidic individuals and families, who lived in small towns without the support of a congregation, while retaining their Hasidic way of life.[39] In addition, the relatively frequent American tours of important European rebbes between 1910 and the 1930s is evidence of the formation of Hasidic communities.[40] These tours were accompanied by mass gatherings of followers in cities across the United States and Canada.

These new world Hasidim were not looking to form new distant Hasidic courts, since the geographical branding was too strong to break. "They live in America but they belong to Lizensk, Mezeritch, or Rishin", in Elie Wiesel's words.[41] In order to maintain their community's way of life, a rabbi was needed, but since Hasidic rabbis were scarce in America, many communities installed a "Stikl Rebbe" as their figurehead.[42] This rabbi was sometimes Hasidic himself, sometimes not; but his role was limited to that of merely a halachic guide: he did not replace the rebbe, who was still in Europe. As a result, the Hasidic communities in America remained dependent on their European rebbes and sought their guidance, or the guidance of other rabbis in the vicinity of the Hasidic court, through the various questions published in the responsa literature.

## Conclusions, questions, and additional remarks

Hasidic responsa communication between America and Europe indicates that Hasidic disciples immigrated to America. Moreover, it accentuates the distinction that has to be made between the immigration of Hasidic disciples and the immigration of their rebbes and Hasidic courts, which remained in Europe until the Second World War. As we have argued, Hasidic peripheries operated in America just as they operated in Europe, through personal voyages, emissaries, and personal letters, which later were referenced in responsa literature. The customary focus of Hasidic research on the figureheads has kept these individual Hasidim under the radar of Jewish historiography. Similarly, Wodzinski and Gellman claim that maps of Hasidism tend to depict only places of residence of famous Hasidic leaders.[43] They add that "an ideal map of Hasidism should represent the distribution of ordinary Hasidic followers rather than simply noting their leaders' places of residence".[44] Although this paper does not offer such a mapping of Hasidic followers, it does prove the existence of such distant peripheries.

Furthermore, Hasidic responsa communication should be weighted as more than just a source proving the existence of American Hasidim. The Hasidic occupation with responsa reflected a general reliance of the Hasidic movement on modern communication and transportation technologies. The existence of efficient postal and telegraph systems, which depended on railways, steamships, and eventually airplanes, was a necessary precondition for exporting east-European modes of Hasidic center-periphery relations to the distant American peripheries. Without these technologies the Hasidic individuals in America would not have remained attached to a specific dynasty. Although the technological perspective of Hasidic communication has not been researched, a preliminary examination of responsa literature suggests that there is a strong correlation between Hasidism and communications technology. The telegraph was first mentioned in a responsa text in 1876 by Yechiel Michel Hevner, who was affiliated with the Stretin Hasidic dynasty. He described his telegraph correspondence in "Nachlah Le'Yisroel" as a means of communication.[45] In the following decade, two additional authors mentioned their telegraph experiences: Yekusiel Yehudah Teiteilbaum, who was the rebbe and founder of the Siget dynasty, and Moshe Teumim, who was the rabbi of Horodenka, which is known for its Hasidic courts.[46] Although the sample size is very small, it hints on a general communicational need of Hasidic leaders that does not necessarily exist in other orthodox sects.

The discussion to this point has ignored the complementary part of the American orthodox community, the Lithuanian Jews, who dominated early twentieth century Jewish life in America. The lack of responsa references to America from their Lithuanian counterparts in Europe reflected the growing strength of American rabbis, and their self-dependence. This corresponds with evidence from other forms of orthodox authority such as "Pesika" (decision), "Semicha" (ordination) and "Haskama" (approval) that signify that by the turn of the century an autonomous American rabbinical hierarchy had evolved.[47] The differences between the self-dependent Lithuanian rabbinate and the externally-dependent Hasidic communities led to a conflict regarding the formation of a unified structure for American Jewry. In 1887, for example, an attempt was made to inaugurate the position of Chief Rabbi of New York, which was offered to Rabbi Jacob Joseph of Vilna. However, Galician and Hungarian Jews did not recognize his authority or the attempt to unite the Jews of America as an autonomous orthodox unit.[48] This might be seen as a conflict over control and power between two factions of the orthodox world, but it can also be seen as an ideological conflict over the idea of authority and its geographical location between the proponents of local autonomy (Lithuanian Jews) and the proponents of European dominance (Hasidic Jews).

Distance and authority are usually inversely correlated; that is, authority is weakened as the distance is greater. That logic would explain the emergence of the autonomous American Lithuanian rabbinate. However, the Hasidic communities in America did not correspond to that pattern, since they preserved their European authorities. The over-representation of Hasidic responsa with regards to America was a reflection of that preservation, caused partially by the unique experience of the Hasidic immigrants, lacking leaders in their new communities. However, the use of long-distance communication was not just a result of the circumstances in a given periphery (America), but rather a necessity of the Hasidic way of life and a fundamental element in the spatial-institutional identity of the Hasidic movement.

## Bibliography

## Notes

1    Judah David Eisenstein, "The Development of Jewish Casuistic Literature in America," *American Jewish Historical Society* 12 (1904): 139-148; Solomon B. Freehof, "An Eighteenth Century American Responsum," *American Jewish Archives* (1953): 121-125.

2    Yaacov Choueka, "Computerized Full-Text Retrieval Systems and Research in the Humanities: The Responsa Project," *Computers and the Humanities* 14 (1980): 154.

3    Various articles in: Sophie Manche, ed., *Communication in the Jewish Diaspora: The Pre-Modern World* (Leiden: E.J. Brill, 1996).

4    Jacob Mann, "The Responsa of the Babylonian Geonim as a Source of Jewish History," *The Jewish Quarterly Review* 7 (1917): 460.

5    See: "Home Page," *Otzar Hahochma,* http://www.otzar.org/; "Home Page," *HebrewBooks. org,* http://hebrewbooks.org; "Home Page," *The Bar Ilan Responsa Project,* http://www.responsa.co.il/.

6    Unrelated references to America could be, for example, an acknowledgment in the book's introduction of family members who live in America.

7    Roger D. Waldinger and David Fitzgerald, "Transnationalism in Question," *American Journal of Sociology* 109 (2004): 1177-1195.

8    Simon Kuznets, "Immigration of Russian Jews to the United States: Background and Structure," *Perspectives in American History* 9 (1975): 35-126.

9    Shaul Stampfer, "The Geographic Background of East European Jewish Migration to the United States before World War I," in *Migration Across Time and Nations: Population Mobility in Historical Contexts,* eds. Ira A. Glazier and Luigi De Rosa (New York: Holmes and Meier, 1986), 220-230.

10   Gur Alroey, "Patterns of Jewish Migration from the Russian Empire in the Early 20th Century," *Jews in Russian and Eastern Europe Countries 57 (2006):* 24-51; Joel Perlmann, "The Local Geographic Origins of Russian-Jewish Immigrants, Circa 1900," *Levy Economics Institute Working Paper* No. 465 (2006); Yannay Spitzer, "Pogroms, Networks, and Migration: The Jewish Migration from the Russian Empire to the United States 1881–1914" (Working paper, 2014).

11  A major problem of comparing the data is the changing borders during this period. Figures from 1900: Isidore Singer and Cyrus Adler, eds. "Statistics," in *The Jewish Encyclopedia: A Descriptive Record of the History, Religion, Literature, and Customs of the Jewish People from the Earliest Times to the Present Day* (New York: Funk & Wagnalls, 1906), 528-536; Figures from 1939: Anglo-American Committee of Inquiry, Report, "Apendix III: Estimated Jewish Population of Europe," in *Anglo-American Committee of Inquiry Report to the United States Government and His Majesty's Government in the United Kingdom* (Lausanne, Switzerland, April 20, 1946), http://avalon.law.yale.edu/20th_century/angcov.asp.

12  Richard H. Rowland, "Geographical Patterns of the Jewish Population in the Pale of Settlement of Late Nineteenth Century Russia," *Jewish Social Studies* 48 (1986): 207-234.

13  The number of responsa titles was calculated from the database of www.hebrewbooks.org.

14  David Assaf, "Hasidism: Historical Overview," in *The Yivo Encyclopedia of Jews in Eastern Europe,* ed. Gershon D. Hundert (New Haven: Yale University Press, 2008), 659-670.

15  Ibid., 661.

16  Simon Dubnow, *Toledot Hahasidut* (Tel Aviv: Dvir, 1967), 3.

17  Marcin Wodzinski and Uriel Gellman, "Toward a New Geography of Hasidism," *Jewish History* 27 (2013): 171-199.

18  Information was gathered from various biographic encyclopedias: *Me'ir Ỿunder, Me'ore Galitsyah: Entsiḳlopedyah Le-Ḥakhme Galitsyah* (Jerusalem: Makhon le-hantsaḥat Yahadut Galitsyah, 1978) [Hebrew]; Yiẓḥak Raphael, Shalom H. Parush, and Yitsḥaḳ Alfasi, *Entsiḳlopedyah La-Ḥasidut* (Jerusalem: Mosad Harav Kook, 1980) [Hebrew]; Yeḥi'el M. Shṭern, *Sefer Gedole Ha-Dorot: Seḳirah Ḳetsarah Ỿe-Tamtsitit Me-Ḥaye Ỿe-Ḥibure Gedole Ha-Dorot Ba-'avar* (Jerusalem: Mekhon "Minḥat Yiśra'el", 1995) [Hebrew]; Yitsḥaḳ Y. Kohen, *Ḥakhme Hungaryah Ỿeha-Sifrut Ha-Toranit Bah* (Jerusalem: Mif'al Moreshet Yahadut Hungaryah, Mekhon Yerushalayim, 1996) [Hebrew]; Baruch Traktin, *Entsiklopedyah Le-Yahadut Romanya* (Jerusalem: Mosad Harav Kook, 2012) [Hebrew].

19  Wodzinski and Gellman, "Toward a New Geography of Hasidism," 195.

20  Samuel C. Heilman, "What's in a Name? The Dilemma of Title and Geography for Contemporary Hasidism," *Jewish History* 27 (2013): 221.

21  Charles L. Bosk, "The Routinization of Charisma: The Case of the Zaddik," *Sociological Inquiry* 49 (2007): 150-167.

22  Heilman, "What's in a Name?" 221.

23  Adam Teller, "Hasidism and the Challenge of Geography: The Polish Background to the Spread of the Hasidic Movement," *AJS Review* 30 (2006): 25.

24  Heilman, "What's in a Name?" 222, 224.

25  David Assaf and Gadi Sagiv, "Hasidism in Tsarist Russia: Historical and Social Aspects," *Jewish History* 27 (2013): 250-252.

26  Teller, "Hasidism and the Challenge of Geography…" 11.

27  Jerome R. Mintz, *Hasidic People: A Place in the New World* (Cambridge: Harvard University Press, 1992), 4.

28  Assaf and Sagiv, "Hasidism in Tsarist Russia…" 252.

29    Ibid., 250; Norbert Gleszer, "Pilgrimages in Jewish Folk Religion in Hungary - from the Chassidic Courts to the Virtual Communities," *Acta Ethnographica Hungarica* 51 (2006): 91-104.

30    Teller, "Hasidism and the Challenge of Geography..." 21-22.

31    Ibid., 23.

32    Steven Lapidus, "The Forgotten Hasidim: Rabbis and Rebbes in prewar Canada," *Canadian Jewish Studies* 12 (2004): 1.

33    Very few important rebbes immigrated prior to 1940. Jeffrey S. Gurock, *American Jewish Orthodoxy in Historical Perspective* (Hoboken: KTAV Publishing, 1996), 52.

34    Jacques Gutwirth, "Hassidism and Urban Life," *The Jewish Journal of Sociology* 38 (1996): 107.

35    Lapidus, "The Forgotten Hasidim..." 14.

36    Lloyd P. Gartner, "Jewish Migrants En Route from Europe to North America: Traditions and Realities," *Jewish History* 1 (1986): 60.

37    Assaf and Sagiv, "Hasidism in Tsarist Russia..." 267.

38    Reuven David Burstein, *Divrei Radach* (Warsaw, 1927); Mordechai Dov Eidelberg, *Chazon LaMoed* (Bialystock, 1923).

39    Lapidus, "The Forgotten Hasidim..." 7-13.

40    Ibid., 5-7; Janet S. Belcove-Shalin, "Introduction: New World Hasidim," in *New World Hasidim: Ethnographic Studies of Hasidic Jews in America,* ed. Janet S. Belcove-Shalin (New York: State University of New York Press, 1995), 9.

41    Elie Wiesel, *Souls on Fire: Portraits and Legends of Hasidic Masters* (New York: Simon and Schuster Paperbacks, 1972), 38.

42    Some Hasidic rabbis immigrated by the end of the nineteenth century, but they were few in number; Belcove-Shalin, "Introduction..." 8.

43    Wodzinski and Gellman, "Toward a New Geography of Hasidism," 173.

44    Ibid., 174.

45    Yechiel Michel Hevner, *Nachlah Le'Yisroel* (Lvov, 1876), 84.

46    Yekusiel Yehudah Teiteilbaum, *Avnei Tzedek* (Lvov, 1885), 230, 275; Moshe Teumim, *Orayan Telisai* (Lvov, 1880), 211. Rahamim Yosef Franko of Hebron mentions the telegraph in 1881 as a response to a question regarding written notification of deaths. I did not include him in my account since it does not mention his use of the telegraph – Rahamim Yosef Franko, *Shut Shaare Rahamim* (Jerusalem, 1881), 76.

47    Menachem Blondheim, "Harabanut Ha'ortodoxit Megala et America: Hageogarfia shel Haru'ach Bemitvim shel Tikshoret," in *Be'ikvot Colombus: America 1492-1992,* ed. Miri Eliav-Feldon (Jerusalm: Zalman Shazar Center, 1997), 483-510 [Hebrew].

48    Daniel Soyer, *Jewish Immigrant Associations and American Identity in New York, 1880-1939* (Detroit: Wayne State University Press, 2001), 116.

Alroey, Gur. "Patterns of Jewish Migration from the Russian Empire in the Early 20th Century." *Jews in Russian and Eastern Europe Countries* 57 (2006): 24-51.

Anglo-American Committee of Inquiry. Report. "Apendix III: Estimated Jewish Population of Europe." In *Anglo-American Committee of Inquiry Report to the United States Government and His Majesty's Government in the United Kingdom*. Lausanne, Switzerland, April 20, 1946. http://avalon.law.yale.edu/20th_century/angcov.asp.

Assaf, David. "Hasidism: Historical Overview." In *The Yivo Encyclopedia of Jews in Eastern Europe*, edited by Gershon D. Hundert, 659-670. New Haven: Yale University Press, 2008.

Assaf, David, and Gadi Sagiv. "Hasidism in Tsarist Russia: Historical and Social Aspects." *Jewish History* 27 (2013): 241-269.

Belcove-Shalin, Janet S. "Introduction: New World Hasidim." In *New World Hasidim: Ethnographic Studies of Hasidic Jews in America*, edited by Janet S. Belcove-Shalin, 1-30. New York: State University of New York Press, 1995.

Blondheim, Menachem. "Harabanut Ha'ortodoxit Megala et America: Hageogarfia shel Haru'ach Bemitvim shel Tikshoret." In *Be'ikvot Colombus: America 1492-1992*, edited by Miri Eliav-Feldon, 483-510. Jerusalm: Zalman Shazar Center, 1997 [Hebrew].

Bosk, Charles L. "The Routinization of Charisma: The Case of the Zaddik." *Sociological Inquiry* 49 (2007): 150-167.

Burstein, Reuven David. *Divrei Radach*. Warsaw, 1927.

Choueka, Yaacov. "Computerized Full-Text Retrieval Systems and Research in the Humanities: The Responsa Project." *Computers and the Humanities* 14 (1980): 153-169.

Dubnow, Simon. *Toledot Hahasidut*. Tel Aviv: Dvir, 1967.

Eidelberg, Mordechai Dov. *Chazon LaMoed*. Bialystock, 1923.

Eisenstein, Judah David. "The Development of Jewish Casuistic Literature in America." *American Jewish Historical Society* 12 (1904): 139-148.

Franko, Rahamim Yosef. *Shut Shaare Rahamim*. Jerusalem, 1881.

Freehof, Solomon B. "An Eighteenth Century American Responsum." *American Jewish Archives* (1953): 121-125.

Gartner, Lloyd P. "Jewish Migrants En Route from Europe to North America: Traditions and Realities." *Jewish History* 1 (1986): 49-86.

Gleszer, Norbert. "Pilgrimages in Jewish Folk Religion in Hungary - from the Chassidic Courts to the Virtual Communities." *Acta Ethnographica Hungarica* 51 (2006): 91-104.

Gurock, Jeffrey S. *American Jewish Orthodoxy in Historical Perspective*. Hoboken: KTAV Publishing, 1996.

Gutwirth, Jacques. "Hassidism and Urban Life." *The Jewish Journal of Sociology* 38 (1996): 105-113.

Heilman, Samuel C. "What's in a Name? The Dilemma of Title and Geography for Contemporary

Hasidism." *Jewish History* 27 (2013): 221-240.

Hevner, Yechiel Michel. *Nachlah Le'Yisroel*. Lvov, 1876.

"Home Page." *HebrewBooks.org*. http://hebrewbooks.org.

"Home Page." *The Bar Ilan Responsa Project*. http://www.responsa.co.il/.

"Home Page." *Otzar Hahochma*. http://www.otzar.org/.

Kohen, Yitshak Y. *Ḥakhme Hungaryah Veha-Sifrut Ha-Toranit Bah*. Jerusalem: Mif'al Moreshet Yahadut Hungaryah, Mekhon Yerushalayim, 1996 [Hebrew].

Kuznets, Simon. "Immigration of Russian Jews to the United States: Background and Structure." *Perspectives in American History* 9 (1975): 35-126.

Lapidus, Steven. "The Forgotten Hasidim: Rabbis and Rebbes in prewar Canada." *Canadian Jewish Studies* 12 (2004): 1-30.

Manche, Sophie, ed. *Communication in the Jewish Diaspora: The Pre-Modern World*. Leiden: E.J. Brill, 1996.

Mann, Jacob. "The Responsa of the Babylonian Geonim as a Source of Jewish History." *The Jewish Quarterly Review* 7 (1917): 457-490.

Mintz, Jerome R. *Hasidic People: A Place in the New World*. Cambridge: Harvard University Press, 1992.

Perlmann, Joel. "The Local Geographic Origins of Russian-Jewish Immigrants, Circa 1900." *Levy Economics Institute Working Paper No. 465* (2006).

Raphael, Yizhak, Shalom H. Parush, and Yitshak Alfasi. *Entsiklopedyah La-Ḥasidut*. Jerusalem: Mosad Harav Kook, 1980 [Hebrew].

Rowland, Richard H. "Geographical Patterns of the Jewish Population in the Pale of Settlement of Late Nineteenth Century Russia." *Jewish Social Studies* 48 (1986): 207-234.

Singer, Isidore, and Cyrus Adler, eds. "Statistics." In *The Jewish Encyclopedia: A Descriptive Record of the History, Religion, Literature, and Customs of the Jewish People from the Earliest Times to the Present Day*, 528-536. New York: Funk & Wagnalls, 1906.

Shtern, Yeḥi'el M. *Sefer Gedole Ha-Dorot: Sekirah Ketsarah Ve-Tamtsitit Me-Ḥaye Ve-Ḥibure Gedole Ha-Dorot Ba-'avar*. Jerusalem: Mekhon Minḥat Yiśra'el, 1995 [Hebrew].

Soyer, Daniel. *Jewish Immigrant Associations and American Identity in New York, 1880-1939*. Detroit: Wayne State University Press, 2001.

Spitzer, Yannay. "Pogroms, Networks, and Migration: The Jewish Migration from the Russian Empire to the United States, 1881–1914." Working Paper, 2014.

Stampfer, Shaul. "The Geographic Background of East European Jewish Migration to the United States before World War I." In *Migration Across Time and Nations: Population Mobility in Historical Contexts*, edited by Ira A. Glazier and Luigi De Rosa, 220-230. New York: Holmes and Meier, 1986.

Teiteilbaum, Yekusiel Yehudah. *Avnei Tzedek*. Lvov, 1885.

Teller, Adam. "Hasidism and the Challenge of Geography: The Polish Background to the Spread of the Hasidic Movement." *AJS Review* 30 (2006): 1-29.

Teumim, Moshe. *Orayan Telisai*. Lvov, 1880.

Traktin, Baruch. *Entsiklopedyah Le-Yahadut Romanya*. Jerusalem: Mosad Harav Kook, 2012 [Hebrew].

Ýunder, Me'ir. *Me'ore Galitsyah: Entsiķlopedyah Le-Ḥakhme Galitsyah*. Jerusalem: Makhon le-hantsaḥat Yahadut Galitsyah, 1978 [Hebrew].

Waldinger, Roger D., and David Fitzgerald. "Transnationalism in Question." *American Journal of Sociology* 109 (2004): 1177-1195.

Wiesel, Elie. *Souls on Fire: Portraits and Legends of Hasidic Masters*. New York: Simon and Schuster Paperbacks, 1972.

Wodzinski, Marcin, and Uriel Gellman. "Toward a New Geography of Hasidism." *Jewish History* 27 (2013): 171-199.

CHAPTER ELEVEN

# For the Love of Language

### Saul Bellow's
### *The Adventures of Augie March*

BARUCH HOCHMAN

I want to propound a simple, possibly self-evident, thesis with regard to Jewish writers in Diasporic languages since the Emancipation. My thesis is simple but it goes against the grain of the prevailing sense that Jewish writers in European languages epitomize the alienation which has marked writing everywhere in the West in modern times. I am thinking of a more and less distinguished series of writers — starting at least with Heine and continuing through Kafka and possibly Proust to the so-called "American-Jewish" writers who took center stage in the United States in the 1950s. I propose that these writers, however richly their work refracts their alienation from all manner of things, were deeply implicated in and even infatuated with the languages they used and the cultures to which these languages belong. Their work reflects not only deep immersion in the languages in which they wrote but also a passion for those languages: a passion which matches and often exceeds that of the most deep-dyed "native sons" of those cultures. That passion frequently tends to be commensurate with alienation from Jewish origins and is a correlative of the assimilation which was the lot of so many Jews in the Western world. And it says much about their place in the world and the emphases — linguistic and otherwise — of their work.

Kafka might be the most poignant example of the intertwinedness of alienation and affirmation in the work of such writers. Self-declaredly alienated from everything — language, faith, nation, even (or especially) himself — Kafka nonetheless wrote German prose of rare distinction: a distinction which seems to have marked the German written in Prague, and by Prague Jews in particular. Only a passionate immersion in a language and its culture could have produced such prose as Kafka wrote.

Regrettably, I touch on Kafka here only to leave him behind — not because he wouldn't have served as well as — or even better than — any other writer to make my argument, but because my very minimal German does not suffice for even rudimentary exemplification. Instead, I will engage with the work of Saul Bellow — specifically, and in some detail, his epoch-making novel, *The Adventures of Augie March*.[1] Bellow's language is my language, and *Augie March*, can serve to make my point, though it will do so in a curiously American, markedly Bellovian way.

It is Bellow's romance with his language — and his alienation from so much else — that I will take as a case in point. It is a curiously anomalous case because the alienation which informs his writing is masked, even while it is marked, by the exuberance, amounting sometimes to euphoria, of its language. Bellow may be taken to represent a cogent instance of the doubleness of which I speak, even as, in his apparent affirmativeness, he also seems to represent a challenge to it.

I will never forget the impact on me of *Augie March* when it first appeared. Like many readers at the time, I was stunned by its vitality: by its imaginative energy, its verbal prodigality, and its literary panache. At the time of its publication in 1953 it seemed a major event in American letters.

*Augie March* opens with a bang of affirmation — with the flare and blare of triumphant selfhood and a flamboyant declaration of affinities which strives to place it in the mainstream of the American literary tradition and its author in the line of writers in "the American grain." At the same time, it employs an idiom which in many ways betrays a radical otherness.

"I am an American," Augie starts —

> I am an American Chicago-born — Chicago, that somber city, and go at things I have taught myself, and will make my record in my own way: first to knock, first admitted; sometimes an innocent knock, sometimes a not so innocent. But a man's character is his fate, says Heraclitus, and in the end there isn't any way to disguise the nature of the knocks by acoustical work on the door or gloving the knuckles.[2]

Already in 1953 the meaning and provenance of this declaration were clear. The bravado of "I am an American Chicago born" declares Augie's affinity with the Whitman who "throws [his] yawp over the rooftops of the world."[3] Augie is setting out to sing a song of himself, with no holds barred: to let it all hang out in the manner of Whitman. "Everyone knows," says Augie,

> Everyone knows there is no fineness or accuracy of suppression; if
> you hold down one thing you hold down the adjoining.[4]

Emphatically, this speaker means to "hold down" nothing: neither his passionate self-involvement nor untrammeled disclosure of who he is: including the fact that, although he is first and foremost "an American," he speaks with a marked, if sometimes elusive, Yiddish inflection. Normative English doesn't accommodate a dangling adjective, like "hold down *the adjoining*" — we expect to be told *what* is adjoining, even as in the preceding paragraph "sometimes an innocent knock, sometimes a not so innocent" leaves us dangling in just that way. "American, Chicago born" is a blatant import from the Yiddish, where a native is a *he-i-gher geborene* — one born here: or rather, a *born-here*-er. And the regurgitative double-entendre of "hold down nothing" is striking in the way it flaunts both an idiomatic crackle and a thoroughgoing strangeness.

Yet even in the alien-ness of his idiom Bellow fills a very American, very Whitmanesque brief. Whitman not only adjures his reader to take to the open road and sing its praises, but also to embrace all the diversity he encounters, including his own inner diversity: all the rifts that cleave his imperiously questing implicitly ramified self which "contain[s] multitudes."[5] Augie, in his way, aspires to such multitudinousness.

The sense of *Augie March*'s Americanness is further enhanced by its close affinity with Huckleberry Finn, both the character and the text he inhabits: an affinity trumpeted by Bellow's echo of Twain's title — *The Adventures of Huckleberry Finn*[6] — as well as by *Augie March*'s ramshackle episodic structure. This affinity is enhanced by the irrepressible innocence, even the boyishness, of its narrator-protagonist — that is, of Augie himself. But it is also confirmed by the way the narrative replays and parodies other familiar American literary sites.

The novel is full of colorful and anomalous "characters": oddballs, eccentrics, outlandish types who echo paradigmatic situations and settings in American fiction: the *lumpen* ambience of the household Augie grows up in; Einhorn, who ends up as a poolroom czar; and the marginal types — often petty criminals — who surround him and Augie, all of them suggesting the worlds of American-Jewish naturalists of the thirties: of writers like Daniel Fuchs and Meyer Levin. The Mexican scenes, and especially the iguana hunting, bring to mind some of Hemingway's depictions of expatriate Americans. The scenes in the lifeboat with Bateshaw summon up the archetypal images in American culture of being storm-tossed at sea, as in Hitchcock's film based on a John Steinbeck novella, *Lifeboat*.[7]

Pervaded by such echoes and analogies *Augie March* lent itself to consideration as a — if not <u>the</u> — Great American Novel. As such, it easily links itself to other resonant American contexts. Alongside the Whitmanesque Open Road emphasis on randomness and on embracing multitudes — an emphasis we find in other writers in Whitman's line, from Carl Sandburg to Alan Ginsburg and the Beats and beyond — we also have the novel's Whitmanesque way of heightening our sense of its richness and the richness of the world it represents by the use of catalogues: of enumerating many items in a string (often not a wholly predictable string) of items.

This effect is augmented by ostentatious use of epithets, allusions, appositives, synonymity and other amplifying strategies. Grandma Lausch, the lodger who lords it over the rather squalid household Augie grows up in, is a modern Machiavelli, but also a Pharaoh or a Caesar, and William Einhorn, the small-time real estate tycoon and operator on all fronts, is a Ulysses, a Caesar and a Machiavelli. Even Winnie, Grandma Lausch's pampered pet, has her own reality-legislating epithets. She is a "pursy overfed dog," who is comically monumentalized by the epithets heaped on her, as though she were a figure in an ancient epic: "*Loud-breathing* and *wind-breaking,* she lay near the old lady's stool."[8]

There are places where Augie heaps up such details in a dizzying way, zooming out into far and exotic places and adverting to remote historical entities to congeal a sense of outlandish splendor — and absurdity. Note the surge of breakneck rhetorical euphoria in the passage where Augie piles detail on detail in describing his brother's flashy girlfriend:

> Extremely young, her face was made up to some thickness of gold tone, lips drawn to a forward point by thick rouge; her lashes and brows seemed to have gold dust sprinkled and rubbed into them; her

hair, golden, appeared added on like the hair of Versailles; her combs were gold, her glasses gold-trimmed and she wore golden jewelry. I was about to say she looked immature, but maybe that means that she didn't bear this gold freight with the fullest confidence; perhaps only some big woman could have done that. Not necessarily a physical giantess but a person whose capacity for adornment was really great. One of that old sister-society whose pins and barrettes and little jars and combs from Assyria or Crete lie so curious and with the wavy prongs and green gnawed bronze in museum cases — those sacred girls laid in the bed by the priests to wait for the secret night visit of Attis or whoever, the maidens who took part in the hot annual battles of gardens, amorous ditty singers, Syrians, Amorites, Moabites, and so on. The line continuing through *femmes galantes,* courts of love, Aquitaines, infantas, Medicis, courtesans, wild ladies, down to modern night clubs or first-class salons of luxury liners and the glamorous passengers for whom chefs plot their biggest soufflé, pastry-fish or other surprises.[9]

The effect, if we wish, is epic as well as comic. As in the Homeric epics, reference to realities in the world outside the space in which the action takes place carries us to other places and other times, and creates the illusion of a capacious world, and, with the heaping up of particulars, a very rich one: a strategy carried over from Homer to Virgil, and on to Milton in the English tradition, and to the hyperbolic, rollicking world that fills Rabelais's comic epic and the hilarities of Till Eulenspiegel — as well of the world of *Moby-Dick,*[10] where the narrative of Ahab's epic whale hunt generates a vision not only of the microcosm which is his ship but also of the cosmos itself and the primordial challenges it presents.

Indeed, Bellow's affinity for Melville (and for the masters of seventeenth century English prose on whom Melville draws so heavily) is felt in the mock-cosmic, often comic scope of Bellow's range of reference. But it is also evoked by the curious affinity between the tonalities of Augie's resonant first-person narrative and those of Melville's Ishmael.

*Moby-Dick* establishes the register of its discourse with Ishmael's opening words. With his "Call me Ishmael," the narrator collars us and carries us into what becomes a tidal surge of language which thrusts far out into the represented world of the novel even as it thrusts into the self-reflexive, philosophizing sensibility of that narrator. "Some years ago," he continues,

> Some years ago — never mind how long precisely — having little or no money in my purse and nothing particular to interest me on shore, I thought I would sail about a little and see the watery part of the world. It is a way of driving off the spleen and regulating the circulation. Whenever it is a damp, drizzly November in my soul; whenever I find myself involuntarily stopping in front of coffin warehouses, and bringing up the rear of every funeral I meet. . . .then I account it high time to go to sea as soon as I can. With a philosophical flourish, Cato throws himself upon his sword; I quietly take to the ship.[11]

In effect, juxtaposition of Ishmael's opening challenge to the reader with Augie's opening thrust — again, "I am American, Chicago born" — serves to foreground the extent to which *Augie March* trumpets its own American-ness as well as the magnitude of its pretensions. But it also underscores the flipside of Bellow's exuberant, ostensibly celebratory sense of life: the dark, depressive, no-exit side which I will now address. There is no eliding the dark side of *Moby-Dick*: the way in which, as Alfred Kazin put it, *Moby-Dick* explores themes of quest and alienation, and uses its opulence of language, as well as other means, to dramatize both the urgency of the quest and the depth of the alienation.

At first, the dark side of *Augie March* hardly registered on readers. Reviewers not only perceived it as a major, even ground-breaking work, but also as a radically affirmative one. In a study called *After Alienation*, published only eight years after *Augie March* first appeared, Marcus Klein identified it, along with a cluster of other works from the fifties, as marking a turn *away* from the alienation which had marked American writing between the wars, and as a celebration of America such as had not been seen in American high culture for many decades.[12] More than 40 years later, on the fiftieth anniversary of its publication (and on the occasion of its appearance in the *Library of America* series), critics were still stressing its affirmations.

In the intervening years Bellow's own extra-novelistic pontifications, among others his Nobel Prize acceptance speech, further served to deflect attention from the bleakness of both the world he represents and of his vision of life itself. Bellow was scathing about critics who lamented the death of the novel and who implied, in a Spenglerian way, that western civilization itself was not only declining but was exhausting itself. At various intervals over the decades, he proposed that his own work bore witness to the genre's continued vitality and implicitly to the vitality of civilization itself.

Yet the fact is that, despite its verbal exuberance, *Augie March* is at bottom a bleak and desolate book — at least as bleak and, essentially, as *beat,* as the long string of novels which followed in Bellow's oeuvre. As Jonathan Wilson shows in *On Bellow's Planet: Readings from the Dark Side,*[13] Bellow's vision, for all the frequent high spirits of its writing, is a depressive one, and Augie, like Bellow's later protagonists, is trapped in a set of binds which prevent him from coming into being as a rich or resonant subject, not only in the "reality" of his life in the novel, but in the imagination of the reader as well. Augie himself cannot break out of the vicious circle of self-contradiction in which he is trapped — of his propensity to declare his independence even while he is subordinating himself to some coercive figure, then to duck out of whatever role that figure casts him in. Nor does the novel itself project a credible world he might live in or emerge from. Augie is clearly conceived as a kind of *Bildung* hero — he speaks from the beginning of teachers and being taught, and makes much of the mentors he attaches himself to. But he is also markedly a picaresque figure, and as such he achieves no significant "education" and undergoes no significant development. The novel itself, moreover, presents no grid of values or alternatives on which Augie's growth could be plotted and within which a point of emergence might be imagined. His world is a marginal one, from his welfare-grounded childhood, to the moment toward the end of the novel when we see him in Rome just after World War II, waiting to conclude a shady deal in American army surplus goods and starting to write, for no apparent reason, the memoir which is the novel we are reading — that is, *The Adventures of Augie March.*

But it is in fact the marginality of Augie's life and the unresolvedness of its issues which links the novel most vividly to its time and its place. Indeed, in this it chimes interestingly with Ralph Ellison's *Invisible Man,*[14] which appeared the year before *Augie March* and which was enthusiastically reviewed by Bellow himself.

Both Bellow and Ellison, on the publication of their work, leapt immediately from a more or less remote margin of the American literary scene to a prominent place at its heart. Both novels center on deeply marginal characters — on outsiders, in fact — desperately in need of confirmation from the center. Their protagonists are not only outsiders but also literal or symbolic orphans, in quest of confirmation from father figures, from authorities with whom they might identify and through whom they might hope to find a viable shape to contain their turbulent inwardness as well as a legitimate, or merely viable, place in the world. But neither can accept such tutelage in the forms in which it is available.

Both novels, moreover, refuse the normative — the classical — novel's expectation that the novel itself constitute a paradigmatic model of the world it reflects or even purports to represent, and this despite its manifest effort to attain at least a limited referentiality. It was a cliché of mid-twentieth criticism that such representation was no longer possible. *The Golden Notebook*,[15] published in 1962, explicitly explores what it regards as the interrelated issued of integrating disparate elements of a person's identity and the difficulty of hammering out a narrative that might resemble the *grand récit* of nineteenth century fiction. Yet both *Augie March* and *Invisible Man* are written with a flamboyance of formulation which suggests an almost magical capacity of language itself to create a world, or at least to create reality in the moment-to-moment.

Beyond that, both novels compensate for their own marginality by displaying a striking virtuosity in wielding the tokens of high culture — American high culture of the moment, but also the high culture of what had come to be defined, in the Great Books tradition, as "Western Civilization." This is true both in terms of the fields of literary and cultural reference in which they place themselves and of the narrative modes they employ. Indeed, both Ellison and Bellow implicitly deny the primacy of their ethnicity even as they furl out their affinity with their communities of origin and trumpet their freedom to work from within terms derived from those communities. *Invisible Man* brims with black folklore and swarms with elements inspired by earlier black writers, yet Robert Stepto, in his book *From Behind the Veil: A Study of Afro-American Narrative*[16] on the emergence of black materials into the arena of normative American culture, has no simple task in exposing the ethnic — *black* — roots of Ellison's novel, owing largely to the salient range of *white* reference, from Sophocles's *Oedipus* to James Joyce.

As for Bellow, the material of *Augie March* and the prose in which it is couched boldly declare their "Jewishness," yet, as in the passage on golden girls which I have cited, Bellow swears allegiance to "Western Civilization" in its Great Books, University of Chicago incarnation, and to the anthropology he had studied and taught. It is within this tradition of Great Books and secular learning that he generally subsumes the biblical and Jewish-historical references, except when he is impelled to render the consciousness of one of his characters — as in the following evocation of immigrant cousin Anna Coblin's relation to the tradition:

> Anna did not object to our going to the movies on Saturday. She herself did not touch money on holy days. She observed them all, including the new moons, from a little Hebrew calendar, covering her head, lighting candles, and whispering prayers, with her eyes dilated and determined, going after religious terrors with the fear and nerve of a Jonah driven to enter frightful Nineveh. She thought it was her duty while I was in her house to give me some religious instruction, and it was a queer account I got from her of the Creation and Fall, the building of Babel, the flood, the visit of the angels to Lot, the punishment of his wife and the lewdness of his daughters, in a spout of Hebrew, Yiddish and English, powered by piety and anger, little flowers and bloody fire supplied from her own memory and fancy. She didn't abridge much in stories like the one about Isaac sporting with Rebecca in Abimelech's garden or the rape of Dinah by Shechem.
>
> "He tortured her," she said.
>
> "How?"
>
> "*Tortured*!"
>
> She didn't think more was necessary, and she was right.[17]

This is masterful in evoking a certain exacerbated immigrant sensibility, but such bracketing of a big chunk of the Jewish tradition in terms of the highly idiosyncratic (if also, in a way, the commonplace) perspective of a rather grotesque character serves to distance Bellow — and us — from that tradition.

In *Call It English*,[18] Hana Wirth-Nesher makes a strong case for the Hebrew/Jewish/Yiddish underpinnings of Bellow's prose — the sort of thing I point out above from the novel's opening paragraphs — and stresses how Bellow's translation from the Yiddish of Bashevis Singer's *Gimpel the Fool*,[19] like his editing with Irving Howe and Eliezer Greenberg of an anthology of stories from the Yiddish, are direct (and major) statements with regard not only to his origins but also to his active affinities. Yet in his fiction Bellow places these elements in an ironic light, even as he embodies and enacts them — more often than not with gusto. It is not surprising that like other artists of his time, he resented being classified as "an American-Jewish" this or that. Like Ellison's use of black folklore and the idiom of black experience, the "Jewishness" of Bellow's writing is assimilated into a mode of discourse which declares itself to be essentially "American" and a part of "Western Civilization," as understood in his time.

If this is so, it is all the more striking that Bellow, like earlier "Jewish writers in Diasporic languages," boisterously celebrated the fact that he had found something like "a home" in language. Part of the novel's euphoria resides in the exuberance with which Augie celebrates his rootedness in the America he represents in his "memoir" and the virtuosity with which he wields its language. Bellow, of course, is not Augie — is not the comically pratfall-taking ingénue through whose mouth he speaks. Yet, as Jonathan Wilson insists, most of Bellow's protagonists not only share a lurking depressiveness and but also bear at least a sneaking resemblance to their creator. It seems to me that for Bellow, as for his protagonists, language, rather than action or thought, provides the prime mode of bringing oneself into being.

Indeed, there is a sense in which Bellow's finding a "home" in language parallels the homing of earlier Jewish "writers in diasporic languages" into the language of their work. There is a sense in which Bellow's and Ellison's need to home in on themselves in this way was one among many signs of the sense of rootlessness which has increasingly characterized the modern world — a sense which finds expression in the disposition of writers to use language as a substitute for the slackening bonds of community.

At this point I would like to suggest (though it involves squinting in a very different direction) that the revival of the Hebrew language and the emergence of Modern Hebrew literature may well reflect an analogous response to such a slackening — in the case of the Hebrew writers, the loosening of bonds to tradition demanded by the Enlightenment (the *Haskala*) — and that it constituted an analogous quest for "home," a quest which had its parallel in the Zionist project of establishing a terrestrial homeland. More than that, I suggest that the remarkable intensity and richness of the work produced in the course of the Hebrew revival (the *Tchiya*), in fiction as well as poetry, reflect the urgency of the quest and may be seen as analogous to the language practice of the "post-Enlightenment Jewish writers" who, like Ellison and Bellow in more recent times, had homed so comfortably into their "diasporic languages."

This "homing" could not have been simple. I take as paradigmatic an anecdote I heard from Dov Sadan when I was his student here in Jerusalem in the early 1950s. Sadan reported that when he served as Agnon's secretary in the mid-1930s, Agnon bemoaned the fact that he couldn't write in a "human," in an existent language: that is, that he had doomed himself to working in a language he had in good part to generate. Agnon's ambivalence toward the Hebrew in which he worked such wonders is reflected the contortedness of a more famous remark of his — the line he delivered when he congratulated Bellow for being awarded the Nobel Prize: "Too bad, though," Agnon supposedly said — in Yiddish, of course — "that you write in an ephemeral language, and not in the language of the Eternity of Israel." It may have been a labor of love to revitalize the Hebrew language, but it is awesome to contemplate the magnitude of the effort that went into it: not only of Agnon, but still more of Mapu and Mendele at the beginning of the "*Tchiya*" — the re-naissance or re-vivication of the Hebrew language — or even, some thirty years after that, of Bialik and Tchernikhovsky, and then of their successor generation, like Alterman, Shlonsky, Avot Yeshurun and their ilk. I assume that part of the opulence of their language reflects the strenuousness of their effort to generate a mode of expression in Hebrew sufficient unto their needs — and unto the needs of the audience they knew they would have, in good part, to create for themselves.

In this perspective, I would like to suggest the "hypertrophy of language" of which I am speaking does not belong only to "Jewish writers in Diasporic languages" or to Jews struggling to rediscover their Hebraic roots as a way of dealing with their own deracination. I would propose that it may well be a universal feature of emergent modernity, and that it is linked to other salient social and cultural realities.

Indeed, one aspect of the cultural moment in which Bellow and Ellison take center stage in American letters in the middle of the last century is the way that moment is marked not only by the movement of writers like Bellow and Ellison from the periphery to the center, but also by the way the center both celebrated and resented the centrality of such writers. I was struck at the time by an essay "On Not Being a Jew" by Edward M. Hoagland which was published in *Commentary* in April 1968,[20] significantly just before Hoagland's marriage to a highly committed and visible Jew who was an editor there — that is, at a journal published by The American Jewish Committee as, among other things, a forum for pondering issues of Jewish life. Hoagland's essay reports the resentment he and John Updike felt when they emerged into the literary arena in the early fifties, and found their natural place had been usurped by the "American Jewish writers." Such resentment did nothing to change the shift in centrality. Quite the contrary. Since that time numerous — and major — writers from still more remote peripheries have usurped the center, and borne home on us the implications of this movement for our sense of dominant and subordinate elements in a literature or even a culture at large.

As the twentieth century moved toward its end, more and more writers from the periphery crowded into the center, including writers in English from a variety of places in the former British Empire: from V.S. Naipaul and Salman Rushdie to Jamaica Kincaid and Zadie Smith. These writers have attained an important place in English letters. Indeed, it seems to be a salient fact of contemporary literary and social life that it is marked by a fluidity which was heralded by the postmodernist celebration of de-centering already notable in the 1960s. Bellow's intrusion on the American literary scene, like Ellison's, heralded a major shift in social and cultural life.

This, of course — and not surprisingly — accords with the transformations in the notion of diaspora with which members of this project have regaled us, and fascinated me: the way in which we have come to think of diasporas, not as displacements from a fixed center, but rather of displacements within displacements, in a social and cultural map which lacks center and no longer aspires to centralities.

Such de-centering is, predictably, a reflex of re-centering at another level. I have no space — but also no adequate tools — to address the "postcolonial" issues which figure in the migration of writers from cultures which speak other languages than English: issues having to do with the identification of the populations of colonized countries with the language of colonization, and the shaping of identities within the moulds of the cultures to which those languages belong. Though I have no tools for dealing with it, it seems worth suggesting that the absorption of Jews into the dominant cultures of the diasporas into which they were thrown can be understood at least partly in terms of other very different but also radically analogous situations. In both cases, the burrowing into the language home the writers have found entails something like the "hypertrophy of language" of which I have been speaking: something which, in English, is still more dramatically evident in the works of writers who crossed a radical language barrier in order to become English writers. (Conrad and Nabokov, with their very different kinds of linguistic virtuosity, may be taken as extreme and supreme examples of the phenomenon.)

Bellow's Canadian, polyglot, Jewish, and Russian antecedents present a different configuration that stirs interesting thoughts about the hybridity of his life as an American author. But that is another subject.

## Notes

1   Saul Bellow, *The Adventures of Augie March* (New York: Penguin Books, 1953).

2   Bellow, *The Adventures of Augie March*, 1.

3   Walt Whitman, *Leaves of Grass* (New York: New American Library, 1955), 55.

4   Bellow, *The Adventures of Augie March*, 1.

5   Whitman, *Leaves of Grass*, 55.

6   Mark Twain, *The Adventures of Huckleberry Finn* (New York & London: Chatto & Windus, 1884).

7   *Lifeboat*, directed by Alfred Hitchcock (Century City, CA: 20th Century Fox, 1944).

8   Bellow, *The Adventures of Augie March*, 1-2.

9   Bellow, *The Adventures of Augie March*, 503-504.

10   Herman Melville, *Moby-Dick* (London: Richard Bentley, 1851).

11   Ibid., 7.

12   Marcus Klein, *After Alienation: American Novels in Mid-century* (Books for Libraries Press, 1962/1970).

13   Jonathan Wilson, *On Bellow's Planet: Readings from the Dark Side* (Rutherford: Fairleigh Dickinson Univ. Press, 1985).

14   Ralph Ellison, *Invisible Man* (New York: Random House, 1952).

15  Doris Lessing, *The Golden Notebook* (London: Michael Joseph, 1962).

16  Robert Stepto, *From Behind the Veil: A Study of Afro-American Narrative* (Chicago, IL: University of Illinois Press, 1991).

17  Bellow, *The Adventures of Augie March,* 27-28.

18  Hana Wirth-Nesher, *Call It English: The Languages of Jewish American Literature* (Princeton, NJ & Oxford: Princeton University Press, 2006).

19  Isaac Bashevis Singer, *Gimpel the Fool,* trans. Saul Bellow (New York: Noonday Press, 1957).

20  Edward M. Hoagland, "On Not Being a Jew," *Commentary* 45, no. 4 (April 1968): 61.

## Bibliography

Bashevis Singer, Isaac. *Gimpel the Fool.* Translated by Saul Bellow. New York: Noonday Press, 1957.

Bellow, Saul. *The Adventures of Augie March.* New York: Penguin Books, 1953.

Ellison, Ralph. *Invisible Man.* New York: Random House, 1952.

Hoagland, Edward M. "On Not Being a Jew." *Commentary* 45, no. 4 (April 1968).

Klein, Marcus. *After Alienation: American Novels in Mid-century.* Books for Libraries Press, 1962/1970.

Lessing, Doris. *The Golden Notebook.* London: Michael Joseph, 1962.

*Lifeboat.* Directed by Alfred Hitchcock. Century City, CA: 20th Century Fox, 1944.

Melville, Herman. *Moby-Dick.* London: Richard Bentley, 1851.

Stepto, Robert. *From Behind the Veil: A Study of Afro-American Narrative.* Chicago, IL: University of Illinois Press, 1991.

Twain, Mark. *The Adventures of Huckleberry Finn.* New York & London: Chatto & Windus, 1884.

Whitman, Walt. *Leaves of Grass.* New York: New American Library, 1955.

Wilson, Jonathan. *On Bellow's Planet: Readings from the Dark Side.* Rutherford: Fairleigh Dickinson Univ. Press, 1985.

Wirth-Nesher, Hana. *Call It English: The Languages of Jewish American Literature.* Princeton, NJ & Oxford: Princeton University Press, 2006.